Baseball's Ultimate POWER

If you have a home computer with Internet access you may:

- request an item to be placed on hold.
- renew an item that is not overdue or on hold.
- view titles and due dates checked out on your card.
- view and/or pay your outstanding fines online (over $5).

To view your patron record from your home computer click on Patchogue-Medford Library's homepage: www.pmlib.org

Also by Bill Jenkinson
The Year Babe Ruth Hit 104 Home Runs

Baseball's Ultimate POWER

RANKING THE ALL-TIME GREATEST DISTANCE HOME RUN HITTERS

BILL JENKINSON

LYONS PRESS
Guilford, Connecticut

An imprint of Globe Pequot Press

For my parents:
For my father, Bill Jenkinson, who taught me to play and love the game of baseball and
For my mother, Nadine Marr Jenkinson, who taught me simply to love.

Copyright © 2010 Bill Jenkinson

Lyons Press is an imprint of Globe Pequot Press.

Cover photos: Babe Ruth (top) © Fotosearch; Manny Ramirez (bottom, third from left) © Mike Ivins/Boston Red Sox; other player photos © National Baseball Hall of Fame, Cooperstown, N.Y.; ball/bat graphics © Shutterstock

Project editor: Jessica Haberman
Layout: Kevin Mak
Text design: Sheryl P. Kober

Library of Congress Cataloging-in-Publication Data
Jenkinson, Bill, 1962-
  Baseball's ultimate power : ranking the all-time greatest distance home run hitters / Bill Jenkinson.
       p. cm.
  Includes bibliographical references and index.
  ISBN 978-1-59921-544-0
  1. Baseball players—United States—Biography. 2. Baseball players—Rating of—United States. 3. Home runs (Baseball)—United States—Statistics. 4. Home runs (Baseball)—United States—History. I. Title.
  GV865.A1J65 2010
  796.357092′2—dc22
                              2009029667

Printed in the United States of America

10 9 8 7 6 5 4 3 2 1

CONTENTS

Preface. VII

Introduction XII

One: The Story of the Tape Measure Home Run 1
Two: Henry, Willie, and Frank 16
Three: Historical Rankings: 40 through 21 25
Four: Top 19th-Century and Negro League Sluggers 50
Five: Historical Rankings: 20 through 11 80
Six: Top 10 Current Sluggers. 111
Seven: Historical Rankings: 10 through 1 143
Eight: The Best of the Best 194

Epilogue 232

APPENDIXES
Appendix A: Top 100 Tape Measure Sluggers 237
Appendix B: Top 100 Longest Drives in Major League Games. 239
Appendix C: Stadium Photographs. 243
Appendix D: Tape Measure Calendar 266
Appendix E: Power Rankings by Position. 283
Appendix F: The Longest of This and the Longest of That. 285

    Singles. 285
    Doubles 286
    Triples 286
    Inside-the-park Home Runs 287
    Fly Outs 287
    Opposite Field Home Runs 288
    Spring Training Home Runs 288
    Postseason Home Runs 289
    All-Star Home Runs 289
    First Career Home Runs 290
    Final Career Home Runs 290
    Home Runs by a Teenager 291
    Home Runs by Player over 40 291

Pinch-hit Home Runs 292

Home Runs by a Pitcher 292

Walk-off Home Runs 293

Appendix G: Power Personified 294

Ten Greatest Individual Combinations of Batting, Throwing, and Running 294

Ten Most Powerful Throwing Arms (Position Players) 295

Strongest Arms by Position 297

Ten Fastest Starting Pitchers 297

Ten Fastest Runners 299

Fastest Runners by Position 302

Ten Longest Hitters Pound for Pound 302

Sources 303

Selected Bibliography 325

Index 330

About the Author 336

PREFACE

Since I researched this book for 30 years, I asked a lot of different folks for help along the way. I trust that my long list of acknowledgements does not strike the reader as indicative of feelings of self-importance. I understand the place of a baseball book, especially compared to works of science and medicine, which may impact quality of life. Yet, there is a niche for this book in the legacy of our national pastime, and I feel proud of what I have accomplished. Accordingly, I wish to recognize the individuals who have helped the most.

Of course, the list starts with my wife Marie, who has assisted at every step along the long journey. Besides reading early drafts and offering suggestions, she has always encouraged me throughout the course of my efforts. I can't recall the number of times that she has accompanied me to the Library of Congress, where she sat for hours at an adjoining microfilm reader looking up accounts of home runs. There aren't many wives who would willingly do that and actually exude positive energy in the process.

I am also indebted to my children and, in two cases, their spouses. That includes Bill, Amanda, Denise, Stephen, David, and Michael. All of my children were good ball players, and the number of baseball experiences that I have shared with each is beyond reckoning. Let it suffice for me to say that I treasure every moment with each of them. In the case of my son-in-law Stephen Stewart, I must acknowledge that his expertise in the field of computer science has been invaluable.

Similarly, I wish to recognize my four grandchildren, who, despite their tender years, are exceptionally supportive. In this regard, I also want to share a personal anecdote. On the afternoon of July 11, 2009, I was in the backyard pitching Wiffle balls to my four-year-old grandson, Alexander. At that moment, his sisters, Katie and Abby, were playing inside with my wife, and Liam, our youngest grandchild, was with his Mom and Dad in the Pocono Mountains. Alex was not hitting as well as usual, and I noticed that he was picking up his back foot during the early stages of his swing. Accordingly, he was losing bat speed. I demonstrated what he was doing wrong, whereupon he smiled and took a practice cut. The difference was significant.

I returned to the mound, and tossed one in. The little fellow swung from his heels and pummeled the ball with everything he had inside his 40-pound frame. The ball flew down the left field line, landed near a paved walkway and rolled under a hedge. I was impressed. Looking down at his happy face, I said, "Alex, you just broke your daddy's distance record for four-year-olds in this yard." I could tell that he was pleased, but he maintained a serious look. After a further moment of contemplation, he looked up and asked, "Papa, are you going to put me in your next book?" Well, Alex, I just did, and nothing could make me happier!

The rest of my extended family has been equally helpful. That especially pertains to my sister, Jean Calhoun, a retired teacher and librarian, as well as my brother, Joe Jenkinson, an unusually wise man and proficient mathematician. Joe is always there to help me with statistical analysis and issues relating to probability. As indicated in this book's dedication, my mother and father were the anchors of my early life. I was similarly blessed with many aunts, uncles, cousins, and grandparents who enriched my existence at every turn. Cousin Tom Stock and best friend Jonathan Herbst have been confidants for decades and have always supported me in all that I do.

Another friend whose help has been essential is historian Bruce Orser. He was the first person to contact me for a discussion of long-distance hitting who gave more than he received. Others would call and ask a question. Receiving the answer to their inquiry, they would provide a curt "thank you," and resume their personal business. Bruce wondered if there was anything that he could do to contribute and hasn't stopped contributing for twenty years. Then there is Tim Reid. After reading my Babe Ruth book, Tim called to offer his appreciation, and we have become personal friends. Along the way, I have learned to value his input, which has been significant. Tim is a fun guy to be around as is his cousin Bob Ward, whom I also consider a valuable ally.

It was during a 2008 trip to Florida, organized by Tim, that I became reacquainted with an old schoolboy buddy by the name of Roy Kerr. He is a retired college professor of Spanish Studies, and he leaped into action at my suggestion that he join the field of baseball history. Roy not only published his own book about 19th-century base-stealing legend Billy Hamilton, but he also read all the early drafts for this book. Roy is the embodiment of that old adage: "If you want something done, ask a busy man to do it."

Father Gabriel Costa was also thoughtful enough to contact me after reading my first book, and he is a truly amazing fellow. Born in Hoboken, New Jersey, Father Gabe is a brilliant mathematician as well as a devout Yankee/Babe Ruth fan. For many years, he has taught math to our finest young men and women at the West Point Military Academy, and, if he offers an opinion on any subject, I listen intently.

During the writing of both of my baseball books, the family of Babe Ruth has been extremely kind to me. Granddaughter Linda Ruth Tosetti and her husband, Andy Tosetti, have been wonderful in every way. If you ever want to see someone energize a crowd about Babe Ruth, attend an event with Linda!

Babe's daughter Julia Ruth Stevens actually lived with her famous dad for many years, and, if there is a living expert on The Bambino, she is the one. Similarly, her son, Tom Stevens, and grandson, Brent Stevens, have afforded me nothing but encouragement and good will. Before moving away from The Babe, I also want to say "thank you" to Mike Gibbons and his entire staff at the Babe Ruth Museum in Baltimore.

Back in the early days of my research, there were very few listings of the career home runs of the various sluggers. The Atlanta Braves had put one together for Henry Aaron, but that was the only one I could locate. As a result, I had to undergo the tortuous process of identifying all the home runs of my subject players before I could begin to research them. Fortunately, the Society for American Baseball Research (SABR) was in its infancy and had obtained the handwritten journals of home run historian John Tattersall. He had laboriously entered every Major League homer beginning in the early 19th century onto sheets of paper, and they were in the custody of one of SABR's founding fathers, Bob McConnell. Bob continued the research, and extended the records all the way back to 1876. Lucky for me, Bob lived in Wilmington, Delaware, instead of Portland, Oregon. I say lucky because I lived about an hour away, in the northern suburbs of Philadelphia. For nearly a decade, I routinely took advantage of Bob's kindness and drove to his house. Once there, I stayed for hours, invading his

basement where the records were stored in cabinets. The patience and hospitality that he and his wife consistently afforded me is something for which I will always be grateful.

Those records have now been computerized, and modern students can access career home run logs on the Internet. The original Tattersall records are now in the care of David Vincent, who is another premier SABR member. David and Bob know more about the history of home runs than anybody else that I know, and this book would not have been possible without their assistance and advice. Further regarding SABR, I am indebted to the entire organization for all that they do. There have been so many members who have helped me that I can't possibly name them all. However, I am particularly thankful to Nicole DiCicco, Phil Lowry, David Stephan, and Bob Bluthardt.

From the scientific standpoint, I must identify Dr. Charles Yesalis, Professor Emeritus from Penn State University. He has graciously counseled me on the subject of steroids and performance enhancing drugs. This is a tough topic, but Chuck has made the process significantly more palatable with his insights and good humor. In the field of physics, I have sought guidance from several different individuals, including Professor Robert Adair of Yale University. He is generally regarded as the father of "baseball physics," and his expertise first clarified the issue of balls in flight for me. On a personal level, Professor Ed Meyer of Baldwin-Wallace College has patiently walked me through this scientific minefield on many occasions despite my admitted density of the subject.

Of course, Major League baseball has been the heart of the story, and there have been hundreds (maybe thousands) of individuals who have contributed in some way. That begins with the players themselves, who, for the most part, have treated me with thoughtfulness and respect. I can not cite every single interview, but I would be remiss if I didn't name a few of the most memorable and enjoyable experiences. That includes personal interaction with Hank Greenberg, Joe DiMaggio, Ted Williams, Mickey Mantle, Ernie Banks, Hank Aaron, Frank Howard, Willie Stargell, Reggie Jackson, Greg Luzinski, Cal Ripken, Paul O'Neill, Fred McGriff, and Adam Dunn. Rocky Colavito was a childhood hero of mine (he actually still is) and has functioned as my chief baseball adviser for this venture. How cool is that?

And don't believe everything that you hear about some guys being lousy communicators. Regardless of their reputations, I was provided with warm and articulate insights from Dick Allen, Jose Canseco, Dave Kingman, and Eddie Murray. Similarly, pitchers might fool you. Despite the fact that the subject of tape measure home runs must be inherently distasteful to them, I have interviewed many who were willing to help in the telling of this story. The most noteworthy were Bob Feller, Warren Spahn, Robin Roberts, Bob Gibson, Nolan Ryan, and Greg Maddux. From the old Negro Leagues, I must recognize my good friend William "Judy" Johnson as being uniquely supportive, while also mentioning Buck Leonard and Buck O'Neil for their graciousness.

The teams themselves have usually been cooperative and helpful. I give special thanks to my hometown Philadelphia Phillies, especially Larry Shenk for setting up all those interviews with visiting players over the course of many years. The Baltimore Orioles, Cincinnati Reds, and Boston Red Sox have been particularly kind to me. Dick Brescianni of the Bosox deserves a hearty pat on the back for arranging my unforgettable meeting with Ted Williams back in 1986, and he has remained a friend during all the intervening seasons. Other teams that have been generous in their assistance are the Atlanta Braves, Arizona Diamondbacks, Cleveland Indians, Kansas City Royals, New York Mets, New York Yankees, Chicago White Sox, Los Angeles Dodgers, Oakland Athletics, Tampa Bay Rays, and Texas Rangers. At the Major League headquarters in New York, I have been helped by many different individuals, but Mike Teevan has always gone the extra yard to make my life easier.

What can I say to my friends at the National Baseball Hall of Fame in New York except "thank you very much." Starting with Bill Guilfoile in the early 1980s and extending to the present time with Jeff Idelson, Jackie Brown, Amanda Pinney, Pat Kelly, Jim Gates, Tim Wiles, and Freddy Berowski, everyone in Cooperstown has been wonderful to me. It is still a genuine thrill every time that I set eyes on the place!

As I have explained whenever I have the chance, I am immensely indebted to librarians from all over the continent. For 30 years, I have been pestering, pleading, and cajoling thousands of them to assist me in my inquiries. I am astonished at the level of kindness and cooperation that I have received in almost every instance. I have lost count of the libraries that have helped me, but the total runs into the hundreds. However, I must pay special tribute to four of them who have led the way. First, my hometown library in Willow Grove, Pennsylvania, known as the Upper Moreland Free Library, has never let me down. The main branch of the Philadelphia Free Library has been a stalwart companion for three decades. The Firestone Library at Princeton University is an extraordinary institution and has become like a second home to me. Thank you Debbie and Coleen. Last, I love the town of Washington, D.C., and the Library of Congress is especially dear to me. I have spent so many hours there that I could walk the halls blindfolded. Thanks to everyone!

On the professional level, I am pleased to express my gratitude to agent Jim Fitzgerald of New York. He is the guy who got me published, and I will never forget that. Of course, without my publisher, Globe Pequot Press along with Lyons Press, there would be no book. Thanks to the entire staff for everything that they have done to make *Baseball's Ultimate Power* the best that it could be. Special mention goes to Jess Haberman and Josh Rosenberg. Then there is my editor, Keith Wallman. For starters, he is a passionate baseball fan, which is a huge plus for a baseball historian writing a book. Second, he is an extremely intelligent man who really knows his job. Most importantly, he genuinely understands my thought processes and makes my work as seamless as possible. Please understand that Keith's presence is found on every page of this work. Let me say it in another way: I have published two books and I hope to do many more. Keith Wallman has been my editor both times, and I hope that I never work with another!

INTRODUCTION

$\mathcal{F}$or as long as I can remember, I have been fascinated with long-distance hitting. My earliest specific memory takes me back to Shibe Park (aka Connie Mack Stadium) in Philadelphia with my dad. It was probably during the 1953 season when I was six years old. The Athletics were still in town, and they hooked up with the Phillies to play an exhibition game. We sat in the lower seats along the left field foul line, which made it convenient for Dad to point out left fielders Gus Zernial (A's) and Del Ennis (Phils).

They were two husky, right-handed power hitters, and it was explained to me that they both hit a lot of home runs. Such an explanation should have been plenty for a six-year-old kid, but not for me. I looked at my father, and asked, "Who hits them farther?" He looked a little surprised, but replied, "I really don't know. They both hit them pretty far. Why do you want to know that?" My response was, "I dunno why. I just wanna know." It seemed perfectly logical to find out who was stronger: Mr. Zernial or Mr. Ennis. Whoever it was would be my favorite.

Having been blessed with a loving and thoughtful father, I was then treated to an oral history lesson that changed the course of my life. Unable to judge the comparative long-distance skills of Zernial and Ennis, Dad still had a lot to say about the general topic. He detailed all the power-hitting glories that he had seen. And there had been plenty. He regaled me with rousing accounts of Babe Ruth and Jimmie Foxx, complete with hand gestures and finger pointing to distant spots all over the ballpark. If the source had been anybody but my dad, I probably wouldn't have believed him. Surely, no one really could hit baseballs that far. But this was my father talking, and absolutely everything he said was chiseled in stone. I was breathless . . . it was just sooo good!

Knowing that the Athletics were leaving Philadelphia after the 1954 season, Dad came through for me again that year. On a warm weekend afternoon, we returned to Connie Mack Stadium for the specific purpose of watching Ted Williams hit a baseball. There was a doubleheader between the A's and Red Sox, and my father stretched our middle-class budget by purchasing tickets directly behind home plate. Teddy Ballgame hit a homer that day, but, to be honest, I spent most of the afternoon stomping empty cardboard cups turned upside down. Yet, I can still recall

Number 9 standing there in front of me and looking very menacing. Of course, the scene was again amplified by Dad's stories. He described seeing Williams launch home runs onto the housetops across 20th Street in right field. More good stuff.

Then along came Stan Lopata. Stan who? Stanley Lopata was a large, powerful man who played catcher for the Philadelphia Phillies from 1948 to 1958. His problem was that he wasn't as good defensively as some of the veteran receivers. But, brother, could he pound a baseball! In 1955, he finally got a chance to prove it. I heard early in the year that Lopata had emerged as the team's longest hitter, so guess who became my new favorite player? Forget Del Ennis; give me Big Stash. Lopata recorded 22 homers that season and followed up the next year with 32. It is unlikely that any catcher in Major League history hit for distance the way that Stan Lopata did in 1956.

Nothing, however, is perfect. Dad and I were in Connie Mack one night in 1955 when Stan came to bat with two out in the 9th inning with men on base. The Phils were trailing by a run or two, so one of Lopata's long bombs would have won it. But he watched three called strikes sail past him, ending the game. Despite his usual sensitivities for my feelings, Dad muttered "that big bum" as we got up to leave. My personal "Mighty Casey" had struck out, and I was devastated. But all was not lost. During a 1956 game, I got to see Lopata slam one far over the 65-foot-high left field grandstand roof, after which, Dad

turned and grinned at me. Oh, sweet redemption! It was also in the summer of 1956 that I experienced the single most important event on my long road of "tape measure" obsession.

In 1956, the Cincinnati Reds were breaking home run records while developing a reputation for having the hardest-hitting roster ever assembled. My Uncle Joe (Dad's brother) had a friend who worked as an usher for the Phillies. It was decided that he would use his connections to arrange an early entrance for me to watch the entire Reds' batting practice. I don't recall the particulars, but, apparently, the visiting team hit first, and the gates were still closed to the public when they started BP. But, there I was, standing along the field level railing just past the third base dugout when those awesome men in their red uniforms came out to practice their hitting. What a show!

That group included muscular Ted Kluszewski, powerful Wally Post, burly Ed Bailey, brawny Bob Thurman, potent Gus Bell, big George Crowe, and rookie strongman-sensation, Frank Robinson. I watched, open-mouthed, for 45 minutes as they smashed ball after ball so far in every direction that I was sure that no other kid had ever witnessed anything like it. It was like seeing miracle after miracle. Those images have never left me; I summon them whenever the subject of great batting strength is mentioned.

The next important step on my personal home run odyssey occurred in 1958. Sometime during that season, I was sitting in my doctor's office waiting to get my tetanus shot. I passed the time by reading a magazine that included an article about charismatic young Cleveland slugger Rocky Colavito. There were graphic descriptions not only about how far he hit the ball, but also how incredibly far he could throw it. Presto! I had a new favorite player. Then, in early October, Dad was reading the *Philadelphia Evening Bulletin* and noticed an advertisement. Turning to me he said, "How would you like to go see the Mickey Mantle–Willie Mays All-Stars this Friday night. Rocky Colavito will be there too." The days of postseason barnstorming tours were almost over back then, but not quite yet. There was a group of Major League stars coming to Connie Mack Stadium on October 10, 1958, and they promoted the event with the names of their two biggest attractions.

Before the game, there was a home run hitting contest that was won by Gil Hodges. But Mickey Mantle made the biggest impression by blasting a ball far over the Philco billboard atop the grandstand roof just left of center field. It was the longest drive that I had ever seen or ever would see. During the game itself, we all got to see Mantle run out a routine ground ball to second base. Years later, I attended the Summer Olympics in Montreal and watched the world's fastest runners compete in the 400-meter sprint relays. They were magnificent, but, over the course of 90 feet, they did not seem to move as inhumanly fast as Mickey Mantle. And, lucky for me, Rocky Colavito threw out a National League runner at third base from the right field foul pole . . . on the fly. That throw left a vapor trail and rendered everyone as incredulous as when Mantle hit his blast. It was a night to remember.

Being a Phillies fan in the late 1950s and early 1960s was not a good thing. One by one, the 1950 Whiz Kids left town. Robin Roberts, Curt Simmons, Rich Ashburn, Del Ennis and, yes, Stan Lopata were all gone. What was left was not particularly entertaining. For a young guy like me, who loved the long ball, it was a desert. Other towns had The Mick, Harmon Killebrew, Willie McCovey, Frank Howard, and the like, but we had . . . well, not much. But then came 1964, and there was Richie Allen. He was my fantasy come to life. The first time that I actually saw him was in an April exhibition game batting against Robin Roberts of all people. Allen smashed one off an ad sign on the left field roof.

Later that season, on June 4 to be exact, I went to Connie Mack Stadium with my younger brother and two buddies to see Richie belt one off Sandy Koufax. We arrived too late to get good seats and wound up sitting high in the left field upper deck. Allen disappointed us that night, but Koufax didn't. He faced the minimum 27 batters on his way to a masterful no-hitter. The only three runs were scored in the 7th inning when huge Frank Howard rocketed a ball to the left field roof directly over our heads. That homer traveled so fast that we almost got whiplash following its flight. What a tremendous shot!

The seasons rolled by, with Richie (later Dick) Allen smashing enough prodigious drives to make up for the submission to Koufax. It was at our family's Fourth of July picnic in 1966 that I announced my conviction that Allen could hit the ball harder and farther than anyone who had ever played. My father smiled benignly, and, while nodding at his brothers, reminded me not to forget about Babe Ruth and Jimmie Foxx. Of course, eventually, even Dick Allen left Philly. However, Greg Luzinski and Mike Schmidt then put on Phillies' uniforms, and I was set for many more years. By the late '70s, I was a dad myself, trying to enrich my children's collective baseball consciousness as my father had done for me. So, when I found myself discussing the history of the tape measure home run with friends, I took it very seriously. I argued for Dick Allen's supremacy while they advocated Mickey Mantle or some other great slugger of their choice.

In order to settle the dispute, I got in touch with the library at the Baseball Hall of Fame in Cooperstown, New York. I assumed that somebody must have done a definitive study on this topic and written a book. There was a book about everything in baseball history. Or so I thought. On this topic, however, there was none, at least not at the Hall of Fame. So, I went next to the Library of Congress in Washington, D.C., but got the same response. No luck. Along the course of my inquiries, I heard the name of Joe Falls, who was a sportswriter for the *Detroit News*.

He reportedly loved the long ball just like me, and, over the years, had written many articles on the subject. I got in touch with Joe, who was a very friendly guy. He freely acknowledged his passion for tape measure home runs, and added that he had personally considered writing a book on the topic, but decided against it. It was just too much work. The research would take years, and then more years after that. This was in 1979. By a coincidence, I soon called the Phillies' business office to inquire about some tickets. I was put on hold while listening to re-creations of great moments in the team's history. One of them focused on Dick Allen's longest home run. The recording described the blow, and then concluded that it had flown 510 feet. "Wait a minute," I thought. I remembered that homer and was certain that it had traveled farther.

The next day found me in the microfilm department at the Philadelphia Public Library where I read old newspaper accounts about Dick Allen. They were informative and entertaining. Hey, this was fun. Without realizing it at that moment, I was hooked. Not fully understanding what I was doing or where I was going, I embarked on an exhaustive study of the history of tape measure home runs. In those early years, I kept bumping into that guy named Ruth. That didn't make much sense to me. While I knew that my dad would not have steered me wrong all those years before, when he had talked about the Babe and Jimmie Foxx, those guys were products of a different age, before improved strength training, nutrition, and equipment. Sure, Ruth was the longest hitter of his era, but he couldn't possibly keep up in purely physical terms with the best modern athletes, could he?

In fact, he did. As time passed, I became more and more fascinated with the Babe Ruth story, and I concentrated on him. Despite everything that had already been written about Ruth, including several qualitative biographies, it was apparent that the whole story had not been told. So, I decided to write my own book about the Babe. It wouldn't be just another biography, however, but a treatise focusing on the man's unique power, extraordinary showmanship, and amazing humanity. That book was published in 2007. However, over all the years since 1979, I have never stopped studying the tape measure home run.

I have spent thousands of hours in various libraries, including the Library of Congress. I have read everything that I could find on this subject from every source that I could identify. Visiting old ballpark sites and tracking down witnesses, I have logged tens of thousands of miles on my cars. The list of experts and witnesses include players, coaches, managers, historians, trainers, batboys, groundskeepers, security guards, reporters, scientists, administrators, scouts, announcers, and plain old fans of every stripe. Along the way, I have been privileged to meet almost every great slugger alive, past and present, from Ted Williams to Ryan Howard. I invite readers to visit the Sources section at the end of the book for further discussion of my research methodology.

Finally, *only 56 years* from the moment when it all started, I have written a book about the history of the tape measure home run. Joe Falls was correct. It did take years and years of intense research to get the job done properly. And, oh yes, you were right, Dad. The Bambino and old Double X are at the top of the list, right where you told me they belonged, back at Connie Mack Stadium on that blessed, summer day in 1953.

One

The Story of the Tape Measure Home Run

*I*n the beginning, power enabled primitive man to simply survive the day. Power remains a basic tool of survival, but now it is so much more. It comes in many forms, and, as a general rule, those who possess it enjoy richer, fuller lives. We see it in politics, warfare, business, and personal relationships. But we also see it as an object of awe, admiration, and entertainment, especially when it comes in the form of muscular speed and strength.

In the realm of fiction, we love hearing about Hercules, Paul Bunyan, and Superman. What biblical scholar doesn't like the story of Samson? Historically, we revere George Washington and Abraham Lincoln primarily for their great deeds and moral authority. But aren't we also fascinated by those shadowy stories about their physical vitality and strength as younger men? Wouldn't it be compelling to see George Washington lift a carriage off the ground to replace a broken wheel? Who wouldn't enjoy watching Abe Lincoln win the county wrestling competition in his youth?

> **Power, pure physical prowess, has inevitably become the main selling point of organized sports.**

Power, pure physical prowess, has inevitably become the main selling point of organized sports. We enjoy expressions of our physical essence: running, jumping, throwing, et cetera. When you factor in our innate sense of competition, athletic games and contests were bound to evolve into a popular phenomenon. The ancient Greeks displayed their core passion by organizing the original Olympic Games. In the Middle Ages, many of mankind's greatest spectacles focused on tournaments featuring jousting and other forms of intense physical competition. In the modern industrial era, Americans continued the tradition by creating a new competition that was appropriate to their time.

The origin of baseball has been somewhat romanticized over time. The truth is that we don't know the exact evolution of the sport. Similar games of ball and stick had been played for centuries around the globe. Then, in 19th-century America, the specific sport of baseball quickly evolved. The first documented game was played in 1840 in the Elysian Fields of Hoboken, New Jersey. By the Civil War, it was played by troops on both sides, and soon became so popular that it developed into a professional enterprise. As baseball quickly grew into our national pastime, the rules were modified and adjusted to facilitate the most attractive form of competition and participation. Essentially, by the turn of the 20th century, the job was finished, and the game was being played much the same way that it is today.

It wasn't a game of power in its early years like it is now. Back then, it was more about coordination, speed, reactions and, yes, a little bit of strength. Yet, power has always been at the heart of the baseball experience. Modern fans have a tendency to think that they lifted the passion for the home run to new levels. In 1998, when Mark McGwire and Sammy Sosa were setting home run records, the baseball world went a little crazy. That pair generated more interest in their sport than anybody else in a long time. Then, along came Barry Bonds with his newly enhanced power matrix, and, for better or worse, America was hooked for the next several years. But, was all this really new? No, not really. Everybody reacted pretty much the same way (even more so) to Babe Ruth as far back as 1919. Yet, America's home run craze started long before that. Ruth certainly elevated baseball's fascination for the long ball, but he wasn't the first man to create a frenzy by pounding horsehide spheres for

prodigious distances. If we carefully look back to the origins of professional baseball, we find that fans have always identified the strongest batsmen for special distinction, even adulation.

Most historians identify 1876 as the start of Major League Baseball, when the National League began competition. There had been a National Association as early as 1871, but it was too disorganized to qualify as a legitimate major league. Even then, however, there was a National Association figure named Lipman Pike who enthralled fans with his long-range clouts. Since his deeds were poorly chronicled, the details of his accomplishments are difficult to evaluate. Nonetheless, his legend still lives in the hearts of purists. The first official Major League home run was hit on May 2, 1876, by Chicago's Ross Barnes at Cincinnati's Avenue Grounds. It was a line drive down the left field line that rolled into an area where spectators watched from their carriages. The final destination of that first four-bagger is our starting point in the evolution of the home run.

Back then, only some big-league fields had outfield fences, typically parks with limited outfield space. During those earliest years, balls hit over the fences weren't even automatic four-baggers. At Boston's South End Grounds on June 6, 1879, Charley Jones blasted a ball over the distant left center field wall for what may have been the longest homer of the decade. Despite the epic distance of the blow, Jones was still required to speed around the bases before the ball was retrieved.

Generally, fans bought tickets to sit in the grandstand behind home plate, but carriages often circled the outfield at the more spacious stadiums where their presence was regarded as too distant to interfere with play. Occasionally, a guy like Ross Barnes smacked the ball far enough to roll where folks were watching, but such instances were regarded as oddities. In David Vincent's authoritative 2007 book, *Home Run: The Definitive History of Baseball's Ultimate Weapon*, he noted that, in 1876, only one home run was recorded for every 500 plate appearances. By 1883, the total had doubled to two per 500, but that number still pales to the 14 per 500 that we routinely see today. Therefore, as a strategic weapon, the home run was not particularly important in the early days of baseball. But that doesn't mean that fans didn't appreciate them.

Of course, the frequency of the long ball continued to increase, and the National League finally addressed the issue of standardization in 1888. A rule was passed that required outfield walls positioned at a minimum distance along the foul lines of 210 feet. That distance was incrementally increased over the years until 1959, when it was permanently fixed at 325 feet. For the sake of historical continuity, some exceptions are allowed. Most notably, the new Yankee Stadium opened in 2009 with the same foul line distances as its predecessor. Since 1888, any ball clearing those standardized barriers has automatically been ruled a four-bagger in recognition of its competitive distinction.

Back in 1880, two virtual giants, Dan Brouthers and Roger Connor, were playing for the Troy Trojans of the National League, and they were immensely popular with contemporary fans. They eventually became great players, but their stature was rooted in the exceptional physical power that both men embodied. Another common misconception held by today's fans is that modern players are significantly stronger than their early predecessors. It's true that the average player of today is bigger than the average player of the 19th century (and probably stronger), but we should not emphasize that disparity for two reasons. First, through careful analysis, it is apparent that the weights of the older players were consistently underreported. Most of us tend to rely on the figures provided in the *Baseball Encyclopedia* as absolute. That is a mistake. The fact that those numbers are often inaccurate is not the responsibility of that publication. They recorded the data that was provided to them. All baseball historians, including myself, use the *Encyclopedia* regularly, and derive great benefit.

Apparently, 19th-century players tended to characterize themselves as fast and agile, since those were the traits that journalists and officials emphasized. If an athlete gave his weight as over 200 pounds, he was sometimes regarded as overweight or even fat. The predictable result was that players were inclined to understate their body mass. Just as common was the policy of recording a man's weight early in his career, perhaps his rookie year, and never adjusting it. Most athletes gain weight from the beginning to the end of their professional lives, but, oftentimes, there is no change to the original record. That still happens today, but not nearly as much as in the old days. The whole thing was rather silly and futile, since fans decide what they like best. Of course, they admire speed and dexterity, but they have always loved power.

On June 27, 1885, Dave Orr (a 250-pound slugger with the era's New York Mets) smashed a tremendous inside-the-park homer to center field at the original Polo Grounds. Reporting the next day, the *New York Times* explained, "The spectators were wild with enthusiasm. They clapped their hands, stamped with their feet and rapped with their canes, threw their hats in the air, and bestowed praise on the successful batter until their throats were hoarse." A generation later, an article about baseball records appearing in the *Washington Post* on August 29, 1909 discussed such diamond rarities as perfect games and unassisted triple plays. It then switched focus to what the readers really wanted. The piece continued, "The long drive . . . is the exploit that lies closest to the heart of the fan. Par-

> **"The spectators were wild with enthusiasm. They clapped their hands, stamped their feet."**
> **—New York Times**

ticularly does he worship at the shrine of the home run." That was 100 years ago, and nothing has changed.

We all know the dramatic results of modern strength training and conditioning. The difference between an athlete who lifts weights and one who doesn't is substantial. Essentially, if two players start at the same strength level, the non-lifter has no chance of keeping up with the one who does. Since we also know that weight lifting was basically unknown to 19th-century ballplayers, we tend to assume that they were not as strong as the modern musclemen. Up to a point, that assumption is true. Today's players are stronger on average than their predecessors. But Brouthers and Connor were as strong as any weight-lifting players of the 21st century. How do we know that? First, we can just look at their photographs. We see lean, but heavily muscled men who tipped the scales at well over 200 pounds. More reliably, we evaluate their power performance curve in the context of their time. Specifically, we study how far they hit baseballs that were far less "lively" than the balls struck by modern players.

Understanding the history of the actual ball used in Major League history is challenging. The so-called "Dead Ball Era" has been designated as extending from 1901 through

1919, but the confusing reality is that the performance of the *ball* had little to do with that designation. Offensive production dropped off significantly in the early 1900s due mostly to rule changes. In 1900, home plate was enlarged from a 12-inch square to a five-sided shape that was 17 inches wide. A year later, foul balls were counted as strikes for the first time, and hitters took a beating. In 1911, the biggest-ever alteration in the ball took place when a cork center was placed inside. Predictably, offensive numbers shot up immediately, but, for a myriad of reasons, the "Live Ball Era" did not officially begin until 1920.

Unfortunately, we do not have exact information about the comparative flight capabilities of Major League baseballs over the course of the game's history. But we do know that the difference from the late 1800s to the early 2000s is considerable. A rough estimate suggests that a ball hit in 2010 would fly about 15 to 20 percent farther than a ball struck with equal force in 1890. There is no way to know for sure. I have arrived at this estimate by polling all the experts I know, and computing the average percentage from those offering an opinion. If that approximation is accurate, that's a big difference. If you add another one-fifth to the total length of the longest drives of Pike, Jones, Brouthers, Connor, Orr, Cal McVey, Cap Anson, Harry Stovey, Jocko Milligan, Sam Thompson, Ed Delahanty, and the other top 19th-century sluggers, you find distances that are compa-

rable to today's best. It is natural to then ask, "How can that be?" If the older guys didn't lift weights, and weight lifting makes such a big difference, how could they hit the ball with the same force?

I have personally struggled with that issue for many years. My findings have consistently indicated the same pattern. With each passing generation, there appears to be more players who can hit the ball beyond a certain linear distance . . . say 400 feet. However, the flight performance of the ball hasn't changed enough to explain the phenomenon completely. It is obvious that the median strength level of Major League players has increased more than the flight capability of the balls they use. Clearly, ballplayers are generally finding ways to get stronger. Yet, there is one extremely important caveat.

My research has also consistently indicated that the strongest players from any past era are as strong as today's muscle-bound behemoths. That has never made much sense to me, but it appears true nonetheless. After years of confusion, the answer is beginning to emerge. It lies in the more demanding physical lifestyles of prior generations and the effectiveness of so-called repetitive function. Players in the same generation as Brouthers and Connor were often farmers or coal miners. They may not have lifted weights in a training center, but the constant use of their musculature in repetitively demanding functions tended to develop prodigious strength. Of course, the results were not always benign.

If their labor was not balanced with proper nutrition and appropriate rest intervals, the effect was to wear out the laborer. But, when the conditions were right, the results were remarkably efficient.

Those old occupations are now difficult to comprehend. Workers in those 19th-century mines and farms often reported for duty before the sun came up and didn't return home until after dark. Miners usually began working at age 12, and farm boys started at a significantly younger age. The first few years in the coal mines generally entailed grueling support jobs, but, by age 16, miners were handed a pick, and expected to slam it into a vein of coal for 12 straight hours . . . every day! Don't even consider the unbearable monotony of those tasks. Ponder the purely physical demands of swinging a heavy tool day after day for 12 consecutive hours. Along with the ingestion of coal dust into their lungs, this draconian lifestyle sent many men into early graves. But the survivors forged physiques of steel-like flesh, capable of doing things that most of us wouldn't even try today.

Some of the best examples of the efficacy of repetitive function are found in military history. In 2005, a group of British Royal Marines were asked to replicate the physical exertions of artillerymen fighting for Napoleon at the historic battle at Waterloo. The outcome was an eye-opener. Those Marines are similar to our own special forces, like Navy SEALs, and are superbly trained. However, when asked to move cannons in the thick mud like the French did in 1815 (as records confirm), they struggled. In fact, in that same Napoleonic Era, we know that The Grand Army trekked into Russia carrying 60 pounds of gear over distances that no modern army can duplicate. How could they do it? Apparently, they did it because they were required to, and they simply got accustomed to doing it. There have also been recent studies of medieval soldiers wielding weapons that modern men struggle to control. Their armor tells us that they weren't that big, but, somehow, they fought with swords and lances that today's athletes can't handle for more than a few moments. When human beings are required to do difficult things, they usually find a way to do them. Somehow, they develop the requisite skills and strength.

Baseball history is replete with examples of men exhibiting immense physical power before the advent of sophisticated strength training. Along with the players already mentioned, the late 1800s featured two powerful sluggers named "Buck." William "Buck" Ewing was born in Ohio in 1859 and grew up in Cincinnati's East End. By 1878, he was working six days a week as a deliveryman for a local distillery. Along with driving his beloved horses, he lifted heavy whiskey barrels 10 hours a day, six days a week. On Sundays, he caught for the local Mohawk Browns, where he was "discovered" by Major League barnstormers in the fall of 1879. By the time he finished his big-league playing career in 1897, Ewing was generally regarded as the greatest baseball player of his era. He stood 5'10" and weighed 185 pounds.

John "Buck" Freeman began life in the coal regions of upstate Pennsylvania in 1871, but learned quickly that the mining life was not for him. At age 16, he ventured into a crude gymnasium in Wilkes-Barre, where he worked tirelessly on the parallel bars. Buck stood 5'9" and tipped the scales at only 170 pounds. After setting the legitimate season home run record in 1899 (with 25), he talked freely about the rigorous lifestyle that had rendered him so potent. He awoke early each morning and hiked 10 to 12 miles over the Pocono Mountains. Freeman also tried to engage in all other forms of intense exertion as often as possible. The combined body mass of the "two Bucks" was relatively low, but it was comprised almost completely of bone, sinew, and steel-like muscle. Despite their physical stature, these men were leviathans in the art of pounding baseballs. In fact, records indicate that these modestly sized old-timers hit the ball with force equal to that of modern powerhouses Barry Bonds and Sammy Sosa. The two Bucks certainly didn't hit long balls nearly as often as their celebrated successors, but, when they hit them, they hit them just as hard.

I acknowledge that the point in discussion is subtle and complex. Athletes are definitely getting bigger, stronger, and faster with each passing year. All the record books confirm this. In every sport, it is difficult to find any performance standard that has not been repeatedly improved with the passage of time. However, in some sports, such as baseball, the incremental improvements are relatively small. More importantly to this discussion, one specific insight needs to be repeated. The average player from the 19th century may be less strong than the average player from the 21st century. But, the strongest players from the 19th century appear to be as strong as the strongest players from today.

Those pioneers, who have already been identified, were succeeded in the early 1900s by men like Honus Wagner, Nap Lajoie, Sam Crawford, Jake Stahl, Gavvy Cravath, and Shoeless Joe Jackson. Their home run totals may seem insignificant by today's standards, but their raw animal power was anything but inconsequential. These men were gifted with superb athleticism, but don't be misled. They also possessed formidable strength and were the glory of their times. Their home run totals were not lower due to a lack of strength, but because of the difference in the way that the game was played. In the beginning, the one-base-at-a-time style of offense was emphasized. Early on, Sliding Billy Hamilton, John

But, the strongest players from the 19th century appear to be as strong as the strongest players from today.

McGraw, Wee Willie Keeler, and others of their ilk provided the blueprint for how runs should be scored. Sluggers were there, and they were very popular. However, they were exceptions, and didn't form the nucleus of the talent pool.

In 1905, Ty Cobb arrived in the big leagues, and his subsequent accomplishments clearly indicate superior batting strength. For example, at Cleveland's League Park on June 25, 1912, Cobb launched a tremendous drive onto a housetop across Lexington Avenue in right field. That ball flew nearly 450 feet; the power was there. If Ty could do it once, he could do it again. Yet, Cobb rarely hit home runs. Why? Swinging for the fences just wasn't fashionable with the purists at that point, and Cobb embraced their old-fashioned techniques. He sublimated power to on-base percentage and base-stealing. Ty choked up on the bat, spread his hands apart, and made a conscious effort to hit line drives to different areas of the field. If the Georgia Peach played today (with the exact same body), he would likely hit at least three times as many homers as he did back then (118). However, early in Ty Cobb's career, the guys were still playing with a ball that resembled a lump of mush. Additionally, the ballparks simply were not designed and constructed with home run production in mind. As late as 1931, when Cleveland's vast Municipal Stadium was built to replace League Park, it featured absurdly long home run distances. Despite continuing in use until 1993, no player ever cleared

Municipal Stadium's original four-base boundary that extended from left center field to right center field. Nobody ever!

Of course, the standards began changing in 1914, when George Herman Ruth entered professional baseball. There doesn't appear to be any rhyme or reason for what happened next. The Babe was a profound abnormality. He was a freak of nature, a biological aberration . . . call him whatever you like. But we really can't learn much from him. Rather, we should just enjoy him. Simply put, Babe Ruth hit the ball harder and farther than anyone else who ever played the sport. He was unique and literally impossible to explain. So, in the story of power hitting, he gets top billing, but doesn't fit into any pattern.

Still, Ruth does serve as the key transitional figure in this story. McGraw and Cobb bitterly resented Ruth for altering the game for which they were the acknowledged masters. From Babe Ruth onward, baseball focused on bigger, brawnier players who scoffed at the old way of scoring. When the Yankees constructed their new playpen in 1923, they did so with Ruth's home run totals in mind. Yankee Stadium ("The House That Ruth Built") was specifically designed with a short right field porch to help The Babe do his thing. But, the other dimensions, by today's standards, were prohibitively difficult. Between 1923 and 2008, when the great Bronx landmark finally closed, the outfield distances were shortened four times. It was Ruth who finally (and permanently) tilted baseball toward the power game, and that sea change is still in effect. Every generation plays in smaller ballparks with livelier baseballs, whereby home runs are easier to hit.

The Bambino was soon followed by Lou Gehrig, who hit the ball with ferocious might, but was not a classic long-distance slugger. The real heir to Ruth's throne was Jimmie Foxx, born on Maryland's Eastern Shore in 1907. He was another guy who never lifted weights as we understand the process today. But Double X still left a legacy of long-distance hitting that has rarely been rivaled. In fact, until Mickey Mantle was born in 1931, the baseball world did not see another physical specimen that could compare to Foxx. Those prodigies combined speed and power to such extreme levels that their deeds now seem fictional. They were two of the most amazing products of human engineering that the athletic world has ever produced. Yet neither of them lifted weights or engaged in modern state-of-the-art strength training. How did they do it?

Again, we return to the farms and mines of America for the answers. Jimmie was raised in Sudlersville, which was in the heart of farm country. In later years, he credited his strong hands and wrists to his frequent milking of cows. His superhuman arms and shoulders were fashioned by hoisting thousands of bales of hay, while engaging in other laborious farm functions. The Mighty Mick was raised in the tiny town of Commerce in northeastern Oklahoma. His father worked in

the local mineral mines, but tried to keep his son from descending into the stygian depths on a daily basis. But the Mantles were not financially secure, and young Mickey had to work.

The younger Mantle wound up near the entrance to the mine as a "screen ape." His task was to break large pieces of mineral ore as they arrived at the surface from the men hundreds of feet below. That was accomplished by smashing the rocks with a 20-pound sledgehammer over and over and over again. Undoubtedly, Jimmie Foxx and Mickey Mantle were born with genetic codes that rendered them naturally strong. But, by the time they reached their late teens, their physiques had been further hardened and sculpted by thousands of hours of intense manual labor. It may not have been pleasant, but the results were astounding.

As Major League Baseball has evolved, one constant has been the fascination for the long ball. The practitioners varied in size and shape, but their popularity never changed. Hack Wilson was short and squat (5'6" and 190 pounds), and Ted Williams (6'4" and 175 pounds in his rookie year) was long and lean. Even the way they arrived at their common skill level seemed to vary from man to man. Williams studied the art of hitting, and then swung a baseball bat whenever or wherever he could. If a pitcher wasn't available, it didn't matter. Young Ted would play imaginary games, taking his rips until it felt perfect. The legendary Josh Gibson of the old Negro Leagues reportedly didn't like batting practice, but still traveled the world to play baseball as often as he could. Somehow, like Williams and all the other great distance hitters, he found a way to generate tremendous bat speed. In the function of hitting tape measure home runs, that's what matters most.

As the years passed, baseball benefited from great talents in every decade. Hank Greenberg came along in the '30s, and was followed by Ralph Kiner in the '40s. Larry Doby was not only the first black player in the American League in 1948, but also one of the great long-distance hitters of any era. Soon after, the '50s witnessed the arrival of Willie Mays, Luke Easter, Hank Aaron, Ernie Banks, and Frank Robinson as well as other great sluggers of color. Something odd then happened in the 1960s. For reasons that we will probably never know, the sport enjoyed the "Golden Age" of tape measure home runs. Without question, there were more men of great power, physically capable of launching baseballs 500 feet, playing in the '60s than in any other decade. Some of them arrived in the 1950s, but spent most of their careers in the following 10-year span. That included such players as Joe Adcock, Harmon Killebrew, Dick Stuart, Frank Howard, Norm Cash, and Willie McCovey. Others actually started in the '60s, and performed into the '70s or even '80s. That group featured Willie Stargell, Dick Allen, Jimmy Wynn, Boog Powell, and Reggie Jackson. And don't forget that Mickey Mantle

spent the second half of his big-league tenure with this group. Available records indicate an enormous number of 450-plus-foot shots by these men.

I first became aware of this apparent 1960s abnormality in the mid-1980s. I sought an explanation, and soon thought I had found one. Most of these '60s strongmen played the majority of their games in enclosed stadiums. By "enclosed," we are not referring to indoor facilities but rather the larger stadiums that wrap their high superstructures around (or nearly around) the outfield perimeter. As far back as the 1920s with additions to ballparks like Yankee Stadium and Comiskey Park, there were arenas where batted balls were sometimes interrupted in mid-flight. But, not until the 1960s, with the wave of newly designed multipurpose stadiums (so-called cookie-cutter structures), were most tape measure shots knocked down so quickly by elevated seating directly behind the outfield fences. Back then, we rarely used the science of physics to estimate how far those balls would have flown if left unimpeded. Instead, there was a lot of grade school arithmetic and guesswork. As a result, long drives from that era were commonly overestimated. I know; I did it myself.

With the eventual guidance of scientists like Robert K. Adair (Sterling Professor of Physics, Yale University), we finally got it right. We came to realize that, when a batted ball has reached its apex (or highest point), it has already used most of its energy and velocity. Accordingly, it falls back to field level in a rapidly declining trajectory. Few people in the baseball world of the '60s (and before) seemed to understand that. For example, witnesses would see a mighty drive collide with some upper tier structure at a height of 80 feet above field level, and assume that it would have flown another 100 feet plus. In fact, the ball was already on its downward arc, and likely had only another 50 feet of flight distance. As a result, most such drives had been over-rated. When I finally learned my lesson, I went back over my records, and downsized hundreds of home runs . . . sometimes by as much as 70 or 80 feet. I then reevaluated the men of the '60s in that reformed context. But, even then, they held up as the mightiest group ever to hit a baseball.

Is it possible that there were more powerful men playing baseball in the '60s than at any other time?

It may have been merely an extraordinary coincidence or it may have been the result of some indeterminate cause, but that crew surpasses any other in tape measure capability. Is it possible that Major League baseballs were more resilient or more aerodynamically efficient during that time? That's highly unlikely. Such a scenario could not have eventuated without public awareness; a livelier ball would have caused *all* offensive production to skyrocket. Except for expansion seasons, that did not happen. As with the case of the individual superiority of Babe Ruth, we have a classic anachronism in the men of the '60s. With each passing year, their deeds seem more remarkable.

Before moving on, there is one theory that should probably be mentioned. Perhaps it doesn't rise to the level of a theory, but rather functions more like a suggestion. As of the early '50s, when the young men of the '60s were pondering their athletic futures, professional football and basketball were not big-time enterprises. If you wanted to get rich and famous playing sports, you had to play baseball, or, in limited cases, become a boxer. However, by the end of that decade, the Baltimore Colts and New York Giants had played their famous NFL sudden-death championship game. In the NBA, the great Boston Celtics' dynasty, with the unrivaled talent of Wilt Chamberlain as their chief nemesis, took hoops to new heights. Suddenly, there were more options for achieving fame and fortune in the sports world. Accordingly, fewer of the country's strongest men found their way onto baseball diamonds. When we also recall that the full circle of baseball integration did not occur until the 1960s, it leads to an intriguing question. Is it possible that there were more powerful men playing baseball in the '60s than at any other time? I don't profess to know the answer. I'm merely asking.

In the '70s, we watched in wonder as Greg Luzinski, Dave Kingman, George Foster, Jim Rice, and Mike Schmidt blasted balls to faraway places. They were succeeded in the '80s by Darryl Strawberry, Mark McGwire, Barry Bonds, Kirk Gibson, Sammy Sosa, Jose Canseco, Cecil Fielder, and Bo Jackson. All through the '90s and into the present, the tape measure honor roll has continued to grow. We have watched Ken Griffey Jr., Frank Thomas, Fred McGriff, Jim Thome, Manny Ramirez, Mike Piazza, Alex Rodriguez, Adam Dunn, Wily Mo Pena, and Ryan Howard emerge as the modern elite. Of course, this entire generation has been tainted by the steroid issue, and that is a cultural tragedy. We will never know the identity of every man who used performance-enhancing drugs, but most of us suspect many of today's athletes.

That issue has created a dilemma for this author. I have publicly expressed my belief that many players since the 1980s have used steroids and human growth hormones. I have even named names. Unquestionably, the issue of performance-enhancing drugs remains a dark cloud over Major League Baseball. Recent revelations about Manny Ramirez and Alex Rodriguez confirm that sad truth. However, this is not a book about drugs, and I don't want the focus of this discourse to head in that direction. Accordingly, steroids will not be addressed in the individual narratives. I will reserve my cynicism for other forums. Of course, I cannot avoid the inevitable inferences that derive from fact. In discussing the power performance curve of some players, it may seem obvious that they have cheated. Whereas I prefer not to overtly discredit anyone, I won't compromise my integrity as an historian to protect them.

I have one final thought about performance-enhancing drugs. Major League Baseball has tried to rectify the problem, but the results have been marginal. There is a mistaken notion that professional baseball has been "cleaned up." It is a fact that progress has been achieved in testing, but there have also been setbacks. For example, in the past, urine specimens were kept indefinitely. That allowed for subsequent, retroactive testing of a player who may have been using an illegal substance whose chemical signature was unknown to scientists at the time of the original test. It was a powerful deterrent against the use of new so-called designer drugs. As a result of the latest agreement between the Players' Union and MLB, that crucial aspect of enforcement no longer exists. I personally doubt that the entire Barry Bonds legal saga would have occurred if specimens were not stored when he testified before a grand jury in 2003. In other words, there is still a lot of work to do before the "Steroid Era" is really over.

Today, as we observe young mega-talents like Prince Fielder and Albert Pujols evolve into tape measure kings, we are engaging in a joyous ritual that has continued for over 130 years. Our fathers, grandfathers, and great-grandfathers did the same thing. They cherished the strongest men of their own times just as we do. And think about this. Our sons, grandsons, and great-grandsons will carry on this same fascination when we are gone. People love power; that will never change. So, it seems fitting to write a book to honor those men who have enriched the game of baseball with their unique and intoxicating ability. Again, this is not a book about home run totals; it is about home runs hit so far that they leave us doubting our senses.

This study is divided into two parts. Part One includes 63 mini-biographies, featuring the strongest of the strong, identifying the most potent batsmen ever to swing a carved piece of wood. They are placed into different chapters, naming the 40 longest hitters in baseball history, the 10 longest-hitting active players, the five mightiest from the the 19th century as well as the five top men from the Negro League era. As the rankings move closer to the top, the mini-chapters become longer. Part One also includes a salute to Hank Aaron, Willie Mays, and Frank Robinson, who deserve their own honoraria in any story about power hitting. It ends with a final narrative chapter of various insights, summaries, and conclusions. Part Two is a compendium of lists of every sort relating to tape measure hitting. Perhaps the two most important lists are the ones identifying the 100 longest hitters and the 100 longest batted balls in baseball history. The Sources section not only establishes where the data comes from, but also discusses the methodology for estimating distances.

Space does not permit the opportunity to recognize every great long-distance hitter in the annals of the game. Since the rankings and selections are the responsibility of a single individual, there are bound to be some oversights and omissions. I have strived to be inclusive, fair, and accurate, but this topic is extremely difficult to quantify. Every man who is even mentioned grew up in an environment in which he was probably the absolute mightiest player. Starting in Little League and continuing through high school, he would likely have been perceived as the strongest hitter that anybody had ever seen. Arriving in the big leagues, he would have performed in such thrilling fashion that his fans regarded him as the best ever. When such players are not rated at the top, or perhaps not included at all, their admirers will be unavoidably disenchanted. For this, I am sorry.

Also, please consider that this topic is naturally infused with a great deal of emotion and personal drama. All of us who have witnessed a genuine tape measure home run have been subjected to the "rush" that it causes. Thereafter, we tend to recall the way our senses were overloaded, and we imbue the memory with particularly ardent passion. In other words, we naturally tend to value our own experiences. If someone recalls a particular slugger as being unusually noteworthy, he almost certainly was. But millions of men (and women) have tried their hand at bashing baseballs, and there is only room to include 63 of them for individual discussion.

It is fair and appropriate, therefore, to question how these rankings have been created. What are the criteria? The truth is that there is no single standard; there is no all-encompassing arithmetical formula. The process begins with the laborious task of studying all or, at least, most of the home runs hit by every great slugger. With the modern hitters, the job is relatively simple. They have played in a time when all of their homers are routinely estimated for flight distance. However, prior to the 1980s, few performers had their power outputs so meticulously documented. In those cases, it is necessary to review the descriptions found in contemporary newspaper accounts for each home run. Obviously, not every homer has been reliably recorded in that fashion, but, after evaluating enough examples (or variables), clear patterns begin to emerge. For example, after reading the descriptions of 400 Henry Aaron home runs, you develop a reasonably accurate understanding of how far he could hit a baseball. You might not know the distance of each individual blow, but you certainly have a reliable picture of his performance parameters.

Once the data was obtained, I tried to develop a sensible system by which to make evaluations. That was the tricky part. I have chosen to implement a three-part standard for judging the batting power of each subject. First, what is the longest single drive that each man is known to have hit? Second, what are the 10 mightiest four-baggers that have been identified for each player? Third, what is their career home run total? When the first two factors are relatively equal, the final ingredient (total homers) is always the tie-breaker. That seems only fair. Some folks might believe that a player's single longest drive represents the best criteria for judging maximum power. I don't. A guy might get lucky, and make optimum contact with a ball that is aided by the coincidence of optimum weather conditions. Player A might strike one of his best-ever shots with a 20-mph tailwind, while Player B never had the same fluky advantage.

I prefer to look at a man's top 10 longest drives. I suggest that a slugger's 10th longest home run is more revealing than his single longest poke. As a result, each subject player has his 10 longest home runs listed immediately after his mini-chapter. Understand, however, that every known bit of information is factored into the ranking system. By way of another example, occasionally, we see a player who didn't hit any balls over 500 feet and few over 450 feet. However, that same fellow might have walloped scores of blows between 400 and 450 feet during a career that

A slugger's 10th longest home run is more revealing than his single longest poke.

is demonstrably noteworthy for exceptional power. Certainly, such a performer needs to be evaluated in a positive light. As a point of reference, 450 feet is the commonly accepted threshold for exceptional long-distance hitting, commonly referred to as a tape measure home run.

So, let's enjoy the phenomenon of long-distance hitting. It represents our essence as sports fans. There is no denying our fascination with power in all its forms. And it's okay to debate or even argue about the quantification process. More than any other sport, baseball, with its affinity for numerical analysis, encourages historical rankings. We cherish that sense of continuity . . . memories passing from father to son, generation to generation. That notion is at the very heart of baseball's lingering appeal. So, remember the guys who gave us the goosebumps. Pass on their names to those who follow, and honor Baseball's Ultimate Power.

Two

Henry, Willie, and Frank

HANK AARON: 755 HOME RUNS— 1954 TO 1976

There is no better way to begin a discussion of baseball's mightiest power hitters than with the great Henry Aaron. "Hammerin' Hank" is not generally known as a tape measure slugger, but it is a fact that he hit the ball with savage regularity for his entire 23-year career. Not only did he record a then-record 755 home runs, he also accrued a lifetime slugging percentage of .555. You can't do

that without pounding the ball game after game, year after year.

Born in Mobile, Alabama, in 1934, Henry was a product of the Jim Crow "Deep South." However, he had an innate aura of inner peace that allowed him to grow into adulthood with an uncommon sense of purpose and determination. That trait, combined with great natural athletic ability, led Hank Aaron into the Major League record book.

Henry was not a large man by professional athletic standards. He stood 6 feet tall, and, for most of his career, played at about 190 pounds. But, as is often the case with great hitters, he possessed powerful hands and wrists. Always considered a superb all-around player, no one envisioned the kind of epic power numbers that Aaron would produce. As a 20-year-old rookie with the Milwaukee Braves in 1954, Hank hit a respectable, but not imposing, total of 13 homers. Smacking 27 the next year, folks took notice. He added 26 in 1956, and received special attention with a pair of twin 450-footers in spring training. Playing in Bradenton, Florida, on March 11, Henry ripped a pair of gigantic shots over the 433 foot sign in dead center field. When Aaron blasted 44 in 1957, at only

Courtesy of the Atlanta Braves

Hank Aaron

age 23, the baseball world knew for certain that Henry was an exceptional power hitter. He never stopped clouting home runs until he retired after the 1976 season.

Aaron's first official tape measure blast occurred on May 7, 1955 at Busch Stadium in St. Louis. Henry bombed one into the shrubbery beyond the 425 foot sign in center field. That blow was a legitimate 450-footer, and erased any lingering doubt about Aaron's pure physical power. As things turned out, Busch may have been Henry's best long-distance launching pad. On July 13, 1963, against Curt Simmons, he actually hit one over those same shrubs. And, on May 25, 1962, Aaron pummeled the ball against the Cardinal image on the towering scoreboard atop the left field bleachers.

In the Aaron era, Forbes Field in Pittsburgh was an exceptionally difficult place for a right-handed batsman to hit home runs. It was 365 feet down the left field line and 457 feet to deepest center. A 12-foot-high brick wall extended around those daunting dimensions, and there was also a 25-foot-high scoreboard in left field that was in play. Nonetheless, Aaron still managed to record 30 homers in Pittsburgh from 1954 through mid 1970, when the Pirates switched to Three Rivers Stadium. Henry's longest at Forbes Field might have been his rocket over the left center field wall on April 22, 1960. He hit it off Pittsburgh ace Bob Friend, who was known to be pretty tough on right-handed hitters. Remarkably, Aaron belted two more

Friend offerings over those bricks on July 21, 1961. Hank then added yet another pair against Friend at Forbes Field on September 23, 1962. Henry Aaron apparently never got the message that he wasn't supposed to bash homers off Bob Friend in Pittsburgh.

In a recent book about Babe Ruth, it has been projected that the Babe would have hit many more homers if playing in modern (and smaller) ballparks. Hank Aaron is entitled to the same fact-based conjecture. The Forbes Field factor has just been discussed, and it is an historical fact that Milwaukee's County Stadium, which Aaron called home from 1954 through 1965, was a difficult place to clear the fences. Accordingly, we should add about another 50 projected home runs to Aaron's career total if plotting his batted balls in today's parks. For the record, among the 193 home runs that Henry recorded at County Stadium, his mightiest probably occurred on July 20, 1960. That was the day that Aaron drove one deep into the bleachers just left of center for a ride of 455 feet.

The most famous distance-shot authored by Hammerin' Hank was his fabled drive into the center field bleachers at the Polo Grounds on June 18, 1962. From the time that this hallowed stadium was renovated in 1923 until it was permanently closed in 1963, only three home runs reached those seats in big-league games. This was one of them. Since it was about 440 feet to the left wing of the bleachers, where the ball landed, this was a drive of about 460 feet. Many baseball fans have heard about this homer, but few know that Aaron blasted one almost as far just two days later while completing the series at the Polo Grounds on June 20. Henry ripped that ball into the upper deck in left center.

Henry Aaron and his Braves teammates moved to Atlanta for the 1966 season, where they occupied what was then called Atlanta–Fulton County Stadium. Fortunately for Aaron, it was a significantly easier place to hit for power than back in Milwaukee. Hank's first homer there was lined into the elevated left field seats on April 29. It came with two out in the 9th inning and won the game against the Astros. Later that season, on July 26, Aaron smashed one over those seats into the club level that was estimated at 458 feet. His longest-ever in Atlanta was his eye-popping 470-foot line drive into the left field upper deck on April 13, 1970.

At Connie Mack Stadium in Philadelphia, Hank launched two balls over the left field roof in 1966. Those blows off Bo Belinsky and Roger Craig were hit respectively on April 20 and June 14. Over the years, he also landed at least six other balls onto that 65-foot-high structure. And that leads directly into another topic for consideration. Aaron recorded 98 triples and 624 doubles during his fabulous career. Predictably, many of them were struck with considerable force. Also at Connie Mack, in 1961, Hank blasted a vicious line drive double off the 420 foot sign in deep left center field that looked like it had been hit with a one-iron. Everyone stared in amazement.

HANK AARON'S 10 LONGEST HOME RUNS

- April 13, 1970—Atlanta off San Francisco's Reberger—Line drive into left field upper deck—470 ft.
- May 25, 1962—St. Louis off Washburn—Off scoreboard atop left field bleachers—465 ft.
- June 18, 1962—New York off Hook—Into center field bleachers—460 ft.
- April 20, 1966—Philadelphia off Belinsky—Over left field grandstand roof—460 ft.
- July 26, 1966—Atlanta off Jackson—Into club level in deep left field—458 ft.
- July 13, 1963—St. Louis off Simmons—Past shrubs beyond center field fence—455 ft.
- May 7, 1955—St. Louis off Moford—Into shrubs beyond 425 ft. sign in center field—455 ft.
- July 20, 1960—Milwaukee off St. Louis's Broglio—High into left center field bleachers—455 ft.
- September 10, 1963—Cincinnati off Tsitouris—Far over center field wall—450 ft.
- April 14, 1961—Chicago off Anderson—Far over left center field bleachers—450 ft.

Make no mistake on this subject: Henry Aaron not only hit baseball's second highest home run total, he hit them long and hard. He clearly deserves to be ranked in the list of the longest hitters in MLB history. His career may best be known for grace, dignity, and consistent athletic virtuosity, but he should also be regarded as a true tape measure king.

WILLIE MAYS: 660 HOME RUNS— 1951 TO 1973

For anyone born before 1960, Willie Mays is generally regarded as the best baseball player that we ever saw. But where does he stand in relation to the focus of this book? For starters, he consistently swung harder than just about anyone who ever played on a regular basis. Mays usually looked like he was coming out of his socks as he swung the bat. That kind of mayhem normally compromises the precision required to center the ball against Major League pitching. Nonetheless, Willie finished his storybook career with a lifetime batting average of .301. That should tell us something about his amazing athleticism.

The first big-league homer that Willie Mays hit came off the great Warren Spahn at New York's Polo Grounds on May 28, 1951. By his own admission, Willie was a nervous 20-year-old rookie who had not fared well in his first few games. Mays believes that Spahn took pity on him, and grooved a "batting practice fastball" right down the middle. Either way, Willie took advantage of the moment

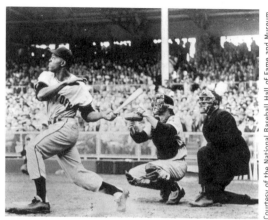
Willie Mays

and pounded the ball onto the towering (80 feet high) roof of the left field grandstand. It was only 273 feet down the left field line at that historic ballpark, but the walls angled out quickly, resulting in power alleys over 400 feet from home plate. In fact, the bullpen in left center field, where Mays would regularly direct many of his best shots, was 440 feet from home plate. All in all, the Polo Grounds was not an easy place to hit home runs.

After recording a very respectable total of 20 homers in his abbreviated first season, Willie Mays missed most of the 1952 and 1953 seasons due to military service. Mays returned in time to start the 1954 season and proceeded to smash 41 home runs. It was a remarkable accomplishment for a 23-year-old who had been out of organized baseball for nearly two years. When it is recalled that Willie had primarily been known for his blazing speed up to that time, it is no wonder that his '54 homer total was so surprising to the baseball world.

Early in that 1954 season, it became obvious that Willie Mays was an athletic prodigy. Willie blasted the ball into the left center field upper deck at the Polo Grounds on May 28 for his first tape measure home run in a Major League game. The ball entered the elevated seats above the 447 foot sign. Almost incredibly, Mays then launched balls to nearly the exact same spot on consecutive days on July 27 and July 28. And he followed that with a potent smash over the left field grandstand roof on September 16.

Willie improved his performance with the astonishing total of 51 home runs in 1955. His longest of the year surpassed the Polo Grounds' roof far from the left field foul line on July 7. It was an imposing display of power. For the record, Mays cleared that roof seven times before the Giants relocated to San Francisco in 1958. However, before departing for the West Coast, Willie also demonstrated his long ball ability all around the National League. His two best as a visitor included a blow off the light tower above the left field scoreboard in St. Louis on July 12, 1956, and a rocket over the 55-foot-high scoreboard in left center in Cincinnati on June 27, 1957.

Playing in the Bay Area for the next 14 years, Mays kept blasting the ball very hard and very far. But it wasn't easy . . . especially after the Giants moved into Candlestick Park. Starting in late afternoon, the prevailing winds at Candlestick tended to blow forcibly across the field from left to right. It was a tough spot for a right-handed power hitter.

But Mays made the most of a difficult situation, and often made a deliberate effort to hit to right field. Overcoming the handicap, Willie finished with 660 home runs. But what might he have accomplished in a friendlier home field? And don't forget those two seasons lost to military service. Surely, we're talking about well over 700 homers.

In San Francisco, Willie's longest at Seals Stadium (1958–1959) was his shot off the top of the center field scoreboard (420 feet away) on September 1, 1958. He also knocked one over the left field bleachers and into the parking lot on May 14, 1959. Mays recorded 29 and 34 home runs in those first two seasons on the West Coast. They were fine totals, but Willie suffered somewhat from the impossibly high expectations that surrounded his arrival in California. Somehow, he eventually lived up to them.

Mays hit his first Candlestick Park home run on May 6, 1960, glancing one off the top of the right field fence. Beginning that season Willie totaled 29, 40, 49, 38, and then 47 homers in 1964. Those were awesome numbers, but the San Francisco fans still wanted more. After all, Mays had hit 51 back in New York in 1955. But, then came 1965, and Willie Mays erased all reservations by blasting his career-best number of 52 home runs. On the long-distance front, Willie reached the 24th row of the remote left field bleachers on September 8, 1961. He also sent balls flying well beyond the 410 foot sign in center field on April 18, 1964, April 19, 1964, May 21, 1964,

April 20, 1965, June 14, 1966, and September 14, 1968.

On the road, Willie bombed balls far over the left center field bleachers at Wrigley Field on May 5, 1962 and April 13, 1963. Returning to the Polo Grounds, where the Mets then called home, Mays surmounted the left field roof twice more: June 2, 1962 and May 5, 1963. At Busch Stadium in St. Louis, Willie uncorked 450-footers on June 2, 1963, August 11, 1964, and August 8, 1965. Mays added drives of comparable length over Connie Mack Stadium's left field roof on April 14, 1965, and over Forbes Field's left field scoreboard on June 12, 1965. However, his best road show occurred on April 30, 1961, at County Stadium in Milwaukee. On this memorable day, Willie Mays blasted four home runs in a ballpark known for its distant fences. Number three landed near the top of the left field bleachers for a blow of 460 feet.

At age 40 on September 26, 1971, Willie lined one 450 feet to dead center at Riverfront Stadium in Cincinnati. He may have been getting old, but Mays still had it. Within two years Willie retired, but not before belting Career Number 660 on August 17, 1973, over the right center field fence at Shea Stadium. Willie Mays then walked away from the game leaving a legacy of speed, skill, showmanship, and power that has rarely been approached in the annals of his sport.

WILLIE MAYS'S 10 LONGEST HOME RUNS

- July 7, 1955—New York off Philadelphia's Negray—Over grandstand roof near left center—480 ft.
- June 14, 1957—New York off Cincinnati's Nuxhall—Line drive over left field roof—475 ft.
- July 12, 1956—St. Louis off Poholsky—Off light tower atop left field scoreboard—475 ft.
- June 2, 1962—New York off Moorhead—Line drive off light tower atop roof in left center—470 ft.
- May 5, 1962—Chicago off Koonce—Far over left center field bleachers—465 ft.
- June 27, 1957—Cincinnati off Gross—Over 55-foot-high scoreboard in left center—465 ft.
- September 8, 1961—San Francisco off Los Angeles's Podres—To 24th row in left field bleachers—460 ft.
- July 27, 1954—New York off St. Louis's Haddix—Into upper deck in deep left center—460 ft.
- April 30, 1961—Milwaukee off Morehead—To top of left field bleachers—460 ft.
- April 14, 1965—Philadelphia off Bunning—Over left field grandstand roof—455 ft.

FRANK ROBINSON: 586 HOME RUNS—1956 TO 1976

Modern fans know that Frank Robinson was a great player. But they have seen him managing and working as a Major League executive for so long that they may have forgotten just how great. The facts confirm that he was one of the best ever, and he certainly pounded the ball viciously for over two decades. Starting with the Cincinnati Reds in 1956, the 21-year-old Robinson became the poster boy for one of the most powerful teams in baseball history. Frank hit 38 home runs that season, and never looked back. The 6'1", 190-pound right-handed powerhouse blasted two drives over the left field roof at the Polo Grounds (May 22 and September 11) in that first season. Perhaps more importantly, Robinson showed that he would not back down from anybody. Pitchers learned early that

Courtesy of the Cincinnati Reds

Frank Robinson

trying to intimidate Frank was futile. For his efforts, Robinson was unanimously voted the National League Rookie of the Year.

In his second season, Frank seemed to get stronger. On September 8, 1957, he cleared the left field bleachers at Busch Memorial Stadium in St. Louis. One week later, Robinson blasted a 485-footer to left center field at Cincinnati's Crosley Field that collided with the second floor of a building across the street. In those days, there was a laundry sign beyond the left field wall at Crosley. That billboard and the building on which it stood were eventually torn down and replaced by a parking lot. But, early in Robinson's career, that sign was a signature plateau for judging long-distance hitting. Frank cleared it several times with the mightiest taking place on May 27, 1959. Later that same year on August 22, also in Cincinnati, Robinson powered one far over the 55-foot-high scoreboard in left center. This drive required great batting strength, but Frank did it many times, including encores on successive days on August 10 and 11, 1962.

No player in the 59-year history of Crosley Field (aka Redland Field) left a more impressive legacy of long home runs than Frank Robinson. His lengthiest was delivered on June 22, 1965. Robby bombed one so far over the center field wall that club officials went in search of witnesses who saw where the ball landed. They were successful. This monumental drive cleared Western Avenue and was measured at 503 feet. On the road, Robinson was equally deadly. At Connie Mack Stadium on May 11, 1965, Frank bombed one onto the 65-foot-high grandstand roof in deepest left center field. The ball rattled around above the 420 foot marker as fans gawked in amazement. Two days later, he reached the same roof in left center field (although somewhat closer to home plate), but this drive was hit against the wind. Returning to Philly on July 3, Frank deposited his third homer onto the rooftop in left center. Robinson hit several other balls to that roof, but doing it three times in the same year as a visitor was exceptional.

During his 10 years in Cincinnati, Frank Robinson averaged more than 32 home runs per season. In 1961, when he belted 37, he won the National League MVP Award. He did everything on a baseball field that a man could do. That included backing up his reputation as one of the toughest guys in the game. At Cincinnati on June 23, 1961, Big Don Drysdale threw a brush-back pitch close to Frank Robinson's head. Drysdale was a menacing 6'6" Dodger hurler with a reputation as a head hunter. But Robinson did not fear him. On his next time up, he tugged his helmet down tight, and proceeded to wallop a long homer. Circling the bases, Frank glared at Don, knowing that this battle was far from over.

When the Reds visited the Dodgers on July 8, Robinson smacked a home run over the center field stockade off Johnny Podres. In the 1st inning the next day, Robbie belted one off Roger Craig. So, when the rampaging Robinson batted in the 6th inning, he had to face Drysdale, who was working in relief. Pre-dictably, Big Don drilled him with a 95-mph fastball. However, the game still wasn't complete. In the 8th inning, Frank smashed yet another homer (off Dick Farrell), giving him seven RBIs for the day. When the Reds returned to The Coliseum on August 16, Larry Sherry plunked Robinson in the 1st inning. As 72,140 fans watched in anticipation, Sherry tried it again in the 3rd inning. Frank evaded the pitch, stepped back into the batter's box, and crushed the next ball far out of the park. For their trouble, Los Angeles lost both games of the doubleheader, as Cincinnati took over first place. Message to the Los Angeles Dodgers: Don't mess with Frank Robinson!

Within a few years, however, the Reds somehow got the idea that Frank was past his prime. After cracking 33 homers in 1965 at age 30, Robinson was traded to the Baltimore Orioles. He then showed the Reds that they had made a mistake. Robinson hit a career-high 49 home runs and won the American League MVP Award. Also in 1966, Frank struck the only fair ball ever to leave Baltimore's Memorial Stadium in an official game. That historic event occurred on May 8 when Frank drove one over the left field bleachers into the parking lot. Touring the American League for the first time, Robinson blasted long balls everywhere he went, including three rockets into the upper deck at RFK Stadium (then called D.C. Stadium) in Washington, D.C. Those homers came on June 6, August 12, and August 14.

As the seasons rolled by, Frank Robinson played intense all-around, winning baseball.

From 1966 through 1971, as an Oriole, Frank averaged 30 homers a year. Turning 35 in 1970, his power was undiminished. He reached the upper deck again in D.C. on June 26, and then sent one through a gap in the hedge in left center at Memorial Stadium on July 8. That drive flew about 450 feet, and Frank directed two more to the same spot in consecutive at-bats on August 27. In 1971, Robinson recorded a measured 453-footer in Anaheim on July 15. Frank moved on to the Los Angeles Dodgers in 1972, and then enjoyed two productive years for the California Angels, adding 54 more homers to his career log. When he was dealt to the Cleveland Indians late in 1974, it was a portent of historic things to come. Robinson was selected to manage the Indians in 1975, becoming the first black field boss in Major League history. Seemingly immune to pressure, Robbie smacked a homer in his first at-bat as player-manager.

Frank Robinson's final career home run (#586) came on July 6, 1976, at nearly 41 years of age, and landed beyond the center field fence in Anaheim. Along the path of his storied career, Frank had performed heroically both on and off the field. Whether facing Bob Gibson in the batter's box, plotting strategy from the dugout, or making tough decisions from Major League headquarters, he did everything with integrity and intensity. While his many accomplishments are too numerous to mention, he is remembered here as one of the most powerful hitters in the game.

FRANK ROBINSON'S 10 LONGEST HOME RUNS

- June 22, 1965—Cincinnati off St. Louis's Gibson—Over center field wall and street—503 ft.
- August 11, 1962—Cincinnati off New York's Hook—High over 55-ft. scoreboard in left center—490 ft.
- September 15, 1957—Cincinnati off Brooklyn's Newcombe—Hit building across street in left center—485 ft.
- May 11, 1965—Philadelphia off Short—Onto roof above 420 ft. sign just left of center—480 ft.
- July 27, 1969—Baltimore off Chicago's Nyman—Deep into bleachers in left center—475 ft.
- June 26, 1970—Washington off Grzenda—Into upper deck in left center—470 ft.
- May 6, 1965—Cincinnati off Los Angeles's Podres—Far over left field wall into parking lot—470 ft.
- May 27, 1959—Cincinnati off Philadelphia's Roberts—High over left field wall and laundry sign—470 ft.
- September 8, 1957—St. Louis off Mizell—Over left field bleachers—460 ft.
- July 15, 1971—California off Messersmith—Line drive far over left field fence—453 ft.

Three

Historical Rankings:
40 through 21

NUMBER 40: FRED McGRIFF—493
HOME RUNS—1987 TO 2004

Batting from the left side, Fred McGriff harnessed great power in his 6'3", 220-pound physique. Toronto's Exhibition Stadium, where McGriff played in his early years, featured half a football field beyond the right field fence. That created lots of open space, but Fred's long shots were rarely calculated for exact distance. Then, on September 2, 1988, somebody took the trouble to measure one of them. The final result was 473 feet. The quantification process changed in 1989, when the Blue Jays moved into the SkyDome. There were five levels in the new ballpark, and Fred regularly sent balls flying into the third and fourth tiers. Playing for the Padres in 1992, McGriff duplicated his earlier 473-footer by slamming one high into San Diego's right center field seats. Fred eventually played for six teams, recording tape measure home runs in at least a dozen Major

---

FRED McGRIFF'S 10 LONGEST HOME RUNS

- June 8, 1987—New York off Rhoden—To 16th row in right field third deck—490 ft.

- September 2, 1988—Toronto off Texas's May—Far over right field fence into football field—473 ft.

- August 28, 1992—San Diego off Pittsburgh's Drabek—High into seats in deep right center—473 ft.

- July 20, 1989—Seattle off Banhead—Into seats beyond center field fence—468 ft.

- May 5, 1999—Tampa Bay off Kansas City's Witasick—Over restaurant in right center—468 ft.

- July 17, 1990—Seattle off Holman—High into third deck in right center—465 ft.

- May 6, 1994—Atlanta off Montreal's Martinez—Off right field press façade—462 ft.

- July 17, 1989—Toronto off California's Petry—To box level in deep right center field—460 ft.

- June 17, 1995—Colorado off Acevedo—Off façade of third deck in right center—460 ft.

- August 6, 1992—San Diego off Houston's Williams—Deep into bleachers in right center—458 ft.

Courtesy of the National Baseball Hall of Fame and Museum

Fred McGriff

League venues. His longest was hit at Yankee Stadium on June 8, 1987, when his towering blast landed in the 16th row of the right field third deck between the second and third exits from the foul pole. That blow occurred early in Fred's career, but he was still belting them to far-off places when he played his final season in 2004.

NUMBER 39: BO JACKSON—141 HOME RUNS—1986 TO 1991 AND 1993 TO 1994

During his brief career, Vincent Jackson epitomized power and athleticism, starring as an NFL running back while launching big-league homers. Sadly, it was a football-related hip injury that forced him into an early retirement. Standing 6'1" and weighing 225 pounds,

Bo batted right-handed. He also threw from the right side while patrolling center field with his blazing speed. After winning the Heisman Trophy in 1985 at Auburn University, Bo surprised most observers by continuing his baseball career. Drafted by the Kansas City Royals in 1986, Jackson played briefly for the minor league Memphis Chicks. His talent was so vast that he was summoned by the Royals later that year. On September 14, 1986, Bo Jackson hit the first and longest home run of his Major League career. It was struck at Royals Stadium, and zoomed to the top of the grass embankment beneath the light tower in deep left center field. It was an astounding blow of 515 feet. Bo would likely have hit a few more in that range if not for his peculiar inside-out swing. He actually lost power by rarely turning on pitches to pull the ball. But that was Bo Jackson; he did things his way.

Courtesy of the Kansas City Royals

Bo Jackson

BO JACKSON'S 10 LONGEST HOME RUNS

- September 14, 1986—Kansas City off Seattle's Moore—Near top of grass in left center—515 ft.

- May 22, 1987—Texas off Loynd—Into top section in center field bleachers—475 ft.

- July 31, 1993—Seattle off Hanson—Deep into center field seats—472 ft.

- June 10, 1987—Minnesota off Blyleven—High into center field seats—466 ft.

- July 17, 1990—New York off Hawkins—High into right center field bleachers—464 ft.

- May 23, 1989—Texas off Ryan—Halfway up bleachers in deep left center—460 ft.

- July 1, 1990—Kansas City off Detroit's Morris—Near top of left field embankment—460 ft.

- May 20, 1994—California off Kansas City's Granger—To 20th row in left center field bleachers—460 ft.

- September 21, 1991—Chicago off California's Abbott—High into left center field bleachers—458 ft.

- June 28, 1987—Kansas City off Seattle's Thomas—To upper fountain in deep right center—455 ft.

NUMBER 38: JOHN "BOOG" POWELL—339 HOME RUNS—1962 TO 1976

Boog Powell's home runs were just as large as the man himself. The slugging left-handed first baseman stood 6'4", and weighed 250 pounds while walloping tremendous drives all around the American League circuit. Boog's longest shot was likely his 490-foot blast to the top of the right center field scoreboard at Kansas City's Municipal Stadium on June 3, 1964. However, Powell's most powerful drive may have been his center field 440-footer three days later at Minnesota's Metropolitan Stadium against a 20-mph wind. If that breeze had been blowing the other way, Boog's homer would have flown over 500 feet.

Four years earlier, during his rookie season with the Baltimore Orioles, Powell cleared the hedge at Memorial Stadium, prompting the groundskeeper to measure that blow at 469

John "Boog" Powell

BOOG POWELL'S 10 LONGEST HOME RUNS

- June 3, 1964—Kansas City off Segui—High off scoreboard in deep right center—490 ft.

- July 18, 1966—Chicago off Pizzaro—Onto right center field grandstand roof—480 ft.

- July 6, 1969—Detroit off McLain—Over 94-foot-high right field grandstand roof—475 ft.

- June 15, 1967—Kansas City off Nash—Over outer wall in right field onto street—470 ft.

- July 26, 1970—Minnesota off Woodson—Off scoreboard in deep right center—470 ft.

- June 22, 1962—Baltimore off Boston's Schwall—Over fence and hedge in center field—469 ft.

- May 14, 1963—Washington off Stenhouse—Into upper deck in center field—465 ft.

- June 25, 1969—Baltimore off Washington's Coleman—Far over fence in right center—460 ft.

- July 21, 1972—Kansas City off Dal Canton—Off right field light tower beyond outer wall—460 ft.

- June 21, 1968—California off Brunet—High into right field bleachers—458 ft.

---

feet. Teaming with Frank and Brooks Robinson, Boog enjoyed great competitive success with those Orioles, winning two World Series. As late as 1975 with the Cleveland Indians, Powell was still smacking tape measure shots, bombing one 450 feet at Kansas City on August 23. While bashing all those long home runs, Boog also earned a fine reputation as a reliable first-sacker, dependable teammate, clutch hitter, and fan favorite. In the baseball world, that is a commendable legacy.

NUMBER 37: JIM RICE—382 HOME RUNS—1974 TO 1989

When Jim Rice arrived in Boston in 1974 to play left field, he succeeded Hall of Fame legends Ted Williams and Carl Yastrzemski.

It seemed like an impossible task, but Rice flourished. Standing 6'2" and weighing over

Jim Rice

Courtesy of the National Baseball Hall of Fame and Museum

JIM RICE'S 10 LONGEST HOME RUNS

- May 5, 1977—Boston off Seattle's Segui—Over screen in left center and onto building roof—495 ft.

- September 13, 1988—Boston off Baltimore's Harnisch—High off light tower in left center—485 ft.

- July 18, 1975—Boston off Kansas City's Busby—Over back wall in center: right of flagpole—475 ft.

- July 13, 1977—Cleveland off Garland—Deep into left field upper deck—470 ft.

- June 19, 1977—Boston off New York's Tidrow—Over screen at 379 ft. sign in left center—470 ft.

- July 2, 1983—New York off Keough—Line drive off third deck façade in left field—465 ft.

- June 16, 1980—Boston off Oakland's Norris—High over left field screen near foul line—465 ft.

- May 4, 1977—Boston off Seattle's Pole—Far over screen in left center—465 ft.

- April 22, 1983—Oakland off Beard—Almost to top of left field bleachers—460 ft.

- August 19, 1985—New York off Bystrom—To third row in left field third deck—460 ft.

---

200 pounds, the right-handed muscle-man started lashing line drives as soon as he donned his Bosox uniform. Jim's signature shots were hit like two-irons, elevating only gradually as they sped in all directions. In fact, if Jim Rice had struck the ball with the same slightly higher trajectory as most of his peers, he would have hit balls even farther. However, nobody from his era hit them harder. Rice enjoyed his peak seasons from 1977 through 1979, when he averaged 41 homers and 128 RBI per year. Of course, many of his greatest drives occurred at Fenway Park. The single longest was a magnificent 495-footer to the rooftop across the street in left center field on May 5, 1977. He also pow-ered dozens of four-baggers into or even over the "triangle" of bleachers in center field at Fenway. He was no slacker on the road either, recording tape measure blasts in every American League town. When Jim Rice retired after the 1989 season, he had amassed 382 home runs, while adding to that incredible legacy that he inherited at the start.

NUMBER 36: JIMMY WYNN—291 HOME RUNS—1963 TO 1977

It is doubtful that any batter in Major League history had a better distance-to-body-mass ratio than Jimmy Wynn. Standing 5'9" and weighing 168 pounds, Wynn was nicknamed

Courtesy of the National Baseball Hall of Fame and Museum

Jimmy Wynn

the "Toy Cannon." He batted and threw right-handed, while playing center field with superior all-around athleticism. Jim grew up near Crosley Field in Cincinnati, and was signed by his hometown Reds in 1962. Drafted by the expansion Houston Colts later that year, he experienced his greatest triumphs inside the Astrodome. Wynn enjoyed his breakout season in 1965 (22 homers), which was the first year of the legendary "Dome." In 1967, Jimmy reached the pinnacle of his athletic career by bashing 37 home runs, while also launching his longest-ever drive. Appropriately, it happened back at Crosley Field. Wynn smashed a gigantic shot on June 10 that cleared the 58-foot scoreboard in left center field before landing on I-75. That epic blow was recorded on film, and the exact landing point can still

JIMMY WYNN'S 10 LONGEST HOME RUNS

- June 10, 1967—Cincinnati off Queen—Far over scoreboard in left center—507 ft.
- July 23, 1967—Pittsburgh off Mikkelson—Over 457 ft. sign in center field—490 ft.
- April 12, 1970—Houston off Atlanta's Niekro—Into yellow seats in left field upper deck—480 ft.
- June 6, 1965—St. Louis off Briles—High off scoreboard atop left field seats—475 ft.
- August 1, 1966—Philadelphia off Culp—Over left field grandstand roof—455 ft.
- June 6, 1967—St. Louis off Washburn—Off scoreboard in left center—452 ft.
- September 9, 1967—Los Angeles off Osteen—Halfway up left field pavilion—450 ft.
- September 7, 1968—Atlanta off Niekro—Into club level in left field—450 ft.
- April 7, 1977—New York off Milwaukee's Travers—Far over center field fence—435 ft.
- August 28, 1965—Pittsburgh off Schwall—Over left field scoreboard—430 ft.

be viewed. It has been measured at 507 feet. Jimmy Wynn clubbed many other magnificent home runs during his notable baseball life, but this one, occurring where he imagined bashing home runs as a child, was the ultimate.

NUMBER 35: HANK GREENBERG—331 HOME RUNS— 1933 TO 1947

Perhaps best known for his personal honor and integrity, Hank Greenberg should also be remembered as one of baseball's mightiest sluggers. Raised in the Bronx, young Henry wanted to emulate Babe Ruth by becoming a powerful batsman. He clearly achieved his goal. Despite missing more than four years during the middle of his career as a result of volunteering for combat duty at the outset of World War II, Greenberg still managed to slug 331 big-league home runs. Although not naturally graceful, Hank stood 6'4" and packed enormous power in his 215-pound frame. As a right-hand-hitting first baseman, Greenberg left a trail of majestic homers in virtually every place he played. His longest may have been his tremendous drive to left center at Boston's Fenway Park on May 22, 1937. That 505-footer sailed across Lansdowne Street, and collided with the top of a two-story building that still stands today. After spending his entire career with the Detroit Tigers, Greenberg played his final season with the Pittsburgh Pirates. Even then, thunder resided in his bat. On July 6,

---

HANK GREENBERG'S 10 LONGEST HOME RUNS

- May 22, 1937—Boston off Ferrell—Over wall left of center; hit building across street—505 ft.

- July 24, 1938—Philadelphia off Potter—Far over left field grandstand roof—495 ft.

- July 6, 1947—Pittsburgh off Chicago's Borowy—Over wall in distant left center—490 ft.

- April 21, 1938—Chicago off Dietrich—Onto left field grandstand roof—480 ft.

- September 14, 1934—Detroit off Washington's Burke—To back of parking lot beyond left field—470 ft.

- August 23, 1938—Philadelphia off Thomas—Over left field grandstand roof—470 ft.

- August 21, 1933—Detroit off Philadelphia's Barrett—Over left field fence, landing a half block away—465 ft.

- June 30, 1940—St. Louis off Kramer—Off scoreboard atop left field bleachers—460 ft.

- May 27, 1938—Chicago off Gabler—Into distant center field bleachers—460 ft.

- September 27, 1938—Detroit off St. Louis's Cox—Into upper deck just left of center field—460 ft.

Hank Greenberg

1947, Hank powered a massive 490-foot shot far over the wall in left center at Forbes Field. Whether bashing baseballs, flying a bomber for Uncle Sam, or serving as a baseball executive, Hank Greenberg did it right.

NUMBER 34: MIKE SCHMIDT—548 HOME RUNS—1972 TO 1989

Despite his historic success as a slugger, Mike Schmidt is not primarily viewed as a power hitter. Schmidt was an excellent baserunner as well as a transcendent defensive third baseman, thereby generating images of athletic virtuosity. Of course, Willie Mays was like that, but there are few others. For the record, Schmitty clubbed drives of at least 450 feet in 10 National League ballparks. His most famous blast (and probably his longest) wasn't even a home run. On June 10, 1974,

at Houston's Astrodome, Mike pummeled one to dead center field that seemed headed for a 500-foot ride. Instead, the ball slammed into a loudspeaker hanging from the roof. Interrupted while still climbing at a linear distance of 329 feet and a height of 117 feet, Schmidt's rocket bounced back toward the infield. As a result, he settled for the longest single in baseball history! Since Mike totaled 548 official big-league homers, this amusing setback probably enhanced his legacy more than it hurt it. Playing his entire career in Philadelphia, Mike naturally recorded the majority of his distance shots at Veterans Stadium, where he hammered eight balls into the distant fifth level and 15 others into the fourth deck. Mike Schmidt may have been a great all-around player, but he was also immensely strong.

Mike Schmidt

MIKE SCHMIDT'S 10 LONGEST HOME RUNS (NOTE THE EXCEPTION AT THE TOP)

- June 10, 1974—Houston off Osteen—Single off loudspeaker on roof in center field—500 ft.
- September 25, 1981—Chicago off Kravec—Line drive into upper center field bleachers—480 ft.
- April 17, 1975—Philadelphia off Chicago's Burris—Off upper deck façade in deep left center—475 ft.
- April 17, 1976—Chicago off Garman—Into upper level of center field bleachers—475 ft.
- August 21, 1974—Cincinnati off Hall—Line drive into elevated yellow seats in left field—470 ft.
- August 31, 1986—Philadelphia off San Francisco's Blue—Line drive to left field upper deck level—470 ft.
- June 1, 1974—Philadelphia off San Francisco's Caldwell—Into upper deck in deep left center—465 ft.
- May 22, 1986—San Diego off Hawkins—Line drive to 27th row in left field lower deck—465 ft.
- June 14, 1977—Cincinnati off Norman—High into seats in dead center field—460 ft.
- July 18, 1975—Philadelphia off Houston's Granger—Deep into left field upper deck near foul line—460 ft.

NUMBER 33: LARRY DOBY—253 HOME RUNS—1948 TO 1958

In 1947, Larry Doby became the first black player in the American League just months after Jackie Robinson had integrated the National League. Although never afforded the same stature as Jackie, Larry also lived the life of a racial pioneer. In fact, Doby's personal social journey created one of the most dramatic scenarios in tape measure history. Washington's Griffith Stadium was situated in an African-American neighborhood that provided Doby with a hero's welcome whenever he visited. Motivated by the positive energy, the 6'1", 190-pound outfielder recorded a higher percentage of his long-distance blasts in this single visitor's venue than in his home ballparks. In this regard, Larry was unique. Swinging from the left side, Doby blasted his longest-ever shot so far over Griffith Stadium's right center field scoreboard that it carried to the roof of a two-story house across an alley and long backyard. This 510-footer in 1951 barely exceeded an almost identical blow from two years earlier. Larry totaled 19 homers at Griffith Stadium, and 12 of them flew over 430 feet. Of course, Doby also pounded tape

LARRY DOBY'S 10 LONGEST HOME RUNS

- May 24, 1951—Washington off Hudson—Over scoreboard in right center and onto house—510 ft.
- May 25, 1949—Washington off Hudson—Over scoreboard in right center and onto house—500 ft.
- May 29, 1955—Kansas City off Shantz—Over right field outer wall into street—475 ft.
- June 19, 1956—Chicago off Baltimore's Moore—Deep into upper deck in right center—465 ft.
- May 19, 1949—New York off Porterfield—High into bleachers in deep right center—465 ft.
- July 1, 1956—Cleveland off Wynn—Far over 410 ft. sign in dead center field—465 ft.
- June 10, 1954—Washington off Stone—Line drive high off right field light tower—460 ft.
- June 4, 1952—Boston off Parnell—Deep into center field bleachers—460 ft.
- August 2, 1950—Cleveland off Washington's Marrero—Far over center field fence—460 ft.
- May 8, 1948—Washington off Hudson—Off loudspeakers atop high center field wall—455 ft.

Larry Doby

measure shots in every American League city. The man was genuinely powerful, but he was also intense, honorable, and principled.

NUMBER 32: KIRK GIBSON—255 HOME RUNS—1979 TO 1995

Starting as an All-American football flanker at Michigan State, Kirk Gibson also played one successful season of baseball for the Spartans. When the Detroit Tigers selected him in the first round of the 1978 amateur draft, Gibson accepted their lucrative contract offer. He brought his aggressive football mentality with him onto the diamond. Standing 6'3" and weighing 215 pounds, Kirk swung savagely from the left side of the plate. On the bases, he ran with shocking speed and

Courtesy of the National Baseball Hall of Fame and Museum

Kirk Gibson

physicality. As a result, he was often injured, but, when healthy, he was highly effective. Gibson left a trail of monstrous home runs everywhere he went. The ideal snapshot of Kirk's career was taken on June 14, 1983, at Tiger Stadium. He blasted a stupendous 515-foot homer over the field roof that landed in a lumberyard across the street. Two innings later, Gibby belted one to the 440 foot sign in center field with a teammate on first base. Both men sped around the bases with the lead runner called out at home. The fire-breathing Gibson arrived a moment later, knocking catcher, ball, and umpire to the ground. Kirk was ruled safe. That combination of power, speed, and aggressiveness exemplified the career of Kirk Gibson.

KIRK GIBSON'S 10 LONGEST HOME RUNS

- June 14, 1983—Detroit off Boston's Brown—Over right field roof and landed across street—515 ft.

- May 10, 1985—Chicago off Seaver—Over right field grandstand roof—510 ft.

- June 16, 1985—New York off Shirley—To back wall atop bleachers in right center—500 ft.

- July 13, 1986—Kansas City off Bankhead—To back of right field bullpen—480 ft.

- September 10, 1986—Detroit off Milwaukee's Bosio—Over grandstand roof in deep right field—470 ft.

- May 1, 1994—Detroit off Chicago's McDowell—Over grandstand roof in right field—465 ft.

- September 6, 1986—Oakland off Andujar—Deep into right field second deck—463 ft.

- April 22, 1984—Detroit off Chicago's Brennan—Liner high into upper deck in right center—460 ft.

- August 30, 1993—Seattle off Nelson—Deep into second deck in right center—452 ft.

- August 3, 1985—Detroit off Milwaukee's Darwin—Onto grandstand roof in right center—450 ft.

NUMBER 31: ANDRES GALARRAGA—399 HOME RUNS—1985 TO 2004

Andres Galarraga had to overcome more than his share of adversity to earn his crown as a tape measure king. Born in Venezuela in 1961, he didn't play his first Major League game until his 25th year. Andres then battled through a series of injuries and illness, including cancer, before retiring with 399 career home runs and the respect of the entire baseball community. Galarrraga was a big man, standing 6'3" and weighing 235 pounds. But he was quick and graceful at first base, where he played defensively. Batting right-handed, he could hit the ball as hard

Andres Galarraga

ANDRES GALARRAGA'S 10 LONGEST HOME RUNS

- May 31, 1997—Florida off Brown—Over exit in left field upper deck—509 ft.

- August 28, 1997—Colorado off Seattle's Oliveras—To concourse in deep left center field—506 ft.

- September 18, 2001—San Francisco off Houston's Oswalt—To top of bleachers in left center—480 ft.

- April 19, 1998—Colorado off Thompson—To top of left center field bleachers—478 ft.

- September 1, 1990—Montreal off Los Angeles's Hartley—To 25th row in left field seats—475 ft.

- July 6, 1993—Colorado off Florida's Hough—High into bleachers in deep left center—473 ft.

- May 26, 1997—Colorado off St. Louis's Petkovsek—To concourse atop bleachers in left—469 ft.

- April 27, 1993—Colorado off Chicago's Bautista—Far over fence just right of center—464 ft.

- September 4, 1993—Colorado off Pittsburgh's Petkovsek—Near top of left field bleachers—460 ft.

- June 25, 1995—San Diego off Valenzuela—To fifth row in left field second deck—455 ft.

as any other modern right-hander with the exception of Mark McGwire. He was similar to Big Mac in another part of his game as well. Andres recorded most of his longest shots well past his 30th year, including his monstrous blast high into Florida's left field upper deck on May 31, 1997. That happened just prior to Galarraga's 36th birthday. He continued to bash gigantic home runs beyond age 40, culminating with a magnificent 480-footer in San Francisco in 2001 after his heroic battle with cancer. Other than his winning smile and great personal courage, Andres Galarraga will best be remembered for the awesome power in his bat.

NUMBER 30: DARRYL STRAWBERRY—335 HOME RUNS—1983 TO 1999

It is true that Darryl Strawberry's career was marked with significant controversy. However, he accomplished things on the diamond that few men have ever rivaled. The sweet-swinging left-hander stood 6′6″, and generated enormous power from his lean but muscular physique. At Montreal's Olympic Stadium on April 4, 1988, Darryl launched a ball off the right field roof overhang that stood 160 feet above the playing field. There is still disagreement about the estimated potential flight distance, but it certainly exceeded 500 feet. Strawberry routinely dented the right center field scoreboard and cleared the right

DARRYL STRAWBERRY'S 10 LONGEST HOME RUNS

- April 4, 1988—Montreal off St. Claire—Off rim of roof high above right field—505 ft.
- October 1, 1999—Tampa Bay off Duvall—Hit pipe hanging from right field roof—490 ft.
- June 17, 1998—Baltimore off Mussina—Off Jumbotron atop bleachers in center—485 ft.
- May 22, 1987—New York off Los Angeles's Valenzuela—Line drive off scoreboard in right center—480 ft.
- October 1, 1985—St. Louis off Dayley—Off clock on upper deck scoreboard in right center—475 ft.
- July 17, 1988—Atlanta off Glavine—To club level in right center past 385 ft. sign—475 ft.
- May 1, 1988—Cincinnati off Perry—Into right field upper deck—470 ft.
- May 12, 1992—Montreal off Haney—Far and high over fence in deep right center—470 ft.
- July 25, 1990—Philadelphia off Carmen—Into 300 level exit tunnel in dead center field—465 ft.
- September 5, 1987—Los Angeles off Valenzuela—Halfway into pavilion in deep right center—460 ft.

Darryl Strawberry

NUMBER 29: EDDIE MATHEWS—512 HOME RUNS—1952 TO 1968

Until Eddie Mathews came along, third base wasn't really a power hitter's position in the minds of Major League teams. It is fair to say that Mathews reinvented that position. Eddie stood 6'1" and weighed 215 pounds, while batting left-handed. Signed at midnight on the day of his high school graduation, the 17-year-old Mathews was coveted by virtually every big-league team. In that first pro season in 1949, at age 17, Eddie slammed 17 home runs in just 63 games. Advancing quickly to the Southern League's Atlanta franchise in 1950, Mathews amazed everyone by thumping 32 homers. After a brief tenure in the Navy, Eddie socked 25 circuits in his rookie year with the Boston Braves in 1952, and followed up sensationally with 47 as a sophomore as the Braves moved to Milwaukee. It was a storybook start to a career that didn't

field bullpen at Shea Stadium during his long tenure with the New York Mets. It should also be recalled that he stole 36 bases during the 1987 season. The man was an athletic marvel. Eventually suffering from illness and addiction, Darryl always seemed to fight back. After missing most of 1997 due to injury, Strawberry played well for the Yankees in 1998, clubbing a 485-footer to center field in Baltimore. Then, almost miraculously, while recovering from colon cancer, Darryl smashed his final regular season homer some 490 feet to right field in St. Petersburg in 1999. Despite extreme adversity, Darryl Strawberry could always pound a baseball.

Eddie Mathews

EDDIE MATHEWS'S 10 LONGEST HOME RUNS

- April 22, 1953—Chicago off Klippstein—Far over right center field bleachers—500 ft.
- June 24, 1955—Milwaukee off Brooklyn's Erskine—To hill beside grandstand in right—485 ft.
- April 30, 1965—Milwaukee off Philadelphia's Herbert—To screen atop bleachers in deep right—485 ft.
- August 11, 1956—Milwaukee off Cincinnati's Jeffcoat—To base of scoreboard in right center—480 ft.
- July 14, 1960—Pittsburgh off Haddix—Onto towering grandstand roof in right—475 ft.
- July 22, 1956—Milwaukee off Philadelphia's Roberts—Over center field fence into trees—470 ft.
- September 21, 1959—Pittsburgh off Friend—Onto right field roof near foul pole—470 ft.
- August 25, 1967—Kansas City off Dobson—Over outer wall in right field—470 ft.
- August 15, 1966—Houston off Zachary—To purple seats in right field fourth level—465 ft.
- April 17, 1960—Philadelphia off Roberts—Over scoreboard in right center—460 ft.

end until 1968. Over the years, Mathews included many tape measure shots among his 512 career homers. Eddie personally labeled his Wrigley Field blast on April 22, 1953, as his personal best. Subsequent research confirmed that this epic smash cleared the third "step-up" atop the right center field bleachers and flew 500 feet.

NUMBER 28: WALLY POST—210 HOME RUNS—1951 TO 1963

Starting as a free agent pitcher in 1946, Wally Post (like Babe Ruth) hit the ball too hard to remain on the mound. Switching to the outfield in 1949, the 6'1", 210-pounder slowly worked his way up to the Cincinnati Reds'

Courtesy of the National Baseball Hall of Fame and Museum

Wally Post

WALLY POST'S 10 LONGEST HOME RUNS

- April 14, 1961—St. Louis off Simmons—Off top of left field scoreboard—520 ft.
- August 23, 1956—Cincinnati off Brooklyn's Newcombe—Over laundry sign in left center—495 ft.
- August 19, 1955—Cincinnati off St. Louis's LaPalme—Over laundry sign past wall in left—490 ft.
- April 16, 1955—Cincinnati off Milwaukee's Burdette—Over high scoreboard in left center—480 ft.
- April 29, 1956 (#3)—Cincinnati off Chicago's Jones—Over scoreboard in left center—475 ft.
- May 22, 1955—Cincinnati off St. Louis's Haddix—Over high scoreboard in left center—470 ft.
- April 29, 1956 (#2)—Cincinnati off Chicago's Rush—Over laundry sign past wall in left—465 ft.
- June 24, 1955—Cincinnati off Philadelphia's Negray—Over laundry sign past wall in left—465 ft.
- August 29, 1955—Philadelphia off Roberts—Over left field grandstand roof—460 ft.
- June 18, 1961—Philadelphia off Baldschum—Over left field grandstand roof—455 ft.

roster before eventually exploding in 1955 and 1956. During those two peak seasons, Wally belted a total of 76 homers, and many of them flew epic distances. Playing right field, the right-handed Post threw almost as hard as he hit. He distinguished himself, however, with the bat in his hands. There was a laundry sign atop a building across the street in left field at Crosley Field. It was a rare occasion for anyone else to clear that distant billboard, but Wally did it routinely. Oddly, Post didn't record his longest-ever during that time. It wasn't until he was well past his prime that Wally pounded his mightiest career homer at St. Louis's Busch Stadium on April 14, 1961. It crashed against the eagle's beak near the top of the Budweiser scoreboard in left field and was immediately labeled as the longest blow ever seen by virtually everyone in attendance. It may have been Wally Post's single longest home run, but there were many other tremendous drives along the way.

NUMBER 27: LUKE EASTER—93 HOME RUNS—1950 TO 1953

Nobody in organized baseball knew exactly when Luke Easter was born. It was likely in 1915, thereby making Easter 35 years old when he hit his first Major League homer. He

LUKE EASTER'S 10 LONGEST MAJOR LEAGUE HOME RUNS

- June 23, 1950—Cleveland off Washington's Haynes—Into upper deck in right center—505 ft.

- July 25, 1950—Cleveland off Philadelphia's Kellner—Into right field upper deck past box seats—480 ft.

- August 19, 1950—Cleveland off Chicago's Holcombs—High into right field upper deck—475 ft.

- June 16, 1951—Washington off Morrero—Over high scoreboard in right center—475 ft.

- June 28, 1950—St. Louis off Johnson—Onto pavilion roof just right of center—465 ft.

- September 13, 1950—Cleveland off New York's Lopat—Over center field fence to bleacher wall—460 ft.

- September 10, 1952—Cleveland off Philadelphia's Bishop—Into right field upper deck—460 ft.

- August 24, 1952—Washington off Masterson—Into center field bleachers—455 ft.

- April 17, 1952—Chicago off Widmar—Liner into right center field upper deck—450 ft.

- June 7, 1952—Philadelphia off Kellner—Over right field fence onto house—450 ft.

Courtesy of the National Baseball Hall of Fame and Museum

Luke Easter

only wound up with 93, and it is fair to wonder why he is ranked with players of considerably more MLB accomplishments. Standing 6'4" and weighing 240 pounds, the left-handed first baseman consistently slammed massive home runs for over a quarter-century while playing professional baseball all over the country. That is why he is listed here. It wasn't Luke's fault that the Major Leagues were not integrated until 1947. He began with the St. Louis Titanium Giants back in the mid 1930s before serving in the U.S. Army in World War II. Easter then landed in the old Negro League in 1946, where he stayed for three years. Signing with the Cleveland Indians in 1949, Luke was slowed by a broken kneecap, which never fully healed. However, he immediately started bashing baseballs as far as anyone in the big leagues. He returned to the minor leagues in 1954, playing in legendary fashion until he retired at nearly age 50. Easter never stopped hitting monstrous home runs, and, if given a fair chance, he may have recorded over 500 homers at the Major League level.

NUMBER 26: GEORGE FOSTER—348 HOME RUNS—1970 TO 1986

George Foster was one of the few men with a weight lifter's physique to excel in Major League Baseball. Standing 6'1" and weighing

Courtesy of the Cincinnati Reds

George Foster

GEORGE FOSTER'S 10 LONGEST MAJOR LEAGUE HOME RUNS

- July 29, 1978—Cincinnati off Philadelphia's Lonborg—Line drive high into left field upper deck—509 ft.
- August 3, 1977—Cincinnati off Chicago's Hernandez—High into left field upper deck—502 ft.
- June 14, 1976—Cincinnati off Chicago's Coleman—Into left field upper deck—492 ft.
- June 27, 1985—Chicago off Sutcliffe—To building across street in left—480 ft.
- September 7, 1977—Cincinnati off San Francisco's Halicki—Off foul pole into left field upper deck—475 ft.
- June 2, 1979—Cincinnati off Philadelphia's Lerch—Into green seats in center field—473 ft.
- August 31, 1980—Pittsburgh off Blyleven—Almost to "Pirate" sign in center—470 ft.
- September 6, 1979—Cincinnati off San Francisco's Griffin—To fourth row in left field upper deck—467 ft.
- August 14, 1981—Cincinnati off San Francisco's Ripley—To second row in left field upper deck—465 ft.
- June 15, 1977—Cincinnati off Philadelphia's Garber—Into green seats in center field—460 ft.

200 pounds, Foster had a classic V shape to his upper torso along with significant muscle definition. That kind of body looks great at the beach, but rarely translates into the kind of athleticism that produces superior bat speed. But George was an exception. His career as a right-handed-hitting outfielder started slowly, but, during his few peak seasons, he was one of baseball's greatest sluggers. At Cincinnati's Riverfront Stadium, it took an extremely powerful wallop to reach the red seats in the upper deck, but Foster accomplished that feat six different times. His single longest career drive was struck there on July 29, 1978 and sailed high into those red seats at a considerable distance from the left field foul pole. It was estimated at 509 feet. However, George was effective wherever he played. In 1977, when he enjoyed his finest year (52 home runs and 149 RBI), Foster was an absolute terror, smashing tape measure homers in every National League ballpark. Although his overall productivity dropped when traded to the Mets in 1982, George Foster remained a feared long-distance hitter until his final playing days in 1986.

NUMBER 25: NORM CASH—377 HOME RUNS—1959 TO 1974

Always a mischievous, fun-loving free spirit, Norman Cash was also a hard-working athlete who pounded baseballs for long distances. Standing 6 feet tall and weighing 185 pounds, the left-handed Cash did not appear physically imposing at first glance. However, his

NORM CASH'S 10 LONGEST HOME RUNS

- July 29, 1962—Detroit off Los Angeles's Botz—Over right field roof to lumber company—515 ft.
- June 11, 1961—Detroit off Washington's McClain—Over right field roof to street—480 ft.
- July 31, 1966—Kansas City off Nash—Over outer right field fence onto street—480 ft.
- August 26, 1967—Kansas City off Hunter—Over outer right field fence to street—480 ft.
- July 20, 1962—Kansas City off Giggie—Over outer right field fence onto street—475 ft.
- July 27, 1962—Detroit off Los Angeles's Grba—Over right field roof to street—475 ft.
- August 15, 1966—Detroit off New York's Stottlemyre—To 11th row in upper deck in center—470 ft.
- May 17, 1969—Minnesota off Grzenda—Off scoreboard in right center—470 ft.
- May 11, 1962—Detroit off Boston's Schwall—Over right field roof to street against wind—465 ft.
- May 18, 1963—Washington off Quirk—Into right field upper deck—455 ft.

Norm Cash

season with elevated offensive numbers, but Cash's performance was exceptional by any standard. Over his long career, Norm proved that merriment and humor were not exclusive to power and production.

NUMBER 24: WALLY BERGER—242 HOME RUNS—1930 TO 1940

Wally Berger is virtually unknown to modern fans, but, in his day, he was one of baseball's mightiest sluggers. Standing 6'2" and weighing 200 pounds, he batted right-handed and performed effectively as a strong-armed centerfielder. In 1928 and 1929, Berger was a Pacific Coast League sensation with Los Angeles, but couldn't make the parent Chicago

thick wrists and forearms told the story of his great power. Playing first base for the Detroit Tigers for most of his career, Norm specialized in distance shots over the towering right field grandstand roof at Tiger Stadium. He cleared that 94-foot-high structure four times, while bouncing balls off the rooftop on a dozen other occasions. His longest ever was struck on July 29, 1962 and traveled 515 feet on the fly, landing in a lumberyard across the street. Cash was just as lethal everywhere he performed. He left a long trail of mighty homers in Kansas City, including three over the outer wall in right field. A career .271 hitter, Norm also distinguished himself in 1961 by winning the Major League batting championship with a lofty .361 average. That was an expansion

Wally Berger

WALLY BERGER'S 10 LONGEST HOME RUNS

- June 16, 1935—Boston off Cincinnati's Johnson—Over left center field bleachers—500 ft.

- June 23, 1930—St. Louis off Johnson—Over left field bleachers—490 ft.

- August 10, 1932—Boston off Pittsburgh's French—Over outer wall in left to RR tracks—485 ft.

- June 23, 1931—Boston off Cincinnati's Benton—Over outer wall in left to RR tracks—480 ft.

- September 5, 1932—Boston off Brooklyn's Heimach—Over outer wall in left to RR tracks—480 ft.

- June 25, 1933—Boston off Chicago's Root—Over outer wall in left to RR tracks—480 ft.

- June 7, 1930—Boston off Pittsburgh's Kremer—Over left field bleachers and outer wall—475 ft.

- July 1, 1937—New York off Philadelphia's Johnson—High over left field grandstand roof—470 ft.

- May 1, 1930—Pittsburgh off Spencer—Far over left field wall into park—460 ft.

- May 30, 1931—Philadelphia off Dudley—Over left field bleachers—460 ft.

Cubs' roster due to their outfield depth. However, after a trade to the Boston Braves, Wally bashed a then-record rookie total of 38 home runs in 1930. Many of them went for great distance, including a 475-footer on June 7 over the outer left field wall at Braves Field. Berger cleared that same obstacle several more times, and also reached every recognized long-distance plateau around the National League circuit. While playing briefly for the Giants in 1937, Wally routinely pounded balls over the towering left field grandstand roof. His career was relatively short (11 seasons) due to a 1936 shoulder injury, but he maintained his great power throughout. As a teammate of Babe Ruth, Berger walloped a home run at

the Baker Bowl on May 30, 1935, during the Bambino's farewell Major League game.

NUMBER 23: MIKE PIAZZA—427 HOME RUNS—1992 TO 2007

It is amazing that a catcher could rank this high on the all-time list of Major League distance hitters. The physical attrition from playing backstop makes exceptional offensive production rare. Along with Josh Gibson of the old Negro Leagues, Mike Piazza is an historic exception. Standing 6'3" and weighing 215 pounds, this right-handed juggernaut absolutely shattered the big-league home run record for a catcher. Starting at Dodger

MIKE PIAZZA'S 10 LONGEST HOME RUNS

- September 26, 1997—Colorado off Holmes—To concourse atop bleachers in left center—504 ft.
- September 4, 1998—New York off Atlanta's Glavine—Far over left center field bleachers—485 ft.
- July 10, 1999—New York off New York's Mendoza—Onto tent beyond left field bullpen—482 ft.
- September 14, 1998—Houston off Lima—Far over fence in dead center field—480 ft.
- September 21, 1997—Los Angeles off Colorado's Castillo—Onto pavilion roof in left center—478 ft.
- June 6, 1994—Florida off Gardiner—Into seats past 434 ft. sign left of center field—477 ft.
- August 16, 1999—San Diego off Hitchcock—High into left field second deck—475 ft.
- July 27, 2001—New York off Philadelphia's Coggin—Over left center field bleachers—473 ft.
- July 30, 1998—New York off San Diego's Hitchcock—To base of message board in left center—472 ft.
- July 30, 1999—Chicago off Trachsel—High over bleachers in deep left center field—471 ft.

Courtesy of the Los Angeles Dodgers

Mike Piazza

Stadium, which Mike called home for many years, Piazza consistently recorded long home runs. In Los Angeles, his single longest soared onto the pavilion roof in left center in 1997, and was estimated at 478 feet. In that same season, Mike reached his career distance apex by blasting a 504-footer in the thin air at Coors Field in Denver. Moving on to the New York Mets in 1998, Piazza started bombing away at Shea Stadium. He belted so many 470- and 480-footers at Flushing that he supplanted Dave Kingman and Darryl Strawberry as the all-time distance king at that ballpark. Over the years, Mike added tape measure shots in every National League stadium where he played. Whenever the question of Major League Baseball's greatest offensive catcher is raised, there can only be one answer.

NUMBER 22: LOU GEHRIG—493 HOME RUNS—1923 TO 1938

Lou Gehrig had the perfect nickname. He was as close to being an "Iron Horse" as any flesh-and-blood man could be. Standing 6'1", this 212-pound dynamo oozed power in every move he made. Batting left-handed and playing first base, Lou was best known for playing 2,130 consecutive games. However, Gehrig should also be remembered as one of baseball's longest hitters. Like Jim Rice from

Lou Gehrig

LOU GEHRIG'S 10 LONGEST HOME RUNS (NOTE THE EXCEPTION AT THE TOP)

- June 7, 1929—New York off Cleveland's Hudlin—Triple off screen in dead center—485 ft.
- May 4, 1929—Chicago off Faber—Over high right field grandstand roof—510 ft.
- June 30, 1931—Detroit off Sorrell—Far over fence in right and onto roof across street—500 ft.
- August 28, 1935—Chicago off Whitehead—Onto high right field grandstand roof—480 ft.
- September 7, 1936—New York off Philadelphia's Rhodes—Almost to top of new right field bleachers—480 ft.
- July 22, 1926—New York off Chicago's Thomas—Past flagpole in deepest center field—475 ft.
- April 19, 1930—Boston off Lisenbee—To top of center field seats—472 ft.
- May 19, 1927—Cleveland off Buckeye—Off high scoreboard in dead center field—470 ft.
- September 10, 1925—Philadelphia off Gray—Onto house roof across street in right center—470 ft.
- May 1, 1934—Washington off Stewart—Over wall and house across street in right—465 ft.

latter years, Gehrig assembled his impressive tape measure resume despite normally striking the ball on a trajectory that was too low to achieve optimum distance. As of 1929, the foul lines at Chicago's Comiskey Park were still 365 feet long, and only Babe Ruth had cleared the symmetrical grandstand roof above them. That changed on May 4, when Lou sent a 510-footer sailing over the top in right field. While establishing the third highest slugging percentage in the game's history at .632, Gehrig crushed the ball with devastating fury all across America. Prematurely struck down by a rare and fatal disease, Lou would almost certainly have exceeded 600 home runs if not for his tragic fate. Modern analysis indicates that Gehrig was initially afflicted as early as mid-1937, but he kept playing until 1939. Lou wasn't just strong in muscle and sinew; he was a giant in heart and soul.

NUMBER 21: RON KITTLE—176 HOME RUNS—1982 TO 1991

Regrettably, Ron Kittle logged only 2,708 Major League at-bats. Partly because of injuries and partly due to a lack of all-around skills, Ron wasn't in the lineup as much as most other established power hitters. But Kittle could pound a baseball! He stood 6'4" and played at 225 pounds, while batting and throwing from the right side. Ron was primarily an outfielder, although he also patrolled first base and served as a DH. He launched massive home runs in every American League park, including his 483-

Ron Kittle

Courtesy of the National Baseball Hall of Fame and Museum

foot bomb on September 13, 1985 in Seattle. But Kittle will always be best remembered for his extraordinary mastery of Chicago's original Comiskey Park. From 1983 through 1990, Kittle bombed seven balls onto the 75-foot-high left field grandstand roof, more than anyone else in history. In fairness to the older sluggers, those stands were positioned closer in Ron's era than when Babe Ruth and Jimmie Foxx formerly visited Comiskey. However, many great modern power hitters, such as Reggie Jackson, Dick Allen, and Greg Luzinski, logged many at-bats at the reconfigured Comiskey Park, and none came close to Kittle's standard. By any yardstick, Ron Kittle was one of baseball's best tape measure sluggers.

RON KITTLE'S 10 LONGEST HOME RUNS

- July 2, 1984—Chicago off Detroit's Rozema—To back of roof in left center—505 ft.
- August 8, 1985—Chicago off Boston's Ojeda—Onto grandstand roof in deep left field—490 ft.
- September 6, 1983—Chicago off Oakland's Codiroli—Onto left field grandstand roof—485 ft.
- September 19, 1983—Chicago off Minnesota's Walters—Onto left field grandstand roof—485 ft.
- September 13, 1985—Seattle off Young—To second row in left center field second deck—483 ft.
- August 1, 1984—Chicago off Boston's Ojeda—Onto left field grandstand roof—480 ft.
- April 18, 1990—Chicago off Boston's Murphy—Onto front roof in deep left field—475 ft.
- April 29, 1984—Chicago off Boston's Nipper—Onto roof near left field foul line—475 ft.
- August 8, 1983—Detroit off Morris—High into upper deck in deep left center—470 ft.
- June 27, 1990—California off Finley—Almost to second deck in left field—465 ft.

Four

Top 19th-Century and Negro League Sluggers

19th Century

NUMBER 5: ED DELAHANTY—101 HOME RUNS—1888 TO 1903

Ed Delahanty was the prototypical 19th-century baseball player. Born in Cleveland in 1857, he was a heavy-drinking Irishman from a large immigrant family, who lived fast and played hard. Standing 6'1" and weighing 190

Courtesy of Jerry Casway

Ed Delahanty

pounds in his prime, his natural good looks belied his complex personality. One of five brothers who made it to the big leagues, he became one of the greatest batsmen that the game has ever produced. Over the course of his turbulent 15-year career, Delahanty consistently hit the ball as hard as anyone of his era.

Oddly, it took young Ed longer to reach his potential than most guys of Hall of Fame stature. He started out fine. The right-handed Delahanty batted .355 for Mansfield of the Ohio State League in 1887, and was tearing up the Tri-State League in 1888. After 21 games in Wheeling, Ed had been hitting .408 with five home runs when the National League Philadelphia Quakers (soon to be Phillies) purchased his contract. He went hitless in his debut on May 22, 1888 and made two errors at second base. For the season over 74 games, Delahanty hit only .228 and made 47 errors. However, he did manage to belt his first big-league homer to deep left center field in Philadelphia on June 13. Limited to 54 games in 1889 due to a broken collarbone, things didn't improve much. Shifting between second base and the outfield, Ed batted .293, and hit no home runs.

The year of 1890 was the sole season of the renegade Players League, and Ed Delahanty spent it with the Cleveland Infants. Playing mostly shortstop, Ed committed the ghastly total of 94 errors, but did bat .298 with three homers. When the league folded after its inaugural campaign, Delahanty returned to the Phillies and, fortunately, found a new position. He switched to the outfield, and, with the exception of one year at first base in 1900 (along with occasional spot duty at other positions), he remained there for the rest of his playing days. In fact, due largely to his superior speed and strong throwing arm, Ed became an excellent left fielder. But Del is remembered as a deluxe hitter, and he was still just an average batsman through the 1891 season. Ed hit only .250 with five homers and a paltry .333 slugging percentage.

Finally, in 1892 in his 25th year, Ed Delahanty made his move. Batting .306, he smacked six home runs and 21 triples, while increasing his slugging rate to .495. Then in 1893, Delahanty made the leap all the way to true superstar. Aided by the new rule that moved the pitcher's mound back 5 feet to 60 feet, 6 inches, he batted .368, clubbed 19 homers and 18 triples, slugged .583, and drove in 146 runs. Those were great numbers, but they would get even better. In 1894, Ed Delahanty and his Phillies teammates had a season that now seems hard to believe. "Big Ed" hit .404, but finished third on his own team in batting average. In fact, the Phils had

four outfielders who bettered the .400 mark: Sam Thompson at .415, utility outfielder Tom Turner (347 at-bats) at .418, and center fielder Billy Hamilton at .403. Delahanty also slugged .585, drove in 131 runs, and scored 149 times.

By the mid-1890s, Ed Delahanty was a feared man. Author Louis P. Masur has quoted pitcher Frederick "Crazy" Schmit: "When you pitch to Delahanty, you just want to shut your eyes, say a prayer and chuck the ball. The Lord only knows what'll happen after that." Once he found his stroke, Del was virtually unstoppable. In 1895, he batted .404, slugged .617, and rapped 11 home runs. The longest sailed over Cleveland's remote left field wall on May 18, which was a feat attained only once before, by Buck Ewing in 1889. Then, on July 13, 1896, Delahanty bombed four homers in one game at Chicago's West Side Park. The first landed in the right field bleachers, but the second topped the scoreboard in right center, earning praise as the longest of the year in the Windy City. Numbers three and four were lined into deep center field, whereupon the speedy Delahanty raced around the bases. He finished that season with a .397 batting average and a slugging mark of .631.

As the years rolled by, so did "The Wild Irishman." His statistics kept mounting along with his legend. In 1899, Ed finally led the National League in batting when he reached the highest mark of his life at .410. On April 19 in Washington, Delahanty went 5 for 6 with a double and homer. Then, on May 13 in Philadelphia, Ed drove out four doubles. In so doing, he became the only man in baseball history to record four home runs in a game and four doubles in another. Batting fourth, directly behind Del that day, was the great Nap Lajoie. Both men smashed the ball viciously all five times that they batted.

Another aspect of Delahanty's baseball life was his ability as a directional batsman. Despite starting out as a dead pull hitter, Big Ed became highly adept at hitting the ball to the side of the field with the nearest fences. In Philadelphia, that was right field, and Del struck the majority of his hometown homers that way. In August 1895, all four of Delahanty's homers flew over Philly's right field wall. However, in an 1899 series in Boston, where the left field fence was very close, Ed lifted consecutive fly ball home runs (June 16 and 17) in that direction. But, as Ed Delahanty continued to flourish on the diamond, his personal life began to unravel. He had managed to keep his drinking and gambling under control, but, in 1900, these habits worsened. Del jumped to the young American League in 1902, and won another batting title. Playing for the Washington Senators, Big Ed batted .376 and walloped 10 homers as he became the first man to lead both Major Leagues in batting. Nobody has duplicated that feat.

Sadly, however, by 1903, Ed Delahanty's life was in complete chaos. Despondent over his mounting debts and evaporating athletic skills, he became intoxicated on a train ride from Detroit to New York on July 2. Ordered off by the conductor on the Canadian side of the International Bridge near Buffalo, Delahanty tried to walk across in the dark. When confronted by a night watchman, Ed somehow fell over, and was swept to his death over Niagara Falls. It was the strangest end for any man who has ever worn a big-league uniform. Not only was Ed Delahanty's life cut tragically short by those bizarre events, they have also tarnished his legacy. Modern fans often think of the man's death instead of his life. That is a shame; his baseball life was extraordinary. Big Ed amassed a lifetime batting average of .346 along with a slugging percentage of .505, which was remarkable in those dead ball days. His 101 home runs were modest by today's standards, but he added 522 doubles and 186 triples. He also stole 455 bases along the way. By any barometer, Delahanty was one of the best players of any age, and certainly one of the mightiest sluggers the game has known.

NUMBER 4: SAM THOMPSON—128 HOME RUNS—1885 TO 1906

Working as a carpenter until age 24, Sam Thompson nearly missed his chance to play professional baseball. For admirers of the long ball, that would have been a big loss. When Thompson finally joined the Evansville team in the North West League in 1884, the franchise folded after he had played only five games. Then, in 1885, Sam started with

Sam Thompson

In 1886, Thompson was the regular right fielder for Detroit, and posted respectable offensive numbers, including eight home runs. Then, in 1887, Big Sam Thompson exploded. Thumping the ball savagely throughout Detroit's 124-game schedule, he led the league in several offensive categories, including batting average (.372), slugging percentage (.571), total bases (311), triples (23), and RBI (166). That runs-batted-in total set the Major League record, and remained the standard until it was surpassed by Babe Ruth in 1921. A big part of his '87 production occurred on May 7, when Thompson slugged two bases-loaded triples. Sam also smacked 11 home runs as the Wolverines won the National League pennant, and then defeated the St. Louis Browns in the forerunner of the modern World Series. Showing his athletic versatility, Thompson also stole 22 bases and threw out 24 runners from rightfield.

Sam came back to earth in 1888, when injuries limited him to 54 games, six homers, and 40 RBI. Detroit folded at the end of the season, whereupon Thompson was acquired by the Philadelphia Quakers. He did well in 1889, but not great. Importantly, however, Big Sam topped the National League with the then-imposing total of 20 home runs. Thompson smacked 14 of those circuits on his home field at Philadelphia's Huntingdon Grounds, which was rebuilt in 1895 and eventually renamed the Baker Bowl. The right field wall after the reconstruction was infamous for its close proximity to home plate (272 feet), but,

Indianapolis of the Western League, where he hit his first professional home run. But, after just 30 games, he was sold to the Detroit Wolverines in the National League. Born in Indiana in 1860, Thompson may have started late, but, once begun, he moved quickly. Batting and throwing left-handed, he had grown into a powerful man of 6'2" and 210 pounds. He possessed a strong, accurate throwing arm, and ran very well for such a big guy—wonderful physical traits that launched him into the Major Leagues after only 35 games in the minors. Sam recorded his first homer on July 28, 1885, off future Hall of Famer and 342-game winner Tim Keefe. In 63 games, he batted .303 and rapped seven homers. He was on his way to greatness.

for most of Thompson's tenure in Philadelphia, it was positioned fairly at 310 feet. On both May 30, 1889, and September 6, 1889, Sam's right field shots landed across the wide breadth of Broad Street near the Reading Railroad station. Those balls flew over 425 feet.

Over the next three seasons, Thompson was a consistent contributor to the renamed Philadelphia Phillies, but he was not at his peak. He averaged over .300, but his home run and slugging-percentage numbers were ordinary. When the pitching mound was moved back in 1893, offensive production went up throughout the league, but Sam was particularly productive. He finished second in batting (.370), third in slugging (.530), and third in RBI (126). He was also among the leaders in homers with 11, the single longest (April 29) again landing near the train station. Then, in 1894, Thompson reached his peak, pacing the best offensive performance by any 19th-century team. His individual numbers bordered on the incredible, while limited to 102 games due to finger surgery in mid-season. Big Sam batted .415, slugged .696, belted 13 home runs and 27 triples, and drove in 147 runs. Almost miraculously, Thompson was one of four Philly outfielders to bat over .400, including fellow slugger Ed Delahanty.

Sam Thompson enjoyed his last great season in 1895, and it was a masterpiece. "The Marvel" paced the 12-team National League in slugging (.654), home runs (18), total bases (352), and RBI (165). He even finished fourth in batting (.392), third in triples (21),

and second in doubles (45). And he did all that in only 119 games! As usual, he was also much more than just a hitter. Often credited with originally perfecting the one-hop outfield throw, Sam accumulated the astounding total of 31 assists from his traditional post in right field. He even mixed in 27 stolen bases along the way. In the area of distance hitting, as usual, Thompson was front and center. He pounded three balls over Philadelphia's center field fence (410 feet) in the month of September alone. The longest came on September 4, when his awesome shot cleared not only the wall but the elevated wires servicing the railroad tracks outside the park.

Big Sam began to slow down in 1896. However, he was still dangerous at the plate, as was the entire roster. In fact, the Phillies of the 1890s probably featured more historically powerful batsmen than any other team in baseball history. In '96, they acquired aging Dan Brouthers, and, until he retired in mid-season, Dan batted fifth, directly behind Ed Delahanty and Sam Thompson. That may have been the mightiest threesome in the annals of the game. Then, when Brouthers left, he was replaced by slugging Nap Lajoie. In 1898, when Thompson retired, his duties were assumed by hard-hitting Elmer Flick. Even Roger Connor spent one season with the Phils in 1892. Those Philadelphia teams never won any pennants, but they certainly could pound the ball.

Due to health issues, Thompson played in only three games in 1897, but returned briefly to the Phillies in 1898. He recorded his final career home run, and, naturally, it was a memory-maker. Playing in the inaugural ball game at Brooklyn's Washington Park on April 30, Sam hit the first-ever homer there. After 14 games, Thompson was hitting .349, but he had grown accustomed to family life back in Detroit. The combination of homesickness and chronic back pain induced him to abandon the rigors of big-league baseball. In May 1898, Sam Thompson quietly returned to the Motor City. However, he still loved the game. Sam played for the Detroit Athletic Club for several more years, and, by all accounts, continued to wallop the ball as long as he took the field. In 1906, just for the fun of it, Thompson appeared in eight games at the end of the season for the Detroit Tigers. He played in the outfield with young Ty Cobb and the great Sam "Wahoo" Crawford, becoming the oldest man, at age 46, to ever hit a triple in the Major Leagues. And consider this: Of all the men who have played big-league baseball, Big Sam drove in more runs per game than anyone else. The actual number is .921 RBI per game, and that is a statistic that cannot be overlooked. It proves conclusively that Sam Thompson was one of the greatest sluggers in baseball history.

NUMBER 3: BUCK FREEMAN—82 HOME RUNS—1898 TO 1907

Pound for pound, John "Buck" Freeman was likely as strong as any player in Major League history. Born in upstate Pennsylvania in 1871,

Buck Freeman

Courtesy of the National Baseball Hall of Fame and Museum

young John worked in the coal mines in his early years as did many other future professional ballplayers of that era. Standing only 5'9", his labors helped to develop his uncommonly efficient 170-pound musculature. Like Babe Ruth, he started as a pitcher, and was also known as a powerful hitter. Unlike Ruth, he was not successful as a big-league hurler, and this delayed his Major League tenure for many years.

Pitching and hitting from the left side, Freeman initially established himself by playing for various semi-pro teams near his hometown of Wilkes-Barre. In 1891, Buck was summoned by the Washington Statesmen of the American Association. However, his poor pitching command ended his initial Major

League experience after just five games. He returned home and kept pitching until 1894 when he finally saw the light, and switched to the outfield while playing for Haverhill, Massachusetts, in the New England League. The result was a .386 batting average along with an astonishing 34 home runs. Still, he was considered merely a minor league talent.

Freeman soon moved to the Toronto Canucks in the Eastern League where he was regarded as a mega-star by his Canadian fans. In 1897 and 1898, Buck led the Eastern League with 20 and 23 homers respectively. The later total was a league record, which led to his return to Washington, D.C. When the minor league season ended, Freeman (along with his manager and four teammates) got a shot with the National League Senators. On September 14, 1898, Buck Freeman smacked one deep into the right field bleachers at National Park. It was a long time to wait for his first big-league homer, but he quickly made up for the lost years.

When Freeman started the 1899 season for the Washington Senators, he had played in only 34 Major League games. In his 28th year, he was still just a rookie, but what happened next was extraordinary. Buck walloped 25 home runs, smashed 25 triples, batted .318, drove in 122 runs, and even stole 21 bases. His .563 slugging percentage exceeded the Major League average (.366) by close to 200 points. His homer total more than doubled Bobby Wallace's runner-up number of 12. In fact, by any reasonable standard, Free-

man set the Major League record that season. Officially, the record had been set back in 1884 by Ned Williamson with 27. But Ned had played at Chicago's Lake Front Park, which had Little League dimensions of 180 feet to left field and 196 feet to right. Accordingly, Buck Freeman's 1899 total of 25 was the bona fide standard until Babe Ruth recorded 29 in 1919.

In the matter of pure power, Buck consistently hit the ball so hard in 1899 that he may have enjoyed the best distance-hitting season of the entire dead ball era. Disdaining the slap-hitting style that dominated baseball thinking in those days, Freeman swung from his heels. The results were dramatic. At Washington Park in Brooklyn, Freeman set the stadium record for home run length by blasting one over 400 feet to right field. He then did the same thing in Louisville, but added about 30 feet to his distance by knocking the ball onto a local distillery. On September 20 at Boundary Park in Washington, Buck clobbered two to the opposite field that were about as long as any hit that year by the league's top right-handed batsmen. Almost incredibly, none of those were his longest of the season. That distinction was earned by an amazing drive to the balcony in center field at Chicago's South Side Park. It was a blow of 440 feet, which was extraordinarily long in the days before the 20th century. Considering all factors, Buck Freeman put on one of the greatest offensive performances in big-league history in 1899.

Sadly for Buck, the National League downsized after the season, and the Senators were disbanded. He was sold to the Boston Beaneaters where he clashed with manager Frank Selee. Freeman played well with six homers and a .301 batting average, but he had no future with that franchise. When the American League opened for business in 1901, Buck simply moved uptown to find his next home. It was with the new Boston Americans (later known as the Red Sox) that Freeman finally found some long-term security. He hit the franchise's first-ever home run on April 30 in Philadelphia, and then christened Boston's brand new Huntington Avenue Grounds on its opening day on May 8. In his first year in the Junior Circuit, Buck belted 12 home runs, batted .339, slugged .520, and drove in 114 runs. He followed that with exceptional numbers again in 1902: 11 homers, .309 batting average, .502 slugging percentage, and 121 RBI. Boston finished in second place both years, and Freeman was pleased.

But, in 1903, Buck led his team to even better things. The veteran right fielder topped the league with 13 home runs, 104 RBI, and 72 extra base hits. His longest drive flew over the right field scoreboard at Chicago's South Side Park on August 20. It was the first time that this structure had been topped, and the ball flew about 435 feet. Buck also became the first man to have led both leagues in home runs. In that glorious '03 campaign, Freeman led the Americans to the World Series title in the first year it was

played. Buck batted .290 in the Fall Classic and slugged three triples. He tailed off in 1904, but was still an offensive force in the context of those times. Freeman hit .280, and recorded seven home runs and 84 RBI. Boston won the American League pennant again, but there was no World Series that year due to the objections of John McGraw. All in all, it was a good year for Buck, but, unfortunately, it would be his last productive one.

As Freeman played in 1905, he was not yet 34 years of age. But, for whatever reasons, he had lost his ability to hit Major League pitching. Perhaps it was his eyesight or some other unknown factor, because it could not have been his conditioning. Buck was a pioneer in the area of exercise physiology, and always kept himself in good shape. In fact, he worked out in a gymnasium and made an overt effort to increase his muscle mass. That was one of the reasons that he could hit a baseball so far, but it certainly didn't fit with the prevailing wisdom of his time. Back then, it was generally considered counterproductive for ballplayers to "bulk up." Regardless of the cause, Freeman hit only five more Major League home runs starting in 1905. Early in 1907, he was sent to Minneapolis in the American Association, where he was a top slugger until he dislocated his shoulder in July 1908. But Buck Freeman loved baseball, and he stayed in the game for many more years as a minor league player/manager and umpire. He had become a legend in his own time, and enjoyed his accomplishments to the end of his days.

NUMBER 2: ROGER CONNOR—136 HOME RUNS—1880 TO 1897

Until Babe Ruth came along, Roger Connor was the leading home run hitter in Major League history. Born in Waterbury, Connecticut, in 1857, Connor grew into an unusually large man for his times, eventually taking the field at 6'3" and 230 pounds. He batted and threw left-handed, and was known as a fine all-around athlete with surprisingly good speed. Roger was also a man of character and integrity, and did much to popularize the game in its early years. He was a true baseball pioneer.

Like many of the early diamond stars, Connor was part of a large Irish immigrant family. Typical of the times, his parents disdained baseball, preferring old-fashioned work. That made it tough for young Roger, and he logged a lot of hours in factories doing back-breaking labor. It wasn't easy, but it helped him to develop his formidable strength. Eventually, Connor's mother relented, and, in 1876, he played a limited number of games for Waterbury. By 1878, Roger had moved to New Bedford, Massachusetts, and, in 1879, Connor made an impressive showing in Holyoke with a .335 batting average. Roger then signed a free agent contract with the National League Troy Trojans in 1880, batting .332, slugging .459, and slamming his first three big-league homers as a third baseman.

Switching to first base in 1881, Roger slipped offensively, but still launched his first epic distance blow. At Chicago's White Stock-

Roger Connor

ings Park on May 11, Connor blasted one to the top of the fence in deepest center field. The ball actually imbedded in the wooden boards 12 feet above field level as Roger circled the bases. Connor improved in '82, which was amply demonstrated by his .330 batting average and .530 slugging percentage. But he averaged just three home runs in those first three seasons, and needed several years to develop into a great home run hitter. But when he hit them, Roger hit them far. When the Troy franchise foundered due to poor attendance, Connor joined the newly formed New York Gothams in 1883. That is where he recorded the most memorable home run of his distinguished career. Oddly, it wasn't even an official four-bagger, but rather an exhibition game homer prior to opening day.

The Gothams, renamed Giants, and the American Association New York Metropolitans played an eight-game exhibition series prior to the '83 season's May 1 opening day. The first contest took place on April 14 in the original Polo Grounds, which had no outfield fences at that time. In the 3rd inning against Tim Keefe, Connor unleashed a tremendous line drive to distant center field that left everyone breathless. He easily circled the bases before center fielder James "Chief" Roseman could retrieve the battered ball. The crowd of 5,584 was so impressed that they arranged a collection and gave the proceeds to Roger as a tribute to his remarkable strength. Connor had recorded only nine big-league homers up to that time, and this was his first game in New York. Nonetheless, the *New York Times* stated that "Connor made one of those long hits for which he is famous." Clearly, his power was already well known.

Roger had a so-so year in 1884, but began a period of steady improvement in 1885. He settled for only one home run, but accrued 15 triples, and batted .371. With limited outfield fences in his home park and irregular home run boundaries league-wide, three-baggers were an essential reflection of Connor's power. In 1886, Roger belted seven homers along with 20 triples, while slugging .540. By that time, he was one of the main men in the world of power hitting. He proved that on September 11 at the Polo Grounds when he bombed one over the outer security wall in right field and onto 112th Street. Such a blow had never been seen until that moment. When he reached home plate, Boston pitcher Charley "Old Hoss" Radbourn stared at him incredulously, and his teammates shook his hand one by one. That historic homer flew about 440 feet.

Although Connor's average dropped to .285 in 1887, he recorded a career high 17 homers along with 22 triples. This magnificent athletic machine also stole 43 bases. At the end of the official schedule, the Giants embarked on one of the most ambitious post-season tours that baseball has ever known. Visiting New Orleans, Los Angeles, and San Francisco, they spent most of the off-season playing baseball. Remember that there were no airplanes or automobiles back then, and the team traveled mostly by way of trains and carriages. The logistics were arduous, but athletes of that era were happy just being paid to play ball. Along the way, Roger Connor walloped longest-ever drives in Los Angeles on November 20 and in San Francisco on December 3. The latter blow may have flown 440 feet to right field. Confirmation of the exact distance is difficult, but, if authenticated, that drive would vie for the distinction of the mightiest drive of the 19th century.

Roger reprised with 14 home runs in 1888, highlighted by three in one game (and six in the series!) at Indianapolis's Athletic Park on May 9. It was only 267 feet to the right field wall, but four of Connor's drives sailed far beyond the barrier. A year later (June 29, 1889), Roger smashed one in the same ballpark that landed nearly a block away. When Connor totaled 13 homers that year, he paced the Giants to their second straight victory in the forerunner of the modern World Series. His best shot cleared the recently erected center field fence at the Polo Grounds on July 11. It was another first-time event. One week later, "Old Reliable" smacked one onto Eighth Avenue in right field, which only he had done before. Connor joined the Players League for the only year of its existence in 1890, predictably posting huge numbers: .349 batting, .548 slugging, and 14 homers. His annual "longest-ever" occurred on July 21 in Buffalo, when Connor's titanic shot sailed over the wall in deep right center.

Returning to the Giants in 1891, Roger had an off year with just seven homers. He then moved over to the Philadelphia Phillies in '92. Showing no sentiment for his former teammates, Connor pounded two homers at the Huntingdon Grounds on April 27 against Amos Rusie. Nicknamed "The Hoosier Thunderbolt" because of his blazing fastball, it has long been asserted that Rusie was the primary cause for the pitcher's mound being moved back to 60 feet, 6 inches for the next season. Returning again to New York in 1893, Roger recorded 11 home runs, but was shipped away for good early in 1894 to St. Louis. It was there in '94, at age 37, that "Dear Old Roger" achieved his highest-ever slugging mark at .552. He accomplished that through a combination of eight homers, 25 triples (another career high), and 35 doubles.

Roger Connor eventually slowed down, but not right away. He enjoyed two more productive seasons, which included 20 additional home runs as well as a brief stint in 1896 as manager. He notched his final career four-bagger on April 29, 1897, against pitching legend Cy Young, and held onto his Major League record of 138 home runs until a guy named Ruth showed up. In his "retirement," Roger became a combination owner/manager/player with Waterbury of the Connecticut League, and shamed the youngsters with a league-leading batting mark of .392 in 1899. It is believed that Connor wore eyeglasses for the first time that year, and one wonders what he might have accomplished if he had donned them in his prime. There are stories of gigantic home runs flying off his bat as late as 1903 when Roger was still competing at age 46 with Springfield in the Massachusetts League. They are probably true, since Roger Connor was one of those rare men whose actual deeds measured up to his legend.

NUMBER 1: DAN BROUTHERS—106 HOME RUNS—1879 TO 1896

Big Dan Brouthers was born in New York's Hudson Valley in 1858, and started playing professional baseball near his home for the Wappinger Falls Actives in 1877. Batting and throwing left-handed, Dan started as a pitcher, but switched to first base within a few years. In that first pro year in 1877, Brouthers was involved in a tragic accident when he collided at home plate with a catcher from another New York team. The man later died, but Dan was exonerated when the incident was judged an accident. Brouthers was a tough customer, yet neither violent nor malicious. In fact, the handsome, mustachioed Irishman was one of the most respected and beloved players of his time.

Dan Brouthers played his first Major League ball for the Troy Trojans in 1879 and recorded his initial home run on July 19 in Cincinnati. During that rookie year, Dan added three more circuits, including an impressive blow over the center field fence in Troy on August 6. Brouthers batted only .274 that season, but still slugged at the then-impressive rate of .429. Those numbers indicate that Dan hit the ball hard when he made contact. But he didn't improve in 1880, playing most of the season for the minor league Baltimore and Rochester teams. It wasn't until Brouthers joined the National League Buffalo Bisons in 1881 that he displayed star-caliber ability.

Dan Brouthers played for five seasons in Buffalo, consistently hitting the ball harder than anyone up to that point in baseball history. During that five-year span, National League hitters slugged at a rate of .340. Starting in 1881, Brouthers led the league five straight times with percentages of .541, .547, .572, .563, and .543. About the only way to quantify the Dan Brouthers of those days is to say that he was the Babe Ruth of the 1880s. He only averaged eight homers per season, but the game was not structured for regular home run production. Some

Dan Brouthers

outfield boundaries were positioned too close to home plate. Others were absurdly far away, and many parks had none at all. What matters from an historical perspective is that Dan Brouthers was hitting the ball as hard as a man could hit it.

Moving to the Detroit Wolverines in 1886, Dan continued to pound the ball. He led the league in slugging for a sixth consecutive time (.581) while batting .370. Now in his prime at age 28, Brouthers stood 6'2", and weighed a muscular 225 pounds. Dan stayed for three seasons in the Motor City, and belted a total of 32 home runs. Many of them were unusually long. On September 10, 1886 in Chicago, Brouthers whacked a single, double, and three home runs. Contemporary accounts confirm that all five blows were hit ferociously. Of note, two of Dan's four-baggers that day stayed inside the grounds. Consistent with the standards of his era, Brouthers sped around the bases 21 times for inside-the-park homers during his days in the big leagues.

On May 17, 1887, Dan came to Philadelphia to play at the Huntingdon Grounds, which were later renamed the Baker Bowl. He drove in six runs with a double and homer to right field along with a long triple to deep left field. Clearing Philadelphia's fence in right (310 feet) was not particularly difficult, but it was a much different story in center (410 feet). Back in the 1880s, 410 feet was a long way to hit a baseball, but Dan Brouthers cleared that daunting distance on consecu-

tive days on May 18 and May 19. Although Big Dan yielded the slugging-percentage crown to Sam Thompson that year (.571 to .562), he still performed at a remarkable level. Along with his 12 home runs, he recorded 36 doubles and 20 triples, while scoring a league-leading 153 runs. However, Brouthers slipped in all areas of performance in 1888, and, at age 30, Dan was regarded by the Detroit management as past his prime. Starting in 1889, Brouthers began an eight-year odyssey during which he played for six different teams. Most players went from team to team in those days, but Dan's travels certainly exceeded the norm. In retrospect, it's difficult to know why. Brouthers was a good soldier and still a solid performer. Of course, his most enduring attribute was his fabulous power.

On May 6, 1889, Dan blasted the first-ever ball over the center field fence at Washington's Capitol Park. Then, visiting Staten Island's St. George Cricket Grounds on June 11, Brouthers lined an awesome shot over the center field fence into an outdoor pageant called "The Fall of Babylon." This drive cleared a high turret that formed part of the spectacle, and was labeled as the longest ball ever struck. The Giants played there briefly while awaiting the opening of the new Polo Grounds. This historic homer came against Hall of Famer Mickey Welch, who earlier struck Dan out for the first time in 33 games. Next, at Boston's South End Grounds on August 20, Dan slugged a ball over the center field wall. That was one of only two drives that ever left the park in that direction. Participating in the Players League in 1890, Dan topped the center field fence at the second Polo Grounds on August 16. That blow was recorded against pitching legend Tim Keefe. A similar thing happened on August 9, 1891, at Recreation Park in Columbus, Ohio. Their right field wall was 400 feet away, and no one had ever cleared it until Brouthers showed up that day. Just nine days later in Boston, Dan smashed a torrid liner over the right field wall, personally assessing the blow as one of his longest.

After two productive seasons with the Brooklyn Grooms in 1892 and 1893, Dan Brouthers had the good fortune to land with the then-dynastic Baltimore Orioles in 1894. They were a rough and tumble bunch who did just about anything (legal or otherwise) to win ball games. And they did a lot of winning in the mid-1890s. They were led by their pugnacious third baseman, John "Mugsy" McGraw, who went on to baseball immortality as the manager of the New York Giants from 1902 through 1932. For whatever reason, Dan was re-energized, and, at age 36, he enjoyed his last great Major League season. Offense was up around the National League that year, but Brouthers was outstanding by any yardstick. He batted .345, walloped nine homers and 25 triples, slugged .560, and stole 40 bases. Dan also smashed the longest drive of his illustrious career. Brouthers warmed up on May 4, 1894, while playing at Baltimore's Union Park. Big Dan unloaded off Brooklyn's

Dan Daub, sending the ball far over the fence at the 365 foot mark in right center. The drive was considered such an accomplishment that the word "here" was soon painted on the fence where the ball had cleared it. However, on July 18, Dan surpassed that same boundary 30 feet closer to center field. To be sure, he was shrinking the Baltimore ballpark like no one before him. But consider this: Between those two historic blasts, Brouthers hit even farther . . . much farther!

On June 16, 1894, at the same Union Park, Dan Brouthers hit what was likely the longest home run of the 19th century. He connected off St. Louis's Ted Breitenstein, and drove the ball on a line drive trajectory over the 16-foot-high wooden fence just right of center field. The ball landed on the sidewalk of Guilford Avenue four doors below 24th Street. It then rolled to 23rd Street with a watchman and club official in pursuit. The drive was so memorable that it was the main topic of conversation 13 years later at a reunion of those legendary Orioles. At that same event in 1907, writers from all three major Baltimore papers confirmed that they had seen the historic blow from their vantage point in the press box. How far did it go? It's impossible to know for sure, but 450 feet is a good estimate. John McGraw later said, "In all my experience in baseball, I have never seen a hit made to equal the one made by Brouthers in Baltimore and don't think I ever will." Considering that the Major League ball did not have a cork center until 1911, this drive was struck with stupendous force.

Dan Brouthers was amazingly powerful that season. Five of his homers cleared Baltimore's distant right field wall, while another sailed over the right center field scoreboard in Philadelphia. His longest as a visiting player flew 40 feet over the right center field wall in Washington on August 1. Naturally, it was categorized as another "longest ever" on Brouthers's career log. But, sadly, this was the last year that Big Dan was able to consistently perform against Major League pitching. When Baltimore sold Brouthers to Louisville in early 1895, management got it right. Dan was out of gas, and struck only two home runs for the remainder of the season. However, before he left the Orioles, Brouthers left one final indelible memory. After training in Georgia, Baltimore scheduled a spring exhibition game against Wake Forest in Raleigh. That contest was played at Athletic Field on April 3, 1895. In the fourth inning, Big Dan bombed one to right field that landed in a nearby cemetery. It was hailed as the city's longest-ever home run, and renowned teammate Hughie Jennings regarded it as even longer than the Oriole Park thunderbolt from the preceding season. Recorded in his 37th year, Dan Brouthers had launched one of the mightiest blows in baseball history.

Brouthers hit his last big-league homer on May 5, 1896, while playing with the Phillies in St. Louis. It was Career Number 106, and flew over the right field fence. When he had not homered again by early July, Philadelphia decided to release the great man. Despite going 4 for 9 in a Fourth of July doubleheader at the Huntingdon Grounds, Dan was sent home. That was typical of management's treatment of players in those days. There was no ceremony or public acknowledgement of past glories . . . just an unfeeling dismissal. But that was not the end of the line for Big Dan Brouthers.

Even though he had lost the quickness to excel at the Major League level, he continued to play competitive baseball until 1906 when he was 48 years old. Starring for Springfield of the Eastern League in 1897, Dan led the league with a .415 batting average. On September 21, he also clubbed another of the longest home runs of his memorable athletic life. Still going strong several seasons later in 1904, Brouthers batted .373 for Poughkeepsie in the Hudson Valley League. On June 1 of that year, at Saugerties, Dan went 6 for 6 with two stirring home runs over the 325 foot mark in right field. Clearly, the man was destined to hit a baseball. And so he did. In a career spanning four decades, Big Dan Brouthers pounded the ball everywhere he went. His tape measure crown is one of the brightest.

Negro League Sluggers

NUMBER 5: LOUIS SANTOP—1909 TO 1926

Louis Napoleon Santop Loftin was born in Tyler, Texas, in 1890, and began his pro baseball career in 1909. Standing 6'4", Louis weighed 240 pounds in his prime. He batted left-handed, but was a right-handed catcher. Both his hitting and throwing power were legendary in their scope. Despite his good-natured disposition, Santop was also a very tough competitor. Sadly, however, his deeds were sparsely documented. As was the case with all Negro League players, Santop's on-field accomplishments received significantly less newspaper coverage than the white Major Leaguers of his era. Accordingly, some of his legendary home runs may be apocryphal.

One legend says that there was an advertising sign situated 440 feet from home plate at the ballpark in Newark, New Jersey. Anyone hitting it with a home run was automatically awarded a new suit of clothes. The story continues that Santop struck it three times in a single game, thereby causing the sign to be removed. That one is a little hard to accept, but it seems likely that Louis hit it once. The legend started somewhere. Of course, there is an opposite consequence to the newspaper problem. For every Santop homer that may have been exaggerated, there is probably an equal (or higher) number of legitimate blasts that were not recorded at all. It is unlikely that historians will ever be able to sort it out.

Louis Santop

Courtesy of the National Baseball Hall of Fame and Museum

Starting in 1909 with the Fort Worth Wonders, he moved on later that same year to the Oklahoma Monarchs, and finished with the Philadelphia Giants. In 1910, he stayed in Philly, catching the legendary Dick "Cannonball" Redding, thus creating the memorable "Kid Battery." Louis then joined the New York Lincoln Giants where he stayed through 1914. Redding followed Santop to the Giants and teamed with "Smokey Joe" Williams to give New York what may have been the hardest-throwing pitching tandem in baseball history. And Louis Santop caught both of them. Remembered mostly for his offensive production, "Top" was also an excellent defensive receiver. And what an arm he had himself! Before games, Louis would prepare by gunning rifle-like throws to all bases while remaining in his crouch. During those memorable years with the Lincoln Giants, Santop also had the honor of playing with the wondrous John Henry "Pop" Lloyd, who is often linked with Honus Wagner as baseball's greatest shortstop.

Switching briefly to the Chicago American Giants in 1915, Santop initiated a five-year odyssey that saw service with the Lincoln Giants (again), Brooklyn Royal Giants, Hilldale (Philadelphia), and U.S. Marine Corps. It was in 1918 that "Top" was drafted by Uncle Sam during World War I and ordered to report to Fort Dix. However, upon undergoing his induction physical, an old baseball fracture was found to have twisted his arm so badly that he was sent home. A few months later, he was recalled by the Marines to perform stevedore duties in Norfolk, which he performed until his discharge in May 1919. It was during this time that Santop received the most colorful nickname of his career. Referencing the famous German siege gun, Louis was called "Big Bertha." It didn't take long to demonstrate the propriety of that nickname. In his first action after returning to civilian life, at New York's Dexter Park on May 25, Santop belted long home runs in both games of a twin-bill against the Bushwicks.

In 1920, Louis Santop returned to the Hilldale Daisies, where he enjoyed his greatest professional success. At Hilldale Ballpark in the suburban town of Yeadon (also referred to as Darby), he was known to hit several homers to distant center field that traveled over 450 feet. However, it was also in 1920 that legendary Hilldale owner Ed Bolden scheduled games in both Camden, New Jersey, and Wilmington, Delaware. Accordingly, Santop had three home fields on which to make his mark. It was at the Camden field on July 23 that Santop began a four-day rampage of massive center field homers. On one of his infrequent "rest days," Louis was called to pinch hit against Norfolk, and won the game with a massive blow far over the middle wall. Two days later at New York's Dyckman Oval against Tesreau's Bears, Santop again bypassed the center field barrier by a wide margin. Then, on July 27 against the Riverside team in their home park, Louis struck only the second ball that ever cleared the distant center field fence. For the record, Louis himself had hit the first. All of these blows flew well over 450 feet, and may have approached the 500-foot plateau.

Back at his other "home fields," Santop collected five hits in the August 14 contest against Lit Brothers at Hilldale Park. On August 23 at Wilmington versus Haridan & Hollingsworth, "Top" rattled the outfield fences in every direction with four booming doubles. Culminating this great season, Louis Santop won his personal showdown with Babe Ruth by collecting three base hits in a barnstorming game against the Bambino at Philadelphia's Baker Bowl on October 7. Every great African-American slugger for the next quarter-century was referred to as the "black Babe Ruth," but Louis Santop was the first.

Ruth usually enjoyed high levels of success against Negro League competition, but, on this occasion, Big Bertha bettered him.

When Santop performed in yet two more home fields late in his career in Philadelphia, he left additional legends of his prodigious power. Playing at 44th and Parkside as well as 48th and Spruce, Louis smashed balls that are still talked about today. In 1925, Santop had to give way to a younger Biz Mackey, who took over as Hilldale's everyday catcher. There was no shame in that since Louis was 35 at the time, and Mackey became one of the Negro League's all-time greats. Santop was released the following year, but had already accomplished enough to eventually enter the Hall of Fame.

As was often the case in the old days, superstar Louis Santop didn't leave the game after his time at the pinnacle of his profession. "Top" founded the semi-pro Santop Bronchos in 1927, occasionally pinch-hitting, and stayed with them through 1931. In 1932, he was the first African-American appointed a Pennsylvania State inspector, and later added broadcasting, bartending, and local politics to his job resume. Santop was also an active member of the Manhattan Elks Lodge as well as a 32nd degree Mason. He died in the Philadelphia Naval Hospital in 1942 as a beloved and respected member of his community. In his heyday, Louis was one of the highest paid performers (reportedly $500 per month) in Negro baseball as well as a fan favorite in both the black and white communities. His pleasant disposition con-trasted with the brutal way that he struck a baseball. Louis Santop was one of baseball's mightiest performers as well as one of its finest ambassadors.

NUMBER 4: JOHN BECKWITH—1916 TO 1938

John Beckwith was a brute. For the most part, that characterization is a reference to his frightening physical capabilities. Standing 6'3" and weighing 230 pounds of mostly muscle, Beckwith could scare anyone with his 38-inch bat. Sadly, however, his behavior was sometimes destructive, both to himself and to his teammates. On the field, he seemed angry much of the time. Sometimes, that state of mind drove him to tremendous production, while, on other occasions, it forced him off the field.

Born in Louisville, Kentucky, in 1902, young John grew into physical manhood so quickly that he was playing semi-pro baseball by age 14. He reportedly played briefly in Havana, Cuba at age 15. Beckwith played often for the Chicago Giants of the Negro Professional League when he was just 17 years old. Batting and throwing right-handed, John started as a catcher, but spent most of his subsequent career as either a shortstop or third baseman. Considering his size and strength, that choice of position was a testimony to Beckwith's superb athleticism. Mostly, of course, he was known as one of the mightiest sluggers in baseball history.

John Beckwith

On May 21, 1921, while visiting the Cincinnati Cuban Stars, John Beckwith cleared the left field wall at Crosley Field (aka Redland Field). The ball kept going and passed over a laundry sign before landing on top of a factory. It was a first time occurrence, and the awed attendees passed the hat, collecting $25 as an honorarium to Beckwith's blast. This drive exceeded 450 feet. Still playing for the Chicago American Giants in 1922, John knocked one over Schorling Park's left field fence on July 4 to beat the Detroit Stars 1-0. That was also a first-ever event, but one month later Beckwith topped the center field wall by 10 feet, thereby shattering the stadium's distance record.

As of October 7, 1923, John Beckwith was still wearing a Chicago uniform. However, on that day at Pyott Park, he was involved in a fight that nearly led to a riot. It is difficult to determine all the consequences of that event, but it was soon reported that Beckwith left town due to "legal trouble." He wound up with the Homestead Grays in 1924, but owner/manager Cum Posey released him in June, whereupon John hooked up with the Baltimore Black Sox. All the while, the "Black Bomber" was bashing baseballs out of sight. There was never any doubt about Beckwith's ability—physical or mental. He was hired by the Black Sox as their manager in 1925, but, almost predictably, assaulted an umpire and was suspended. Beckwith remained as a player with Baltimore until July 8, 1926, when he was traded to the Harrisburg Giants. Despite his vast talents, no team kept John Beckwith for long.

However, there was one brief respite from the seemingly never-ending conflict. In 1927, playing with the legendary Oscar Charleston in Harrisburg, John Beckwith enjoyed a season of uninterrupted production. Beckwith actually took over from Charleston as player/manager for that one season, and the two giant egos functioned in a reasonably compatible fashion. Although the statistics are unreliable, it is believed that John slammed over 70 home runs against a combination of Negro League, semi-pro, and minor league competition. Based on the relatively benign events of '27, Cum Posey brought Beckwith back to the Homestead Grays in 1928 and 1929.

On June 16, 1928, at Pittsburgh's Forbes Field, the Grays hosted the Beaver Falls Elks, and Beckwith bombed one over the distant left field wall. The *Pittsburgh Courier* reported that "Beck" was the first Gray to hit one out of that cavernous ballpark in years, but he was only warming up. On July 28 against the team from Jamestown, John rocketed a ball over the wall 11 panels to the right of the left field scoreboard. In essence, Beckwith's massive shot left the premises in almost dead center field near the 457 foot mark. Then, playing winter ball in southern California after the season, which he usually did, John walloped one at Los Angeles's White Sox Park that had to be seen to be believed. It cleared the left field wall and an adjoining house before landing on the second house outside the stadium. This epic blow on January 20, 1929 was estimated at 500 feet.

That brings us to the most interesting of all the reported long home runs hit by John Beckwith. It is believed that he once smashed a ball over the far-off left field bleachers at Griffith Stadium in Washington, D.C, which then collided with an advertising sign atop those left field seats. If true, that means that John Beckwith did basically the same thing that Mickey Mantle did in 1953, when the Mighty Mick started his own long-distance legend. Did it really happen? Again, we do not have an exact date. But we do have the testimony of some reliable Negro Leaguers who provided the details. After striking the sign in deep left field, the ball bounced back

into the bleachers. That means that this drive flew about 460 feet before it was interrupted in mid-flight about 50 feet above the playing field. Those dynamics translate into a blow of some 510 feet. It's up to the reader to decide if he or she believes the legend.

What we know for certain is that John Beckwith recorded a lifetime batting average of .366 against Negro League competition. Known as a dead pull hitter, he compiled that number despite dealing with extreme defensive shifts. He is also credited with hitting .330 in exhibition games versus Major League pitchers. In 1930, Beckwith signed with the New York Lincoln Giants, and played for the great Pop Lloyd. Using the Catholic Protectory Oval as his primary home field, John extended his tape measure legacy. On March 30, he larruped a pair of four-baggers with one passing far over the fence in left center. It was compared for length with one that Beckwith had smacked the year before as a visitor (June 2, 1929) that soared over the flagpole near center field. Unfortunately, John fractured his leg while sliding on June 14, 1930. He returned to play part-time in the Negro League World Series later that year against young Josh Gibson and the Homestead Grays. However, Beckwith was never quite the same after this injury.

John Beckwith played in the Negro League until 1938, seeing service on six more rosters. He finished his baseball days as a player/manager with the White Plains Crescents near New York City in 1941. He then worked briefly as a policeman in the Big Apple, but reportedly succumbed to his demons. It is said that he became lost in a world of prostitution, bootlegging, and gambling. John Beckwith was one of the most gifted baseball players that America has ever produced. Negro League star Ted "Double Duty" Radcliffe said of him, "Nobody hit the ball any farther than him: Josh Gibson or nobody else." He struggled with issues unrelated to the quality of his play, but, with a bat in his hands, he was a performer of epochal proportions.

NUMER 3: NORMAN "TURKEY" STEARNES—1923 TO 1940

Norman Thomas Stearnes was born in Nashville, Tennessee, in 1901, and became one of baseball's greatest all-around players. He was a marvelous defensive center fielder who could run, throw, and hit. Norman stood 6 feet in height, and weighed only 170 pounds, but his lean, muscular frame generated tremendous bat speed and prodigious power. Hitting and throwing left-handed, "Turkey" Stearnes left an impressive legacy of tape measure home runs. There is some confusion about the source of his intriguing nickname, but it probably originated in childhood from the way he ran. "Turkey" tended to flap his arms while running with a "herky-jerky" motion. But it was only a matter of style. He also used a rather awkward stance while batting (wide open with his right toes pointing up and out), but he was extremely effective. Norman was a masterful performer whose accomplishments transcended his quirky mannerisms.

Turkey Stearnes began his pro career in 1921 with the Montgomery Grey Sox in the Negro Southern League. He moved quickly up the ladder, and, after spending a year in Memphis, played for the Detroit Stars in 1923. In 60 games, Stearnes batted .365, and slugged 17 home runs. That was a remarkable total for a 22-year-old rookie of that era. Usually competing in about 75 league games a year, he averaged 18 home runs per season. Stearnes's batting average for the decade was

Norman "Turkey" Stearnes

close to .360 with a high of .378 in 1929. And other than "Cool Papa" Bell of the St. Louis Stars, he was regarded as the best center fielder and baserunner in Negro League baseball. His single longest drive during that time may have been his epic shot over the center field fence at Detroit's Mack Park on August 2, 1926.

Stearnes moved to the New York Lincoln Giants in 1930, but returned to Detroit in mid June. However, before leaving, Turkey slammed long homers at both the Protectory Oval (May 11) and Dexter Park (May 30). Upon his homecoming back in the Motor City, Norman discovered that he had inherited an imposing field on which to play. Until that time, the Stars had played at Mack Park, but it had been damaged in a 1929 fire. When Hamtramck Stadium opened in 1930 with its 450-foot right field boundary, Ty Cobb (believe it or not) threw out the first ball for the inaugural Negro League game. In the city's first-ever night game on June 27, 1930, Norman tried his best to be the first to clear that right field wall, but he would have to wait. Then, visiting the Nashville Elites, Stearnes walloped homers on consecutive days (July 12 and July 13) over their distant center field fence.

The season had already been eventful for Norman by the time September arrived, but that was a particularly historic month in Negro League history. In the East, Pop Lloyd's New York Lincoln Giants with John Beckwith squared off against Oscar Charleston's Homestead Grays and young slugger Josh Gibson in their version of the World Series. In the West, Stearnes and his Detroit Stars engaged the St. Louis Stars with Mule Suttles for western supremacy. In the process, Turkey bashed three homers, driving in 11 runs and batting .481 in seven games. Included in those impressive numbers were two enormous home runs. On September 16 in St. Louis, Norman blasted the ball 500 feet to right field off Ted Trent. Back in Detroit five days later, Turkey realized his wish by thumping a 475-footer over the right field fence.

On June 28, 1931, Norman essentially reprised that deed by walloping another shot out of the park in Detroit. This one came off Satchel Paige, and won the second game of a twin-bill by a 1–0 score. Next, at Cleveland's vast new Municipal Stadium on August 30, he hit the longest ball in a five game series with the Homestead Grays. His triple off the distant bleacher wall in right center flew about 465 feet. Turkey then settled in with the Chicago American Giants for the next four seasons (1932–1935). Norman was a quiet and pleasant man who seemed happy just to do his job well. Even though he seldom socialized with the other league players, they both liked and admired him. Stearnes eventually married the niece of fellow Negro League stalwart, Ted "Double Duty" Radcliffe, and Ted couldn't say enough good things about him. In fact, Radcliffe saw what might have been Norman's longest-ever home run when both men were participating in the Cuban

Winter League. Radcliffe saw Stearnes launch an astounding drive far over the center field wall in Camaguey that landed in a nearby lake. He estimated the distance at 520 feet.

In 1933, Stearnes was joined on the Chicago American Giants by George "Mule" Suttles. With the "Mule" hitting from the right side and the "Turkey" batting from the left, they formed one of the most powerful (and colorfully nicknamed) tandems in baseball history. Those Giants enjoyed a remarkable season. On August 20, Stearnes sealed their 28th straight victory with a timely home run against Nashville. The two great sluggers stayed together through 1935, when Turkey took final advantage of the protection he received from batting in front of Mule. Seeing a lot of good pitches, Stearnes compiled an amazing batting average of .430. At age 35 in 1936, Turkey Stearnes finally started to slow down. Playing for the Philadelphia Stars, he batted under .300 (.298) for only the second time in his career. In 1937, with both the rejuvenated Detroit Stars and Chicago American Giants, he stormed back to .383. But he was older now, and no longer could consistently sustain that level of excellence. He dropped down to .292 with Chicago and Kansas City in 1938. His home run output also decreased, but Norman never lost his great power. He finished his Negro League competition with the Monarchs in 1940, but he still managed to blast five home runs in just 30 games.

Like so many of the early superstars, both black and white, Norman Stearnes didn't leave the game entirely when he stepped down from the top rung. He played semi-pro ball in Detroit and Toledo through 1945. Then, when one career ended, Stearnes began another. Always an industrious man, Norman often worked seasonally in the auto industry even during his glory years. Upon his retirement from baseball, Stearnes spent the next 29 years in the employ of the Ford Motor Company. In the baseball arena, it is obvious that he was held in very high esteem by his peers. Seemingly, every former Negro Leaguer campaigned for Norman's entry into the Hall of Fame, and it finally happened in 2000. Who could deny him? He compiled a lifetime average of .359 along with 185 home runs in 905 games. During his documented 14 games versus white Major Leaguers, Stearnes batted .313 with four homers. Using any criterion, Turkey Stearnes was one of the best and most powerful performers in the annals of his sport.

NUMBER 2: GEORGE "MULE" SUTTLES—1923 TO 1944

George Suttles was born in rural Alabama in 1900, and, as a young man, worked long hours in Southern coal mines. It was there that he developed his prodigious strength. By his late teens, he was also playing baseball in the Birmingham area, where he soon established his new profession. In his prime, George stood 6'2" and weighed about 230 pounds. Batting and throwing from the right side, the amiable

Courtesy of the National Baseball Hall of Fame and Museum

George "Mule" Suttles

Suttles moved from team to team in his early years, but eventually settled with the Birmingham Black Barons in 1923. Showing power akin to that of a mule, he received the nickname that he kept for life.

In those early years with the Black Barons, George was an outfielder. His home run totals were not impressive in 1923 and 1924, but he consistently hit the ball hard. Suttles used Rickwood Field in Birmingham as his home park, where the fences were prohibitively distant from home plate. George seemed to come into his own in 1925, when he blasted 13 home runs and batted .331 in 74 league games. But, when Mule moved to the St. Louis Stars in 1926, he really took off. Taking advantage of the cozier dimensions in Stars' Park in St. Louis, Suttles smashed a

league-leading 27 homers in 87 games. However, his success was not just the result of a change in stadiums. George was reaching his athletic prime, as could be recognized by his lofty .418 batting average.

Mule also enjoyed switching from the outfield to first base. Although he occasionally returned to outfield play, George functioned primarily as a first-sacker for the rest of his career. Remaining in St. Louis for the remainder of the 1920s, Mule Suttles became the greatest power hitter in the Negro League. From 1926 through 1930, Suttles averaged over 18 league homers per year, while batting close to .400. Proving that he didn't need the short left field boundary in St. Louis to produce, George blasted a homer against his former Birmingham mates on May 28, 1929 that resolved any lingering questions about his power. Blasting the ball far over the center field fence at Stars' Park, "Mule" established a new distance record.

It was also around this time that George Suttles hit what is believed to be the longest home run of his storied career. Playing winter ball in Cuba in 1928–1929, he is reported to have pounded an extraordinary drive to center field at Tropicana Park in Havana. Some say that this drive eventually landed in the harbor, and there are legends of super-human distances in the 600-foot range. Those claims are almost certainly bogus, but it is likely that this stupendous drive flew well over 500 feet. Like all of baseball's greatest sluggers, from Babe Ruth to Mark McGwire, there is significant hyperbole surrounding the deeds of Mule Suttles. But that is not George's doing; he just hit them.

From 1930 through 1932, George Suttles was a baseball nomad. Starting with those St. Louis Stars, he moved on to brief stints with the Baltimore Black Sox, Washington Black Senators, Detroit Wolves, and Washington Pilots. However, one factor remained constant. The Mule crushed the ball wherever he went. Suttles then landed with the Chicago American Giants in 1933 where he played for three seasons. That was also the year that the Negro League staged its first annual East-West All-Star Game at Comiskey Park in Chicago. The game evolved into a personal showcase for Suttles, who always seemed to rise to special levels of achievement. In fact, George enjoyed the high point of his professional life during the subsequent 1935 contest, when his home run off Martin Dihigo won the game in the 11th inning. His final statistics for seven East-West appearances stood at .412 in batting average and .941 for slugging. The longest homer hit by Mule during this time was probably his enormous clout on August 20, 1935, at Western League Park in Des Moines. It cleared the trees beyond the center field fence for a ride of over 500 feet.

When Suttles joined the Newark Eagles in 1936, he found his permanent baseball home. With the exception of short stays with Indianapolis and New York, George would remain there until he retired from the game after the 1944 season. Playing mostly at Ruppert Stadium, Mule left a trail of gigantic shots that are now legendary. On August 21, 1936 in a man-to-man showdown with Josh Gibson, Suttles ripped a 460-footer past the center field fence. During the 1930s, Suttles also spent most of his off-seasons competing in the California Winter League. Actually, Mule was there eight different years, and he compiled an extraordinary record. Many Major Leaguers similarly spent their winter months in that same league. For example, Larry French pitched there for several seasons, and Suttles is known to have clobbered a 475-foot home run against him in 1936. When George's final winter numbers are totaled, they show some impressive conclusions. He batted .378, slugged .869, and bombed 64 homers.

Another highlight in Mule's career was his participation in Newark's "Million Dollar Infield" starting in 1938. George held down first base, while Dick Seay played second with Willie Wells at shortstop and Ray Dandridge at third base. When all the dust finally settled, Suttles, Wells, and Dandridge were elected to the Hall of Fame in Cooperstown, and Seay was recognized as one of the greatest-ever defensive infielders. It was an historic combination. By 1941, at age 41, Mule Suttles should have been slowing down. However, in that single season with the New York Black Yankees, he was still pounding the ball with amazing power. He reportedly struck 500-foot-plus homers at Nashville on June 15 and Paterson, New Jersey, on August 2.

Eventually, as Mule finally began to slip as a player, his reputation as an old-fashioned good guy was recognized. He became the Eagles' player/manager in 1943 and 1944, and used his reputation to motivate his players to live up to his personal standards. One of them, Clarence Israel, said, "He was considered my dad. Suttles was the most gentle person I ever saw." However, even at age 43, the savage power was still intact. On August 8, 1943, in another game against rival Josh Gibson at Griffith Stadium, George pounded a screaming liner into the center field bleachers for a ride of 445 feet. On the matter of that historic batting power, Chico Renfroe of the Kansas City Monarchs stated, "He had the most raw power of any player I've ever seen. He went after the ball viciously. When he swung, you could feel the earth shake."

Josh Gibson

Courtesy of the National Baseball Hall of Fame and Museum

NUMBER 1: JOSH GIBSON—1930 TO 1946

There are so many legends about the exploits of Josh Gibson that it is difficult to separate fact from fiction. However, during the 1980s, decades after his death, every surviving member of the old Negro Leagues attested to his tremendous power and overall offensive brilliance. In addition, there are more than enough confirmed accounts from primary sources to establish Josh as the greatest power hitter of the Negro League era. He was a man of almost unlimited ability who

achieved things on the baseball diamond that are worthy of the boundless legends.

Born in Georgia in 1911, Josh soon moved to Pittsburgh, the city he called home for the rest of his short life. Young Gibson was a great multisport athlete, but chose baseball as his favorite endeavor. By 1930, at age 18, he was already well known as the star catcher for the semi-pro Crawford Colored Giants. The top black team in the Pittsburgh area was the legendary Homestead Grays, who already had a starting backstop in Buck Ewing. But he was injured on July 25 while playing under a problematic portable lighting system that the

Kansas City Monarchs had brought with them to Pittsburgh. That prompted Grays' manager Cum Posey to summon young Josh, who was coincidentally sitting in the stands. He was an immediate sensation.

Often playing at Forbes Field when the Major League Pittsburgh Pirates were on the road, the Homestead Grays and Josh Gibson competed in a ballpark with prohibitively difficult home run boundaries. It hardly mattered to the right-handed Gibson. He stood 6'1" and weighed 194 pounds. Later, in his prime, Josh played at 225 pounds. On September 13, 1930, against the Baltimore Black Sox, young Gibson smashed a ball over the 457 foot mark in center field at Forbes Field. It was the first of many tape measure blasts that would set the youthful Hercules apart from all other Negro League performers. By the end of September, Buck Ewing had recovered from his injured finger, but the formidable Gibson had essentially taken his job. A highly anticipated 10-game "World Series" was about to start between the Grays and New York Lincoln Giants, and Gibson played every inning.

In the first game, played at Forbes Field on September 20, Gibson smacked a triple off the left field scoreboard, followed by a tremendous homer over it. Five days later at Bigler Field in Philadelphia, Josh hit a monumental shot over a house across the street in left field. Within 48 hours, on September 27, 1930, at Yankee Stadium, Gibson connected off the Giants' Connie Rector. The ball sped like a bullet to left field, landing in the back of the bullpen 460 feet from home plate. That two-week sequence of power hitting was an extraordinary accomplishment for an 18-year-old man.

In his second pro season in 1931, Josh Gibson solidified his position as one of baseball's top young sluggers. On June 13 against Homewood, he belted a long homer over the distant left center field wall at Forbes Field in one of the Grays' many nonleague games. Gibson also contributed long-distance shots in games at Charleroi, Pennsylvania (July 6), and Cleveland (October 4). Josh was impressive enough to catch the eye of local black entrepreneur Gus Greenlee, who decided to use his dubious fortune to supplant the Homestead Grays as Pittsburgh's top team. Greenlee founded the new Pittsburgh Crawfords, and hired many of the top black players of the day, including Josh Gibson. In his first year with the Crawfords in 1932, Josh belted eight home runs, and batted .325 in games against Negro League competition, while adding 26 additional homers versus the remainder of the schedule. That year he achieved another distance feat during an event before the July 30 game at Greenlee Field (the Crawfords' home park). Taking part in field events with the Baltimore Black Sox, Josh won the "long throw" contest. Never considered a great defensive backstop (he was solid), Gibson always possessed a powerful and accurate throwing arm.

By 1933, the Pittsburgh Crawfords were the most heralded team in Negro baseball.

Along with Josh Gibson, they featured player/manager Oscar Charleston, who many believed to be the best all-around player (black or white) in the country. Batting left-handed, Charleston was nearly as powerful a batsman as Josh. Future Hall of Famers Judy Johnson and "Cool Papa" Bell similarly distinguished the lineup. Of course, the Crawfords also included the wondrous Satchel Paige as part of their pitching staff. He teamed with Gibson for four years as a battery combination that now seems more like myth than reality. Predictably, those two developed a friendly rivalry, and, when facing each other as adversaries in later years, they staged some epochal personal battles.

Gibson's top performance that year occurred on July 23 during a doubleheader against the Chicago American Giants. Playing on neutral turf at League Park in Cleveland, Josh accumulated eight base hits, which included a tremendous and dramatic home run to center field. In 1934, Josh's top effort came at Pittsburgh's Greenlee Field on June 9, when he clubbed three long homers. However, less than a month later on July 4 at the same site, Gibson had the honor of catching what might have been Satchel Paige's greatest game. Facing the rival Homestead Grays in the first part of a holiday twin-bill, Satch pitched a no-hitter, fanning 17 while facing only 29 batters.

Josh Gibson kept getting better, and, in Chester, Pennsylvania, on August 5, 1935, smacked a pair of 500-foot shots to the railroad tracks in left field. On May 10, 1936, Gibson walloped three home runs at New York's Dyckman Oval in a doubleheader versus the Cubans. The first was a shot to the concession roof in right field, while the second was a towering drive over the 75-foot-high center field backdrop. Number three landed high in the left field bleachers near the scoreboard. Twenty days later, Josh defeated the Philadelphia Stars on their home field at 44th and Parkside with a 10th inning blast over the barrier in center. And, on June 14 in that same season, Gibson rocketed two homers at Cleveland's League Park, where four-baggers were hard to come by for right-handed batters. In 1937, Josh returned to the Homestead Grays, but also played five weeks in the middle of the season for Ciudad Trujillo in the Dominican Republic. In the process, he batted over .400.

The single most acclaimed homer of Josh Gibson's storied life never happened. It has been alleged for decades that Gibson once drove a ball completely out of Yankee Stadium. In truth, although Gibson was immensely powerful, he never struck such a blow, and never claimed to have done so. In a 1943 interview, Josh personally identified his 460-footer in 1930 as his longest Yankee Stadium drive. At that same time, he labeled his July 24, 1938 blast in Monessen, Pennsylvania as his absolute longest. The ball cleared the center field fence at Tin Plate Field so impressively that Mayor James Gold ordered a measurement. After passing through the top of a large tree and clearing a garage, it had landed in a flower bed at the office yard of the Page Steel Company. That drive was recorded at the specific distance of 536 feet. As an encore, Gibson pounded four home runs in a single game just four days later in Zanesville, Ohio. Nothing changed in 1939 as Josh continued to demonstrate his supremacy over all other Negro League sluggers. That was apparent on July 16 at Washington's Griffith Stadium as Gibson launched three titanic shots into the distant left field bleachers.

Accepting a better financial deal, Josh Gibson played the 1940 season in Caracas, Venezuela. When that schedule ended in early August, Josh returned home with the intention of playing with the Grays during their many unofficial exhibition games. When Negro League execs said no to that prospect, Josh switched to Veracruz, Mexico, until the end of 1941. In 94 games that year, Gibson slugged 33 home runs, while batting .374 and winning the MVP Award. During these years, Josh also ventured to Cuba and Puerto Rico to play winter baseball. Along the way, he is known to have pounded 500-foot shots at La Boulanger Park in Santa Clara, Cuba, and Escobar Stadium in San Juan, Puerto Rico.

In 1942, Josh came home again to the Homestead Grays, and remained with them until his premature death in early 1947. It was during these years that he teamed with Buck Leonard to form one of baseball's great power tandems. Leonard played first base, and batted from the left side, while batting

third or fourth in the lineup. However, during that '42 season, Gibson wasn't the same player that Pittsburgh fans had watched during the '30s. Plagued by various health issues, Josh was thought to be past his prime. When he suffered a nervous breakdown on New Year's Day 1943, many regarded Gibson as completely washed up at age 31. However, it is a mark of greatness to respond to adversity. And Josh Gibson not only responded to his problems in 1943, he overwhelmed them by enjoying one of baseball's greatest-ever individual seasons.

At that time, the nation was fully engaged in World War II, and strict gasoline rationing was in force. As a result, the Grays had to forsake their emblematic team bus, playing fewer games in Pittsburgh and more in Washington. All visiting teams found it easier to travel to Union Station by train, and the D.C. fans used the capital's extensive public transportation system. In all, the Homestead Grays played 38 games at Griffith Stadium in 1943, compared to only 11 back in Pittsburgh. It worked out well. Attendance soared, as did their star catcher.

In those 38 Griffith Stadium contests, Gibson recorded 10 home runs. That may sound merely excellent, but, in fact, it was absolutely sensational. The left field bleachers at Griffith were 400 feet away, and it was 455 feet to the deepest angle just right of center field. Playing a full American League home schedule that year, the entire Washington Senators team hit only nine homers on their home field. Josh averaged about 440 feet per Griffith four-bagger in '43, which provides some further scale to his accomplishment. As always, exact numbers are hard to establish for the old Negro Leaguers, but, in 55 documented games that season, Gibson hit close to .500. Batting mostly in the cleanup spot, directly behind Buck Leonard, he was unstoppable!

Although handicapped by headaches and dizziness due to hypertension during the latter years of his career, Gibson remained a great slugger to the end of his days. In 1944 and 1945, Josh continued belting long home runs, clearing the left field grandstand roof at Philadelphia's Shibe Park on August 7, 1945. As late as May 22, 1946, Gibson slammed a 490-foot homer at Forbes Field. But great musculature is not an antidote for high blood pressure, and Josh tragically succumbed to a stroke at age 35 on January 20, 1947, at his mother's home in Pittsburgh. Sadly, he passed just three months before Jackie Robinson broke the color barrier in Major League Baseball.

In 1982, Buck Leonard gave his list of the longest homers that he had personally seen Josh hit. It included a drive onto a mountain in Welch, West Virginia, a blast over the center field scoreboard in Newark, New Jersey, the '38 homer in Monessen, a shot to the 28th row of the left field bleachers at D.C.'s Griffith Stadium, and a mighty poke over the tennis court at YMCA Field at 44th and Parkside in Philadelphia. Leonard was certain that all of them flew over 500 feet. Can anyone reasonably dispute his assertions? Buck was a grounded and realistic individual who was not given to exaggeration. More importantly, Josh Gibson was a real life Samson, who could hit baseballs like only a few others in the history of his sport.

Five

Historical Rankings: 20 through 11

NUMBER 20: DICK STUART—228 HOME RUNS—1958 TO 1969

Richard Lee Stuart was a colorful character, but he was also one of the most powerful batsmen in baseball history. Known as much for his poor fielding as for his batting proficiency, he was often called "Dr. Strangelove," "Stonefingers," or "Iron Glove." Stuart was a brash, talkative individual who made people laugh at his amiable antics on and off the field. It is a tribute to his memory that he is regarded with affection by his former teammates. But, first and foremost, Dick Stuart is remembered because he could pound a baseball like few other men.

A native of northern California, the 6'4", 220-pound, right-hander took a long time to make it to the Major Leagues. Stuart was a sub-par outfielder and a slow baserunner, so, despite his obvious power, he was a questionable big-league prospect. He played minor league ball in 1951 and 1952, and then spent two years in military service. Returning to organized baseball, Dick hit 33 home runs for three different minor league teams in 1955. Then, despite tearing up the Western League for Lincoln with an astounding 66 homers in 1956, Stuart was still regarded as unready

for the majors. Some of those homers were legendary for their distance, especially in high-altitude Pueblo, Colorado. Dick added 45 home runs for three more minor league squads in 1957 before moving up to Salt Lake City in 1958. Finally, after blasting 31 circuits in just half a season, he was summoned to the Pittsburgh Pirates.

Switching to first base to minimize his defensive liability, Dick Stuart drove one into Wrigley Field's right center field bleachers on

Dick Stuart

July 10, 1958, for his first Major League home run. It had been a long wait, but Stuart made up for the lost time. He soon demonstrated conclusively that he could do things with a bat that most big leaguers could only imagine. On successive days at Cincinnati's Crosley Field (August 16 and 17), Dick bombed 450-footers over the center field wall and left center field scoreboard. Returning to Wrigley on August 19, Dick walloped a ball over the left center field seats that went for another ride of about 450 feet.

In that first abbreviated season, Stuart recorded 16 homers. Along the way, Dick also proved himself at home in Pittsburgh. At Forbes Field on July 29, Stuart beat the Cubs with a 450-foot bases-loaded triple to deepest center field. After the game, he declared that he would eventually clear the 457 foot sign that he had just short-hopped. Most of Dick's teammates laughed at that notion. Two days later, Stuart bashed one high over the distant left field scoreboard. Then, on September 10, Stuart clubbed the ball over the remote wall in left center. That drive left the park about 410 feet from home plate and still cleared the trees outside the stadium. It was a majestic blow of about 475 feet, and left the Pirates shaking their heads. However, they had to wait one more year to fully comprehend the vast talent they were witnessing.

On May 1, 1959, Dick Stuart faced Cardinal relief ace Jim Brosnan in the 9th inning at Forbes Field. The game was on the line, and Stuart felt that he still had a lot to prove. A moment later, Brosnan's slider was sailing a hundred feet above the left field scoreboard, which was situated about 375 feet away. To this day, nobody knows exactly where in Schenley Park the ball finally landed, but folks are still guessing. The best estimate for the total flight distance is 520 feet. Veteran stadium watchers summoned up memories of Babe Ruth, Mickey Mantle, and Ralph Kiner to try to figure out who had hit the longest homer in park history. They were still working on the problem on June 5 when Stuart added another piece to the puzzle. This time he surpassed the brick wall over that 457 foot sign just left of center field. It was the first time in the stadium's 50-year Major League history that this feat had been accomplished.

Chicago Cub center fielder George Altman estimated that the ball had cleared the wall by 25 to 30 feet. Left fielder Walt Moran, who probably had an even better view, said it was more like 40 to 50 feet. Pirate shortstop Dick Groat said that the other players were "numb and amazed." And Lou Boudreau said simply that it was the longest drive that he had ever seen in his long career. It probably landed in the adjoining Little League field about 515 feet from where it started. It had taken Dick Stuart longer than he wanted, but he had finally proven his vast capabilities. For the record, he added a 495-footer halfway up the huge slope of seats in left center field at the Los Angeles Coliseum on June 26.

In truth, 1959 was to be the highlight of Stuart's tape measure odyssey, but he would still improve in overall production and productivity. Dick hit 23 homers in 1960, including a June 12 shot into the center field bleachers in St. Louis. That was the year that the Bucs defeated the mighty New York Yankees in a classic seven-game World Series. Stuart then rose to 35 homers in 1961 along with 117 RBI, while batting .300 for the only time in his Major League career. His best long ball was lined over the 430 foot mark in center field on September 13 at the Los Angeles Coliseum. Dick dropped down to only 16 homers in 1962, but, in retrospect, it worked to his advantage.

Traded to the Red Sox, Stuart took advantage of the nearby Green Monster at Fenway Park. He enjoyed his best season in 1963 by slugging 42 home runs and knocking in 118 runs. Dick reached the upper deck at D.C. Stadium on April 13, and hit one of the longest-ever homers at Fenway on June 14. That ball sailed far over the left field wall, and landed near the back of a building in the direction of the Massachusetts Turnpike. However, during spring training in 1964, Stuart acknowledged that he couldn't hit the ball as far as in the past. That was an interesting insight considering that he was hitting them more often than ever. He followed up with 33 homers and 114 RBI that season, but, sadly, it was Stuart's last great year.

Moving on to Philadelphia in 1965, Dick topped the left field roof on July 2 at Connie

---

DICK STUART'S 10 LONGEST HOME RUNS

- May 1, 1959—Pittsburgh off St. Louis's Brosnan—High over left field wall and far into park—520 ft.
- June 5, 1959—Pittsburgh off Chicago's Hobbie—Over wall at 457 ft. sign in deep left center—515 ft.
- June 26, 1959—Los Angeles off Podres—Halfway up high slope of seats in left center—495 ft.
- June 14, 1963—Boston off Baltimore's Pappas—To back of building beyond wall—485 ft.
- September 10, 1958—Pittsburgh off San Francisco's Grissom—Over wall and trees in left center—475 ft.
- July 3, 1961—Cincinnati off Maloney—Over scoreboard and clock in left center—470 ft.
- June 7, 1962—Pittsburgh off Los Angeles's Sherry—Far over left center field wall and into park—470 ft.
- April 13, 1963—Washington off Rudolph—Deep into left field upper deck—465 ft.
- July 2, 1965—Philadelphia off Cincinnati's Arrigo—Over left field grandstand roof—460 ft.
- June 12, 1960—St. Louis off Simmons—High into center field bleachers—455 ft.

Mack Stadium. He recorded 28 homers for the year, while teaming with fellow long-distance master Dick Allen. But it never seemed quite good enough. Due to his one-dimensional play, and, perhaps also due to his eccentric behavior, Dick Stuart never stayed long in any one place. Dick went from team to team, even whacking 33 home runs for Japan's Taiyo Whales in 1967. He finished in 1969 during a brief stint with the California Angels. Stuart drilled his final homer (Number 228) over the right field fence on April 14, raising his right arm as he rounded the bases. Perhaps Dick should have hit more homers, but the combined length of those blows surpasses that of any man with a comparable total. Dick Stuart was a true King of the Tape Measure.

NUMBER 19: JOSE CANSECO—462 HOME RUNS—1985 TO 2001

Jose Canseco had a way of focusing the spotlight on himself during and after his tumultuous career. He arrived in the big leagues at the end of the 1985 season and immediately started whacking tape measure home runs. On the field, Jose spent the next 16 years winning pennants and World Series, moving from team to team, and setting performance records. Off the field, he always had something provocative to say, while spending time with rock stars and driving sportscars at breakneck speed. After he retired, Canseco remained in character by writing a book in

Jose Canseco

Courtesy of the National Baseball Hall of Fame and Museum

which he named himself and other great stars of his sport as chronic steroid users.

Jose Canseco Jr. was born in Havana, Cuba, in 1964, but soon moved with his family to Miami, Florida, where he grew up. Drafted in the 15th round of the 1982 amateur draft, Jose quickly signed with the Oakland Athletics. His rapid ascent through the minors was facilitated by his decision to begin using steroids after the 1984 season. In 1985, Canseco started at Double-A Huntsville, where he clubbed 25 home runs and drove in 80 runs in just 58 games. He was promoted to Triple-A Tacoma in mid-season, but, before leaving the Southern League, Jose recalls pounding two tape measure homers in a game at Birmingham. While competing in 60 games in the Pacific Coast League, Canseco batted

.348, smacked 11 homers, and totaled 47 RBI. Predictably, he was then summoned to the Big Show by the Athletics.

Naturally, Jose's very first Major League home run was a whopper. On September 9, 1985, at the Oakland Coliseum, Canseco pounded the first pitch he saw far over the fence in dead center for a drive of 450 feet. At Comiskey Park in Chicago on September 22, Jose lined one off the light tower atop the left field grandstand roof. That poke was estimated at 480 feet. Canseco then launched one to the 34th row of the left center field bleachers back in Oakland on September 26. It was a majestic drive of 495 feet, and may have been the longest that Jose ever hit. Despite striking out at an alarming rate, Canseco clouted his first three homers for tape measure distance. No one else ever started like that.

In 1986, Jose hit 33 home runs, and won the Rookie of the Year Award. In Anaheim on April 21, Canseco went deep into the right center field bleachers for a remarkable opposite field drive of 450 feet. And on August 5 in Seattle, Jose almost reached the second deck in straightaway center field with a rousing poke of 470 feet. He followed up with 31 dingers in 1987, and three of them stood out. Two went about 460 feet. The first one flew into center field in Detroit on July 21 and the second was directed to left center at Oakland on August 5. But the best of the year came on June 28 in Cleveland's Municipal Stadium. It was a scorching line drive that smashed into

the upper deck façade near left center for a 490-foot ride.

Jose Canseco started the 1988 season as a star, but he ended it as a superstar. His tenure at that exalted level didn't last long, but he made the most of it. On September 23, Jose stole two bases to make his total 40 for the year. In so doing, he became Major League Baseball's first-ever member of the "40-40 Club." He had already hit his 40th homer the week before, thereby becoming an historical icon. The hulking, 6'4", 240-pound Canseco may have been immensely powerful swinging from the right side, but he was also startlingly fast on the bases. Of course, as Jose was making history, he was also bombing baseballs to far off places. His drives of over 450 feet were recorded in Seattle on April 13, Oakland on May 9, Minnesota on June 3, and Texas on June 9 and September 7.

After breaking a bone in his left wrist during spring training in 1989, Canseco dropped off to only 17 homers. However, much of the disappointment was offset by winning the World Series. Jose came back with 37 home runs in 1990, and did even better in 1991 with 44. Probably the longest of that two-year span flew to center field at the SkyDome in Toronto on May 22, 1990. After getting knocked lopsided, the ball descended onto the restaurant roof above the fence for an estimated 480-footer. Canseco added blasts of 469 feet in Cleveland on July 8 and 465 feet in Oakland on July 25. By this time, however, the controversy in Jose's life was starting to outpace his on-field production. On August 31, 1992, Canseco was traded to the Texas Rangers, starting a seven-city odyssey during the second half of his career. On September 15, Jose reached the left field roof at Tiger Stadium in Detroit to demonstrate that he would remain strong regardless of the uniform he wore.

During his time in Arlington, Canseco recorded many long drives, but thumped his longest on June 13, 1994. It flew over the fence in left center field, cleared the entire length of the bullpen, and struck the back wall. It was quite a wallop, and measured 488 feet. Spending the next few years with the Boston Red Sox, Jose kept building his

long-distance resume, including a blast of 463 feet over the Green Monster on July 17, 1996. Canseco then spent one season with the Toronto Blue Jays, where he fashioned his highest-ever home run total. Smacking 46 circuits in 1998, Jose's exploits were largely overshadowed by the record battle in the National League between former teammate Mark McGwire and Sammy Sosa.

In that one year, Canseco almost equaled his famous 1989 LCS homer of 484 feet into the fifth deck in the SkyDome. Jose delivered balls into that same level on July 19 and September 5. Plus, he did it again on April 12, 1999, when playing for the Tampa Bay Devil Rays. Before leaving Tampa, Canseco reached the catwalk

---

JOSE CANSECO'S 10 LONGEST HOME RUNS

- September 26, 1985—Oakland off Chicago's Bannister—To 34th row of bleachers in left center—495 ft.
- June 28, 1987—Cleveland off Huismann—Liner off façade of second deck near left center—490 ft.
- June 13, 1994—Texas off Seattle's Hibbard—Off back wall of bullpen in left center—488 ft.
- October 7, 1989—Toronto off Flanagan—To fifth row in fifth deck in left field—484 ft.
- September 22, 1985—Chicago off Davis—Line drive off light tower on left field roof—480 ft.
- May 22, 1990—Toronto off Wills—Onto restaurant roof above fence in dead center—480 ft.
- September 15, 1992—Detroit off Kiely—Onto 94-foot-high left field grandstand roof—475 ft.
- April 22, 2000—Tampa Bay off Anaheim's Ortiz—To catwalk in left center—472 ft.
- July 19, 1997—Oakland off Minnesota's Rodriguez—High into bleachers in left center—470 ft.
- April 12, 1999—Toronto off Lloyd—Deep into fifth level in left field—470 ft.

108 feet above the playing field in left center for an eye-popping homer of 472 feet on April 22, 2000. Jose was then shipped to the New York Yankees on August 7. Although he didn't play much, he did have the pleasure of winning his second World Series.

Canseco wrapped up his Major League career in 2001 while hitting his last 16 home runs for the Chicago White Sox. His final circuit-shot flew over the center field fence on October 3 at Yankee Stadium, fixing his tally at 462. At age 37, Jose felt that he had a few more good years left in his lethal bat. When he didn't get the chance, Canseco offered his personal belief that he was being "black-balled" because of his outspoken behavior. He may have been right. Either way, it had been an amazing run, filled with many ups and downs. One thing is certain: No baseball fan will ever forget that Jose Canseco had played the game.

NUMBER 18: CECIL FIELDER—319 HOME RUNS—1985 TO 1998

Cecil Fielder got off to a slow start in the Major Leagues, hitting a total of just 31 home runs in his first four seasons. In fact, after playing part-time for the Toronto Blue Jays from 1985 through 1988, Fielder spent the 1989 campaign with the Hanshin Tigers in Japan. Cecil belted 38 homers that year, and many were unusually long. His many Japanese admirers affectionately nicknamed him the "Wild Bear."

Upon returning to the U.S. with the Detroit Tigers in 1990, Cecil Fielder exploded as a Major League slugger. The burly 6'3" right-handed-hitting first baseman blasted 51 home runs, including several that traveled exceptional distances. The left field grandstand at Tiger Stadium was constructed in 1938, and the 90-foot-high roof was positioned about 360 feet down the left field foul line. Of course, that distance increased as it angled out toward center field. It was such a remote target that only two balls had landed there in its 52-year history. Fielder narrowly missed that roof on July 24, when his towering drive dipped just beneath the front edge, landing high in the left center field upper deck. However, Cecil kept on swinging, and pounded one onto that structure just right of the light tower on August 25. It was a blow of about 510 feet. Just before his 27th birthday, Cecil Fielder had arrived as a legitimate tape measure home run hitter.

Cecil put together another great season in 1991, when he recorded 44 more homers. If anything, he seemed even stronger. Now nicknamed "Big Daddy," Fielder made his mark all around the American League circuit. After recording 450 (plus)-footers in Boston and Kansas City (July 4 and July 19), Cecil sent one on a genuinely epic journey at Milwaukee's County Stadium on September 14. His tremendous drive sailed completely over the high left field bleachers and landed in the outside concourse. That shot was measured at 502 feet. It was the only time in the 48-year history of that ballpark that an official home run cleared those left field seats. It was a whopper. At home, he had been just as forceful. On June 29, Fielder belted one off the roof façade in left field that caromed down through an exit in the upper deck.

In 1992, Big Daddy had another productive year. Among his 35 dingers were blows in the 420 to 430-foot range in Texas, Cleveland, Minnesota, Chicago, and Detroit (several). By this time, he was also an RBI machine, averaging 130 ribbies over the previous three seasons. On defense, Fielder was stationed at first base for about half his games, when he wasn't used as a designated hitter. Cecil Fielder was very powerful, but he was not fleet of foot. With his problematic weight issues, he was paid to hit. Anything else was considered a bonus.

By 1993, Cecil's homer total had dipped to 30, but he continued hitting more drives that were notable for extra length. In that one remarkable season, Fielder hit two balls in Detroit over the 440 foot sign in dead center (May 4 and July 20), and, almost unbelievably, three more onto the left field grandstand roof. Those classic drives occurred on May 16, June 14, and July 2, and each was estimated at almost 500 feet. Only eight game balls ever reached that distant plateau in its 62-year lifespan, and Cecil Fielder recorded almost half of them in that one memorable campaign. He added his fifth and final roof-topper the following year on May 4, 1994. In that same year, on April 10, Cecil had

Cecil Fielder

Courtesy of the National Baseball Hall of Fame and Museum

launched a towering drive to the sixth row of the left field upper deck at Yankee Stadium. And, why not? All great American League sluggers were expected to earn their distance spurs in the "House That Ruth Built." Cecil Fielder took care of that obligation with this 475-footer.

In 1995, Fielder reached the center field seats two more times at Tiger Stadium. Those blows were hit on May 7 and May 28. In Milwaukee on May 9, Cecil bombed one 15 rows into the bleachers just left of center field. But Fielder's increasing weight was becoming more of an issue. He was officially listed at 240 pounds, but most observers felt that he weighed much more. When Cecil Fielder stole a base for the first time in his Major

League career on April 2, 1996, it was noted that this event occurred in his 1,097th game. It was the longest stolen base famine in the annals of the sport. But, as stated, Big Daddy was never known for his speed. Back on July 4, 1991, at Fenway Park, Fielder had lined a 420-foot cannon shot against the center field wall that resulted in a single.

However, the fans never seemed to care. They thoroughly enjoyed Cecil's one-dimensional game and reveled in his awesome power. Four days after that belated first stolen base, he crushed a 450-foot homer in a game that was played in Las Vegas. The Tigers eventually traded Cecil to the New York Yankees later in the 1996 season, which concluded for him with a very respectable

total of 39 home runs. Included among them was a 450-foot drive into "Monument Valley" in left center field on September 19. Sadly, it was Fielder's last great season, although he wasn't quite finished yet.

Big Cecil recorded his 300th Major League homer at Yankee Stadium on his 34th birthday on September 21, 1997. And, in his final year in 1998, mostly playing for the California Angels, Cecil was still lethal with a bat in his hands. Fielder's girth was more of a problem than ever, but he hadn't lost his ability to produce bat speed. On April 21 in Anaheim, Cecil knocked one onto the bullpen roof past the left field fence. Next, Fielder almost cleared the lofty left field bleachers at Comiskey Park II on May 13, and then powered a

CECIL FIELDER'S 10 LONGEST HOME RUNS

- August 25, 1990—Detroit off Oakland's Stewart—Onto left field roof right of light tower—510 ft.
- September 14, 1991—Milwaukee off Plesac—Over high left field bleachers onto concourse—502 ft.
- June 14, 1993—Detroit off Cleveland's Bielecki—Onto back of left field grandstand roof—495 ft.
- July 2, 1993—Detroit off Texas's Whiteside—Onto left field roof right of light tower—485 ft.
- May 16, 1993—Detroit off Baltimore's Mussina—Onto left field roof left of light tower—480 ft.
- May 4, 1994—Detroit off Texas's Reed—Onto left field roof near foul line—475 ft.
- July 4, 1991—Boston off Darwin—Off the top of left field light tower (near lights)—470 ft.
- May 13, 1998—Chicago off Sirotka—To top of left field bleachers—465 ft.
- April 10, 1994—New York off Hernandez—Into left field upper deck—465 ft.
- May 28, 1995—Detroit off Chicago's Baldwin—Over center field fence into seats—460 ft.

ball high over the 413 foot mark in Arizona on June 9. Fielder's last official home run (Number 319) was smacked into the left field bleachers at Kansas City on July 27, 1998. He tried to keep it going in 1999, when he belted three spring homers with the Toronto Blue Jays, but his diminishing skills left him off the final roster. It had been quite a career.

By the time Cecil walked away, he had already done something to secure his legacy that no other tape measure slugger has yet to do. He had fathered a son, who is now one of baseball's longest hitters. There have been other father-son home run hitters such as the Bells (Gus and Buddy), the Griffeys (Ken Senior and Ken Junior), and the Bonds (Bobby and Barry). However, not until Cecil Fielder was succeeded by Prince Fielder has baseball experienced successive bona fide long-distance sluggers of the same bloodline. Many players have hit more homers than Cecil Fielder, as Prince probably will, but very few have hit them farther. Fans always liked the affable big man, and he put on quite a show wherever he played.

NUMBER 17: BARRY BONDS—762 HOME RUNS—1986 TO 2007

Barry Bonds is arguably the most provocative and controversial player in Major League history. Although disliked by most Americans, Bonds is generally held in high esteem by the folks living in the Bay Area. He also remains well liked by many people from Pittsburgh, where he began his career, as well as by many Giants fans wherever they are found. Whether you love him or hate him, Barry has been virtually impossible to ignore. For better or worse, he is woven into the fabric of modern American culture like no other contemporary ballplayer. However he is regarded as a person, his athletic greatness cannot be overlooked.

Barry Bonds has always been strong. You can't hit home runs at the Major League level without being much stronger than the average male, and his overall athleticism has been exceptional even by big-league standards. However, has he always been particularly strong compared to other Major League players? No, not really. Upon arriving in Pittsburgh in 1986, Barry Bonds instantly became one of the best all-around players in the majors. He also hit more home runs than the typical big leaguer, but he didn't hit them farther. He had to wait another 14 years for that.

Barry's first career homer occurred on June 4, 1986, in Atlanta, and it landed just beyond the left center field fence. Bonds hit the ball hard consistently for the next couple years, but waited until April 17, 1988 at Chicago's Wrigley Field to record his first tape measure home run. Aided by a strong tailwind, this shot landed in the upper center field seats for a drive of about 460 feet. When Barry was traded to the San Francisco Giants in 1993, he reached a then career high of 46 homers. He was obviously one of the game's preeminent power hitters as well as its best all-around player. But, despite that special stature, Barry didn't record his second tape measure homer (confirmed at 450 feet or more) until July 18, 1995. That one landed deep in the right field upper deck at Candlestick Park in San Francisco. But again, this blow was wind-driven, as was Bonds's third tape measure drive, hit on June 20, 1997, also at Candlestick.

Then, on June 6, 2000, at Anaheim, Barry smashed the ball high into the bleachers in right center. It was an imposing drive of about 485 feet, and was hit with only negligible wind. Bonds had waited a long time, but he had finally arrived as a long-distance hitter. Over the course of the next few years, he made up for lost time. Barry established the

Barry Bonds

all-time season home run record the following year by knocking the astonishing total of 73 balls out of various parks. The one on May 3, 2001 flew over the bleachers in Pittsburgh for a ride of 462 feet. That was followed by a 451-footer in San Francisco on June 7, a 485-footer in Denver on September 9, and one of 454 feet in Houston on October 4.

Then, in 2002 at age 38, Barry Bonds enjoyed the best tape measure season of his long career. He hit fewer homers (46) that year, but mostly because pitchers started walking him with record frequency. When Barry hit them, they flew farther than ever. He started off at Dodger Stadium on April 2 and 3 with four homers, including drives of 443, 447, and 459 feet. In early June, Bonds was particularly impressive. He blasted a prodigious blow to the base of the scoreboard atop the right field bleachers in San Diego. That drive of 482 feet on June 5 was followed three days later by a towering homer of comparable length into the right field upper deck in Yankee Stadium. Barry kept bombing away, and finished the year with the two longest officially estimated homers of his big-league tenure. One of three homers he recorded in Colorado on August 27 flew far beyond the center field fence and was judged at 492 feet. Bonds hit one in the same direction at Pac Bell Park in San Francisco on September 9, and it was calculated to have flown 491 feet. Since the earlier drive was enhanced by Denver's altitude, it is apparent that the latter one was struck with more force. It came down

BARRY BONDS'S 10 LONGEST HOME RUNS

- August 27, 2002—Colorado off Stark—Far over center field fence and trees—492 ft.
- September 9, 2002—San Francisco off Los Angeles's Perez—Far over fence in center to backdrop—491 ft.
- October 20, 2002—Anaheim off Percival—Into exit tunnel in right center field bleachers—485 ft.
- September 9, 2001—Colorado off Elarton—Far over fence in deep right center—485 ft.
- June 5, 2002—San Diego off Tankersley—To base of scoreboard atop seats in right—482 ft.
- June 8, 2002—New York off Lilly—To 20th row in right field upper deck—480 ft.
- June 6, 2000—Anaheim off Etherton—High into bleachers in right center—480 ft.
- September 13, 2003—San Francisco off Milwaukee's Davis—Over right field bleachers (arcade) into cove—480 ft.
- August 8, 2003—San Francisco off Philadelphia's Mesa—Over right field arcade and far into cove—475 ft.
- July 7, 2003—San Francisco off St. Louis's Stephenson—Over center field fence and concession stand—471 ft.

at the base of the center field backdrop and was a real rocket.

Barry did more of the same in subsequent seasons. He started right away in 2003 with an April 1 drive of 463 feet high into the right field bleachers in San Diego. That was followed by a similar bolt of 475 feet at Comiskey Park II on June 10, but his best work was reserved for his worshipful fans from the Bay Area. Barry splashed balls of 457, 460, and 475 feet into McCovey Cove along with a 471-footer over a concession stand in center field on July 7. He saved his season-longest for September 13, when his 480-footer again soared over the right field arcade and into the water.

Despite walking an all-time record 232 times in 2004, Barry continued bombing away. He kept the home folks happy by plopping several more wet souvenirs into McCovey Cove, including drives of 470 feet on April 13 and 450 feet on August 3. However, his most impressive performance of the year occurred in Atlanta on August 29, when he bashed two balls to right center for homers of 462 and 467 feet. Due to serious knee problems, Bonds missed most of 2005, but still managed to power one into the right field upper deck at RFK Stadium in Washington on September 20. Continuing his recovery in 2006, Barry survived the Philadelphia boo-birds on May 7 by reaching the façade of the third deck in right center. That homer at Citizens Bank Park was a 470-footer. By the end of that month, Bonds passed Babe Ruth's career home run total by knocking one into a throng of his loyal and delirious fans in center field at Pac Bell Park.

In 2007, when Bonds supplanted the great Henry Aaron as baseball's all-time home run leader, Barry was still blasting. In the season that he turned 43 years of age, Bonds drove one to the tenth row of the center field bleachers in San Francisco on May 5. That blow was estimated at 452 feet and demonstrated conclusively that Barry Bonds was still a formidable long-distance hitter despite his advancing years. Bonds's record-breaking 756th homer on August 7 at Pac Bell Park flew into the center field bleachers as fans around the country argued over the legitimacy of the event. Regardless of their position on this provocative subject, they had witnessed baseball history in an intensely emotional fashion. That is a Bonds legacy that no one can dispute.

Regarding pure power, Barry may not have hit his homers as far as a few others, but he has now hit more than anyone else. The final act, number 762, was recorded in Denver on September 5, 2007, and topped the left center field fence. It was remarkably similar to the first one that Bonds hit 21 years earlier in Atlanta. And, starting in 2000, his tally of long-distance hitting compares favorably with that of any other contemporary player.

NUMBER 16: JOE ADCOCK—336 HOME RUNS—1950 TO 1966

Any conversation about Major League Baseball's strongest men must include the name of Joe Adcock. He stood 6'4", and weighed anywhere from 220 to 240 pounds during his career. It was all sinew, bone, and muscle. Born in Louisiana in 1927, Joe attended LSU as a two-sport star in baseball and basketball. Realizing that baseball was his first calling, Adcock signed with the Cincinnati Reds as an amateur free agent in early 1947. It took him two years to become productive as a pro, but he had a big year (19 home runs and 116 RBI) in 1949 with Tulsa in the Texas League.

Joe then broke in with the Reds in 1950. In his first game on April 23 at Forbes Field in Pittsburgh, the brawny right-hander blasted a double off the top of the wall in distant right center. That was an opposite-field blow of 435 feet, and sent a message. Watch out for this guy! His first four-bagger landed at the top of the left field bleachers in St. Louis on July 5. In his second year, on April 27, 1951, Adcock replicated his first extra-base hit when he smashed a ball to the exit gate at Forbes Field. Joe ran well for a big man, and, this time, he circled the bases. During Adcock's first three seasons, he played out of position. Although a good first baseman, Joe had to play left field due to the presence of burly Ted Kluszewski. If anyone ever added up the muscle shared by two teammates, the top prize would probably go to the duo of Joe

Adcock and Big Klu. But Joe wanted to play first base, and he wanted to play more. So, he insisted on a trade. After averaging just 10 homers a year from 1950 through 1952, Adcock was sent to the Milwaukee Braves in 1953. Subsequently, his career blossomed.

On April 29 at the Polo Grounds in New York, Joe Adcock did something that had not been done in a big-league game since that old ballpark had been renovated in 1923. Babe Ruth had knocked a couple of balls into the old center field bleachers back in 1921, but no one had done it since. Adcock not only reached the left wing of those newer seats, but he made it all the way to the 10th row. It was an imposing drive of 476 feet. Joe recorded 18 homers that year, and several of them were huge. He banged out 440-footers in Cincinnati on July 1 and in Chicago on August 15. But his second longest of the season was delivered on July 18 at spacious Forbes Field. Adcock walloped the ball over the center field wall just right of the 457 foot sign for a ride of about 470 feet.

In 1954, 9 of Joe's 23 homers were struck at Ebbets Field in Brooklyn. More importantly, four came in one game on July 31 to tie the Major League record. Adcock also added a double off the top of the left field wall for a record 18 total bases. That standard lasted until 2002 when Shawn Green amassed 19. Joe ripped his final Brooklyn homer on September 10 by slamming a tremendous drive high into the Ebbets Field upper deck in left center. Not coincidentally, Adcock's season

came to an early conclusion the next day, when Dodger hurler Don Newcombe broke his left thumb with an errant pitch. Joe probably wasn't surprised, since he had been struck on the head by Dodger Clem Labine after his four-homer game. In those days, teams didn't react kindly to anyone dominating them. Adcock was having a similar year in 1955 when he was struck in the arm by a pitch from the Giants' Jim Hearn on July 31 in Milwaukee. Hearn was the same guy that Joe had victimized for his historic Polo Grounds homer in 1953. Adcock's arm was fractured, and he missed the remainder of the year. Just two weeks before in New York, Joe had blasted a massive homer into the upper deck above the

Joe Adcock

Courtesy of the Atlanta Braves

447 foot sign in left center. He also chased Willie Mays to the bleacher fence for a drive of similar length in the same game. It may have been that display that finally prompted the retaliation from Hearn. Does this sound like a pattern? Adcock was evolving into a dangerous slugger who never gave an inch at the plate. That made him a marked man in the baseball world of the 1950s.

In 1956, Adcock stayed healthy and enjoyed his best year with 38 homers. As usual, he tore things up at Ebbets Field with eight four-baggers, including the longest of his career. The 1953 Polo Grounds homer may have been Joe's most famous blow, but it was not his longest. That distinction was earned by Adcock's mighty blast over the 83-foot-high left field grandstand roof in Brooklyn on June 17, 1956. Joe's epic effort flew high over that roof at the 350 foot mark between the foul pole and light tower. It was recovered in a nearby parking lot and flew about 510 feet. It was the only ball that ever cleared that roof in its 28-year history. Exactly one month later in a game at Milwaukee's County Stadium against New York, Joe was drilled on the wrist by Giant pitcher Ruben Gomez. Adcock decided enough was enough. In a rage, he charged Gomez, and chased him off the field into the dugout. Facing Jim Hearn (the guy who ended his 1955 season) two days later, Joe completed the message. He walloped a 1st inning grand slam, later adding another homer and double. That eight RBI performance warned National League pitch-

ers to think twice about throwing at the big Cajun. Later in the year in Milwaukee (August 29), Adcock socked a 460-foot drive over the center field fence. The hitters' background was then comprised of a tall stand of pine trees known as "Perini's Woods," and that is where Joe's shot landed.

Two years later on August 3, 1958, Adcock actually reached the second row of trees for an even lengthier drive of 470 feet. It was one of many that Joe hit in Milwaukee that flew well over 450 feet. On the road, Adcock remained just as effective. He again cleared the wall at the 457 foot sign in Pittsburgh on July 3, 1959, and somehow topped the 64-foot-high scoreboard in right center in Philadelphia on April 14, 1960. In that same place, Joe cleared the left field grandstand roof on both July 20, 1961 and July 21, 1962. He also sent two balls over the center field shrubbery in St. Louis on July 14, 1961 and May 25, 1962. Adcock's longest at Wrigley Field was probably his massive blast far over the bleachers in left center field on September 3, 1962. That was a blow of about 500 feet.

Joe was traded to the Cleveland Indians in 1963, and spent the last few years of his career in the American League. His strength was undiminished as he smashed tremendous home runs all around the circuit. The longest two were slammed as a California Angel in his final year, 1966. On July 4, Adcock hit a bullet just under the left field roof at Detroit. At nearly 39 years old, Joe acknowledged, "Now that was pretty good. I think it was

JOE ADCOCK'S 10 LONGEST HOME RUNS

- June 17, 1956—Brooklyn off Roebuck—Far over high left field grandstand roof—510 ft.

- July 4, 1966—Detroit off Lolich—Line drive into upper deck just under left field roof—505 ft.

- September 3, 1961—Chicago off Ellsworth—Over left center field bleachers and across street—500 ft.

- September 2, 1966—California off Washington's Humphreys—Off light tower in deep left center—495 ft.

- July 21, 1962—Philadelphia off Hamilton—Over billboard on roof in left center—490 ft.

- April 29, 1953—New York off Hearn—Into left wing of center field bleachers—476 ft.

- July 3, 1959—Pittsburgh off Witt—Over wall at light tower in deep left center—475 ft.

- August 3, 1958—Milwaukee off San Francisco's Antonelli—Into trees past center field fence—470 ft.

- July 18, 1953—Pittsburgh off Waugh—Over wall near 457 ft. sign in left center—470 ft.

- September 10, 1961—Milwaukee off Pittsburgh's Sturdivant—To top of bleachers in left center—465 ft.

the hardest one I ever hit." He then rattled the light tower in Anaheim on September 2. That monstrosity passed over the 396 foot sign in left center; both of those blasts were realistically estimated at 500 feet. When Joe retired at the end of the season to manage the Cleveland Indians, he had recorded 336 home runs. Only a few men in baseball history could claim to have hit the ball harder.

NUMBER 15: SAMMY SOSA—609 HOME RUNS—1989 TO 2007

Sammy Sosa did not enjoy immediate success in his Major League career. Born in the Dominican Republic in 1968, Sammy ben-efited from the rich baseball environment of his native land. He became a talented player at an early age, but gave no indications of developing into a record-breaking power hitter. Drafted in 1985 as an amateur free agent, Sosa never hit more than 11 home runs in a minor league season. Starting with the Texas Rangers on June 16, 1989, the 20-year-old right-handed-hitting outfielder hit his first home run five days later. Facing Roger Clemens, Sosa knocked one into the nets above the Green Monster at Fenway Park, but it was only one of four that year. Sammy was traded to the Chicago White Sox a month later. He remained with the Chisox for the next two years where he recorded a combined total of

25 homers. Sosa was then swapped to the Chicago Cubs for George Bell on March 30, 1992, but hit only eight home runs for that year. Sammy didn't assert himself until his fifth season, in 1993, when he belted 33 homers.

Even then, Sammy was not yet a tape measure type. He hit one 438 feet in Cincinnati on July 21, 1993, and his only noteworthy distance drive in 1994 came in altitude-enhanced Denver on April 22. Things remained pretty much the same in 1995, when Sosa's longest went 458 feet at Coors Field on August 17. Sammy added a 444-footer in Miami on August 30, but really didn't quite measure up to the big boys. Then, along came 1996, and the world saw a different Sammy Sosa. He looked bigger and stronger, and the results confirmed the observations. Sosa hit a then-career-high 40 home runs, and several of them surpassed that special 450-foot threshold. Included in that group were 460-foot shots at Wrigley Field on April 17, May 5, and July 30. In 1997, Sammy hit another 36 homers that were topped by a 463-foot blast over Wrigley's left center field bleachers on May 18.

Then, in 1998, Sammy Sosa shocked the baseball world with his accomplishments. Who could have foreseen? As everyone now knows, he engaged in an historic home run duel throughout the season with Mark McGwire. Sammy eventually finished as the runner-up, but he amassed the astounding total of 66 home runs. Plus, many of those were absolute rockets! In fact, Sosa pummeled at least four balls in the 480-foot range, including two over

Sammy Sosa

Courtesy of the National Baseball Hall of Fame and Museum

the left center field bleachers in Chicago on September 13. The others flew out of the park in San Francisco on August 10 and in Denver on August 30. Number 66 was blasted 462 feet into the left field fourth deck at the Houston Astrodome on September 25, 1998.

Sammy, however, was just getting started. He ripped another 63 four-baggers in 1999 with the longest, hit on August 20, landing 501 feet from home plate. The ball had taken flight over Wrigley Field's left center field bleachers. On the road, on May 8, Sammy reached the left field upper deck at Riverfront Stadium in Cincinnati. Even better, nine days later in Miami, Sosa bombed two homers in one game, each flying about 465 feet. The first topped the 434 foot sign in deep left center field. The second surpassed the center field fence and disappeared into an exit tunnel.

Sammy Sosa "slipped" back to 50 homers in 2000. He started on April 7 in Cincinnati by knocking a 445-footer into the seats just left of center. Then, on April 18 in Montreal, Sammy hit one about the same distance that cleared the center field television platform. He kept hitting them very far all year with his final dinger landing in the upper deck in St. Louis on September 16. Then, almost incredibly, Sammy roared back to his former ethereal standards by bashing 64 home runs in 2001. That list was accented by 465-foot blows to left center field in Pittsburgh on July 19 and in Los Angeles on August 4. But, the best of the bunch was a 471-footer that hit halfway up the green backdrop in center field at Atlanta on September 1. At season's end, Sammy could say that he was the only player in Major League history to total 60 or more homers in three different years.

When Sammy permanently returned to mere mortal status in 2002 with 49 homers, he was still as strong as ever. He rammed a 484-foot drive to the flagpole in deep left center at Pittsburgh on April 12. Everybody hits the ball a little farther at mile-high Coors Field in Denver, but Sosa went a little beyond that on August 10. In reverse order, Sammy blasted four-baggers 411 feet, 468 feet, and 491 feet.

Despite continuing to drop back closer to normalcy with 40 homers in 2003, Sammy Sosa created his *pièce de résistance* at Wrigley Field on June 24 of that year. He thundered the ball heavenward toward left center

field, which he had done many times before on his home turf. Sammy had often cleared the bleachers in that direction, but this was different. With the aid of a strong tailwind, this ball kept going when the others had descended. It flew over Waveland Avenue and splattered onto the surface of Kenmore Street with a bunch of local ball-chasers in pursuit. As is the case with every great distance hitter from Babe Ruth to Barry Bonds, Sammy has sometimes had the length of his homers exaggerated. That phenomenon occurred again in this instance, but the actual facts are impressive nonetheless. Originally reported at 536 feet, it is likely that this blow flew about 520 feet.

Also in 2003, Sosa recorded a 470-foot center field homer on June 18 in Cincinnati and a magnificent 484-foot drive to left field on July 20 in Miami. Sammy still had a lot more to do, but his power clearly diminished after that season. Sosa smacked another 35 home runs for the Cubs in 2004, but the distances were waning. His longest went 454 feet at the modern Comiskey Park in Chicago on June 27, but his second longest went a modest 434 feet in San Diego on May 15. When Sosa moved on to the Baltimore Orioles for the 2005 season, he hoped for a rebirth of his glory days. It didn't work out. After hitting only 14 homers with the longest traveling 430 feet, Sammy retired.

He sat out the whole year in 2006, but fashioned a comeback in 2007 with the Texas Rangers. He experienced moderate success

---

SAMMY SOSA'S 10 LONGEST HOME RUNS

- June 24, 2003—Chicago off Milwaukee's Vizcaino—Over bleachers and street in left center—520 ft.
- August 20, 1999—Chicago off Colorado's Astacio—Far over bleachers in left center—501 ft.
- October 8, 2003—Chicago off Florida's Penny—To upper bleachers in dead center field—495 ft.
- August 10, 2002—Colorado off Chacon—To top of bleachers in left center—491 ft.
- May 4, 1999—Chicago off Colorado's McElroy—Far over bleachers in left center—485 ft.
- April 12, 2002—Pittsburgh off Williams—Far over fence in left center to flagpole—484 ft.
- July 20, 2003—Florida off Almanza—Deep into left field upper deck—484 ft.
- August 30, 1998—Colorado off Kile—Over left field bleachers and hit scoreboard sign—482 ft.
- August 10, 1998—San Francisco off Brock—High into left center field bleachers—480 ft.
- September 13, 1998—Chicago off Milwaukee's Patrick—Over left field bleachers and across street—480 ft. (**Note:** It was one of two 480-footers on this date.)

---

by launching 21 home runs with the longest flying 439 feet. However, the high point clearly occurred on June 20 in Texas as Sosa hit Career Home Run Number 600. It landed in the right center field bullpen and traveled 395 feet. When his career finally ended at the conclusion of the 2007 season, Sammy Sosa had 609 homers. The last one also soared over the right center field fence in Texas on September 26. That was a lot of long balls, and many of them were struck so far that they will never be forgotten.

NUMBER 14: RALPH KINER—369 HOME RUNS—1946 TO 1955

Ralph Kiner's Major League career didn't last long, but, during his 10 seasons, he was one of the great power hitters of all time. Born in Santa Rita, New Mexico, in 1922, Ralph grew up in Alhambra, California. He was signed by the Pittsburgh Pirates in 1941 as an amateur free agent. Kiner was making modest but steady progress in the minor leagues when Uncle Sam called him to military service from 1943 through 1945. Upon the conclusion of World War II, Ralph finally began his big-league career as a 23-year-old rookie in 1946.

At 6'2" and 200 pounds, Ralph Kiner was a mediocre outfielder who batted from the right side. Despite being a dead pull hitter, Kiner hit his first Major League home run onto the roof of the right field pavilion at Busch Stadium in St. Louis on April 18, 1946. He then resorted to form by blasting his second homer far over the distant left field scoreboard at Forbes Field in Pittsburgh one week later. The ball actually topped that structure by 30 feet and landed about 450 feet away. It was the first of many tape measure drives in Ralph's meteoric career. In that first year, he totaled 23 homers, which was good enough to lead the National League. But, there were some drastic changes in Pittsburgh for the 1947 season, helping Kiner to become the Senior Circuit's most feared slugger.

The outfield walls in Pittsburgh were generally positioned far away. It was a short distance down the right field foul line at Forbes Field, but that rarely benefited Kiner. He almost always hit to left and left center field where it was an absolute graveyard. However, the Pirates obtained veteran slugger Hank Greenberg for 1947, and decided to aid Hank by placing an inner fence in left field. That shortened the home run boundary to a normal 330 feet, and the new home run territory was called "Greenberg's Garden." Hank had a good year, hitting 25 homers, but Ralph zoomed up to 51. In '47 alone, Kiner landed 13 balls in the inviting "Garden." When Greenberg retired after the season, the inner fence stayed, but the left field homer

Ralph Kiner

Courtesy of the National Baseball Hall of Fame and Museum

territory was renamed "Kiner's Kitchen" or "Kiner's Corner."

Of course, not all of Ralph Kiner's Pittsburgh homers were routine. He knocked lengthy drives over the left field scoreboard on June 15, July 23, August 13, August 15, August 16, and September 11. In 1948, Kiner belted 40 more home runs, and his pattern was similar to the preceding year. Many landed in his "Kitchen," but many others left the ballpark completely. A good example took place on July 15, when Ralph powered one over the bricks in left center field at the 424 foot mark. In the next season, "Mister Slug" put on his best show yet. Kiner hit 54 home runs in 1949, and several were genuine tape measure beauties.

Up to that time, no one had ever cleared the 50-foot-high scoreboard in left field at Braves Field in Boston. Ralph did it by a wide margin on May 8, and, almost did it again by overcoming a stiff incoming wind on August 24. There are still stories about how far those balls traveled, but we will never know for sure. It is likely, however, that number one passed over the railroad tracks outside the park for a ride of about 510 feet. Due to the adverse breeze, number two probably landed about 475 feet from home plate. Kiner added drives in the 450-foot range in Brooklyn on July 20, in Philadelphia on August 26, in New York on August 31, and in Chicago on September 3. It was an amazing season.

Ralph kept going in 1950 with 47 more homers, including the single longest of his career. On April 22, Ralph crushed a ball far over the left field scoreboard that headed deep into adjoining Schenley Park. It appeared to be still rising when it soared out of the stadium. A late-arriving radio announcer saw the ball land near the "Pipes of Pan" statue in the park, but it is probable that it had already landed and was in the process of bouncing. But, considering all factors, this drive likely flew somewhere around 520 feet. Kiner also hit memorable blows over the remote left center field wall on May 9, May 30, June 11, July 14, August 10, and August 15.

"Mister Slug" cranked out 42 more homers in 1951 as he remained on top of the slugging world. Not only did he clout a 450-foot bomb over the roof at New York's Polo

Grounds on June 2, he recorded a fly out of comparable distance to Willie Mays in the same game. Ralph had an equally entertaining day at home on July 8. He started off in batting practice by breaking the hour hand on the scoreboard clock with a savage line drive. In the actual game, he recorded two doubles and a homer that just missed striking the clock again. This time, his liner roared over the left field wall into the park. Kiner's longest of the '51 season was a 495-foot blast over the trees in left center on August 5. Veteran coach Benny Bengough declared that he had never seen anything hit farther.

When Ralph Kiner led the Major Leagues with 37 homers in 1952, it marked the sixth straight time that he claimed that distinction. No one in baseball history has done the same. Ralph's most imposing long-distance feat involved a 440-footer on June 11 off Boston's Max Surkont at Forbes Field. Not bad, but it was followed by a 460-foot moon shot off the same guy that caromed high off the light tower on July 13. Despite such impressive batting prowess, Ralph was slowing down just a bit. Always a tough salary negotiator, Kiner may have pushed the Pittsburgh brass too far in 1953. It is said that his trade to the Chicago Cubs on June 4 was prompted by financial issues. Nonetheless, he still ripped 35 homers, including a tremendous shot over Wrigley Field's left center field bleachers on September 15. Among Ralph's 22 four-baggers in 1954 was a huge drive over the 50-foot scoreboard at Crosley Field in Cincinnati on April 25.

RALPH KINER'S 10 LONGEST HOME RUNS

- April 22, 1950—Pittsburgh off Cincinnati's Peterson—Over left field scoreboard and far into park—520 ft.

- May 8, 1949—Boston off Hogue—Far over left field scoreboard and RR tracks—510 ft.

- August 5, 1951—Pittsburgh off Philadelphia's Konstanty—Over left center field wall and trees—495 ft.

- September 3, 1949—Chicago off Chipman—Far over left center field bleachers—485 ft.

- August 15, 1950—Pittsburgh off Cincinnati's Blackwell—Over wall at light tower in left center—480 ft.

- August 24, 1949—Boston off Spahn—Liner against wind over left field scoreboard—475 ft.

- August 31, 1949—New York off Jones—High into upper deck in deep left center—475 ft.

- July 14, 1950—Pittsburgh off New York's Maglie—Line drive over left center field wall—470 ft.

- July 20, 1949—Brooklyn off Newcombe—Liner deep into upper deck in left center—465 ft.

- June 11, 1950—Pittsburgh off Philadelphia's Donnelly—Into light tower in deep left center—465 ft.

By this time, Kiner was suffering from a nerve problem in his back, and it would soon end his career. He played in Cleveland in 1955, but was limited to 18 home runs while playing in severe pain. Ralph was still strong though. On May 3, he smashed a ball against an incoming breeze from Lake Erie that soared far over the left center field fence before landing 435 feet from home plate. He called it quits after hitting his 369th and final homer on September 10, 1955, over the left field wall at Fenway Park in Boston. Ralph was not yet 33 years old at the time. Without that disabling back ailment he could have accomplished much more, but Ralph Kiner still retired with one of the truly great power resumes in big-league history.

NUMBER 13: DAVE KINGMAN—442 HOME RUNS—1971 TO 1986

Dave Kingman was born in Oregon in 1948 and grew up with a complex, introverted personality. He was one of those guys who people couldn't figure out. Generally known for having lousy relations with the media, there were some in the press corps who liked him a lot. On the field he was regarded as one-dimensional, a fellow who was indifferent to his defensive and baserunning duties. He was also criticized for his low batting average and high strikeout totals. While he did have those flaws, Kingman could consistently pound baseballs to faraway places, so he rightfully has a place of honor here.

After starring in college at Southern Cal, Kingman was drafted by the San Francisco Giants in 1970. Assigned to Phoenix in 1971, Dave reportedly slammed a massive home run through the window of a National Guard Armory in Little Rock. He was certainly tearing things up, because, when he was called up by the Giants on July 30, Dave had already struck 26 homers. On the very next day at Candlestick Park, Kingman knocked one into the left field seats with the bases loaded for his first Major League home run. The following day, on August 1, 1971, Dave hit two more. It was quite a start. By the time the month

Dave Kingman

ended, Kingman had also recorded his initial tape measure shot. That one was launched at Shea Stadium in New York on August 25 and cleared the left field bullpen before landing on a bus. That ball flew 460 feet and marked the 6'6", 215-pound Kingman as a real powerhouse.

In his first three full seasons with the Giants, the right-handed enigma hit a total of 65 homers, which wasn't up to expectations. But when he hit them, he hit them far. A typical day's work occurred on August 6, 1972, in a doubleheader at Candlestick Park in San Francisco. After striking out six straight times, he knocked one over the center field fence and deep into the seats. Dave then lined a ball into the left field second deck at Cincinnati's Riverfront Stadium on August 19. When asked about his handiwork, Kingman stated calmly that this drive was the "hardest I hit all year." Indeed. Dave rarely recorded his home runs on line drives, but this vicious smash sailed over 450 feet.

In those early Giant years, Kingman's single longest four-bagger was his tremendous poke on September 12, 1973, high into the seats in left center field in Atlanta. It was a drive of about 475 feet. During that time, Kong's primary defensive position was at third base, but he didn't play it well. When he was traded to the Mets in 1975, they featured him in the outfield and increased his plate appearances. The result was a 36-homer season. As sometimes happens, Dave hit his best shot during spring training in Fort Lauderdale.

Facing the Yankees on March 12, Kingman thumped a prodigious drive over the second fence in left field, the ball landing at the back of a practice field. New teammate Tom Seaver labeled the blast "absolutely incredible," and compared it to Reggie Jackson's historic Detroit All-Star homer.

Dave then showed up in 1976 expecting a good year. After hitting a routine first home run at Shea Stadium, Kingman came to Wrigley Field on April 14 to play the Cubs. What he got was the longest home run that he would ever hit, the first of many such tape measure shots in the Windy City. Dave swung with a distinct uppercut, and tended to lift the ball at an unusually high trajectory. That wasn't good when the wind was blowing in, but, when it was blowing out, it was very good. And it was blowing out on April 14, 1976 . . . hard!

Kingman connected in the 6th inning, and the ball took off toward left field like it would never come down. It almost didn't. The ball passed far over Waveland Avenue and ultimately struck the side of the third house up on Kenmore Avenue. This drive has been erroneously reported at various unrealistic distances, but it needs no hyperbole. The landing point has been authentically confirmed, and the Cubs have been gracious enough to measure the distance to the house. Since that figure is slightly in excess of 530 feet, we can safely estimate this epic blast in the 540-foot range. Few balls in Major League history have flown so far. For good measure,

Dave added a 465-footer into the trees across Waveland Avenue the very next day.

Then, along came 1977, and Dave Kingman played for four different teams. In truth, this was the pattern that marked his entire career, but four teams in one year was a lot even for "Sky King." He still recorded 26 homers with his longest bouncing against the outer fence in left center field in New York on May 13. That 495-footer was just a little longer than a foul ball that he struck off the roof ring in Montreal on June 1. The blow was later surveyed and found to have been fair. Playing for the Chicago Cubs in 1978, Dave hit 28 dingers. One of three hit on May 14 in Los Angeles flew 460 feet, clearing the left field bullpen at Dodger Stadium. His longest, however, took off at the "friendly confines" at Wrigley Field on August 15. That is when Kingman recorded his second 500-foot home run by again pummeling a ball well past Waveland Avenue.

In 1979, Dave Kingman enjoyed his best year ever by blasting 48 home runs. Several of them traveled 450 feet or more. But injuries limited Dave to just 255 at-bats and 18 homers in 1980, whereupon he was shipped back to the Mets. It was there that Kingman bombed what was probably the second longest drive of his intriguing baseball life. At Shea Stadium on August 14, 1981, Dave smashed the ball over the 396 foot sign in deep left center. It did not return to ground level until it short-hopped the outer fence 515 feet from home plate.

DAVE KINGMAN'S 10 LONGEST HOME RUNS

- April 14, 1976—Chicago off Dettore—To third house past Waveland Ave. in left field—540 ft.
- August 14, 1981—New York off Philadelphia's Christenson—Almost to outer fence in deep left center—515 ft.
- August 15, 1978—Chicago off Atlanta's Garber—Into trees in left field past Waveland Ave.—500 ft.
- May 13, 1977—New York off Los Angeles's Rhoden—Over bleachers in left center to outer fence—495 ft.
- June 1, 1977—Montreal off Brown—Fair ball off roof ring in left field (ruled foul)—480 ft.
- September 12, 1973—Atlanta off Morton—Deep into raised seats in left center—475 ft.
- April 20, 1979—Chicago off Montreal's Rogers—Over Waveland Ave. in left field—475 ft.
- April 27, 1976—New York off Atlanta's Morton—Far over left field bullpen—470 ft.
- June 21, 1977—San Diego off Pittsburgh's Candelaria—Liner into second deck in left field—470 ft.
- September 2, 1986—Oakland off New York's Rasmussen—Almost to top of left field bleachers—465 ft.

And so it went for the remainder of Dave's career. Wherever he went, he hit lots of home runs (including 37 in '82), but he could never find a permanent home. He played his final three seasons as a designated hitter with the Oakland Athletics from 1984 through 1986, where he belted 100 home runs. He left his calling card at Yankee Stadium on August 17, 1984, by smashing a 455-foot drive to the back of the bullpen in left center. Finally, on September 2, 1986, Dave bombed one near the top of Oakland's left field bleachers. It was a 465-foot shot, and his final tape measure homer in a big-league uniform. Although still potent at bat, Kingman had no Major League job in 1987. He finished with 442 home runs. It's too bad that he didn't find a way to improve his overall game or his personal reputation just a little bit. If he had, Dave would certainly have made it into "The 500 Club," and probably into the Hall of Fame. Even without such conjecture, he still earned a place on his sport's all-time power list, and that can't be taken away from him.

NUMBER 12: TED WILLIAMS—521 HOME RUNS—1939 TO 1960

Was Ted Williams the best hitter who ever played? Most informed observers believe that the facts identify Babe Ruth as the greatest ever, but, even if they're right, Teddy Ballgame is right behind him. Williams hit 521 home runs, and almost certainly would have totaled about 700 without four and a half years of military service. He finished second to Ruth in slugging percentage, and was first all-time in on-base percentage, just ahead of the Babe. What else can be said? How about this? Despite his slender frame, Ted Williams was one of the strongest hitters who ever picked up a bat.

Ted was seemingly born to hit. After becoming a neighborhood legend while growing up in San Diego, Williams played his first full season of pro ball with the Pacific Coast League Padres in 1937. While still in his 19th year, he managed to hit 23 home runs. Moving up to Minneapolis of the American Association in 1938, Ted clubbed the imposing total of 43 homers. When Boston fans heard about his spring exploits as a rookie with the Red Sox in 1939, they could hardly wait to see him. He did not disappoint them. On April 23, he lined his first homer 425 feet into Fenway Park's right center field bleachers on his way to a 31-homer season. His highlight occurred on May 4 at Tiger Stadium when he blasted two long right field four-baggers. Number two sailed high over the towering grandstand roof and hit the second floor of the taxi-cab build-ing across the street. It was a stunning drive of about 490 feet.

Williams dropped off to 23 home runs in 1940, but roared back with 37 in 1941 while batting .406. Ted was whippet-thin as a young man, standing 6'4", and weighing only 175 pounds. Batting from the left side, he didn't give the appearance of being unusually strong. But the "Splendid Splinter" could produce tremendous bat speed, and the results were undeniable. On May 7, 1941, Ted blasted one high into the right center field upper deck at Comiskey Park in Chicago. It was an impressive blow of about 440 feet, but paled compared to what followed. Williams won that same game in the 11th inning by slamming the ball to the top of the grandstand roof above where the first

Ted Williams

homer landed. That eye-opener sailed about 505 feet.

Ted reprised his act in 1942 with another outstanding year while belting 36 homers. He probably best displayed his power by knocking a pair of 450-foot homers to the housetops across 20th Street at Shibe Park in Philadelphia. Those two right field drives happened on May 19 and May 29. Williams seemed unstoppable, but fate intervened. He missed the next three years due to military service in World War II and did not return until the start of the 1946 season. With his former commander-in-chief (Harry Truman) in attendance at Griffith Stadium in Washington, D.C., Ted came home to big-league baseball on April 16. In the 3rd inning, he teed off to straightaway center field, where the ball landed in the tenth row of the bleachers. Such a shot had not been seen in the nation's capital since Babe Ruth stopped coming to town. It was a giant clout of 470 feet. When interviewed in Winterhaven, Florida, in 1986, the then 67-year-old legend recalled the moment by jumping up and grabbing a bat. While showing off his ageless swing, he described what happened. "It was a low and away slider, and I went down and nailed the sonovabitch."

Later that season, Ted Williams hit the longest home run of his remarkable career. It occurred on June 9 at Fenway Park in Beantown. Taking advantage of a helping breeze, Williams unloaded toward the distant right field bleachers. The ball kept going and going until it conked a fan in the head who was sitting in either the 33rd or 37th row in section 42. There is still some question on this point. Yet, even in the lower plateau, this drive computes as a 522-foot masterpiece, confirming its status in Red Sox lore. It should also be noted that Ted had hit a 500-footer just three weeks earlier in St. Louis. That drive on May 18 landed on a roof on the far side of Grand Avenue in right center.

The years rolled by, and nobody except Uncle Sam could restrain Ted Williams. Despite already serving his country for three years, he was called back to duty during the Korean War. This time he saw some heavy-duty combat as a pilot, and missed another season and a half. Upon returning to the Red Sox in August of 1953, many observers felt that Williams was finally over the hill. Not so. On August 30 and 31 at Cleveland's vast Municipal Stadium, Ted slammed terrific shots into the right field upper deck. Then in 1954, Williams smacked 29 homers in just 117 games while batting .354. Just to remove any lingering doubt about his power, Ted recorded a 480-foot blast to the 22nd row of Fenway's bleachers on May 29. He also ripped one about 5 feet farther at Philly's Shibe Park on September 3.

Would this guy ever slow down? Not for a long time. As late as 1957 at age 39, Ted Williams hit 38 home runs while leading the Major Leagues with a .388 batting average. When hampered by injuries in 1959, Ted did suffer an off year, but his pride brought him

TED WILLIAMS'S 10 LONGEST HOME RUNS

- June 9, 1946—Boston off Detroit's Hutchinson—To 33rd row of right field bleachers—522 ft.

- May 7, 1941 (#2)—Chicago off Rigney—To back of grandstand roof in right center—505 ft.

- May 18, 1946—St. Louis off Kinder—Onto roof across street in right center—500 ft.

- August 7, 1958—Boston off Washington's Clevenger—To the 25th bleacher row in right—495 ft.

- May 4, 1939 (#2)—Detroit off Harris—Over right field roof and hit second story across street—490 ft.

- September 3, 1954—Philadelphia off Portocarrero—Onto house across street in right center—485 ft.

- May 29, 1954—Boston off New York's Byrd—To 22nd bleacher row in right center—480 ft.

- July 23, 1955—Chicago off Byrd—Onto right field grandstand roof—480 ft.

- July 2, 1958—Boston off Washington's Pascual—To 15th bleacher row in center field—480 ft.

- April 16, 1946—Washington off Wolff—To 10th row in center field bleachers—470 ft.

back in 1960, and he went out on top at age 42. In that implausible finale, Williams batted .319 while thumping 29 homers in a mere 113 games. In storybook fashion, he clubbed a 420-foot home run at Fenway Park in his very last at-bat on September 28, 1960.

In the 17-plus seasons leading to that moment, Ted mastered every established distance plateau around the American League. In his limited history at Municipal Stadium in Kansas City, he still managed to join the elite list of men to hit a home run onto Brooklyn Avenue beyond the outer fence in right field. He reached the far side of Grand Avenue in St. Louis three times along with the housetops across 20th Street in Philadelphia twice as

often. In Cleveland's Municipal Stadium, Williams rammed seven balls into the right field upper deck despite usually playing at League Park through 1946. He also reached or cleared Tiger Stadium's right field roof seven times. Ted drove 13 homers into Yankee Stadium's right field upper deck, while launching 17 to Comiskey Park's upper deck or rooftop.

If Williams had returned in 1961, when expansion elevated offensive production, his numbers would have been even higher. Instead, he retired, leaving everyone wondering if we would ever see another hitter like Teddy Ballgame. Williams stayed close to his sport by coaching and managing for a number of years after his time as a player. To the end of his days, Ted Williams embraced the science of hitting with unparalleled passion. Based on his performance, we should remember him with the same fervor.

NUMBER 11: GREG LUZINSKI—307 HOME RUNS—1971 TO 1984

Appropriately known as "The Bull," Greg Luzinski was the physical opposite of Ted Williams. He stood 6'1" and was as thick as a tree trunk at about 240 pounds. Luzinski swung from the right side, and, unlike the temperamental Williams, always seemed to keep his emotions on an even keel. In one way, however, they were almost exactly alike. They both hit baseballs so hard that witnesses often shook their heads in amazement. Born in Chicago in 1950, Greg became a schoolboy sensation at Notre Dame High School in suburban Niles, Illinois. He was drafted in the first round of the 1968 amateur draft by the Philadelphia Phillies and quickly asserted himself in their farm system.

After winning two minor league home run titles, Luzinski got some significant playing time (100 at-bats) with the Phillies late in 1971. It didn't take him long to begin establishing the greatest long-distance legacy in the history of Philadelphia's Veterans Stadium. On September 7, Greg pounded one into the left field upper deck (fifth level) for a drive of about 455 feet. Five days later, he added one of similar length over the left field bullpen at Shea Stadium in New York. Not bad

for a 20-year-old. In his formal rookie season in 1972, Luzinski recorded 18 homers, and two of them were enormous.

On May 16 at Veterans Stadium, Luzinski connected off a Burt Hooton knuckleball, and smashed it to dead center field. In keeping with their hometown roots, the Phillies had placed a replica of the Liberty Bell at the 500 level. This extraordinary drive collided with it for a 505-foot home run. Then, on September 3 in Atlanta, Greg unloaded in the direction of left center field, where the club level was raised high above the field and over 450 feet from home plate. So, when Luzinski's drive landed there, it caused quite a stir. Why not? It was a poke of about 500 feet. Greg increased his production in 1973 and recorded 29 homers. His longest collided with a seat in the fifth row of the Vet's left center field upper deck. That was a shot of 495 feet. Luzinski injured his knee in 1974, missing most of the season, but 1975 was his best year to date.

Among Greg's 34 circuits were rockets of 475 and 445 feet in Philly on July 5 and August 17, as well as a 450-footer in Montreal's Jarry Park on August 2. Moving on to 1976, Luzinski fell back to 21 homers, but his power was in full force. He ripped another ball into the left center field upper deck at Veterans Stadium on May 8, and then bashed another shot over the left field bullpen in New York on August 1. The latter drive also cleared a bus parked lengthwise and bounced on one hop over the outer fence into the parking lot. Both homers had flight distances of about 485 feet.

Greg Luzinski

In 1977, Greg Luzinski enjoyed the best season of his career. While batting .309 and driving in 130 runs, he clubbed 39 home runs. At this point, he teamed with Mike Schmidt to give the Phillies one of the best power tandems in baseball. The Phils had some outstanding teams, winning three division championships in the late '70s, but it seemed that they would never win their first World Series. At least in 1977, it wasn't Greg's fault. Along with his great overall numbers, he blasted what was probably the longest homer of his life. On May 21 at Houston's Astrodome, he scorched a line drive that didn't stop until it crashed into a yellow seat in the fifth row of the upper deck in field. It's impossible to know how far this eye-popping screamer would have flown, but a conservative esti-

mate is 515 feet. Luzinski also added one of the longest-ever drives in LCS history when he blasted one between the flagpoles in dead center field at Dodger Stadium on October 4.

There was more of the same in 1978 when Greg belted 35 homers. They were best exemplified by his 460-footers at Dodger Stadium on June 12 and at Candlestick Park on September 1. The Los Angeles bolt landed in the loge level (second deck) in left field where few balls have ever visited. The San Francisco blast soared high over the left field fence and descended about halfway up the bleachers. In describing that homer, the *Philadelphia Daily News* used the word "tremendous," the *Philadelphia Bulletin* said "vicious" and the *Philadelphia Inquirer* decided on "titanic." The *San Francisco Chronicle* was impressed with hometown hero Jack Clark's poke high into the seats, but added that Luzinski's went about 15 rows higher.

Greg's play slipped some over the next few seasons, but there were compensations. Included in his 18 four-baggers in 1979 were two tremendous drives at Three Rivers Stadium in Pittsburgh. On April 18, he knocked one into the left field upper deck, and, on August 5, he blasted a ball to the base of the scoreboard in center field. They were respective drives of 480 and 490 feet. More importantly, Luzinski and the Phillies won their first-ever World Series in 1980 even though Greg was again somewhat sub par with 19 home runs. But, of course, some of them were rockets. Luzinski powered a screaming line drive all the way to the third row of the center field seats at The Vet on

GREG LUZINSKI'S 10 LONGEST HOME RUNS

- May 21, 1977—Houston off McLaughlin—Liner to fifth row in left field upper deck—515 ft.
- May 16, 1972—Philadelphia off Chicago's Hooton—Off Liberty Bell at center field upper deck—505 ft.
- September 3, 1972—Atlanta off Kelley—To club level in left center—500 ft.
- August 28, 1983—Chicago off Boston's Boyd—Onto left field roof and bounced over—500 ft.
- July 11, 1973—Philadelphia off Atlanta's Freeman—To fifth row in upper deck in deep left center—495 ft.
- August 5, 1979—Pittsburgh off Blyleven—To base of center field scoreboard—490 ft.
- May 8, 1976—Philadelphia off Los Angeles's John—Into upper deck in deep left center—485 ft.
- August 1, 1976—New York off Apodaca—Over left field bullpen and bus—485 ft.
- April 18, 1979—Pittsburgh off Robinson—To second row in left field upper deck—480 ft.
- June 26, 1983—Chicago off Minnesota's Oelkers—Onto left field grandstand roof—480 ft.

April 22. That was a line drive of about 460 feet, which is a feat of brute strength that few men can equal.

The Bull was sent off to the White Sox in his hometown of Chicago in 1981, and that is where he spent the final four years of his Major League tenure. In that time, he averaged 21 homers a season, and, predictably, some of them were huge. Four of his shots landed on the towering left field grandstand roof at Comiskey Park, including three in 1983 alone. Home plate had been moved up since Ted Williams had played there, but it was still a very tough target to reach. To illustrate this point, it should be understood that those four roof-toppers ranged from 475 feet to 500 feet. In that same season, on August

22, Greg nearly cleared the left field bleachers in Kansas City, a feat that had never previously been accomplished.

Greg Luzinski hit his final home run into the left field bleachers in Toronto on August 28, 1984. All together, he bashed 307 out of the park. If he had hit more, he probably would be ranked in the all-time distance top ten. Greg is right there with the men ranked 7th through 10th in terms of pure power, but the common sense tie-breaker is the total number of career home runs. That is where the others have a significant advantage. Either way, a considerable number of Luzinski's four-baggers were exceptional in their length, and he surely earned the right to wear his crown as one of the Kings of the Tape Measure.

Six

Top 10 Current Sluggers

NUMBER 10: J. D. DREW—216 HOME RUNS—1998 TO 2009

J. D. Drew's baseball career has seen a series of ups and downs. As a star at Lowndes High School in Georgia, he was drafted by the San Francisco Giants in the 20th round of the 1994 amateur draft. Drew preferred to go to college, which was a good decision. He became a freshman All-American at Florida State University, which quickly improved his prospects. As a sophomore, J. D. (which stands for an inverted David Jonathan) achieved first team All-American status. Then, in his junior season in 1997, Drew batted .455, while repeating as All-American and winning the Golden Spikes Award as America's outstanding college player.

On February 1, 1997, while playing against UNC-Charlotte on his home field in Tallahassee, J. D. Drew did something that made Major League scouts begin to drool. Using a metal bat, J. D. sent a towering drive to right field that cleared the fence by about 100 feet before landing in a tree. The ball had flown close to 550 feet. Of course, the metal bats used in college propel the ball much farther than their wooden counterparts in professional ball, but 550 feet is still an amazing distance. More

importantly, it was one of 30 home runs that Drew recorded that season. Accordingly, when the amateur draft took place on June 3, the Philadelphia Phillies used the second overall pick to select J. D. Drew.

However, Drew and agent Scott Boras had other ideas. They demanded a signing package that the Phils had already vowed not to offer. Essentially, Philadelphia dared J. D. not to sign, and he accepted the challenge. Drew played for the Saint Paul Saints of the independent Northern League for the rest of the '97 season, and cycled back into the 1998 draft. This time, he was picked by the St. Louis Cardinals (fifth overall), who proceeded to give him his money. J. D. raced through the Double-A and Triple-A Cardinal affiliates,

J. D. Drew

making his Major League debut on September 8, 1998, in St. Louis. That just happened to be the night that Mark McGwire made history by breaking the single-season home run record. Drew then recorded his first Major League four-bagger the next day in Cincinnati.

When J. D. Drew came to Philadelphia's Veterans Stadium for the first time on August 10, 1999, he was placed under tight security. Many Philly fans had not forgiven Drew's rejection and berated him passionately. In response, J. D. ripped a 434-foot home run before leaving town. It was a typical blow from the bat of the 6'1", 200-pound outfielder, who batted from the left side. During his first few years in the big leagues, Drew belted several homers in the 430 to 450-foot range. However, although he played well, J. D. had been preceded into St. Louis by such lofty expectations that he had a difficult time living up to them. A series of debilitating injuries only made it harder for Drew.

J. D. played 135 games in 2000, recording 18 home runs along the way. At that point, he started hearing the whispers that he wasn't living up to either his potential or his paycheck. However, when his games played slipped to 109 in 2001, he offset that disappointment by bashing 27 home runs. Included in that impressive total were a 440-footer in St. Louis on May 13 and a 468-foot bomb four days later in Pittsburgh. Then, early in the 2002 season, J. D. Drew blasted a ball high off the scoreboard at the upper deck level in right center field at Busch Stadium. That mammoth drive on April 12 was estimated at 496 feet and labeled Drew as a legitimate tape measure slugger.

In 2003, J. D. played in only 100 games. However, he seemingly reached the apex of his power performance curve by bashing a series of lengthy blows on his home turf in St. Louis. His rather modest figure of 15 home runs included 457- and 471-foot drives at Busch Stadium on May 31 and September 10. However, those two shots were dwarfed by the monstrous blast Drew pounded off the scoreboard's video screen on May 16, 2003. That drive to right center field was judged at 507 feet and established the high point for distance in J. D.'s career. For those who witnessed this event, it was an unforgettable sight.

Drew was traded to the Atlanta Braves in 2004 and enjoyed his most successful campaign. Playing in a then-career-high 145 games, J. D. smacked 31 homers, but the distance of his single longest drive dropped to 445 feet. This phenomenon has been seen before and raises a question that only the player himself can answer. It is extremely difficult to center a ball against competitive Major League pitching. Sometimes, this already difficult function becomes even tougher when the hitter swings with all his strength. It seems likely that J. D. Drew opted to take "a little off" his swing in order to achieve higher overall efficiency.

J. D. then spent two seasons with the Los Angeles Dodgers, where his performance was regarded as mediocre. He recorded a total of

J. D. DREW'S 10 LONGEST HOME RUNS

- May 16, 2003—St. Louis off Chicago's Clement—To video sign in right center field upper deck—507 ft.

- April 12, 2002—St. Louis off Houston's Miller—Off scoreboard at right center field upper deck—496 ft.

- September 10, 2003—St. Louis off Colorado's Elarton—Into right field upper deck—471 ft.

- May 17, 2001—Pittsburgh off Ritchie—Over right field bleachers—468 ft.

- July 26, 2008—Boston off New York's Pettitte—Deep into right center field bleachers—460 ft.

- May 31, 2003—St. Louis off Pittsburgh's Wells—Off right field video board—457 ft.

- May 7, 2005—Cincinnati off Ortiz—Far over center field fence—455 ft.

- July 2, 2005—Los Angeles off Arizona's Vazquez—Into center field pavilion—448 ft.

- July 3, 2009—Boston off Seattle's Hernandez—Into center field bleachers—446 ft.

- August 12, 2004—Atlanta off Milwaukee's Sheets—Two sections deep in right field seats—445 ft.

35 homers with his longest at Dodger Stadium being computed at 448 feet on July 2, 2005. When Boston decided to sign Drew to a rather costly free agent contract in 2007, some members of Red Sox Nation had misgivings. Perhaps unfairly, they regarded J. D. as a little "soft." His inability to consistently stay in the lineup along with a seemingly casual playing style led to the doubts. Those perceptions only got worse as Drew recorded just 11 homers in 140 games during the 2007 campaign.

However, all that changed quickly when J. D. smacked a crucial grand slam homer against Cleveland in the ALCS. In fact, Drew played inspired ball throughout the postseason, helping lead the Bosox to another World Series championship. In 2008, J. D. slammed a 460-footer deep into Fenway Park's right center field bleachers on July 26, which harkened back to the days of Ted Williams. When Drew then overcame a painful back injury to again play exceptional October baseball, the process of acceptance appeared complete. His fall resume was highlighted by a timely 437-foot home run off Angel relief ace Francisco Rodriguez. J. D. continued his consistent performance for the Red Sox in 2009, which was highlighted by a 446-foot shot into Fenway Park's center field seats on July 3. It had been a long time since 1997, when J. D. Drew spurned his first chance to play Major League Baseball. Sometimes, the road appeared too long and arduous for him to stay the course. However, his power and persistence have finally prevailed.

NUMBER 9: ALBERT PUJOLS—366 HOME RUNS—2001 TO 2009

Albert Pujols is one of the greatest right-handed hitters in baseball history. That is saying a lot, but his numbers are indisputable. Born in the Dominican Republic in 1980, Albert moved to New York in 1991 and then on to the Kansas City area, where he starred in high school, American Legion, and college baseball. In fact, as a senior at Fort Osage High School in 1998, Pujols batted .660 along with eight home runs, despite being intentionally walked nearly half the times he came to the plate. He was drafted by the St. Louis Cardinals on June 2, 1999, in the 13th round of the amateur draft, and has proven to be an exceptional bargain.

© Shutterstock

Albert Pujols

Albert's quiet self-confidence has always served him well. He turned down the Cards' initial offer of $10,000 and opted instead to play in the Kansas Jayhawk League in the summer of 1999. That took guts. If he had failed, he might never have had another chance to play professional baseball. Instead, he exceeded the Cardinals' expectations, whereupon they gladly signed Pujols to a significantly enhanced offer of $70,000. In 2000, Albert soared through the St. Louis farm system, playing in Peoria (A), Potomac (AA), and Memphis (AAA). His combined season totals included a .314 batting average, 19 home runs, 96 RBI, and a .543 slugging percentage.

Reporting to spring training in 2001, Pujols had just turned 21, and was regarded as a long shot to make the Cardinal roster. But Albert Pujols is a determined man. He not only made the team, but he went on to win the National League Rookie of the Year Award. He hit his first Major League home run on April 6 in Arizona, and finished the year with 37. Albert's other numbers were equally dazzling: .329 batting average, 130 RBI, 112 runs, and a .610 slugging percentage. Probably his longest homer of that remarkable freshman campaign was his prolific shot over the temporary backdrop in St. Louis on August 20. The Cardinals were in the process of building their new stadium, and Pujols launched one over the 40-foot-high temporary canvas in dead center. It was a drive of 450 feet.

Albert confirmed his legitimacy in 2002 by clubbing another 34 home runs and knocking in 127 runs. In the process, he recorded 450-footers in New York and Pittsburgh on April 23 and May 25. After just two big-league seasons, Pujols was regarded as a genuine star. Then, along came 2003, and folks didn't know how to quantify this guy. In an astounding display of offensive firepower, "Prince Albert" blasted 43 homers, batted a league-leading .359, and slugged at the rate of .667. He also drove in 124 runs and scored 137 times! Pujols unloaded two more 450-footers in St. Louis on May 3 and September 10, but recorded his longest drive in Cincinnati on August 31. Albert uncorked a blow of 477 feet high into the left field sector that was recognized as the season's longest at Great American Ballpark.

Despite being hampered by a painful heel injury in 2004, "El Hombre" kept pounding away at a prodigious pace. He increased his home run output to 46 while maintaining his usual lofty standards in all offensive categories. His drive of 456 feet at Coors Field in Denver on September 26 was particularly noteworthy. Having started his career as a third baseman, Albert was switched briefly to left field and then finally moved to first base in 2003. He was a little tentative in the beginning, but, by 2005, Pujols was attacking the ball as aggressively on defense as he always had on offense. Accordingly, his contributions in the field received more and more attention. In addition, the 6'3", 230-pounder

stole a career high 16 bases. Combined with his 41 home runs and customary overall offensive production, Albert Pujols won the National League Most Valuable Player Award in 2005. It was richly deserved.

By this time, Albert was drawing inevitable comparisons to other historic ballplayers who had shone brilliantly early in their careers. Men like Ted Williams and Joe DiMaggio were frequently mentioned. In fact, Pujols's numbers through his first five seasons were as good as anyone ever at a comparable stage. In 2006, he got even better. Starting on April 3 at Citizens Bank Park in Philadelphia, Albert smashed the ball relentlessly all year. He belted two long left field homers that opening day, but it was the second one that startled the sellout crowd. It was lined all the way to the distant second deck in left, and estimated at 455 feet. Proceeding through the schedule, Pujols recorded 445-foot shots in Washington on September 5 and St. Louis on September 27.

For the season, Albert ripped 49 homers (most of them over 400 feet), batted .331, and slugged away at a .671 clip. He drove in 137 runs and scored 119. Pujols struck out only 50 times, which is extraordinary for a man of his great power. Continuing his defensive progression, Albert was awarded his first Gold Glove. Most importantly, Pujols led the St. Louis Cardinals to a World Series championship over the favored Detroit Tigers in the fall. At age 26, Albert Pujols had already done just about everything that could be done on a ball field; he was on track to become one of the all-time greats in his field of endeavor.

Pujols slipped just a little in 2007, but was still magnificent. Slamming 32 homers and batting .327, Albert remained the poster boy for National League right-handed batsmen. He walloped a tremendous 471-foot shot in a return visit to Philadelphia on July 13 that cleared the seats in deep left center. Two days later in the same park, Pujols reached the top of the brick backdrop in straightaway center field for a 453-footer. When Albert added 37 dingers in 2008 despite suffering from a painful, year-long right elbow injury, he proved again that he was one tough dude. Pujols is truly talented, but his grit and determination may be his finest traits. His single longest shot in '08 soared over the center field fence in Milwaukee on May 9. It was a typical drive that sailed 450 feet.

Following off-season elbow surgery, Albert seemed more dominant than ever. He began the 2009 campaign by routinely banging 440- and 450-footers all around the National League circuit. When he launched a 465-foot rocket off Randy Johnson at St. Louis on June 30, Pujols attained his long-distance peak for the season. Entering the 2010 season, Jose Alberto Pujols Alcantara is only 30 years of age. Barring unforeseen events, he is headed toward the Mount Olympus of baseball immortals. His on-field performance and off-field humanitarianism have rarely been equaled. Even if he stopped playing now, his resume would certainly place him in Cooperstown.

ALBERT PUJOLS'S 10 LONGEST HOME RUNS

- August 31, 2003—Cincinnati off Serafino—To top of batter's eye in center field—477 ft.
- July 13, 2007—Philadelphia off Romero—Over back brick wall in deep left center—471 ft.
- June 30, 2009—St. Louis off San Francisco's Johnson—Into left field upper deck—465 ft.
- April 25, 2009—St. Louis off Chicago's Patton—To top of left field bleachers—458 ft.
- September 26, 2004—Colorado off Gissell—Deep into left center field bleachers—456 ft.
- July 15, 2007—Philadelphia off Eaton—High off brick backdrop in center field—453 ft.
- April 23, 2002—New York off D'Amico—Over left field bullpen—452 ft.
- May 3, 2003—St. Louis off Montreal's Vargas—To club window below left field upper deck—452 ft.
- May 25, 2002—Pittsburgh off Anderson—Far over fence near left field foul pole—450 ft.
- April 3, 2006—Philadelphia off Fultz—Line drive into left field upper deck—450 ft.

NUMBER 8: PRINCE FIELDER—160 HOME RUNS—2005 TO 2009

Having a successful Major League slugger as your father is a mixed blessing. Prince Fielder was born in Ontario, California, in 1984, one year before his father, Cecil, made it to the big leagues. Growing up, Prince was a regular visitor to Major League clubhouses and even took occasional batting practice with the pros. Obviously, many doors were open to him that were not available to boys with average dads. However, there was a down side. No matter what he did in his youth, there was always somebody telling him that his father had done it better. Finally, after the 2007 baseball season, Prince left those concerns in his rearview mirror. It took a while to get there.

As he was concluding his high school career in Florida, young Fielder was chosen by the Milwaukee Brewers in the first round of the 2002 amateur draft. He signed quickly and went to work in a rookie league. He did well and moved rapidly up the Brewers' minor league chain. By 2005, Prince had made it to the top (Triple A) level, playing in the Pacific Coast League with the Nashville Sounds. In just 103 games, Prince belted 28 home runs and drove in 86 runs. The Brewers called him up on June 13, needing Fielder to serve as their designated hitter during interleague play. Staying until June 25, 2005, in Milwaukee, Prince hit his first Major League homer, a booming 430-footer to right field. He soon returned to Nashville, but was summoned

Prince Fielder

Scott Boehm/Getty Images

back on August 15, finishing the season with the Brewers.

Batting from the left side, Prince Fielder, at 6 feet even, was 3 inches shorter than his famous dad, but his girth was even stouter. Papa Cecil had always battled weight problems, and his son was actually heavier at a comparable age. So, there were still reservations about Prince's athletic future. However, when the Brewers traded incumbent first baseman Lyle Overbay in the off-season, it gave Fielder the chance to prove himself. He did not fail. He played 157 games in his official rookie season in 2006 and slugged 28 home runs. Prince posted decent batting and slugging averages (.271 and .483) and shocked everyone by stealing seven bases. That was five more than Cecil's career total. Okay, he ran faster than his slow-footed daddy, but could he hit a baseball as far?

On May 12, 2006, at Miller Park in Milwaukee, Prince Fielder faced the Yankees' Jose Lima in the 4th inning. A moment later, a baseball was flying far over the right center field fence. It eventually smacked into the "Road Runner" sign atop the seats, and was estimated at 475 feet. Baseball fans had their answer: There were now two Fielders who had hit tape measure home runs in a Major League game. Prince followed that gem with a 471-foot blast over the right center field bleachers in Pittsburgh later that same month (May 29). In fact, Prince's total of 28 dingers for that season was only three less than Cecil's grand total for his first four seasons combined. About the only thing that Senior had done that Junior had not done was to record an historic 50 home run season. But Prince was only 22 years old. If he would ever reach such lofty heights, it wouldn't be anytime soon. Or so everyone thought.

Prince Fielder started well in 2007 by ripping his first homer on April 3 off Randy Wolf of the Dodgers. He finished the month with six. Then, on May 4, he knocked one 445 feet into Miller Park's right center field seats, and really seemed to take off. He added a pair two days later and showed up at Dodger Stadium in Los Angeles on May 21 with three more under his belt. In the 2nd inning versus Brett Tomko, Fielder unloaded. Prince rocketed the ball toward right center field (his favorite

long-distance direction), and it easily scaled the outfield fence. In fact, it didn't land until it almost reached the top of the pavilion, which amounted to a 462-foot journey. In the 9th inning against Takashi Saito, Fielder sent one 430 feet in the same direction. For the month, Prince finished with 13 home runs.

Fielder delivered eight more in June, but slipped to just three in July. At 260 corpulent pounds, it was thought by some observers that Prince was too heavy to stay strong for the entire season. But Fielder stormed back with nine homers in August, including a 450-footer in Houston on the 10th. Beginning the month of September, Prince stood at 39 circuits, and needed another 11 to reach the 50 plateau. It was a lot to ask a ballplayer at the age of 23. On September 7 in Cincinnati, Fielder smoked a 446-foot shot to right field and seemed strong as a bull. When he bombed one 472 feet off a girder in deep right center field in Milwaukee on the 24th, he stood at 48. The drama ended the next day, when Prince walloped his final two home runs against the St. Louis Cardinals. Prince Fielder had reached 50 homers at a younger age than any player in Major League history. Any lingering doubt about living up to his father's legacy was permanently dispelled.

No player, regardless of age, could continue that pace. It was no surprise then, when Fielder dipped to 34 homers in 2008. Those numbers still kept Prince near the league leaders, and he continued to be regarded as one of baseball's best young sluggers. Naturally,

PRINCE FIELDER'S 10 LONGEST HOME RUNS

- May 12, 2006—Milwaukee off New York's Lima—Off "Road Runner" sign in deep right center—475 ft.

- September 24, 2007—Milwaukee off St. Louis's Wainwright—High off girder just right of center field—472 ft.

- May 29, 2006—Pittsburgh off Duke—Over bleachers in right center—471 ft.

- June 30, 2009—Milwaukee off New York's Santana—Onto concourse in right center field—470 ft.

- April 18, 2006—Houston off Miller—To eighth row in right field upper deck—465 ft.

- May 21, 2007—Los Angeles off Tomko—High into pavilion in right center—462 ft.

- October 5, 2008—Milwaukee off Philadelphia's Blanton—Onto concourse in deep right center—462 ft.

- September 16, 2006—Washington off Astacio—To third row in right field upper deck—453 ft.

- July 13, 2007—Milwaukee off Colorado's Francis—High into right center field seats—450 ft.

- September 16, 2008—Chicago off Dempster—Over right field bleachers—450 ft.

his power also remained exceptional. At San Francisco's Pac Bell Park on July 19, Fielder splashed a 446-foot drive over the right field arcade into McCovey Cove. On September 16, he cleared Wrigley Field's right field bleachers with a 450-foot shot. Then, in the playoffs versus Philadelphia, Prince walloped a drive onto the concourse in deep right center field at Milwaukee. That 462-footer was his longest of the season.

In 2009, Fielder seemed unstoppable. On June 30 in Milwaukee, he walloped a 460-foot shot onto the right center field concourse against Johan Santana of the Mets. Less than two weeks later, Prince won the annual All-Star Game home run derby in St. Louis. Included in his impressive array of mighty clouts were tremendous drives computed at 496 and 503 feet.

Entering the 2010 season, Prince Fielder had been in the Major Leagues for less then five years. In that short time, he had already amassed 160 home runs and distinguished himself as one of the most promising power hitters in the history of the game. At age 26, his potential has few limits. Who knows where the man will wind up when he hangs up his spikes?

NUMBER 7: FRANK THOMAS—521 HOME RUNS—1990 TO 2008

Thomas is a big man. Yes, he is physically imposing at 6'5" and 275 pounds, but his stature goes way beyond mere size. Wherever he goes, whether competing on the field, speaking in the clubhouse, or just walking into a room, his presence seems larger than life. And so it is when he's hitting a baseball. As of 2008, Thomas had been in the big leagues for 19 years, and had been smashing the ball mercilessly the entire time. Frank didn't play in 2009, but, since he has not officially retired, he is grouped with other active players.

Frank Edward Thomas was born in Columbus, Georgia, in 1968, and starred at Columbus High School in football, baseball, and basketball. He accepted a football scholarship to Auburn University and played tight end as a freshman. When Thomas suffered a football-career–ending injury, he feared the prospect of losing his scholarship. However, Auburn stood by him, allowing Frank to switch his focus to baseball. By the time Frank Thomas left campus, he had set the school record by clouting 49 career home runs and had earned the South East Conference MVP Award. As a collegian, he was permitted to use an aluminum bat, thereby leaving a trail of frighteningly forceful home runs.

The Chicago White Sox used the seventh overall pick in the first round of the 1989 amateur draft to obtain the rights to Thomas. He was a right-handed-hitting first baseman with a seemingly unlimited future. He progressed rapidly, and made his Major League debut on August 2, 1990. Despite hitting for average, it wasn't until August 28 and 80 at-bats that he recorded his first big-league homer. It was a line shot into the left field bleachers at Minnesota's Metrodome. In that abbreviated season, Frank belted seven circuits and batted .330. Those numbers were not a fluke. In his first two full seasons, Thomas batted well over .300, slugged well over .500, drove in over 200 runs, and ripped a total of 56 home runs.

Entering the 1993 season, the "Big Hurt" was already a star. In that season, he took

Frank Thomas

© Ron Vesely/Chicago White Sox

the giant step up to superstar status. Batting .317, slugging .607, amassing 128 RBI and 41 home runs, Thomas easily won the American League Most Valuable Player Award. During that time, he launched several drives in the 450-foot range, including a 454-footer at the modern Comiskey Park on July 23. It was an exceptional year, but was soon superseded by his 1994 accomplishments. Despite having his season cut short by the infamous labor dispute, Frank Thomas blasted 38 home runs, drove in 101 runs, and scored 113 times. However, his best numbers included his .353 batting average and .729 slugging percentage.

Frank won his second straight AL MVP Award in 1994, and his power was now becoming a Chicago institution. He sent a stream of mighty blows high into the Comiskey Park bleachers in all directions. As he aged, Thomas became more of a dead pull hitter, but, in his younger years, he sprayed his homers from foul pole to foul pole. In '94 alone, Frank sent 15 of his four-baggers to the opposite field along with five others to straightaway center field. However, his longest was directed to the front edge of the left field roof at Detroit's Tiger Stadium. It was a drive of 463 feet.

Like Albert Pujols, Frank Thomas was so successful in his early Major League career that he was often compared to the game's most historic figures. In retrospect, that all seems fair. He settled into a pattern of consistent production that will clearly result in a first ballot ticket to Cooperstown. In 1995 and 1996, Frank banged 40 homers while working on his tape measure resume. On May 20, 1995, he knocked one almost to the top of Comiskey's left field bleachers for a ride of 460 feet. Then, on September 20, 1996, Thomas sent another ball to almost the same spot. Despite pulling a muscle in his side in the summer of 1997, and spending time on the disabled list, Frank still recorded 35 home runs. Once more, his longest drive was a towering blast to the top of the left field seats in Chicago. This blow occurred on September 8 and was judged at the distance of 453 feet.

In an effort to prolong his career, Thomas was switched from first base to designated hitter in 1998. Frank didn't care for the move, which actually decreased his offensive production. He dipped to 29 homers, and, perhaps more noteworthy, fell below the .500 plateau in slugging for the first time. However, he started the season in fine form, when he blasted his longest drive as a visiting player on April 4 at Tampa Bay's Tropicana Field. Batting in the 4th inning against Dennis Springer, Thomas unleashed all his vast strength, and blasted the ball in a towering parabola toward left field. It rose majestically and then caromed off a catwalk that was suspended from the roof. The ball careened into foul territory but was ruled fair based upon where it had been interrupted. Frank trotted around the bases as his epic blow was conservatively estimated at 475 feet.

After years of consistent production, Thomas entered the roller coaster stage of his career in 1999. Hampered by right foot and

FRANK THOMAS'S 10 LONGEST HOME RUNS

- July 23, 2002—Chicago off Minnesota's Santana—Onto concourse atop left field bleachers—495 ft.
- April 4, 1998—Tampa Bay off Springer—Off catwalk below left field roof—475 ft.
- May 16, 1992—Chicago off Baltimore's Milacki—To top of left field bleachers—466 ft.
- July 5, 1994—Detroit off Boever—To front edge of left field roof—463 ft.
- May 20, 1995—Chicago off California's Sanderson—To fourth row from top of bleachers in left—460 ft.
- July 3, 2005—Oakland off Zito—Into left field second deck—460 ft.
- August 4, 2003—Chicago off Kansas City's Field—High into left center field bleachers—454 ft.
- September 8, 1997—Chicago off Milwaukee's Karl—Near top of left field bleachers—453 ft.
- April 7, 2007—Tampa Bay off Silva—High into left center field seats—453 ft.
- July 23, 1993—Chicago off Milwaukee's Miranda—High into left center field bleachers—451 ft.

ankle injuries, Frank hit only 15 homers that season. He rebounded superbly in 2000 by enjoying career highs with 43 home runs and 134 RBI. For his noble efforts, Thomas finished second in the MVP balloting, won the AL Comeback Player of the Year distinction and was voted onto the White Sox All-Century team. But things fell apart again in 2001, when an early season triceps tear limited him to just four homers. Repeating the up-and-down cycle, Frank whacked 28 home runs in 2002, and actually recorded the longest drive of his career. Facing Johan Santana (of all people) in Chicago on July 23, Thomas finally cleared the left field bleachers. He had come close many times, but, with this 495-foot thunderbolt, he finally made it all the way.

Things got even better in 2003, when the Big Hurt smacked 42 homers, including several in the 450-foot vicinity. But, when he dropped off for two straight seasons in 2004 and 2005 (combined total of 30 homers), his relationship with the White Sox finally soured. He moved on to Oakland in 2006, and unexpectedly soared all the way back to 39 home runs.

After signing with Toronto in 2007, Frank displayed his enduring power by blasting a 453-foot shot into the upper left center field seats at St. Petersburg's Tropicana Field on April 7. Visiting Minnesota on June 28, 2007, Thomas recorded his 500th career home run by smacking a 400-footer into the bleachers in left center field. Frank returned to Oakland in 2008, where he added seven more homers, including number 521 in Detroit on August 9. That may be the final four-bagger in the remarkable career of Frank Thomas, but, considering his resilience, it wouldn't be a shock if he came back again in 2010.

NUMBER 6: WILY MO PENA—77 HOME RUNS—2002 TO 2008

On June 14, 2004 at Philadelphia's Citizens Bank Park, a large crowd assembled early. Local hero Jim Thome was one home run short of 400 for his career, and Cincinnati Reds superstar Ken Griffey Jr. was sitting at 499. They had come to see history. During batting practice, thousands congregated in "Ashburn Alley" above and beyond the outfield bleachers, where there were several eating establishments. Most of the talk focused on Thome and Griffey. But, suddenly, a ball flew from home

Wily Mo Pena

plate, and headed to left center field. It kept going long after everyone thought it would stop, and eventually cleared the alley before short-hopping a souvenir shop on the far side. All the talk about Thome and Griffey quickly stopped, and a buzz circulated in the crowd. "Who hit that ball?" At first, no one seemed to know. Then, slowly, the answer began to circulate. It was young Wily Mo Pena of the Reds.

That drive would have flown about 515 feet if unobstructed by stadium structure and permitted to return to field level. It's true that it's easier to hit home runs in batting practice than in actual games. However, since batting practice pitchers don't throw as hard as pitchers in competitive situations, there is less energy transferred to the bat, making it more difficult to hit for epic distances. Wily Mo Pena is a legendary batting practice hitter who is known to have recorded "longest-ever" blasts almost everywhere he has appeared. He hasn't done badly in games either. If he can somehow avoid injuries and stay in the lineup, Wily Mo will probably rank among the mightiest hitters ever to play the game.

Like so many of today's stars, Pena was born in the Dominican Republic. That was in 1982, and he grew so rapidly that the New York Mets signed him as an amateur free agent in 1998 at 16 years of age. That deal was voided in early 1999, whereupon the Yankees signed Wily and sent him to a rookie league. He batted .247 and managed only seven homers, but word spread about the distance of those few four-baggers. After a sub-par 2000 season, Pena was traded to the Cincinnati Reds in 2001, where he enjoyed a successful campaign (26 home runs) with their A-Level affiliate. When Wily performed reasonably well the next year at Double-A Chattanooga, the Reds brought him up for a late-season evaluation. It was on September 12, 2002 at Riverfront Stadium that Pena recorded his first big-league home run.

At 6'3" and 245 pounds, Wily Mo is a fearsome sight standing from the right side of the plate. Holding the bat far back in his stance, he seems to dare the pitcher to throw the ball anywhere within his reach. After overcoming a nasty hamstring injury, Pena did well in his brief stay at Triple-A Louisville in 2003, and then whacked five home runs in an 18-day period with the Reds in September. By 2004, Wily was finally ready for serious Major League participation and performed very well. In 110 games, he rocketed 26 home runs and slugged at a .527 rate. His longest of the season was launched on August 14 at Cincy's Great American Ballpark (later named Cinergy Field), which had opened a year earlier. It flew high into the seats in left center and was estimated at 473 feet.

Playing all three outfield positions in 2005, Pena had another solid season. But, considering his vast ability and potential, it really wasn't up to the expectations of the Cincinnati fans or management. He fought off more injuries and belted 19 homers along with a .492 slugging percentage. It's not difficult to identify Wily's single longest blow of

that year. He smashed one on April 17 in Cincinnati that landed high in the second deck in deep left center. It was a 502-foot gem that finally put Pena's remarkable strength on official display. Then, on June 29 in St. Louis, Pena crushed a ball two-thirds of the way up the center field backdrop that was estimated at 492 feet. It was another awesome shot.

The Reds seemed to lose patience in the spring of 2006 and traded Wily Mo to the Boston Red Sox. Unfortunately, he suffered another debilitating injury, this time in the form of a left wrist tendon that required surgery. Pena returned to action on July 30, and, within 24 hours, bombed a monstrous drive far over the Green Monster at Fenway Park in Boston. That shot was judged at 475 feet. Visiting Kansas City on August 8, Wily Mo pounded the ball to the aisle atop the left field bleachers for a homer that was conservatively estimated at 460 feet. Pena was again awe-inspiring, but his final total for the year stood at just 11 home runs.

Things stayed pretty much the same in 2007. On April 17 in Toronto, Wily Mo dropped some jaws by blasting a 470-foot homer to the top of the restaurant in dead center field. As of August 17, Wily was averaging 440 feet per home run, but there had been only five of them. He was shipped off to the Washington Nationals, where he was immediately installed as the regular left fielder. Pena responded two days later with a drive against the left field upper deck façade at RFK Stadium in D.C. On

September 10, Wily Mo rapped two homers versus the Marlins in Miami, and it was the shorter of the two that left everyone incredulous. In the 3rd inning off Scott Olsen, Pena sent a scorching line drive down the left field line that third baseman Miguel Cabrera tried to intercept. He attempted a leaping catch, but just missed. The ball kept flying like a bullet until it topped the outfield fence. There are occasional stories of infielders trying to leap for balls that leave the park. But they are mostly that . . . just stories. Once they are carefully researched, their validity fades away. Not this one; it really happened. It was a display of power that was reminiscent of Babe Ruth.

Wily Mo Pena was provided with an opportunity to show his mettle in 2008, but injuries again rained on Pena's parade. He tore his left oblique muscle during spring training, and then hit rock bottom with season-ending left rotator cuff surgery on July 14. For the entire year, Wily Mo recorded only two home runs, although one was a 441-foot scorching line drive into Washington's left field seats. Both the Nationals and Pena had hoped for 500 at-bats in 2008 and the chance to finally utilize his vast ability to maximum advantage. Obviously, it didn't happen, and, considering his apparent proclivity for injury, it is fair to wonder if Wily Mo will ever succeed as a Major League baseball player. Released by

WILY MO PENA'S 10 LONGEST HOME RUNS

- April 17, 2005—Cincinnati off Houston's Duckworth—High into second deck in deep left center—502 ft.

- June 29, 2005—St. Louis off Morris—High off backdrop in dead center field—492 ft.

- July 31, 2006—Boston off Cleveland's Byrd—To back of parking lot beyond left field wall—475 ft.

- August 14, 2004—Cincinnati off San Diego's Beck—High into seats in left center—473 ft.

- April 17, 2007—Toronto off Chacin—To top of restaurant in dead center field—470 ft.

- August 8, 2006—Kansas City off Hudson—To aisle atop left field bleachers—460 ft.

- August 12, 2006—Boston off Baltimore's Benson—High over wall in deep left center field—458 ft.

- September 18, 2004—Cincinnati off Chicago's Maddux—Far over center field fence—454 ft.

- August 10, 2006—Kansas City off Hernandez—Over fountain in deep left center field—451 ft.

- July 2, 2005—Cincinnati off Houston's Rodriguez—High into left center field seats—450 ft.

Washington in early 2009, Pena was signed to a minor league contract by the New York Mets. Sadly, that venture didn't succeed either. However, as of 2010, Pena is still just 28 years old, and there is realistic hope for a better future. His power is beyond question. If Wily Mo Pena stays healthy for just one full season, we may witness one of the great tape measure displays in the annals of his sport.

NUMBER 5: ALEX RODRIGUEZ—583 HOME RUNS—1995 TO 2009

Alex Rodriguez has been building a baseball resume since high school that can compare favorably with anyone who has ever played the sport. Is he the greatest ever? No, not quite. Compare his career slugging percentage and OPS with those compiled by the all-time leaders, and that question is readily answered. But he has always played infield, where offensive numbers are not generally as impressive as for outfielders. All in all, he has been magnificent, and certainly ranks among the top 10 players in baseball annals. He has also hit the ball with exceptional power.

Born in New York City in 1975, Alexander Emmanuel Rodriguez lived his early years in the Washington Heights section of town. At age four, his family moved back to their ancestral home in the Dominican Republic before finally settling in Miami, Florida. There, young Alex became a legend at Westminster Christian High School, winning a prep national championship in his junior year. As a senior, Rodriguez batted .505, hit nine home runs, and stole 35 bases in 33 games, while earning the USA Baseball National Player of the Year Award. Not surprisingly, Alex was taken first overall by the Seattle Mariners in the 1993 amateur draft.

In 1994, Rodriguez played for six different teams. His transcendent ability rocketed him through all three levels of minor league ball (A, AA, and AAA) in just a few months. On July 8 in Boston, he made his first big-league appearance. Of course, that season was cut short by the players' strike, whereupon Alex was sent to Calgary for more experience.

Alex Rodriguez

Photo by Jeanne Newman

He completed the year by playing winter ball back in the Dominican Republic. When the '95 campaign opened, Rodriguez was assigned to the Mariners' top affiliate at Triple-A Tacoma in the Pacific Coast League. In just 54 games, he batted .360, belted 15 home runs, drove in 45 runs, and slugged at the rate of .654. Obviously, minor league competition could not contain him. He was summoned back to the Big Show, and, at age 19, Alex recorded his first Major League homer on June 12, 1995, at the Seattle Kingdome.

In 1996, the year that Alex Rodriguez turned 21 years of age, he compiled numbers that are hard to believe. Playing shortstop, the 6'3", 200-pounder smashed 36 home runs and 54 doubles, while batting .358 and slugging .631. Along the way, he drove in 123 runs and scored 141 times! In Detroit on April 9, he drove a ball into the lower center-field seats for a 446-foot poke, and smacked a 448-footer in Toronto on June 25. Batting from the right side, Alex went to the opposite field with outside pitches, and still drove the ball out of the park. For such a young man, he had an amazingly sophisticated game. His future seemed limitless.

All the early indicators proved accurate. Over the next four years (1997 through 2000), Rodriguez continued to play superior defense at shortstop, while averaging 37 home runs a season. His longest drive in that time was a 465-footer into the Kingdome's left field second deck on April 6, 1998. But Seattle is a small market franchise, and the Mariners simply couldn't afford to keep Alex under contract. He was granted free agency and signed with the Texas Rangers for the 2001 season, where he somehow elevated his game to even higher standards. Still playing the defensively demanding position of short-stop, Alex recorded consecutive home run totals of 52, 57, and 47 from 2001 through 2003. For a man at his position, those totals represent some of the most extraordinary statistics in baseball history. Included in those 164 homers were dozens of drives in the 440-foot range. However, despite Rodriguez's individual brilliance, the Rangers still weren't winning, and, on February 16, 2004, the inevitable happened.

In one of baseball's biggest-ever transactions, Alex was traded to the New York Yankees for Alfonso Soriano. A-Rod was returning to the city of his birth and would finally play on a stage big enough for his vast talents. Of course, the Yanks had Derek Jeter entrenched as their shortstop and captain, which meant that Alex needed to move to third base. Predictably, Rodriguez easily handled the transition and banged out 36 home runs during his first season in pinstripes. If there were any noticeable changes, it was that Alex appeared to be getting stronger. After clouting a 456-footer to the second tier restaurant in Arizona on June 17, he reached the seventh row of the left field upper deck at Yankee Stadium on July 10. That 462-foot shot was believed to have been his longest in over six years.

In 2005, Rodriguez slammed 48 homers and won his second American League MVP Award, the first coming with Texas in 2003. Alex turned 30 that year, but his power was still rising. He bombed a 460-footer over Boston's Green Monster on July 17, and then attained his career-longest at Yankee Stadium on August 13. Facing Juan Dominguez of the Rangers in the 3rd inning, he walloped the ball far over the left field fence to the ambulance parking area near the outer stadium wall. It was such a monstrous blow that the Yanks measured the exact distance at 487 feet. The next day, he slammed one 453 feet into the visitors' bullpen in left center. The day after that in Tampa Bay, A-Rod launched one off the roof catwalk in deep left center. That blow was hard to estimate, but it certainly would have flown over 450 feet if unimpeded. That was three tape measure shots in as many days.

When Rodriguez added 35 home runs in 2006, he included another ball to the same distant sector as the year before in Yankee Stadium. This drive on June 15 landed just a few feet shorter than its predecessor and was computed at 480 feet. Always a tireless worker in the weight room, Alex now weighed 225

ALEX RODRIGUEZ'S 10 LONGEST HOME RUNS

- August 13, 2005—New York off Texas's Dominguez—Over back wall in deep left field—487 ft.
- June 15, 2006—New York off Cleveland's Lee—Over back wall in deep left field—480 ft.
- August 9, 2008—Los Angeles off Lackey—High onto boulders beyond left center field fence—468 ft.
- June 30, 2008—New York off Texas's Feldman—Into monument area in left center—467 ft.
- April 6, 1998—Seattle off New York's Pettitte—To second row in left field upper deck—465 ft.
- June 17, 2007—New York off New York's Hernandez—Over visitors' bullpen in left center—464 ft.
- July 10, 2004—New York off Tampa Bay's Brazleton—To seventh row in left field upper deck—462 ft.
- July 17, 2005—Boston off Wakefield—High over Green Monster just left of center—460 ft.
- April 16, 2008—New York off Boston's Buchholz—Into visitors' bullpen in left center—460 ft.
- August 15, 2005—Tampa Bay off Fossum—Off roof support in deep left center—458 ft.

pounds, and his strength was unquestioned. Next, in 2007, he reached Olympian performance levels by blasting 54 homers, while winning his third MVP title. Rodriguez replaced the legendary Jimmie Foxx on August 4 as the youngest player in Major League history to reach the 500 home run plateau. Alex kept going in 2008 (recording drives of 460, 460, 467, and 468 feet), and he seems destined to ultimately supplant Barry Bonds as baseball's all-time home run champion.

Rodriguez ran into his first serious roadblock starting the 2009 season, battling a serious hip injury along with embarrassing revelations about prior steroid use. Yet, he finished strong by winning his first World Series. Barring further serious injury or illness, Alex will probably exceed 800 homers before he retires. Under any circumstances, that is a wondrous accomplishment, but, considering his defensive responsibilities, it borders on the incredible. A-Rod is a player for the ages who hits the ball as hard as any man who has ever patrolled the left side of the infield.

NUMBER 4: MANNY RAMIREZ—546 HOME RUNS—1993 TO 2009

On October 16, 2007, during the American League Championship Series at Cleveland's Jacobs Field, Manny Ramirez drilled a home run 430 feet to right center field. That's a long way for a right-handed hitter to drive a base-

ball. More importantly, it was Manny's 23rd postseason homer, which is more than anyone else in Major League history. Ramirez has a reputation for his zany antics, which are usually explained by saying that it's just a matter of "Manny being Manny." Okay, the man is a little goofy. But think about that postseason statistic. It tells us that Ramirez is a great clutch hitter as well as a very strong batsman.

Manuel Aristides Ramirez was born in the Dominican Republic in 1972, moving to the Washington Heights section of New York City in 1985. By 1991, Manny finished his exceptional schoolboy career at George Washington High, where he was named the city's player of the year. Ramirez was the first round pick of the Cleveland Indians in the 1991 amateur draft. He did well in the Class-A Carolina League in 1992 and was promoted to the Double-A Eastern League the next year. In 1993, after 89 games with the Canton-Akron Indians, Manny had belted 17 home runs and driven in 79 runs. Cleveland then moved him up to the Triple-A Charlotte Knights in the International League to see what he could do. It didn't take him long to show them. Over the next 40 games, Ramirez hit 14 home runs and slugged at a .690 clip. The Indians then summoned him to the Big Show, where he made his first appearance on September 2, 1993. One day later, Manny recorded his first two Major League homers. On a day of splendid irony, they were hit at Yankee Stadium in front of hundreds of friends from his old neighborhood, which was situated minutes from the landmark ballpark. At age 21, he had arrived.

In his rookie year in 1994, Ramirez played in only 91 games, but still clubbed 17 home runs and slugged .521. When he competed in 137 games in 1995, his homer and slugging outputs increased to 31 and .558 respectively. It was in that year that Manny hit his first Major League tape measure job by belting a 450-footer in Baltimore on August 14. At 6 feet and 200 pounds, he was only average size for a big-league slugger, but Manny knew how to swing the bat. He blasted 33 dingers in 1996 and upped his slugging percentage to .582. He took a step backward in 1997, when he dropped off to 26 home runs, but still bashed his longest drives to date. On July 1 at Houston's Astrodome, Ramirez reached the left field upper deck with a 470-foot shot.

Manny not only rebounded in 1998, but actually elevated his production to superstar stature. He banged out 45 homers, drove in 145 runs, and accrued his highest-yet slugging percentage of .599. In 1999, Ramirez's ascendancy continued. He bombed another 44 home runs, including a 471-footer at Cleveland on September 19, and knocked in the extraordinary total of 165 runs. Manny also slugged at the rate of .663. Ramirez sustained some injuries in 2000, and his participation dropped to 118 games. However, when on the field, he was better than ever, posting a career-high slugging percentage of .697 while drilling 38 homers and recording 122 RBI. Those numbers from 1998 through 2000

Manny Ramirez

Photo by Mike Ivins/Boston Red Sox

were sensational, and when he became a free agent, the Boston Red Sox outbid the Indians and anxiously signed him to a contract on December 19, 2000.

The relationship between "Man-Ram" and the Red Sox was somewhat controversial, but it was also extremely productive. In that first season in 2001, Manny bashed 41 home runs, and a few of them were gigantic. At the Toronto SkyDome on June 2, he drilled a 454-footer against the façade of the left field fourth deck. The next day he topped that. Facing Chris Carpenter in the 4th inning, Ramirez blasted the ball into the fifth level just right of an exit. It was estimated at 491 feet. Those were impressive shots, and the pattern continued when the Blue Jays visited Boston's Fenway Park later that month. On June 23, 2001, Manny smashed an offering from Chris Michalak high over the left field wall. It seemed headed to the Massachusetts Turnpike, when it clanged off the light tower 100 feet above field level. That prodigious drive was judged at 501 feet.

Ramirez and the Red Sox kept plugging away in 2002 and 2003: the team winning lots of games and the player hitting lots (33 and 37) of home runs. Entering 2004, Boston had not won a World Series since Babe Ruth was in town in 1918. That was 86 years earlier, and the Red Sox Nation was past the point of impatience. Manny Ramirez didn't worry about such things. In fact, Manny didn't seem to worry about anything. Often criticized for his indifferent performances in left field and on the bases, Ramirez was known for intensity in only one area . . . hitting a baseball. He showed up early to prepare for batting practice and prided himself on being one of baseball's top sluggers. Manny shone again in 2004 by smacking 43 homers. The Sox had added designated hitter David Ortiz to their arsenal, and their firepower finally compared favorably to the Yankees. Ramirez blasted homers in the 455-foot range on May 4 in Cleveland and September 27 in Tampa Bay, and finally led Boston to a long-awaited World Series championship. It was the sweetest form of vindication for both the team and their temperamental cleanup hitter.

Manny returned in 2005 and bashed 45 more homers. His season-longest came on April 19 against Blue Jays' ace Roy Halladay, and landed in the parking lot beyond the Green Monster in left field. That ball did not land until it had flown 470 feet. Yet, that

MANNY RAMIREZ'S 10 LONGEST HOME RUNS

- June 23, 2001—Boston off Toronto's Michalak—High off light tower in left field—501 ft.

- June 3, 2001—Toronto off Hamilton—High into left field fifth deck—491 ft.

- July 26, 2007—Cleveland off Lee—Far over center field fence—481 ft.

- October 7, 2007—Los Angeles off Los Angeles's Weaver—High onto green center field backdrop—473 ft.

- September 19, 1999—Cleveland off New York's Cone—To top row in left field seats—471 ft.

- July 1, 1997—Houston off Minor—Into left field upper deck—470 ft.

- April 19, 2005—Boston off Toronto's Halladay—Over left field wall into parking lot—470 ft.

- October 1, 2005—Boston off New York's Johnson—Far over Green Monster to parking lot—463 ft.

- October 1, 2005—Boston off New York's Gordon—Over center field bleachers to back wall—463 ft.

- May 4, 2004—Cleveland off Davis—To top of left field bleachers—459 ft.

one was only 7 feet longer than a matching pair of 463-footers launched against the Yankees during a late-season showdown at Fenway Park on October 1. Ramirez slowed down a little in 2006, when some nagging injuries limited him to 130 games and 35 homers.

Then in 2007, he slipped even further. But on July 26 in Cleveland, Manny sent out a reminder that his superior ability was still intact. He unloaded a monstrous 481-foot homer to dead center field that served as a precursor to his postseason performance. During that October run, Manny Ramirez batted .341, and rapped four home runs, including a majestic 473-foot drive to the green backdrop adjacent to the boulders in Anaheim. In so doing, Ramirez led the Red Sox to their second World Series victory in three years. Slipping again in early 2008, he was shipped off to the Los Angeles Dodgers. But Manny decided to be Manny, and went on a rampage, batting a torrid .396 and slamming 17 homers in 53 games. Several of those home runs flew in the 440-foot range.

Who knows where Manny goes from here? In 2009, he suffered the indignity of missing 50 games for violating MLB's Joint Drug Agreement. Before serving the suspension, however, he drilled a 457-footer over the elevated railroad tracks in left field at Minute Maid Park in Houston. That blast against Astros' ace Roy Oswalt was delivered on April 22. Obviously, the ability is still there. Turning 38 in 2010, Manny Ramirez appears to have a lot of gas left in his tank.

NUMBER 3: RYAN HOWARD—222 HOME RUNS—2004 TO 2009

Batting and throwing left-handed, the 6'4", 245-pound Ryan Howard consistently punishes baseballs like few men before him. Born in St. Louis in 1979, Ryan starred at Lafayette High School and Southwest Missouri State before being picked by the Philadelphia Phillies in the fifth round of the 2001 amateur draft. He moved rapidly through the Phils' organization, winning MVP honors in 2003 and 2004 at A-Level Clearwater and AA-Level Reading. Howard also starred at Triple-A Scranton–Wilkes-Barre in the International League later in 2004 and wound up with 46 minor league homers.

Not surprisingly, Ryan made a "cup of coffee" appearance with Philadelphia late that same year, and smacked his first big-league home run at Shea Stadium on September 11, 2004. It was a rousing shot over the 396 foot sign in deep right center field. Howard certainly appeared ready for Major League play, but the Phils had veteran slugger Jim Thome entrenched at first base. Accordingly, Ryan returned to Scranton–Wilkes-Barre in 2005, and was in the process of tearing things up when Thome injured his right elbow. Batting a remarkable .371 after 61 games, Howard was quickly summoned by the Phils. This was his unexpected opportunity to shine. The result? Ryan Howard slugged 22 homers and drove in 63 runs in 88 games, while winning the National League Rookie of the Year Award.

Included among his four-baggers were some highly impressive drives. On August 28, Ryan slammed a ball 40 feet up the center field backdrop in Arizona. He also reached the right field upper deck in Washington on October 1. However, his longest was also one of many timely blows that helped to win ball games. On August 10, 2005, Howard ripped a 9th inning grand slam at Dodger Stadium to win 9–5. That rocket landed in the upper blue seats in deep right center and was estimated at 454 feet. The Phillies then did right by everyone by moving the popular Thome to the White Sox before the 2006 season. Jim recovered from his injuries and found a

Ryan Howard

good home in the Windy City. Ryan became an instant mega-star in the City of Brotherly Love.

As of April 23, 2006, Ryan Howard was regarded as a powerful batsman, but, by the end of that day, he was known as a super-stud. Citizens Bank Park had opened in Philadelphia in 2003. It had a hitter-friendly environment with relatively easy outfield dimensions, and looked like a good place for Howard to function as a home run hitter. However, there were some locations within the ballpark that did not seem reachable. One of them was "Ashburn Alley" beyond the tall brick batter's backdrop in center field. Named for Phillies' Hall of Famer Richie Ashburn, the alley serves as a food court and meeting place. In that direction, it is 450 feet from home plate, and elevated another 30 feet above field level.

Facing Florida's Sergio Mitre in the 4th inning, Ryan delivered a baseball to that land of hot dogs, handshakes, and cheese-steaks as fans gasped in amazement. That magnificent blow was estimated at 486 feet. Another remote plateau inside the park was the third deck in right field. Even Barry Bonds had been unable to place a ball there during batting practice. He had reached the façade a few times but couldn't make it all the way despite slamming away in those competitively benign circumstances. That all changed on June 20, 2006, when Ryan Howard squared off against veteran right-hander Mike Mussina of the Yankees. Batting in the

RYAN HOWARD'S 10 LONGEST HOME RUNS

- April 23, 2006—Philadelphia off Florida's Mitre—Over brick backdrop in dead center—486 ft.

- June 20, 2006—Philadelphia off New York's Mussina—To first row in right field third deck—481 ft.

- April 5, 2008—Cincinnati off Mercker—To top of backdrop just right of center—479 ft.

- June 27, 2007—Philadelphia off Cincinnati's Harang—Over brick backdrop in dead center field—472 ft.

- May 30, 2009—Philadelphia off Washington's Martis—To first row in right field upper deck—471 ft.

- August 31, 2006—Washington off Astacio—To third row of upper deck in right center—470 ft.

- June 30, 2007—Philadelphia off New York's Sosa—To top of second deck in deep right center—468 ft.

- July 15, 2006—San Francisco off Hennessey—Over 421 ft. sign in deep right center—460 ft.

- August 30, 2007—Philadelphia off New York's Hernandez—Just over alley railing left of center—460 ft.

- August 19, 2006—Philadelphia off Washington's Ortiz—To back wall of visitors' bullpen in center—458 ft.

1st inning, Ryan connected perfectly, and momentarily watched his handiwork fly away to right field. The normally modest young man apparently understood the force he had just unleashed. But he quickly regained his focus, lowered his head, and began trotting around the bases as the ball crashed into a seat of the first row in that top tier. This awesome poke was judged at 481 feet. Before the season ended, Ryan Howard recorded a club record total of 58 home runs. He also won the National League Most Valuable Player Award, and established himself as one of the baseball titans of the modern era.

Howard kept bombing away in 2007, when, despite a stint on the disabled list, he amassed 47 home runs. He started slowly, and several observers suggested that the cause was Ryan's sudden avoidance of opposite field hitting. Throughout his brief career, Howard had hit a high percentage of his homers to left center field. Early in '07, this was not the case. However, two days after returning from the DL on May 27 in Atlanta, Ryan parked one in the seats just left of center. The next day, back in Philly, he belted a ball into the lower deck in left center. Howard had found his stroke, and was back on track for the rest of the season.

As usual, the big guy excelled during interleague play, and blasted a 451-foot shot into Cleveland's second deck in right center field on June 19. At home, Ryan cleared the center field brick backdrop for the second time. This occurred on June 27, and resulted in a 472-foot estimate. He added a 468-footer to right center three days later. Perhaps his most impressive home park power performance came on August 30, when Howard climaxed a streak of opposite field homers. On this day, he drilled one just left of center that skipped over the railing fronting Ashburn Alley for a ride of 460 feet. Despite pulling almost everything to the right side for the first month-and-a-half of the season, Ryan finished with 15 opposite field home runs. When Ryan Howard hits to all fields, he is virtually unstoppable.

Upon starting slowly again in 2008, Howard was required to adjust once more. Although Ryan recorded his longest drive of the year on his first homer of the new campaign, his 479-footer to right center field in Cincinnati did not lead to early season success. By mid-May, he was struggling to produce, but Ryan appeared to widen his stance and shorten his stride. In so doing, he dropped off in distance, but significantly upped his efficiency. Howard wound up with 48 home runs and led the Philadelphia Phillies to their first World Series Championship in 28 years.

Showing genuine character and commitment, Ryan lost about 20 pounds during the off-season AFTER signing a multiyear contract. With his increased athleticism, he not only fielded better in 2009, but even consistently hit the ball farther than in '08. His 471-foot right field upper-decker at home on May 30 aptly demonstrated his renewed vigor. Ryan Howard hadn't turned 30 years of age when the 2009 season concluded. He will probably be with us for many years to come, and his final legacy will likely be historic.

NUMBER 2: JIM THOME—564 HOME RUNS—1991 TO 2009

In an era when many big-league ballplayers are regarded as selfish and self-serving, Jim Thome stands apart. In one poll, he was voted as one of the three friendliest players and, in another study, he was selected as "Best Teammate" in Major League Baseball. Jim wears his pants rolled up above his calves just like the old-timers and gives interviews without expecting anything in return. On the field, he swings with all his might, and sends baseballs flying in every direction. In short, Thome is the ultimate "throwback."

Jim was born in Peoria, Illinois, in 1970, and starred in both baseball and basketball at Limestone High School. He then attended Illinois Central Junior College, where he continued his mastery of both sports. Drafted by the Cleveland Indians in the 13th round of the 1989 amateur draft, Thome stayed with college ball for a while longer. He then did well enough in 27 games with the Class-A

Clearwater team in 1991 to motivate the Indians to call him up in September. Jim took the opportunity to record his first big-league homer, driving one into the Yankee Stadium right field grandstand on October 4, 1991.

Thome started 1992 at Double-A Canton/Akron, but was quickly promoted to Triple-A Colorado Springs. At 6'4" and weighing 225 pounds, Jim was expected to hit home runs. For whatever reason, Thome did little of that in 1992 despite batting well over .300. He again played for Cleveland at the end of the year, but was assigned to the Charlotte Knights in the AAA International League in 1993. This time, the left-handed-hitting third baseman flexed his large muscles and belted 25 homers in just 115 games. That warranted yet another summons from the parent club, and, this time, Jim stayed for good. In 47 games, Thome socked seven home runs and batted .266, allowing him to begin the 1994 season as the starter at the "hot corner."

That season was cut short by a labor dispute, but, in only 98 games, Jim walloped 20 homers. Thome continued to grow and upped his total to 25 four-baggers in 1995 while leading the Indians to the American League pennant. At this point, Jim Thome was an established big-league power hitter, but, when the 1996 season ended, he was a genuine star. On May 21 at Cleveland's Jacobs Field, he ripped one into the second deck in right field for a drive of 454 feet. At Baltimore's Camden Yards on July 26, Jim sent a ball soaring far over the right center

Jim Thome

© Ron Vesely/Chicago White Sox

field wall, landing halfway across the Eutah Street promenade. It then bounced against the B&O Warehouse after flying 460 feet. Those were only two of 38 homers, which combined with a .311 batting average and .612 slugging percentage.

Thome switched from third to first base for the 1997 season, but his power output stayed the same. He cracked 40 home runs, including a 455-footer on July 12 to the back of the right field upper deck in Minnesota. That was followed by three years of consistent slugging, where Jim averaged 33 dingers per season. The longest individual drives each year included a 483-foot blast on May 31, 1998 in Toronto to the third level just right of center field above the restaurant. Also featured was the absolute longest poke in the baseball life of Jim Thome, which flew off his bat in Cleveland on July 3, 1999. That epic blow cleared the fence in center and bounced through a gate on its way to Eagle Avenue. The actual flight distance was computed at 511 feet. The lengthiest in 2000 also took place at Jacobs Field and traveled 479 feet to right field on July 17. At age 30, Jim wasn't going to get any stronger, but he was about to become even more productive.

Thome had been consistently superior from 1998 through 2000, but escalated his effort to consistently great from 2001 through 2003. In those latter three years, Jim slammed 49, 52, and 47 home runs respectively. In 2001, he recorded drives in Cleveland that sailed 473 feet on May 8, 472 feet on July 6, and 462 feet on July 7. Then, in his peak performance year in 2002, Thome slugged at a .677 clip, while hitting matching 470-footers on May 30 and July 26 in Cleveland. Despite those exceptional exploits, or perhaps because of them, Jim left the Indians to sign a lucrative long-term contract with the Phillies. He did not disappoint his new employer.

In 2003, Thome whacked 47 homers in his new uniform, and many of them flew a long way. He hit one at Shea Stadium on July 10 that cleared the bleachers in left center. That was an opposite field poke of 445 feet. Philadelphia fans had not seen such raw power since the days of Mike Schmidt and

JIM THOME'S 10 LONGEST HOME RUNS

- July 3, 1999—Cleveland off Kansas City's Wengert—Far over fence in center and hit pillar—511 ft.

- May 31, 1998—Toronto off Hentgen—Over restaurant in deep right center—483 ft.

- July 17, 2000—Cleveland off Houston's Miller—To auxiliary bleachers in right center—479 ft.

- May 30, 2002—Cleveland off Detroit's Greisenger—Over fence in center to picnic area—474 ft.

- May 8, 2001—Cleveland off Kansas City's Henry—Far over fence in deep right center—473 ft.

- July 6, 2001—Cleveland off St. Louis's Morris—High into right field seats—472 ft.

- July 26, 2002—Cleveland off Detroit's Santana—High into right field seats—470 ft.

- April 7, 2000—Tampa Bay off Guzman—Off "C" ring on center field roof—465 ft.

- June 4, 2008—Chicago off Kansas City's Hochevar—Over shrub backdrop in dead center field—464 ft.

- July 7, 2001—Cleveland off Seattle's Veres—Deep into right field seats—462 ft.

Greg Luzinski. That was the final season for Veterans Stadium, and Jim recorded the last Vet four-bagger by reaching the right center field seats on September 27. Citizens Bank Park opened on April 3, 2004, with an exhibition game against the Cleveland Indians. Jim struck the stadium's first homer by planting the ball into the ninth row of the second deck in right field. For the year, Thome belted 42 home runs, including a bunch of 450-footers into that same second deck.

Unfortunately, Jim was bit by the injury bug in 2005, and dropped to just seven homers. He suffered a season-ending case of right elbow tendonitis whereupon the Phils called up minor league sensation Ryan Howard to take his place. The young phenom won the National League Rookie of the Year Award. With two sluggers at the same position, Philly worked out a trade with the Chicago White Sox. However, before he left, Jim recorded one final tape measure shot for the fans who had come to love him in the City of Brotherly Love. On July 9, 2005, Thome smoked a 455-foot beauty to the eighth row in the right center field second deck.

From 2006 through 2009, Jim was making friends and pounding homers in the Windy City. Career Number 500 sailed to left center field in Chicago on September 16, 2007. At age 38 in 2008, Thome pounded 34 homers, including two shots to center field that were measured at 461 and 464 feet. In 2009, he was still going strong, recording two home runs and seven RBI on July 17 in Chicago. The

second of those two homers sailed over the vine backdrop in center field, and was measured at 460 feet. As the seasons have rolled by, two things have stayed constant in the baseball world of Jim Thome. First, wherever he plays, both fans and players love the guy. Second, he keeps hitting the ball for prodigious distances. Now, nearing the end of his playing days, the man has earned his lofty ranking among modern ultra-strong sluggers.

NUMBER 1: ADAM DUNN—316 HOME RUNS—2001 TO 2009

Born in Houston in 1979, Adam Dunn is a prototypical Texan. Standing 6'6" and weighing 275 pounds, it is no wonder that his home runs are as big as his home state. But Dunn is not just large; he can also run with surprising speed and throw with power and accuracy. Accordingly, Adam has always been an outstanding athlete. At North Caney High School, he excelled not just in baseball but also in football as one of the top prep quarterbacks in America. Scouts assumed that football would be his first choice, and, as a result, he slid to Cincinnati's second round pick in the 1998 amateur draft. The Reds would soon benefit from their gamble.

Accepting a football scholarship to the University of Texas, Dunn was red-shirted in his freshman year at Austin in the fall of 1998. Hoping to displace starting quarterback Major Applewhite during spring drills in 1999, Adam suffered a disappointment. The

Adam Dunn

ergy Field. It flew 425 feet into the green seats in right field and initiated a startling series of events. During the month of August alone, the imposing rookie belted 12 homers. For the entire 2001 season (minor and Major Leagues), Dunn struck a total of 54 home runs, and most of them flew over 400 feet. He played left and right fields, stole bases, and showed a level of athletic maturity that was rarely seen in first-year players. It all climaxed on October 2 in Chicago's Wrigley Field, when Adam launched a massive blast over the right center field bleachers that flew nearly 500 feet. It had been a truly eventful campaign.

In 2002, Adam Dunn hit the solid, but unspectacular, total of 26 home runs. He seemed well on his way to significant improvement in the next year, when he blasted Number 27 on August 15, 2003. However, he also injured his thumb on that same date, thereby ending his season prematurely. Earlier on that fateful day, Adam had rocketed a 454-foot homer in Cincinnati, which was actually 10 feet shorter than his blast on June 14, 2003, in the same place. This all led to Dunn's breakout season in 2004. Adam upped his homer output to 46, while also batting .266, slugging .569, walking 108 times, stealing six bases, scoring 105 times, and driving in 106 runs. Amidst the triumph, there was one dark cloud. Dunn struck out a then-record 195 times. That was the biggest flaw in his game, and will likely remain so for his entire career. But his power is the best countermeasure.

Longhorns had just recruited Chris Simms, another Prep-All-America QB, and head coach Mac Brown experimented with Dunn at tight end. That did it. As the Cincinnati Reds reacted gleefully, Adam Dunn gave up the sport of football. It then took less time than expected for the left-handed-hitting slugger (he throws from the right side) to make it to the big leagues. After successful stints with minor league franchises in Billings, Rockport, Chattanooga, and Louisville, Adam was called up to the Reds on July 20, 2001 at age 22. Up to that time, he had batted .334 and slugged 32 homers, including 460-footers in Indianapolis and Louisville.

Adam Dunn recorded his first Major League home run on July 27, 2001 at Cincinnati's Cin-

During his noteworthy 2004 season, Adam hammered home runs of 449, 450, 452, and 458 feet. That was an impressive performance, but then came August 10 at Cinergy Field. In the 4th inning against the Dodgers' Jose Lima, Dunn connected perfectly, driving the ball just right of center field. On and on it flew, soaring high over the fence, clearing the batter's backdrop and eventually landing at the rear of a pavilion before rolling into the Ohio River. Club officials investigated thoroughly and concluded that the ball had flown the astounding distance of 535 feet. Some cynics dispute that final tally, but independent research confirms that, even if there has been some inadvertent hyperbole, it is minor in scope. Without doubt, this drive traveled well over 500 feet in the air.

With the advent of the 2005 season, Adam Dunn settled into a period of remarkable consistency. Despite his best efforts, the strikeouts continued, but so did the high percentage of walks. Dunn is an aggressive hitter, but his aggressiveness is tempered by discipline and self-control. He regularly runs high pitch counts, which is most unpleasant

ADAM DUNN'S 10 LONGEST HOME RUNS

- August 10, 2004—Cincinnati off Los Angeles's Lima—Out of stadium just right of dead center—530 ft.
- September 27, 2008—Arizona off Colorado's Rusch—Line drive high off scoreboard in center field—504 ft.
- October 2, 2001—Chicago off Farnsworth—Far over bleachers in right center—490 ft.
- April 6, 2006—Cincinnati off Pittsburgh's Grabow—Between pillars in deep right center—479 ft.
- September 20, 2001—Cincinnati off Chicago's Duncan—To scaffold on new stadium in right center—475 ft.
- July 28, 2009—Milwaukee off Villanueva—Onto concourse in deep right center field—473 ft.
- September 11, 2007—Cincinnati off St. Louis's Mulder—High off backdrop in dead center—471 ft.
- May 4, 2005—Cincinnati off St. Louis's Cali—Far over center field fence—470 ft.
- May 17, 2008—Cincinnati off Cleveland's Kobayashi—To top row in right field bleachers—468 ft.
- June 16, 2005—Cincinnati off Atlanta's Smoltz—Far over center field fence—465 ft.

for opposing pitchers, and, despite his modest batting averages, his on-base percentages have been surprisingly high. Upon reaching base, he doesn't just stand there. Although he doesn't steal as many bases these days (19 stolen bases in 2002 and 1 in 2008), he still runs well, and scores a lot of runs. He has experimented at first base, but has settled into corner outfield as his permanent position. Most observers, however, feel that Adam is now an indifferent defender. His essence is his power.

From 2005 through 2008, Dunn hit exactly 40 home runs each year. Many of them were majestically long. In '05, they included drives in Cincy of 464, 465, and 470 feet. They were followed by comparable blows at Cinergy Field in 2006 that flew 458, 460, and 479 feet. That last one was a real eye-opener. It flew between the pillars atop the seats in deep right center, and bounded out of the stadium on April 6. On the road, Adam recorded a 460-foot shot to right center in Denver's Coors Field on May 4, 2006. There was more of the same in 2007, as Dunn mastered Cinergy Field with four-baggers of 453 and 455 feet. He then bettered those blasts on September 11 by slamming a 471-footer high off the center field backdrop. As a visitor, Adam poked one 450 feet in Pittsburgh on April 27, broke some scoreboard lights with a 460-footer in New York on July 15, and reached Milwaukee's right field top deck with a 455-foot shot on August 17.

Dunn was fortunate to play in a hitter's ballpark in Cincy, and, during his brief stay

in Phoenix, he enjoyed the benign conditions at Chase Field. On September 27, 2008, he smashed a sizzling line drive through the 1,086-foot altitude to the scoreboard in straightaway center field. The ball clanged off the so-called Jumbotron 67 feet above the field at a linear distance of 408 feet. Since this blow was actually timed at 3.94 seconds of flight time, it was reliably estimated at 504 feet. In 2004, Richie Sexson had launched one even higher off the scoreboard, but, since his was a high fly, it was judged at 495 feet.

Dunn moved on to the Washington Nationals for the 2009 campaign where he enjoyed another highly productive season. Considering his vast natural power, Dunn will continue to build his legacy of long distance clouts wherever he takes the field. On a return visit to Arizona on May 9 and 10, 2009, Dunn poled a pair of bookend shots to either side of that same scoreboard, which were respectively measured at 462 and 465 feet.

HONORABLE MENTIONS

It was difficult to limit this list to only 12 current sluggers. Baseball is gifted with the talents of so many powerful performers that a case for top-10 inclusion could be made for many players who didn't make the list. Veterans like David Ortiz and Carlos Delgado have enjoyed remarkably successful careers as sluggers, but their long-distance resumes didn't appear quite as impressive as some others. That doesn't mean that they are not as strong as those making the list. They may have fashioned their swings for peak efficiency at the expense of a few feet of linear distance on their batted balls.

Young guns like Nelson Cruz, Mark Reynolds, and Justin Upton can hit the ball as far as anyone playing today but haven't been around long enough to compile a lengthy career tape measure log. Reynolds has hit tape measure shots so regularly since arriving in 2007 that he seems to be heralding the second coming of Jimmie Foxx. Check back in a few years, and several of the younger sluggers will almost certainly rank higher. Here is a partial listing of other power-hitters who should also be recognized:

- Lance Berkman
- Russell Branyan
- Nelson Cruz
- Carlos Delgado
- Ken Griffey Jr.
- Vladimir Guerrero
- Travis Hafner
- Josh Hamilton
- Andruw Jones
- Mark Reynolds
- Richie Sexson (currently inactive)
- Gary Sheffield
- Justin Upton

Seven

Historical Rankings:
10 through 1

NUMBER 10—REGGIE JACKSON—563 HOME RUNS—1967 TO 1987

Ask this question to a group of middle-aged baseball fans: "What is the longest ball you ever saw hit?" The most common answer might be: "Reggie Jackson's 1971 All-Star shot in Detroit." Indeed, it was an awesome drive, and it was authored by the first man on the final list of baseball's strongest-ever batsmen. Reginald Martinez Jackson was born in 1946 in the suburbs of Philadelphia and grew into a 6-foot, 210-pound bundle of left-handed-hitting muscle. He combined power and showmanship like no one else since Babe Ruth.

After starring in football, track, and baseball at Cheltenham High School, Jackson enrolled at Arizona State University in 1964 on a football scholarship. However, after his freshman year, he focused only on baseball in order to pursue his ambitions to play in the big leagues. He excelled on the diamond and was taken as the second overall pick in the 1966 amateur draft by the Kansas City Athletics. Reggie continued his rapid ascendancy with instant success at both Class-A Modesto (1966) in California and Class-AA Birmingham (1967) in the Southern Association. When

summoned to the Major Leagues for the first time in June 1967, Jackson had just turned 21 years of age. He recorded his first big-league home run for the Athletics on September 17 of that season by knocking a ball over the right center field wall in Anaheim.

By the start of Reggie's official rookie season in 1968, the Athletics had relocated to Oakland, California. Jackson belted 29 homers that year, including four drives high into the

Reggie Jackson

right center field bleachers during visits to Yankee Stadium. However, the longest of the bunch was struck back in Anaheim on September 1. It took a majestic flight high into the right field bleachers, and was estimated at 489 feet. That tremendous blow stamped Reggie Jackson as one of baseball's longest hitters, but it was only the beginning.

Reggie spent much of 1969 on pace to break Roger Maris's then-record home run total of 61. He eventually cooled off, but still finished with the impressive total of 47. On May 30, Jackson lined one off the façade of the right field second deck in Oakland, and then reached that second deck on August 2. Both shots approximated 450 feet in flight, and their distance focused attention on the strength of the young hometown slugger. On the road, Reggie was even more lethal. Jackson cleared both the inner and outer right field fences in Kansas City on June 16 when his 480-footer landed on Brooklyn Avenue. That was outstanding work, but it was about 30 feet short of Reggie's even mightier blow in the same park on April 20.

On this day, the sophomore star recorded the first of two historic home runs off the tops of American League scoreboards. The Kansas City moon shot collided with the top of the board in deep right center field at a linear distance of 440 feet. In a rather odd coincidence, Reggie smashed another drive on July 5 in Minnesota that was remarkably similar. The Twins' ballpark featured a scoreboard that was positioned just like the one used by the newly formed Kansas City Royals. They were both constructed just right of center field and towered about 60 feet above the ground, close to 450 feet from home plate. In Minneapolis, Jackson's blast struck a beer sign just a few feet below the top. These two classic four-baggers were wind-aided, but that is the case with most historically long home runs. They traveled about 510 feet and 520 feet respectively, and proved that this 23-year-old prodigy was already one of the strongest hitters in the annals of his sport.

Reggie Jackson had an off year in 1970 when he feuded with mercurial A's owner Charles Finley for much of the season. However, he still managed to club 23 homers, including a couple in the 450-foot range. The first was launched deep into the right field upper deck at RFK Stadium in Washington on May 2, and the second landed in the center field upper deck near the flagpole at Tiger Stadium in Detroit on August 30. It was in that same ballpark in the Motor City that Reggie Jackson reached the pinnacle of his long-distance career the following season.

Jackson hit 32 homers in 1971, but it was his All-Star four-bagger on July 13 for which he is probably best remembered. Facing Dock Ellis in the 3rd inning, Reggie lined one with all his might toward the 90-foot-high grandstand roof in right center field. The ball gave the appearance of rising until it struck the light tower on the roof, before ricocheting back onto the field. Many seasoned observers instantly labeled this blow as the longest they had ever witnessed. It's impossible to know exactly how far the ball would have flown if left unimpeded, but the best estimate is about 540 feet. It was certainly struck with savage ferocity. Jackson also recorded a 460-footer to center field in Oakland on May 22 as well as a 475-footer into the right center field upper deck in Chicago's Comiskey Park on July 6. It was a memorable year.

Led by their charismatic outfielder, the Oakland Athletics had become a great team by this time. From 1971 through 1975, they topped the American League West, and they won the World Series three straight years from 1972 to 1974. Along the way, Reggie Jackson settled into a pattern of consistent power production. He averaged 30 home runs per year and always managed at least one legitimate tape measure shot per season. On June 23, 1972, Nolan Ryan defeated the Athletics with a masterful two-hitter in Oakland. Ryan spent most of the game blowing hitters away with his legendary 100-mph fastball, but tried to trick Reggie Jackson with a slow curve in the 1st inning. That was a big mistake! The ball struck a green canvas atop the center field bleachers for a ride of 475 feet. On July 20, 1973, Reggie deposited one of Gaylord Perry's offerings to Oakland's top bleacher row in right field for a total flight of about 480 feet. Apparently, Hall of Fame pitchers posed no special impediment to Reggie Jackson.

On August 28, 1974, Reggie clubbed a pair of 425-foot homers to right field at Mil-waukee's County Stadium, but they were considered petite compared to two monstrous foul blasts. On that day as well as the day before, Jackson pounded 500-foot shots into the newly constructed right field upper deck. Reggie then finished his tenure in Oakland by pounding 36 homers in 1975. Charley Finley could no longer afford to meet the payroll of his star-spangled roster and started to dismantle his dynastic team. Before he left, however, Reggie visited Anaheim on June 28, 1975, where he launched a 430-footer to center field and a 453-footer to the back of the bullpen in right field.

Reggie would spend only one year at his next stop in Baltimore, but he made it count. He clubbed 27 homers in 1976, including a 500-footer high off the back wall of the right field bullpen in Kansas City on July 20. It was a respectable year, but only a prelude. In 1977, Reggie Jackson put on the pinstripes of the New York Yankees, and it seemed like a perfect match. It was never easy for Reggie in New York, since controversy followed him everywhere. But Jackson did not shy away from the spotlight, which had never shined brighter than in the Big Apple. Reggie recorded 32 homers in his first year with the Yanks along with five more against the Dodgers in the World Series. The final three occurred on consecutive swings on October 18 at Yankee Stadium, with the last one landing on the black backdrop in center field. That 465-foot beauty paced the Yankees to their first World Series championship in 15 years.

REGGIE JACKSON'S 10 LONGEST HOME RUNS

- July 13, 1971—Detroit off Pittsburgh's Ellis—Line drive off light tower on roof in right center—540 ft.
- July 5, 1969—Minnesota off Perry—High off scoreboard in deep right center—520 ft.
- April 20, 1969—Kansas City off Bunker—High off scoreboard just right of center—510 ft.
- July 20, 1976—Kansas City off Gura—Off top of back wall in right field bullpen—500 ft.
- September 1, 1968—Anaheim off Wright—Far over right field fence—489 ft.
- June 16, 1969—Kansas City off Butler—Over outer right field wall onto street—480 ft.
- July 20, 1973—Oakland off Cleveland's Perry—To top row of right field bleachers—480 ft.
- July 6, 1971—Chicago off Bradley—High into upper deck in deep right center—475 ft.
- June 23, 1972—Oakland off California's Ryan—Off green backdrop in center field—475 ft.
- April 15, 1983—Minnesota off Viola—Far over center field fence—472 ft.

Reggie stayed with New York for four more years, and again averaged about 30 homers a season. He didn't get any weaker during that time. Jackson regularly lofted balls deep into the upper (third) right field deck at Yankee Stadium. On one occasion, May 9, 1979, Reggie went the other way, depositing a homer beyond "Death Valley" into the bullpen in left center. Jackson did just as well on the road. On May 6, 1980, he smacked one to the 20th row past the 392 foot sign near center field in Milwaukee. Then, on July 11 in Texas, Reggie reached the 10th row of the green seats in center field against a strong incoming breeze. Each of these drives traveled about 450 feet.

At age 36, Reggie Jackson played for the California Angels in 1982. He stayed there for five years and hit 123 home runs as he wound down his exceptional career. Jackson had a habit of hitting long homers in Anaheim as a visitor, and nothing changed as a hometown performer. On May 12, 1982, Reggie bombed a homer halfway up the bleachers in right center, and, on October 2, 1982, he reached the green backdrop in dead center. Both of those blasts soared somewhere around 465 feet. When Jackson reported to work in Anaheim on June 10, 1983, with a 102-degree fever, he was judged too weak to play. However, when called to pinch hit in the 10th inning, he responded with a 470-foot clout to right center. Reggie reached the same area on May 28, 1984, with his 10th career grand slam. Four months later, Jackson recorded Career Number 500 with a 420-foot drive high in the right field terrace. On August 19, 1985, Reggie knocked one into the "football seats" just right of center. Referencing his latest masterpiece after the game,

Jackson remarked, "I can't hit it any better." To round out his Anaheim tape measure resume, Reggie logged a pair of 450-footers in 1986 (September 18 and 21).

Jackson spent his final season back in Oakland in 1987. Just before his 41st birthday, Reggie showed that he still had it. On April 30, he dented a bleacher seat four rows from the top in right field. That was a 460-foot shot. Finally, on August 17, 1987, Reggie Jackson hit his 563rd and last Major League home run. It was a fitting climax. He directed it to right field in Anaheim while wearing an Athletics uniform. That was the exact way it all started back in 1967. Reggie Jackson was a unique player. He oozed talent, flair, drama, timing, and charisma, but, more than anything else, he succeeded because of his extraordinary power. He hit them often and he hit them far. During his 21 seasons in the big leagues, Jackson sent baseballs flying into oblivion everywhere he played. Everybody enjoyed the show, perhaps Reggie more than anyone else.

NUMBER 9: HARMON KILLEBREW—573 HOME RUNS—1955 TO 1975

Harmon Killebrew was born to hit home runs. Recommended to the original Washington Senators by a real senator from his home state of Idaho, Harmon was signed before his 18th birthday. Due to some archaic roster rules of that time, Killebrew spent most of his first five seasons (1954–1958) sitting on the Washington bench. Even in his few early plate appearances, he displayed enormous power. While still only 18 years old on June 24, 1955, Harmon hit his first Major League home run at Griffith Stadium in Washington, D.C. The left field fence was situated almost 400 feet from home plate back then, and, yet, Killebrew's shot traveled to the 24th row in the bleachers. It was a stunning drive of about 470 feet, but it was only an indicator of better things to come.

Harmon finally got his chance in 1959 at age 23, and he took full advantage. He led the American League with 42 home runs, and many of them were genuine leviathans. On the road, Killebrew belted 450-footers in Chicago, Cleveland, Kansas City, and Boston as well as a 470-footer into the parking lot in Kansas City on July 27. At home, he drove one two-thirds of the way up the distant left field bleachers for a 465-footer on May 20, but later topped that distance twice. On June 19, Harmon reached the 28th row, and on July 11, he knocked one into the 26th row. Those blows were estimated at 490 feet and 485 feet respectively, and identified Killebrew as the strongest right-handed batsman in the American League.

Harmon dropped off to "only" 31 homers in 1960, but that output was remarkable in the overall context. First, he suffered two serious muscle pulls (one in his hamstring and the other in his left shoulder), which curtailed much of his playing time in the first half of the season. Second, he switched defensive positions. Originally signed as a second baseman, Killebrew filled out his 6-foot frame with about 210 pounds of muscle, thereby making middle-infield play somewhat impractical. He moved to third base for his breakout season in 1959, but then played more than half the time in 1960 at first base. Harmon was next stationed in left field, but then spent the rest of his career moving back and forth between first base, third base, and, near the end, designated hitter. Harmon Killebrew may have been a defensive gypsy, but he was always a great slugger.

Included among Harmon's 31 dingers in 1960 were two that were especially noteworthy. He launched one off the façade of the left field roof at Detroit's Tiger Stadium on September 11. That target was about 372 feet away and 85 feet high, and, since the roof had never been reached, it was regarded as quite a poke. However, the homer on August 6 at Chicago's symmetrical Comiskey Park was even more impressive. Any drive to either rooftop in left or right field was regarded as historic, and records were kept for every roof-topper. Since Killebrew's shot on this occasion didn't reach the roof, it has largely been forgotten. That's too bad since Harmon personally rated it as the hardest ball he ever hit. Facing Herb Score in the 3rd inning, Killebrew smashed a sizzling line drive toward the left field upper deck. The ball appeared to be rising when it crashed into a vertical support beam just under the roof. It then

Harmon Killebrew

Courtesy of the National Baseball Hall of Fame and Museum

caromed all the way back to the shortstop as Harmon jogged around the bases. This home run was struck with brutal ferocity, and probably would have flown around 500 feet.

In 1961, when the Senators relocated to Minneapolis–Saint Paul, they became the Minnesota Twins. Harmon Killebrew felt right at home and blasted 46 home runs. His first-ever at Metropolitan Stadium, recorded on April 30, thudded halfway up the batting eye in dead center field for a masterful 475-footer. The left field bleachers had not been topped with a second deck at that time, and Killebrew blasted one near the top to the 39th row on May 10. That was a drive in the 480-foot range. As a visitor, Harmon peaked in Kansas City from September 8 through 10, where he clubbed three homers between 450 and 470 feet. Killebrew kept getting better, and ripped

48 homers in 1962. And on August 3 in Detroit he eclipsed his roof façade shot from two years earlier. This time, he actually reached the towering left field rooftop, which no hitter had done since its construction in 1938. That memorable drive was judged at 505 feet.

Harmon added 45 more four-baggers in 1963, which featured twin 450-footers into the left field grandstand at Cleveland's Municipal Stadium on May 17 and 18. He also reached the left center field upper deck at D.C. Stadium (later renamed RFK Stadium) on August 26. There was a new Senators franchise in Washington by then, and Killebrew did well when returning to his original Major League home. He had hit a comparable homer high into the left field upper tier in the same park the year before. He, of course, sparkled in his current house as well. Harmon planted another ball into the 39th row of the left field bleachers at Metropolitan Stadium on June 18 for one more 480-foot homer.

Among Killebrew's 49 home runs in 1964 were a few beauties hit on the road. He bashed one high off the left center field light tower at Fenway Park on May 17, and then cleared the hedges in the same direction at Baltimore's Memorial Stadium exactly one week later. Both of those shots were recorded at about 470 feet. Harmon dislocated his left elbow midway through 1965, but still salvaged a 25-homer season. He drove a couple of 400-footers into the left field grandstand at Yankee Stadium on June 20, but they were dwarfed by a double and triple hit on the same visit to the Bronx. It was 457 feet to deepest left center and 466 feet to dead center in "The House That Ruth Built" in those days, Killebrew hitting two 455-footers in those respective directions. When Harmon rebounded with 39 home runs the following year, it was good news for Twins' fans. His single best shot landed near the base of the giant "A" frame scoreboard in left center field at Anaheim. That drive on June 20, 1966, was measured at 476 feet.

"Killer" ripped 44 more in 1967, and set the all-time Metropolitan Stadium distance record along the way. The left field bleachers had been topped with a second deck two years earlier, and it was doubtful that the higher deck would ever be reached by a batted ball. That changed on June 3, when with the help of a strong tailwind, Harmon cannonaded one into the second row for an eye-popping blast of 522 feet. In the long history of that ballpark, no home run was judged to have flown as far. And, amazingly, Killebrew dented the upper deck façade during the next game for a 510-foot follow-up.

Harmon was playing in the All-Star Game on July 9, 1968 when he was the focus of a gruesome sight. In stretching for a throw at first base, he split too far, and tore his groin in an excruciatingly painful injury. He sagged to a then-career low 17 home runs, but came roaring back with 49 homers in 1969. That matched his career high, and, at age 33, it was a most gratifying comeback. His raw strength was still intact as well. Killebrew

HARMON KILLEBREW'S 10 LONGEST HOME RUNS

- June 3, 1967—Minnesota off California's Burdette—To second row in left field upper deck—522 ft.
- June 4, 1967—Minnesota off California's Sanford—Off façade of left field upper deck—510 ft.
- August 3, 1962—Detroit off Bunning—Onto left field grandstand roof—505 ft.
- August 6, 1960—Chicago off Score—Line smash off girder under left field roof—500 ft.
- June 19, 1959—Washington off Detroit's Foytack—To 28th row in left field bleachers—490 ft.
- July 11, 1959—Washington off Baltimore's Brown—To 26th row in left field bleachers—485 ft.
- May 10, 1961—Minnesota off Baltimore's Stock—To 39th row in left field bleachers—480 ft.
- June 18, 1963—Minnesota off Chicago's Fisher—To 39th row in left field bleachers—480 ft.
- June 20, 1966—Anaheim off Brunet—To base of A-frame scoreboard in left—476 ft.
- April 30, 1961—Minnesota off Chicago's Shaw—Halfway up backdrop in center field—475 ft.

again banged one halfway up the center field backdrop in Minnesota on July 17 that calculated to a ride of 475 feet.

When Harmon Killebrew smacked 41 home runs in 1970, it looked like he might go on forever. There was even talk of him breaking the Bambino's then-career record of 714 four-baggers. And why not? He was just 34 years old and full of vigor. He demonstrated that with 450-footers in Anaheim on July 12 and in Detroit on August 2. However, Harmon had limitations like everyone else, and soon began the same inevitable decline that all athletes experience. He dropped to 28 homers in 1971 and failed to hit a bona fide tape measure shot for the first time since the '50s. But he did record Career Number 500 on August 10 in

front of his appreciative home fans. There was still plenty of fire left in the furnace.

Killebrew logged the highly respectable total of 26 home runs in 1972, and, at least for a time, regained his tape measure status. On July 1, Harmon unloaded to left field at Comiskey Park, and did something that he had never done as a younger man. He reached the left field roof, thereby earning the final spur on his impressive long-distance resume. Since that structure (the grandstand roof, not the ballpark) was built in 1927, it had served as the perfect barometer for judging great power hitters. If Killebrew had not gone there, he obviously would still be rated among the best, but this 470-footer was icing on his cake. Harmon then finished the year with a rocket of

455 feet into Comiskey's left center field upper deck as well as a 460-foot bomb onto a shed beyond center field in Kansas City. Those two drives were hit on September 5 and 9.

Killebrew's 1973 season was pretty much a lost cause as injuries and age shackled him to just five home runs. He did better the next year with 13, but it was clear that Father Time was closing in. He still managed to belt one 434 feet into Minnesota's center field seats on May 5, 1974, but that campaign was his last as a member of the Twins. The Killer came back for one final season in 1975, and played for the Kansas City Royals where he had always performed well. At age 39, he slugged 14 homers in his farewell year, including Number 573 back in Minnesota on September 18. That 405-foot drive into the seats in left center provided him his final trot around the bases, and it seemed fitting that it took place in that location. The Minnesota fans had supported, honored and, yes, in many cases, come to love Harmon Killebrew. He was their original hometown hero, and that was never going to change.

Killebrew remains the man with the fourth highest career home run percentage in baseball history. He also hit those homers with such consistent and spectacular power that few in his sport can rival him for plain old-fashioned strength. Harmon had a kind and temperate disposition, but not when he was swinging the bat. In those brief moments, he was transformed into a vision of athletic violence, pounding baseballs into oblivion.

NUMBER 8: WILLIE McCOVEY—521 HOME RUNS—1959 TO 1980

Standing 6'4", and displaying long rippling muscles, left-handed-hitting Willie McCovey was an imposing sight every time he came to bat. In his very first Major League game on July 30, 1959, against future Hall of Famer Robin Roberts at San Francisco's Seal Stadium, McCovey went 4 for 4, including two rousing triples. He was born on January 10, 1938, in Mobile, Alabama, and tried to enlist in the Navy as a young man. Fortunately, his mother intervened, and he signed a contract with the then New York Giants in 1955.

Willie recorded 102 minor league home runs, including 29 in just over half a season in Phoenix of the Pacific Coast League in 1959. That was when he was summoned by the then San Francisco Giants, and that

Willie McCovey

is when he first met Mr. Roberts. In just 52 games, McCovey smashed 13 homers, batted .354, and won the National League Rookie of the Year Award. One of those four-baggers was hit off Warren Spahn in Milwaukee on August 20, and flew over the right field bleachers. It landed under the scoreboard 465 feet away and marked the genial giant as a menacing offensive force.

After starting so gloriously as a 21-year-old phenomenon, instant stardom was expected of Willie in his second season in 1960. It didn't happen. In fact, it took three more years before McCovey took the big step to Major League stardom. It's not that he wasn't good; he averaged 17 homers a year from 1960 through 1962. But the fans in San Francisco wanted their own homegrown superstar. Sure, they loved Willie Mays, but they felt they had inherited him from his former patrons in New York. They longed for Willie McCovey to be their San Francisco stud. It took a little longer than they wanted, but they got their wish. And while waiting for that big breakout in 1963, McCovey was also inching up the ladder of tape measure immortality.

On September 9, 1960, McCovey blasted one to the back wall atop the high right field bleachers at Crosley Field in Cincinnati. No one is known to have cleared those seats at their highest point during a game, but this 480-foot rainmaker by Willie came closer than any other. At Candlestick Park on September 9, 1961, long before that windswept arena was partially sheltered by the right

field grandstand, McCovey pummeled the ball far over the right field fence. It was hit off Don Drysdale and landed 475 feet from home plate. And at Sportsman's Park in St. Louis on May 10, 1962, versus the great Bob Gibson, Willie sent one soaring so far over the right field pavilion that it landed on the opposite side of Grand Avenue. That was another 475-footer. McCovey wasn't yet hitting them as often as his fans had hoped, but he certainly was hitting them far.

Then, along came 1963, and Willie McCovey really asserted himself. He ripped 44 home runs, and many of them were cross-country beauties. Willie recorded 450-footers on the road at Wrigley Field on April 13 and at the Polo Grounds on July 17. At Candlestick, he did even better. On June 28, he flew one over the right field fence that bounced into the parking lot. That 460-footer was special, but not as much as his final four-bagger on September 26. That missile passed over the 375 foot sign on the right center field fence and landed three rows from the top of the bleachers. Altogether, that shot flew about 485 feet. And consider this: McCovey achieved this level of offensive success despite playing out of position on defense. Normally a first baseman, starting in 1962 and lasting through 1964, Willie played mostly in left field due to the presence of Orlando Cepeda (another slugging first-sacker) on the Giants' roster.

In 1964 McCovey had a bad year—assorted issues and injuries limited him to just 18 home runs—but he still left his distance mark. Visiting Connie Mack Stadium in Philadelphia on July 29, Willie knocked one to dead center field that collided with the wall at the 447 foot mark. That robust double was followed by a homer the following day that traveled about the same distance in the same ballpark. However, this poke was directed to right field, where it topped the 32-foot-high wall, sailed over 20th Street, and landed on a housetop. McCovey rebounded nicely in 1965 with 39 home runs, including several of his trademark long-distance blasts. The Mets had moved into Shea Stadium by that time, and Willie caromed one halfway up the huge scoreboard in right center field. That blow of 460 feet happened on August 27, but he had smashed one just as far 17 days earlier in San Francisco before leaving for the East Coast. That right field rocket collided violently with the Candlestick Park foul pole, and, according to the *San Francisco Chronicle*, "It nearly knocked the pole down." Then, on September 8, back in Frisco, McCovey bombarded the ball almost into the parking lot beyond right field for a journey of 490 feet. Swinging his 33-ounce, 35-inch bat, Willie made such perfect contact that he later said, "That was as squarely as I ever hit a ball."

Although most sluggers reach their distance-hitting primes in their mid-twenties, Willie McCovey, at age 28, was just entering his in 1966. Soon after the Cardinals moved into their new home at Busch Stadium, Willie and his friends came calling. On June 29, McCovey hoisted one of his 36 homers that year over the fence in straightaway center field that descended at the base of the backdrop 460 feet away. It was quite a poke. However, it faded from memory when Willie returned on September 4 and planted one into the far off upper deck in right center field above the scoreboard. Miraculously, the ball was struck on a line drive trajectory that resulted in a 515-foot journey. Willie kept pace at home on September 16 by blasting the first-ever home run over the bleachers in right center. That 505-footer was regarded as the longest ever struck at Candlestick Park. Combining both distance and drama, McCovey finished the season with what was the most memorable homer of his brilliant career. With the pennant on the line at Pittsburgh's Forbes Field on October 1, Willie won the game with an 11th inning laser over the exit gate in deepest right center field. The ball flew 465 feet and concluded one of the best tape measure seasons of that era.

Facing Jim Bunning at Connie Mack Stadium on May 22, 1967, Willie continued to add to his long ball legacy. Recording his seventh of 31 seasonal home runs, he teed off with all his might. The ball raced through the air and passed over the center field side of the 64-foot-high scoreboard situated in deep right center. That amazing blast was estimated at 510 feet. McCovey also added homers in the 460-foot vicinity in Cincinnati, Pittsburgh, New York, and, of course, a few times in San Francisco.

Willie followed up with 36 more homers in 1968 that included consecutive 475-footers

WILLIE McCOVEY'S 10 LONGEST HOME RUNS

- September 4, 1966—St. Louis off Jackson—Into upper deck in right center at scoreboard—515 ft.

- May 22, 1967—Philadelphia off Bunning—Over high scoreboard in deep right center—510 ft.

- September 16, 1966—San Francisco off New York's Fisher—Over right center field bleachers—505 ft.

- June 6, 1969—San Francisco off Philadelphia's Wise—Almost to outer wall in right center field—500 ft.

- June 22, 1969—Atlanta off Neibauer—To eighth row in right field upper deck—500 ft.

- September 8, 1965—San Francisco off Houston's Taylor—Far over right field fence to outer wall—490 ft.

- September 26, 1963—San Francisco off Philadelphia's Brown—To top of bleachers in right center—485 ft.

- September 9, 1960—Cincinnati off Maloney—To wall atop high right field bleachers—480 ft.

- September 9, 1961—San Francisco off Los Angeles's Drysdale—Far over fence in right near outer wall—475 ft.

- May 10, 1962—St. Louis off Gibson—Over right field pavilion and across street—475 ft.

to right field at Candlestick Park on April 28 and May 1. He next added a pair of 450-foot tracers off Jim Bunning back at Forbes Field on June 23. Moving on to 1969, McCovey enjoyed the finest season of his career. He achieved a lifetime high of 45 home runs, while winning the National League MVP Award. That total included the usual assortment of monster shots in the Bay Area, highlighted by blows of 450 feet and 500 feet against Rick Wise of the Phillies on June 6. The lesser of the two (#1) landed near the top of the right center field football bleachers, while the longer one (#2) was lined over those bleachers, landing near

the outer wall adjacent to the parking lot. Willie also did something that no one else ever did in the history of Fulton County Stadium in Atlanta. He hit two balls into the remote upper deck in the same season. They were launched on June 22 and September 11, with the first landing in the eighth row in right field. That 500-footer may have been the longest ever struck in the Atlanta ballpark.

The Giants began construction of their new right field upper deck in 1970 when their veteran first baseman clubbed 39 home runs. Naturally, Willie explored that territory with several batted balls ranging up to 470 feet. At Dodger Stadium on May 16, McCovey ripped a 460-footer into the right field loge. That prompted venerable Los Angeles manager Walter Alston to say, "For pure strength, McCovey is the strongest man in the National League." Sadly, however, Willie was suffering from arthritis in his right knee along with pain in his right shoulder. When McCovey reported for duty in 1971, he was 33 years old and was past his prime. He was still a great hitter and would enjoy many more productive seasons, but he would never again perform like a superstar. Willie totaled 32 homers over the course of the next two years, including the first ball lofted into the new upper deck on April 21, 1971.

Battling back with 29 circuits in 1973, McCovey banged right field upper-deckers on May 8, June 27, August 7, and September 23. An era came to an end in 1974 when Willie McCovey was traded to the San Diego Padres. He rewarded his new employer with 22 home runs that were highlighted by 450-foot center field drives in Pittsburgh on August 10 and Montreal 10 days later. Willie added 23 four-baggers in 1975, but dropped all the way down to a measly seven homers in 1976. As a saving grace on May 5, he was able to splash a ball into the 460-foot distant swimming pool outside Jarry Park in Montreal. When he returned to the Giants at age 39 in 1977, it seemed like a mere courtesy whereby McCovey could finish his Hall of Fame career with his original team.

But Willie McCovey had one last treat saved for Giant fans. He summoned up all his fading physical reserves, and bashed 28 home runs. Loving the game, Willie played through more and more pain from his arthritic knees in both 1978 and 1979 while totaling 27 four-baggers. He tried one last time in 1980 at age 42, but it was just too much. However, he did belt Career Number 521 on May 3 in Montreal before retiring from the game. That final home run flew far over the right field fence, and meant that McCovey had recorded homers in four different decades from 1959 through 1980. Not bad for a shy 17-year-old kid who thought that he would earn his keep by joining the Navy.

NUMBER 7: WILLIE STARGELL—475 HOME RUNS—1963 TO 1982

Wilver Dornel Stargell was a great slugger, but, perhaps more importantly, he was a class act. Born in Earlsboro, Oklahoma, on March 6, 1940, Willie had some Native-American blood mixed in with his predominantly African-American heritage. He grew up in the San Francisco area, and spent his minor league years hopscotching all over the map. By the time he became a Pittsburgh Pirate, where he would spend his entire Major League career, Willie could relate to anyone. That was a key factor in his success as a team leader, resulting in six NL East titles and two classic World Series championships.

Willie Stargell

grandstand roof. The ball struck a girder just under the roof as Stargell lumbered around the bases with everyone gulping in disbelief. It was an extraordinary blow, and instantly labeled Willie as one of the most powerful men in his sport. After the game, Stargell said, "It was the best ball I ever hit." The drive would have flown about 505 feet, and was one of 21 hit that year by the likeable young star.

Willie improved to 27 home runs in 1965, including a May 28 shot of 455 feet over the right field bullpen at New York's Shea Stadium. Then, on June 24 at Dodger Stadium in Los Angeles, Stargell struck three homers in one game (two off Don Drysdale), and nearly added a record-tying fourth. His 8th inning double landed on the railing in left field, thereby missing number four by inches. The Dodgers' ballpark would repeatedly witness optimum performance by Willie Stargell.

Forbes Field, meanwhile, had a cozy 309-foot right field foul line, but it was not a good place to call home for even a left-handed hitter. The dimensions in every other direction were prohibitive. That is proven by the fact that Willie recorded only 41 percent of his home runs in that ballpark until the Pirates moved into Three Rivers Stadium midway through 1970. Stargell liked to hit outside pitches toward left center field, but there was a 415-foot power alley along with a 15-foot brick wall out there. Willie still managed to belt a 450-footer on July 8, 1966 over that obstacle. Earlier in the day, Willie had hit the

After clubbing 27 home runs at Columbus in the International League in 1962, Stargell was summoned to Pittsburgh. The 6'3", left-handed-hitting outfielder was still rather lean at 190 pounds, but he eventually filled out to a muscular 225 pounds. Willie didn't play much in that first abbreviated season and hit no homers. But he returned in 1963 to hit 11 four-baggers, including Career Number One at Chicago's Wrigley Field on May 8. The ball flew rather routinely into the right field bleachers, and did nothing to establish Stargell as one of baseball's mightiest batsmen. That distinction would have to wait one more year.

On May 11, 1964, at Forbes Field in Pittsburgh, Willie smashed a torrid, rising line drive toward the 86-foot-high right field

457 foot sign in deepest center on one hop for an inside-the-park homer. Stargell had immense power, but no hitter (righty or lefty) could surmount that wall on a regular basis. The lengthiest of Willie's 33 circuits that year was smacked on May 28 at the Astrodome in Houston. It flew to the 30th row of seats in right center and was estimated at 490 feet.

Willie dipped to just 20 home runs in 1967, but his batting strength was reaching full flower. Just like contemporary National League slugger Willie McCovey, Stargell took a little longer than most to attain optimum power. Despite recording fewer homers in his 27th year, it was obvious that Willie was pounding them farther than ever. On June 7, Willie hammered a ball high over the 436 foot sign in right center at Forbes Field. That was a wallop of 480 feet and impressed Pittsburgh fans for its longevity. But then came July 3 in the same ballpark. Stargell squared off versus Don Drysdale, orbiting a ball to deepest center field against the nasty right-hander. Almost unbelievably, it kept going and going until it cleared the 457 foot sign by a wide margin. The horsehide finally landed in an adjoining Little League field for a flight of 520 feet. Those two historic drives were more than sufficient for a great tape measure season, but Willie was just loosening up. Six days later, he launched the ball to the top of the towering right field roof for the first time in his career. Then, against all odds, Stargell did it again on August 18! Those matching 475-footers culminated the greatest single season distance-hitting performance in the annals of Forbes Field. For the record, in the last half-century, a ball managed to land on that grandstand roof an average of only once every four-plus years.

Willie Stargell then seemed to settle into a groove of consistent production. There was no greatness yet, but he was solid. Willie averaged 28 home runs from 1968 through 1970, as the Pirates and their slugging left fielder waited for their moment. Actually, Stargell really wasn't the star of his own team. That honor was reserved for Roberto Clemente, who had played for Pittsburgh with such notable élan since 1955. But Willie was fine with that, especially considering that his niche as the mightiest Pirate was totally secure. Stargell kept knocking balls all over Forbes Field until it appeared that it had shrunk. Willie airmailed the right center field wall on June 14 and July 24, 1969, as well as surmounting the wall in center on April 13 of that same year. He then landed balls onto the right field roof on July 4, 1969, August 26, 1969, and April 25, 1970. Stargell somehow even topped that 86-foot-high building on August 19, 1969, and April 20, 1970. The eight aforementioned drives flew anywhere from 460 feet to 510 feet. It's no wonder that the Pirates moved into Three Rivers Stadium in the middle of the 1970 season; Willie Stargell had rendered Forbes Field obsolete. Along the way, Willie was still blasting on the road. At Jarry Park in Montreal on July 16, 1969 Stargell nailed a 465-footer over the right field scoreboard and into a swimming pool. While visiting Dodger Stadium on August 5, 1969, Willie recorded the longest-ever home run in the ballpark that has housed those Dodgers since 1962. The ball soared over the right field pavilion and landed 506 feet from home plate. And in the final days of Crosley Field in Cincinnati on May 1, 1970, Stargell thumped one to the top of the right field bleachers.

In an era when the National League oversaw the building of many so-called cookie cutter stadiums, nothing changed for Willie Stargell. Willie happily accepted the move into brand new Three Rivers Stadium, where he lined the ball off the façade of the top deck in right field on August 9, 1970. Teammate Al Oliver watched the rapid trajectory, and later said, "If somebody had tried to catch the ball, his hands would have come off." Bill Mazeroski added, "I've never seen a ball hit harder in my life." This 510-foot masterpiece demonstrated that Stargell would rule his new playpen in the same way that he had dominated the old one. As usual, events evolved similarly when Willie played his away games. On June 13, at Jack Murphy Stadium in San Diego, Stargell almost reached the scoreboard atop the bleachers in right center. Two days later, back at Dodger Stadium, Willie hammered one of his best shots to the top of the pavilion in right center. Both of those wallops were estimated at 480 feet.

When Willie Stargell played his first full season in Three Rivers Stadium in 1971, he recorded a career-high total of 48 home runs.

It was not a coincidence. Getting away from those daunting Forbes Field dimensions was a tonic for Willie. For example, he thumped three imposing drives to center field from April 21 through April 27 that flew from 420 feet to 455 feet. Back at Forbes, two would have been outs with the third merely an extra-base hit. At Three Rivers, they resulted in Stargell jogging around the bases with home runs. And Willie did just fine when he pulled the ball to right field as well. He deposited horsehides into either the third or fourth decks on April 21, May 30, June 20, and June 23 for drives of anywhere from 440 feet to 500 feet. At Veterans Stadium in Philadelphia on June 25, Stargell rocketed a ball through an exit tunnel in the 600 level in right field. It was the only such drive in the 33-year history of that venue. As a fitting climax to this serendipitous season, the Pittsburgh Pirates defeated the Baltimore Orioles in a dramatic seven-game World Series.

Besides hitting another 33 long homers in 1972, Willie did something else of particular note. He played first base more than he played the outfield. Stargell resumed his outfield duties for the following two seasons, but in 1975, he returned to the first sack for the rest of his days as a ballplayer. "Pops" as he was now often called, stormed back to the top of the slugging world with 44 dingers in 1973. On May 31, he bombed the ball to the fourth row in section 512 in the top deck in right field for what may have been the longest drive ever hit in Three Rivers

Stadium. That 500-footer was almost equaled by Stargell's center field blast on June 19, which was definitely the longest-ever in that direction at Three Rivers. Willie also reached the right field pavilion roof at Dodger Stadium on May 8, and drilled another through a tunnel under the scoreboard in San Diego on July 12. Those balls ate up 490 and 480 respective feet of real estate.

From 1974 through 1978, Stargell averaged 21 home runs per season. That wasn't bad, but it signaled the inevitable decline faced by every athlete. Many of those homers were long, and one was genuinely noteworthy. On May 20, 1978 at Olympic Stadium in Montreal, Willie crushed the ball into the right field upper deck past the auxiliary scoreboard. That magnificent 515-foot rocket was the only upper-decker in any direction in the 28-year history of that ball yard. Then, in 1979, 39-year-old Willie Stargell was reborn. He led his team to a second World Series title while being voted co-winner of the National League MVP Award. Willie socked 32 homers, many of them in clutch situations, including his last tape measure shot on July 4. That drive into the right field upper deck at Busch Stadium in St. Louis was estimated at 510

WILLIE STARGELL'S 10 LONGEST HOME RUNS

- July 3, 1967—Pittsburgh off Los Angeles's Drysdale—Over wall in center into Little League field—520 ft.

- May 20, 1978—Montreal off Twitchell—Into right field upper deck—515 ft.

- August 19, 1969—Pittsburgh off Houston's Wilson—Over 86-foot-high right field roof—510 ft.

- August 9, 1970—Pittsburgh off New York's Taylor—Liner to façade of upper deck in right—510 ft.

- July 4, 1979—St. Louis off Knowles—Into upper deck in right center—510 ft.

- August 5, 1969—Los Angeles off Foster—Over pavilion roof in right field—506 ft.

- May 11, 1964—Pittsburgh off Cincinnati's Ellis—Liner off girder under right field roof—505 ft.

- April 20, 1970—Pittsburgh off Houston's Bouton—Over 86-foot-high right field roof—505 ft.

- June 25, 1971—Philadelphia off Bunning—Into exit in 600 level in right field—505 ft.

- May 31, 1973—Pittsburgh off Atlanta's Gentry—To fourth row in upper deck in right—500 ft.

feet. By the time Stargell struck his 475th and final homer, while playing at Riverburgh Stadium in Cincinnati on July 21, 1982, he was dearly loved by the entire Pittsburgh community. Pops had become the unquestioned head of the Pirate "family" where his legacy of physical power and dignified leadership will likely never be seen again.

NUMBER 6: MARK McGWIRE—583 HOME RUNS—1986 TO 2001

Mark McGwire was always a powerful man as well as a great home run hitter. In truth, however, it wasn't until mid-career that he displayed the nearly superhuman strength for which he is now usually remembered. In fact, if McGwire were judged for his accomplishments as a distance hitter prior to his 32nd year, he wouldn't make it into the top-30 list. But, in his final seven seasons from 1995 through 2001, Mark consistently pounded the ball so far that he rivaled even the one and only Babe Ruth for distance supremacy. For this reason, it is more difficult to rank Mark McGwire than anyone else, but sixth place seems like a fair judgment.

Born in Pomona, California, on October 1, 1963, Mark David McGwire became an All-American baseball player at USC. Competing in 149 games from 1982 through 1984, he recorded 54 collegiate home runs. Moving on to Modesto of the California League the following year and then to both Huntsville (Double A) and Tacoma (Triple A) in 1986,

Mark added 48 minor league homers. By August 20, 1986, it was apparent that this guy was going to hit with power wherever he played. That was when the Oakland Athletics called him up to the big leagues. Just five days later, at Tiger Stadium in Detroit, the 6'5", 220-pound McGwire did what the A's expected him to do: He belted a home run. And it was a beauty! The ball passed just over the 440 foot sign in dead center field for a lengthy ride of 450 feet.

Something odd happened next. In fact, that "something" happened over almost the entire course of the following decade. Despite smashing many home runs, Mark McGwire did not hit an official homer significantly farther than his first Major League four-bagger until 1995. In his first full season in 1987, the right-handed-hitting first baseman set the rookie record by walloping 49 home runs. It was an amazing performance for anyone, but especially for a rookie not yet turned 24 years of age. And make no mistake; many were slugged very far. At Exhibition Stadium in Toronto on May 27, McGwire bashed a homer about 450 feet into the seats in deep left center field. He matched that distance and direction at Municipal Stadium in Cleveland on June 27. That represented excellent distance, but it certainly wasn't historic.

In 1988, Mark added 32 home runs, which included a 455-footer at Boston's Fenway Park on May 17 along with a 440-footer at Milwaukee's County Stadium on June 22. Then, in 1989, McGwire socked 33 dingers with his

Mark McGwire

Mark McGwire finally remained healthy for most of a full season, and he returned to form with 39 homers. Or did he? Actually, he didn't return to his old self; he eclipsed his own level of optimum power by a considerable margin. At Minnesota on May 12, Mark shot one so far to center field that he broke his personal distance record. His drive of 463 feet was then duplicated at Fenway Park on June 11 when he thumped the ball high over the Green Monster in left field. They were followed by drives of 452, 450, 459, 460, 457, and, finally, 467 feet. That last one was smacked to the top of the left center field bleachers in Oakland on September 20, 1995. While most sluggers achieve their optimum distance in their mid-twenties, or occasionally in their late twenties, Mark McGwire became the first notable power hitter in baseball history to do that after age 30. And this was just the start of more to come . . . much more.

Mark soared all the way up to 52 home runs in 1996, and he also sent them farther than even the year before. He landed a ball on the left field roof in Detroit on April 28 that was estimated at 462 feet. Before the season ended, McGwire shattered his own personal best several times. He reached 470 feet in Chicago, 475 feet in Minneapolis, 473 feet and 481 feet (both on September 22) in Seattle, and 488 feet at the Skydome in Toronto. That eye-popper settled into the seventh row of the fifth deck, proving unequivocally that Mark McGwire was a certifiable tape measure hitter.

longest flying an estimated 450 feet to center field on September 24 at Minnesota's Metrodome. And so it went for five more years. Mark drilled 39 homers in 1990. His longest that year settled into the second row of seats in the left field upper deck in Oakland. That 450-footer remained the longest known home run recorded by Mark McGwire until July 4, 1994. On that day Mark visited Yankee Stadium and deposited a ball into the bullpen in left center field near the monuments. That drive traveled 452 feet. From 1991 through 1994, McGwire recorded homer totals of 22, 42, 9, and 9. Mark was hampered by injuries in '93 and '94, but his peak distance remained constant even when he felt well. And then came 1995!

In 1997, Mark finally reached the ultimate distance plateau. He delivered 58 homers with too many (15) flying over 450 feet to describe each individually. What happened on June 24 at the Seattle Kingdome, however, must be discussed. McGwire tore into a 97-mph Randy Johnson fastball and orbited it to left field. The ball landed at the back of the second deck over a clock and was initially estimated at 538 feet. That figure was argued back and forth by physicists and scientists of other disciplines, and was eventually reduced to a more practical 505 feet. But, no matter, Mark had made it to 500 feet. And that's the point where all the great distance hitters must go to earn their stripes. Traded to the St. Louis Cardinals on July 31, McGwire kept going long. He smashed a 500-footer in Miami on August 22 and then a 504-footer at Busch Stadium in his new hometown on September 2. But Mark still wasn't finished. Back at Busch on September 16, McGwire crunched one off the top of the scoreboard in left center that was judged at 517 feet. After that shot, nobody could doubt Mark's 500-foot credentials.

MARK McGWIRE'S 10 LONGEST HOME RUNS

- May 12, 1998—St. Louis off Milwaukee's Wagner—To fourth row in left center field upper deck—535 ft.
- May 16, 1998—St. Louis off Florida's Hernandez—Off façade of press level in dead center—535 ft.
- September 16, 1997—St. Louis off Los Angeles's Martinez—To top of scoreboard in left center field—517 ft.
- July 17, 1998—St. Louis off Los Angeles's Bohanan—Into exit tunnel in left field upper deck—511 ft.
- August 26, 1998—St. Louis off Florida's Speir—To top of backdrop in center field—509 ft.
- June 24, 1997—Seattle off Johnson—To top of second deck over clock in left field—505 ft.
- September 2, 1997—St. Louis off Chicago's Navarro—High off scoreboard in left center—504 ft.
- April 23, 2000—St. Louis off Colorado's Karl—Over scoreboard to upper deck in left center—502 ft.
- August 30, 1998—St. Louis off Atlanta's Martinez—Between backdrop and Coke sign in center—501 ft.
- August 22, 1997—Florida off Saunders—To eighth row in left field upper deck—500 ft.

What happened next, in 1998, is now the stuff of legend. Not only did Mark McGwire shatter Roger Maris's season home run record by hitting 70, he did so while blasting balls consistently farther than anyone in the past three-quarters of a century. Mark essentially warmed up until May 12 with his longest until then being a 462-footer. Then he got serious. McGwire thundered the ball all the way to the fourth row in section 389 in the left center field upper deck at Busch Stadium, resulting in a 527-foot estimate. Only four days later, on May 16, 1998, Mark rocketed another drive with all his might that headed toward dead center field. The ball struck an advertising sign on the façade of the press level, whereupon everyone (both media and fans) instantly demanded an estimate. But there was one problem. The landing point was so distant that it had not been included in the Cardinals' stadium distance grid. Not wanting to keep everyone waiting until the next day, club management made their best guess which was 545 feet. Subsequent investigation indicates that both of these Herculean drives would have flown about 535 feet if allowed to return to field level. They were probably the two longest homers in McGwire's career, and they were hit in the same week. Talk about strong!

And that's the way things went for the rest of the season as Mark battled Sammy Sosa for the home run championship of the world. Of course, McGwire won—70 to 66 in a duel that baseball historians will study in perpetuity. Both men hit the ball with savage fury, but Mark hit them the hardest. During the remainder of that epic campaign, McGwire added 500-footers in St. Louis on July 17 (511 feet), August 26 (509 feet), and August 30 (501 feet). On the road, he also played the role of the human launching pad. At Veterans Stadium on May 19, Mark drilled a center field 440-footer, a left field 451-footer, as well as a left center field 471-footer. Visiting the Astrodome on June 18, he knocked one 449 feet into the left field upper deck. On June 25, McGwire dented a crossbeam near the corner of the left field scoreboard at Jacobs Field in Cleveland for a ride of 461 feet. At Jack Murphy Stadium in San Diego on July 20, Mark reached the third row in the left field second deck. That was good for 458 feet and was followed by a 452-footer at Coors Field six days later. Three Rivers Stadium in Pittsburgh came next with a 465-foot shot just right of center on August 22. Last on the list was Joe Robbie Field in Miami where McGwire boomed four homers in just over 24 hours on September 1 and 2. In order, they flew 450 feet to dead center, 472 feet in the same direction, 497 feet over an exit in the left field upper deck, and 458 feet into the seats in left center. Would it be too melodramatic to conclude with, "And, on the seventh day, he rested"?

Mark McGwire was almost as lethal in 1999, but there isn't room to give the same detail as for 1998. He recorded 65 home runs, and his two most impressive blows happened on the road. On May 22 at Dodger Stadium, Mark delivered one to the top of the pavilion in left center. The ball bounced out of the ballpark and was estimated at 484 feet. Then, at Shea Stadium in New York on August 22, Big Mac bounced one off the top of the huge scoreboard in deepest right center field. Mark was a pull hitter, so this 495-foot super-bomb directed the other way was very, very special.

Injuries began overtaking McGwire again in 2000. He had suffered from various foot and leg problems for years; he had added so much muscle mass in his upper body that his legs now appeared worn out. Mark was a passionate weight lifter, but he always tried to balance that with a strict stretching regimen. However, there was nothing that he could do to ward off the tendonitis then ravaging his right knee. Weighing somewhere around 265 pounds, the constant pounding on his joints was just too much. He still managed 32 home runs that year, but the end was near.

Entering the 2001 season, Mark McGwire's pain had become nearly unbearable. He missed much of the early season, but still displayed awesome hitting ability by whacking 29 homers in just 400 at-bats. In fact, after Mark logged his final career home run in Milwaukee on October 4, he retired with the highest home run per at-bat ratio in Major League history. Stepping aside just after his 38th birthday, Mark left the game riddled with controversy and doubt, but also imbued with awe and wonder. He was, unquestionably, the longest hitter of the modern era.

NUMBER 5: DICK ALLEN—351 HOME RUNS—1964 TO 1977

Although Dick Allen was an amazing athlete, his Major League numbers were merely very good, but not sensational. Accordingly, most modern fans hardly know him, and his legacy has been sadly misplaced. But he was the real deal. Starting as a youth in western Pennsylvania, where he was a spectacular basketball talent as well as an enormously gifted baseball player, Dick could do anything in the arena of sports. His iconoclastic behavior often compromised his athletic production, but he never failed on the field. Most importantly to this story, Richard Anthony Allen could pound a baseball like few other men in the history of the national pastime.

Dick Allen

There is a legend that 17-year-old Dick Allen hit two 500-foot home runs in a semi-pro game in 1959. Ordinarily, such a story would be labeled as nonsense. However, the tale originated with John Ogden, who was not a frivolous man. Ogden was born in 1897 and pitched for the International League Baltimore Orioles from 1919 to 1925, where he teamed with Lefty Grove. Playing there for Jack Dunn, the discoverer of Babe Ruth, Ogden eventually earned a promotion to the big leagues, and competed against the Bambino. Decades later, in 1959, Ogden was scouting for the Philadelphia Phillies and traveled to Wampum, Pennsylvania, to watch Allen play. That is where Ogden saw Richie (as he was then called) smash two tremendous homers that he (Ogden) personally measured after the game. Perhaps some hyperbole crept into Ogden's memory when he described these events in a *Philadelphia Bulletin* interview printed on July 1, 1969. Clearly, he was emotionally invested in Allen. In 1960, the Phillies signed the right-handed slugger to a huge bonus based on Ogden's passionate recommendation. But John Ogden never changed his story and went to his grave saying that Dick Allen was the only player he ever saw who hit the ball as hard as Babe Ruth.

Working his way quickly to the big leagues, Dick played in 1963 at the Triple-A level with the Arkansas Travelers in Little Rock. He enjoyed a huge year, belting 33 home runs and winning the team MVP Award.

Although most Arkansans were kind to Allen, he was still subjected to some intense racial bigotry, and suffered the emotional scars. When he became a regular for the Phillies in 1964, he was tried at third base, which was a new position for him. He started in the organization as an infielder, but had soon been switched to the outfield. Switching back to the infield as a Major League rookie wasn't easy, and he made numerous throwing errors. Predictably, he was loudly booed by the Philly fans. This was standard behavior in the City of Brotherly Love, but young Allen didn't understand that. Before long, he retreated behind a wall of defensive behavior and never really came out during the remainder of his tumultuous career.

Regardless of the personal turmoil, Dick Allen struck baseballs prodigious distances wherever he played. With Little Rock, he pounded a ball far over the scoreboard in left center field at Indianapolis on August 24, 1963. The following spring, as he prepared for his first Major League season, Dick mangled a baseball so hard in Tampa that it smashed into the lights atop a pole in left field. That ball appeared to be rising when stopped in mid-flight 360 feet away and 96 feet high. Everyone was guessing the potential flight distance, starting with 500 feet, when a few of Dick's former Little Rock teammates took their fun away. They calmly stated that, although the Tampa blow was genuinely impressive, it was nothing compared to Allen's minor league blast in Indianapolis.

Dick Allen hit 29 home runs in 1964 and won the National League Rookie of the Year Award. On May 31 at Connie Mack Stadium in Philadelphia, Dick recorded his first official big-league tape measure drive. Standing 5'11", Dick was 195 pounds of mighty right-handed muscle. On this May night, he launched one into a stiff incoming breeze that flew high over the double-deck left field grandstand as well as a rooftop billboard. There was a tower behind the billboard with a transformer situated about halfway up to the lights. Dick's roaring blast collided with that transformer at a height of 100 feet and 380 feet from home plate. Again, estimates started flying, but it would take another year to get a real fix on Allen's extraordinary power.

Back at Connie Mack on May 29, 1965, Dick was at it again. He hit another rocket, this time soaring over the Coca Cola billboard on the roof in left center. Phillies' publicist Larry Shenk quickly went outside to investigate and found a reliable eyewitness to the landing point on Woodstock Street. The final math worked out to 529 feet. Almost incredibly, Allen reprised that mind-blowing deed just 12 days later by thumping another ball over the left field roof. This one shot over the Cadillac billboard, just missing the same light tower that had been struck the year before. Shenk also duplicated his recent performance and identified a responsible witness to where the ball dropped onto a parked convertible. This time the flight was computed at 504

feet. Dick Allen was only 23 at this time, but was hitting confirmed 500-plus-foot home runs against the best pitchers in the game.

The higher that a player is ranked on the historical distance list, the harder it is to include all the deeds of that player. And so it is with Number Five. By 1966, Dick Allen was pummeling so many tape measure shots that space will permit only the highlights on his resume. On April 29, Allen separated his right shoulder sliding and missed almost a month of play. The problem was that he could not throw the ball. Since Dick was able to swing the bat, he was sent out to left field where strong-armed shortstop Bobby Wine ran out to assist him. Using this bizarre system at New York's Shea Stadium on May 30, Allen demonstrated that even though he couldn't throw, he really could still hit the ball. He nailed one to dead center field where it thudded halfway up the backdrop 460 feet away. Despite the missed games, Allen wound up with 40 home runs, including 12 of over 450 feet. One of those came off Sandy Koufax at Dodger Stadium on July 27, and went screaming 465 feet into the palm trees beyond the left field bullpen.

On June 6, 1967, Dick Allen learned that teammate and close friend Bob Uecker had been traded. Venting his anger, he thundered the longest homer of his unlikely career by smashing the ball over the Philco billboard near the center field end of the grandstand roof. Unfortunately, no witness to the landing could be found. The ball disappeared over the roof 420 feet away at a height of about 90 feet and was described by all onlookers as a line drive. Coach George Myatt saw Mickey Mantle's epic 1953 blast in Washington, D.C., and opined that Allen's ball was hit farther. No one knows the exact distance, but 540 feet would be a good guess.

Dick Allen's career almost came to a tragic end before that 1967 season concluded. Pushing a stalled car after a rainstorm on August 24, he lacerated two tendons in his right hand when it accidentally broke through the glass of a headlight. The injury ended Allen's season with 23 homers, and, although he returned to full-time play in 1968, he never completely healed. Accumulating 33 and 32 homers respectively in 1968 and 1969, the "Wampum Walloper" could still knock them a country mile. He clanged one off a light tower against Nolan Ryan at Shea Stadium on July 15, 1968, but the ball still landed 490 feet away as confirmed by multiple observers in the visitors' bullpen. On June 17, 1969, Dick slammed one of his many homers over the Coke sign in left center at Connie Mack Stadium. When he faced fire-balling Bob Veale of the Pirates four days later against a strong wind, it was assumed that it would be humanly impossible to do it again. This wind factor has been authenticated by fellow tape measure king, Willie Stargell, who then watched Allen clear that distant billboard. In 1983, Willie rated this drive as the longest he ever saw, despite having a hard time believing that it actually happened.

After six stormy seasons in Philadelphia, Dick Allen was finally traded. By then a credible first baseman, he went to work for the St. Louis Cardinals where he delivered 34 homers. The one at Montreal's Jarry Park on July 3, 1970, landed in a camera platform that was high above the ground and 448 feet away in center field. Moving on to the Los Angeles Dodgers in 1971, Allen managed only 23 circuits before again being handed his walking papers. His first two homers in Dodger blue went flying far over the center field fence before passing between the two flagpoles. But his longest occurred on August 20 during a return trip to Philly where games were then played at Veterans Stadium. Dick smote one on a line just left of the Liberty Bell replica hanging from the upper deck in center field. It was a monumental blow of almost 500 feet.

Dick Allen had one brief shining moment of baseball Camelot. In 1972, he played for friend and manager Chuck Tanner with the Chicago White Sox and won the American League MVP Award while striking 37 homers. After the season, he signed a three-year contract that was the most lucrative to date in baseball history. But Allen was never destined to enjoy peace of mind. After belting 16 homers, including a May 1 moon shot onto the Comiskey Park rooftop, Dick ended his season on June 28 with a first base collision that broke his left fibula. Everything seemed back on track in 1974. Allen produced what may have been the second longest home run ever hit at Tiger Stadium on July 6. He

DICK ALLEN'S 10 LONGEST HOME RUNS

- June 6, 1967—Philadelphia off Chicago's Niekro—Over third sign atop roof in deepest left center field—540 ft.
- July 6, 1974—Detroit off Lemanczyk—Liner off roof façade in deep left center—535 ft.
- May 29, 1965—Philadelphia off Chicago's Jackson—Far over sign on grandstand roof in left center—529 ft.
- August 19, 1966—Philadelphia off New York's Friend—Liner over sign on left field grandstand roof—515 ft.
- June 15, 1966—Cincinnati off O'Toole—Liner over high scoreboard in left center—510 ft.
- June 21, 1969—Philadelphia off Pittsburgh's Veale—Far over sign on left center field roof—510 ft.
- August 22, 1964—Philadelphia off Pittsburgh's Bork—Liner over left field roof between first two signs—505 ft.
- June 10, 1965—Philadelphia off Los Angeles's Podres—Far over sign on grandstand roof in left field—504 ft.
- June 16, 1967—Philadelphia off Pittsburgh's Law—Liner far over sign on left field grandstand roof—500 ft.
- May 1, 1973—Chicago off Cuellar—To light platform on left field grandstand roof—500 ft.

whipped his 38-ounce war club with stunning velocity and crushed the ball on a torrid line off the roof façade at its furthest point in deepest left center field. That ball would probably have flown about 535 feet. When Dick recorded his 32nd homer on August 16, it appeared certain that he would better his personal record. But it was not to be. Allen soon complained of extreme fatigue, and "retired" from baseball on September 14. The White Sox family was devastated. But Allen decided to "un-retire" in 1975, and played for parts of the next three years. However, he amassed only 32 more home runs. When he hit them, they still went a long way, but his vast skills were eroding. Three months after his 35th birthday, in June 1977, he retired again . . . this time for good. He left as he entered, as a total enigma, but also as one of the most gifted and powerful performers that the game has ever known.

NUMBER 4: FRANK HOWARD—382 HOME RUNS—1958 TO 1973

Frank Howard was one of the biggest men to ever play in the Major Leagues. Standing 6'7" and weighing close to 300 pounds as a veteran, he was a mountain of a man. But his size was not a natural batting advantage. If it were, we would see more huge players on this list. Most extra-large athletes have slower reflexes, lesser coordination, and an overall problem with quick muscle function. All those attributes are essential in hitting baseballs for long distances. So Howard actually had to overcome some obstacles because of his size. And he did it in style. When it came to smashing the ball, Frank was beautiful to behold.

After starring in baseball and basketball at Ohio State University, Frank Howard was assigned to the Class B team in Green Bay by the Los Angeles Dodgers. This was in 1958, and Frank quickly made his mark by belting 37 home runs. Recalled after his MVP minor league season, the right-handed Howard recorded his first Major League homer off Robin Roberts at Connie Mack Stadium on September 10. It was a massive drive against a billboard atop the left field grandstand roof. Frank returned to the minors in 1959, but was promoted to Double A Victoria in the Texas League. He didn't stay long. After thumping 27 homers, he was shipped off to Triple A Spokane in the Pacific Coast League. Even there, the competition was overmatched as Howard added 16 more circuits. As he had

the year before, Frank got a late season look by the Dodgers, and, like the year before, smoked a 450-foot home run. This one was lined into the left center field bleachers in St. Louis on September 22.

Howard next played winter ball in the Dominican Republic, and initially started the 1960 campaign back in Spokane. But there was nothing more for him to prove in the minors, and, at age 23, he became a permanent big leaguer for the Dodgers on May 13, 1960. Along the way, Frank had left a trail of monstrous home runs at every stop. That included such places as Green Bay, Rochester (MN), Victoria, Austin, Spokane, Vero Beach, Pedro San Marcus, and Japan (as a collegian).

Frank Howard

Courtesy of the National Baseball Hall of Fame and Museum

Some of those drives are still being discussed today. And, sure enough, Howard's first homer as a full-time Major Leaguer was yet another tape measure blast. On May 17 off Bob Buhl at County Stadium in Milwaukee, he clubbed one far over the center field fence and into a cluster of pine trees. But all this had been just a tease. Just eight days later in Pittsburgh, Frank Howard really connected.

At Forbes Field on May 25, 1960, Frank walloped the ball far over the distant brick wall in left field. It eventually landed in adjoining Schenley Park at the prodigious distance of 520 feet from home plate. Originally, there were reports that the ball had flown even farther since a local newsman, arriving late at the ballpark, saw it land. However, as is often the case with eyewitness reports, it was later determined that the ball had bounced before entering the man's line of vision. Frank didn't need any enhancements. He reached the 48th row of the left field bleachers at the Los Angeles Coliseum on June 11 and then the 31st row of the left center field bleachers in Milwaukee on June 24. Both blows traveled in the 475-foot range and were two of Howard's 23 homers for the year.

"Hondo" had an off year in 1961 when he dropped to just 15 home runs, but the giant outfielder still hit them far. On May 7, Frank distinguished himself again at Forbes Field by launching a missile over the left field wall. He then lined the ball against the scoreboard on top of the left field bleachers at Busch Memorial Stadium in St. Louis on July 22. Those

drives were estimated at 455 feet and 480 feet respectively. Howard fared much better in 1962, blasting 31 home runs. He unloaded particularly long drives in Cincinnati, Philadelphia, and Houston, but reserved some of his best for the hometown fans. The Dodgers started playing in Chavez Ravine that year, and Frank knocked two far over the fence in dead center at new Dodger Stadium. Those twin 450-footers were delivered on September 9 and 26.

Over the course of the next two seasons, Frank Howard did reasonably well. He hit a total of 52 homers, but that wasn't good enough. Considering his vast size and superlative power, the expectations had evolved in a proportionate scale. Everyone wanted and expected Howard to be a superstar, and he was merely very good. As a result, he was traded to the Washington Senators at the conclusion of 1964. But before he left the National League, he passed out a few more of his calling cards. Frank hoisted one over the left center field roof at New York's historic Polo Grounds on August 16, 1963. In Philadelphia on June 4, 1964, Howard teamed with Sandy Koufax to beat the Phils 3–0 in one of the fastest games in recent memory. His line drive to the grandstand rooftop in the 7th inning off Chris Short provided the only scoring. Koufax pitched to only 27 men while hurling a masterful no-hitter.

After two years in Washington, it appeared that the Dodgers had been right. Frank Howard had hit 21 homers in 1965 and 18 in 1966.

He was a solid Major League player, but visions of stardom appeared unlikely to materialize. Predictably, his chief value to the local fans was his ability to hit tape measure shots. They kept track of his drives into the distant upper deck areas in symmetrical D.C. Stadium. During that two-year period, Howard sent six balls there. But his best were clubbed on the road. On July 18, 1965, Frank pounded the ball toward deep left field at venerable Yankeee Stadium. It kept going until it collided with a chair in the fifth row of the left field upper deck near the center field end in section 34. Only Jimmie Foxx and Mickey Mantle were known to have hit comparable balls at the Bronx ball yard. This drive ended its ride 70 feet above the field at a linear distance of 440 feet from where Howard started it. Twelve days later at Municipal Stadium in Kansas City, Frank struck again. This time, the ball landed on the batting cage in center field, and it was actually measured at 516 feet. That was about the same length as the New York rocket.

Something interesting then happened in 1967. Frank Howard attained a career high of 36 four-baggers and looked very comfortable in the process. He bombed three more into the upper deck regions, including two nearly incredible shots. The first was directed to center field on April 24, and the second reached the walkway in left center field on September 24. Keeping another date with history, Frank also cleared the Green Monster at Boston's Fenway Park on June 10. This drive went by way of the far end, near center field,

and landed on the building across Lansdowne Street. It was the same structure that was previously visited by guys named Foxx and Ruth. Appropriately, Frank Howard became a celebrity in the nation's capital, and earned the nickname "Capital Enforcer."

The good times got even better in 1968 with 44 more balls flying out of American League ballparks. This time, four homers found their way into the upper deck level along with four others into the mezzanine just beneath that top deck. As usual, Howard was every bit as effective as a visiting player. He bashed two in Cleveland on May 16 that were noteworthy. The first landed in the 12th row of the lower deck in far-off left field (475 feet), and the second rested in the alley between the left field grandstand and the center field bleachers (470 feet). Municipal Stadium always was known as a tough home run park, but Frank cut the place down to size. Forty-eight hours later at Detroit's Tiger Stadium, Howard banged two more. Number one soared through an exit in the right center field upper deck, and number two landed on the 94-foot-high left field upper deck. It was a rare blow that was judged to have flown 510 feet.

Finally, Frank Howard was regarded as a superstar. He did nothing but enhance that image by slugging a career-best 48 homers in 1969. The upper deck total was increased by four as was the mezzanine count by three. Those upper-deckers flew a minimum of 420 feet for a ball into the first row at the foul

FRANK HOWARD'S 10 LONGEST HOME RUNS

- September 24, 1967—Washington off Detroit's Sparma—To walkway in left center field upper deck—535 ft.
- July 7, 1969—Washington off Cleveland's Williams—To fourth row in center field upper deck—530 ft.
- April 24, 1970—Washington off California's Messersmith—To exit in left center field upper deck—525 ft.
- April 25, 1966—Washington off Chicago's John—To second row in center field upper deck—522 ft.
- May 25, 1960—Pittsburgh off Umbricht—Far over left field wall into Schenley Park—520 ft.
- July 30, 1965—Kansas City off O'Donoghue—Onto batting cage in center field—516 ft.
- July 18, 1965—New York off Mikkelsen—Into upper deck near left center—515 ft.
- May 18, 1968—Detroit off Lolich—Onto 94-foot-high left field grandstand roof—510 ft.
- August 25, 1971—Anaheim off May—Far over center field fence—506 ft.
- August 16, 1963—New York off Craig—High over grandstand roof in left center—505 ft.

line, but increased to as much as 535 feet for a drive to the lateral walkway in left center. In fact, Frank's stupendous drive all the way to the fourth row in dead center on July 7 went almost that far. It was a truly epic blast. Then, in 1970, Howard enjoyed his final year at peak efficiency. He smoked 44 additional homers and celebrated with his richest harvest of upper deck shots. He somehow propelled six balls there as well as four others into the mezzanine. The single longest flew into an exit at the walkway level in left center. Struck on April 24, this 525-footer was yet another drive of legendary proportions.

Howard dropped off to 26 homers in 1971 and logged his final two upper-deckers. At Comiskey Park on Chicago's South Side on July 25, Frank nearly reached the roof when his prolific shot struck a vertical pillar just left of center field. And on August 25 in Anaheim, Howard drilled the ball so far to center that Angel officials just had to measure it. The result was a computation of 506 feet. That event offers a good insight into the man's extraordinary batting power. Despite playing only on occasion in Anaheim, Frank Howard registered a list of homers that flew 440, 452, 468, 475, 495, and 506 feet. The Senators didn't start competing there until 1966, so Frank compiled that record as a visiting player in just six years. By any barometer, Howard was a distance-hitting freak.

The Senators moved to the Dallas, Texas, area for the 1972 season. Sadly, Frank was no longer a star player, and his new fans never saw him at his best. He managed only 10 homers and was sold to the Detroit Tigers toward the end of the year. Howard improved slightly in 1973, but still hit only 12 home runs. He did record his final two tape measure blasts by nailing comparable 460-footers into the left center field upper decks in Detroit and Chicago on June 12 and August 26. His last Major League homer (Number 382) sailed into the screen above the Green Monster in Boston on September 8, 1973.

After his days as a player, Frank Howard stayed active by coaching and managing in the big leagues for many years. He is regarded with affection and respect, but, mostly, he is still viewed with a sense of awe. That is appropriate, because he earned it.

NUMBER 3: MICKEY MANTLE—536 HOME RUNS—1951 TO 1968

Mickey Mantle. Just say the name, and any reasonably informed baseball fan will envision a likeable, All-American wonder-boy oozing speed and power. Born in rural northeast Oklahoma in 1931, Mickey was raised by his loving dad to escape life in the local mines. To do this, young Mantle needed to develop his extraordinary skills, and father Mutt saw to that. He taught Mickey to bat from both sides of the plate, and pitched to him even when his own underground labors left him near the

Mickey Mantle

brink of exhaustion. Despite setbacks along the way, it all worked out.

Mickey played football, basketball, and baseball at Commerce High School, but his gridiron participation nearly resulted in tragedy. An infection from a leg injury almost caused the loss of the limb. Fortunately, he recovered, and signed a modest contract with the New York Yankees upon graduation in 1949. Playing shortstop later that year at Class D Independence, Mantle hit seven home runs in 89 games. In 1950, he moved up to Class C ball in Joplin, Missouri, where he began to shine. In 137 games, Mickey slugged 26 homers and batted .383. That earned him an invitation to the Yankees' 1951 rookie camp in Phoenix, but he had virtually no chance to make the parent club. He was just 19 and very raw. Mantle had shown great defensive potential at Joplin with his strong arm and blazing speed, but he had also committed many errors. However, almost immediately, manager Casey Stengel switched Mickey to the outfield, and focused on watching the kid hit. He could hardly believe his eyes!

Against all odds, Mantle was still on the Yankee roster when they played an exhibition game at Bovard Field in Los Angeles on March 26. But what could Stengel do? The boy had belted three long homers and batted close to .500. The contest on that day was scheduled against USC, whose players were mostly older than Mickey. But, in the case of Mickey Mantle, age meant little. He proceeded to smash titanic home runs from both the right and left sides that are revered to this day. The one to left field sailed over 500 feet, and the latter ball to right field flew much farther. There will be more discussion of these events in the final chapter. By the time the Yankees completed their spring games at Ebbets Field against the Dodgers, Mantle had clubbed nine home runs. He had also made the team as the starting right fielder.

At first, he didn't do well. He was just a frightened country kid playing at Yankee Stadium beside the legendary Joe DiMaggio. Although his play was erratic, the power was unmistakable. Mickey hit his first Major League home run at Chicago's Comiskey Park on May 1, 1951, and it was a whopper. The ball was lined 450 feet into the center field end of the right field grandstand. Three days later, Mantle blasted one about 25 feet farther to right field at Sportsman's Park in St. Louis. Still, he seemed lost, and, on July

15, Mick was sent to the Yanks' top affiliate in Kansas City. Happily, that wasn't far from Mantle's home, and his dad was able to visit him, delivering a much-needed pep talk. Playing for the Blues in just 40 games, Mickey went on a tear. He batted .364, drove in 50 runs, and bashed 11 home runs, including a July 31 moon shot over the light tower in Toledo. By August 20, he was recalled to New York, and never looked back.

Mantle moved to center field in 1952 with the retirement of DiMaggio. He hit 23 homers and played well, but it was a bittersweet year. Mutt Mantle passed away in early May, succumbing to Hodgkin's disease at age 40. It was a devastating emotional blow to the still-shy 20-year-old, but Mickey challenged himself to persevere in his father's memory. He succeeded. In August, Mantle finally received the last word on his military status. The Korean War was raging, and Uncle Sam badly needed able-bodied recruits. The problem was that Mickey Mantle was not regarded as physically fit. The osteomyelitis in his leg required daily treatment, and Mantle's draft board decided to permanently categorize him as "4-F." It is worth noting that Mickey played his entire professional career on legs that were not sound enough for military service.

Despite the handicap, in 1953, Mantle demonstrated such extraordinary power that fans began to regard him as a kind of superman. It started at Forbes Field in Pittsburgh on April 9. Playing an exhibition game shortly before opening day, Mantle launched an amazing drive from the left side that cleared the towering right field grandstand. It passed out of sight about 100 feet in height and about 400 feet away, resulting in a 510-foot estimate. Just eight days later at Griffith Stadium in Washington, D.C., Mickey belted one from the right side that flew about the same distance. This was the famous blast over the left center field bleachers that has traditionally been regarded as a 565-footer. That distance was the result of a clever publicity gambit by Yankee publicist Red Patterson, but the data clearly refutes his claim. However, Mickey was just getting started. He topped the left field bleachers in St. Louis on April 28 for a 500-foot ride. At Shibe Park in Philadelphia on July 6, Mantle smashed the ball over the left center field roof onto a house across Somerset Street. That was a monstrous blow of 525 feet. Not ignoring the hometown folks, Mickey completed his tape measure journey at Yankee Stadium on September 12. His 20th of 21 home runs landed in the far end of the left field upper deck. The seat that blocked the final stages of the flight was measured at 425 linear feet and 80 feet above ground. At that distant point, the ball was still traveling so fast that it ricocheted 60 feet back onto the field! Estimated at 515 feet, this drive was hard to believe. And don't forget; this guy was not yet 22 years old.

Mantle improved to 27 homers in 1954, but the Yankee faithful were getting a little impatient. These were the folks who

had watched guys named Ruth, Gehrig, and DiMaggio. When Mickey didn't produce in like fashion in those first few years, they occasionally vented their frustration by booing his frequent strikeouts. It wasn't easy inheriting that legacy, but Mantle stayed the course. That season, he belted a couple drives over 450 feet into the right field upper decks in Cleveland and New York on August 5 and September 2. However, his most interesting shot didn't result in a home run. On April 18 at Yankee Stadium, the "Commerce Comet" ripped a 470-foot triple off the center field wall under the Ed Barrow plaque. It was a reminder of just how difficult it was to knock it out of the park in that direction. Like Babe Ruth and all other Yankee sluggers, Mickey benefited from a few "cheap" homers down the nearby foul lines each year. But he lost more then he gained due to the prohibitive distances from center to left center.

Mickey Mantle took the big step from talented youngster to established star in 1955. He hit 37 home runs, topped .600 in slugging for the first time (.611), and recorded his career high in outfield putouts (372). Mickey also did his usual long-distance thing. At Comiskey Park on June 5, he bombed one to the base of the light tower atop the left field roof. On June 21 at Yankee Stadium, Mantle slugged a homer all the way to the ninth row of the center field bleachers beyond the 461 foot sign. Both of those shots flew around 500 feet. That was terrific stuff, but it didn't measure up to what happened in 1956. If

Mickey became a star in '55, he exploded to true superstardom the very next year. Some of his astral type numbers included 52 home runs, .353 batting average, .705 slugging average, 130 RBI, and 132 runs scored. Mantle also led the Yankees to their fourth World Series championship in his six years on the team. Along the way, he smacked a bunch of high megaton four-baggers.

It began on opening day in Washington on April 17. Batting left-handed against Camilo Pascual, Mickey launched two magnificent drives over the 30-foot wall in center field. The first cleared the 408 foot sign in dead center, while the second disappeared at the 438 foot mark a little to the right. There were reports that number one landed on the roof at 2014 Fifth Street, confirming the extraordinary length of 530 feet. Four days later in New York, Mantle drove the ball to the 20th row at the far end of the right field upper deck. Then, back at Yankee Stadium on May 30, Mickey victimized Pascual and the Senators again. He clubbed one high into the right center field bleachers off Camilo in the second game of the doubleheader. However, he had done even better in game one versus Pedro Ramos. His historic shot collided with the right field roof façade, 117 feet above ground and 370 feet from the starting point. Since the trajectory was that of a high fly, this ball probably would have flown just shy of 500 feet. Worth noting, it was the first homer to reach that rarified plateau since the grandstand was completed in 1938. Also during that impressive 1956

campaign, Mantle added drives in the 475-foot range in Kansas City (May 21), Detroit (June 18), Cleveland (September 16), and Boston (September 21).

Mickey came back to earth in 1957, but still struck 34, generally lengthy, home runs. Several of them flew about 460 feet, including balls that short-hopped the distant bleacher wall in Cleveland on June 5 and 6. Similarly, Mantle knocked one over the hedge beyond the center field fence at Memorial Stadium in Baltimore on August 10. In 1958, Mickey and the Yankees won yet another World Series after a one-year hiatus. The still-youthful center fielder put on a show by circling the bases at near light-speed after ripping a 450-foot shot to the flagpole in center. That display occurred on May 9, and was the second of Mantle's 42 homers for the season. For reasons already discussed, Mickey tried to avoid hitting fly balls to center field when playing at home. That lesson was reinforced on May 10 as he flied out to Washington's Albie Pearson 440 feet away in the 1st inning. If that seems like tough luck, consider that Mantle flied out again to Pearson in the 4th inning. That time, Albie was 460 feet from home plate. Mickey had an off year in 1959 with 31 home runs, giving the Yanks some cause to worry. Despite his veteran status, he was just 28 years of age. Still, there were growing concerns about the seemingly endless string of nagging injuries that plagued him. In truth, Mantle was holding up magnificently considering that his legs were in poor shape when he started. His entire career would be a war of attrition against those afflictions.

Mickey had a solid 40-homer season in 1960. That included a 480-foot blast to the upper deck in right center field at Cleveland's Municipal Stadium on July 20. He also continued his good work in the Motor City by bashing one through the light tower on the right center field roof at Tiger Stadium on September 10. Through no fault of Mickey Mantle, some of his home runs have been exaggerated for distance. This is one of them. It was a tremendous wallop, flying about 500 feet, but it could not have traveled farther in the air. Then, in 1961, Mickey blasted a career high of 54 homers, spending the summer locked in an epic home run battle with teammate Roger Maris. Mantle eventually settled for second best as Roger broke Babe Ruth's record with 61 homers. All American League offensive numbers were up that year because of expansion, but Mickey's statistics were awesome by any measure. He batted .317, slugged .687, drove in 128 runs, and scored 132 times. Of course, Mantle also banged out some eye-popping distance drives.

On June 21, 1961, Mickey thumped a pair of 475-footers at Municipal Stadium in Kansas City. The first banged off the scoreboard in deep right center, and the second cleared the outer right field wall before landing on Brooklyn Avenue. Batting from the left side on June 30 at Yankee Stadium, Mickey again dented the center field wall for another inside-the-parker. The following day, batting

righty, he slammed the ball over the 457 foot sign into the bleachers in deepest left center. The day after that, Mantle launched one of his seven homers of the season that landed in the right field upper deck. Considering that the Yanks won the Series again, it was a heck of a year. Yet, it was the last time that Mickey would play 150 games, making it a watershed season in a negative manner.

After totaling 30 home runs in 1962, Mantle hoped for better results in 1963. Sadly, it didn't happen. Breaking his foot on June 5, Mickey missed much of the season, and managed only 15 four-baggers. But for true tape measure addicts, it was not a lost year. After warming up with twin 450-footers in Baltimore (May 11) and New York (May 15), the Mighty Mick thundered the longest and mightiest official home run of his life. It happened on May 22, 1963, at Yankee Stadium as he batted left-handed against Kansas City's Bill Fischer. As he said many times in later life, he connected with all his power and a perfect swing, making optimum contact in the process. The ball sped upward in a savage line trajectory and momentarily looked as if it would clear the right field roof. Ultimately, it smashed into the ornamental roof façade not far from where Mantle's 1956 blast had collided with the same structure. The difference, and it was a big difference, was that this '63 blast was a line drive. That was demonstrated by the fact that the ball caromed back to the second baseman. The estimate for this extraordinary blow has been debated by physicists, baseball experts, and common fans ever since. It should be noted that it has been scientifically proven that the ball was on its way down when it struck the façade. Prudent judgment places the projected flight distance at 540 feet.

To everyone's relief and satisfaction, Mickey rebounded to enjoy his last great season in 1964. While slugging 35 home runs, he batted .300 and drove in 100 runs for the final time. He also still patrolled the cavernous center field region at Yankee Stadium. In his 33rd year, Mantle remained a force on the baseball diamond. That fact was evident when Mickey smacked one against the edge of the left field roof at Tiger Stadium. Taking place on July 24, it was the longest drive that Mantle ever hit in that direction in Detroit. Then on August 12, Mickey belted his longest-ever center field drive in New York. Standing in the left side of the batter's box, Mantle pounded the leather so far over the 461 foot sign that it came down in the 12th row. It was estimated at 512 feet. When the Yankees lost the World Series in seven games to the St. Louis Cardinals in the fall, Mickey was magnificent. He batted .333 and ripped three homers. That fixed his final Series' total at 18 circuits, which remains the record to this day.

Playing in the Houston Astrodome in an exhibition game on April 9, 1965, Mantle logged the first Major League home run ever struck indoors. It was a rousing 400-foot line drive into the seats in right cen-ter. Mickey delivered just 19 home runs that year, and his overall play was in decline. But his power seemed ageless. On June 22, he again topped the 457 foot marker in left center, which nobody else had done in recent memory. Knowing that those pain-ravaged legs couldn't last forever, the Yankees staged "Mickey Mantle Day" on September 18 at the stadium. It was a testimony to New York's respect for the man that the event attracted a sellout despite the Yanks' dismal position in the standings. Then, happily, there was somewhat of a renaissance in 1966. Playing in only 108 games due to various ailments, Mickey whacked 23 home runs. There were times when the guy could hardly throw or run, but there was still thunder in his bat. On May 14 in Kansas City, he hit the outer wall in right center field. And, on July 8 in New York, Mantle topped the center field fence for the final time.

Switching to first base in 1967, Mickey clubbed 22 homers. Career Number 500 sailed into the right field lower deck at Yankee Stadium on May 14. The original Washington Senators were then playing in Minnesota as the Twins, but there was a new Senators' franchise in the capital. They played at D.C. Stadium, which was eventually renamed after Robert F. Kennedy. Since Mantle couldn't seem to resist hitting tape measure shots wherever he played, he hammered a ball to the second row in the left center field upper deck. That was a blow of 462 feet. At home on July 25, Mickey visited the 12th row of the bleachers past the auxiliary scoreboard in left center. That 455-footer was the final tape measure homer that Mantle would record.

He hit his final 18 homers in 1968, including two more into the right field upper deck. After smacking a homer in game one of a June 29 twin-bill in New York, Mickey was sitting out the second game. When called upon to pinch hit in the 8th inning, the old warrior slammed a 450-foot drive near the monuments in center field. It won the game 5–4. A young Mantle would have circled the bases, but, nearing age 37, Mickey limped into second base before leaving for a pinch runner. The end was near. Home run Number 536 was lined into the right field lower deck in New York on September 20, 1968. It was the last time that New Yorkers would watch Number 7 perform this treasured ritual. It took them a long time, but they had come to love Mickey Mantle. As the years rolled by, they had understood the great pain that he endured in playing for them. In fact, when Mickey Mantle died in 1997, he was the most beloved baseball player in the country. It was an honor that he had earned.

MICKEY MANTLE'S 10 LONGEST HOME RUNS

- May 22, 1963—New York off Kansas City's Fischer—Line drive off right field roof façade—540 ft.

- April 17, 1956—Washington off Pascual—Over high center field wall onto house—530 ft.

- July 6, 1953—Philadelphia off Fanovich—Far over grandstand roof in left center—525 ft.

- September 12, 1953—New York off Detroit's Hoeft—Liner high into far end of upper deck in left—515 ft.

- August 23, 1956—New York off Chicago's LaPalme—To 20th row in left field upper deck—515 ft.

- August 12, 1964—New York off Chicago's Herbert—To 12th row in center field bleachers—512 ft.

- April 17, 1953—Washington off Stobbs—Over left center field bleachers—510 ft.

- September 21, 1956—Boston off Sullivan—To bleacher wall atop center field bleachers—510 ft.

- June 21, 1955—New York off Kansas City's Kellner—To ninth row in center field bleachers—505 ft.

- April 28, 1953—St. Louis off Cain—Over left field bleachers; landed across street—500 ft.

NUMBER 2: JIMMIE FOXX—534 HOME RUNS—1927 TO 1945

Jimmie Foxx looked like a Greek god, and hit baseballs with the force of Zeus hurling thunderbolts from Mount Olympus. Nevertheless, he remains somewhat unknown to modern fans. That is a cultural tragedy, since James Emory Foxx is an immensely important figure in the history of the national pastime. Born in Sudlersville on the Maryland Eastern Shore in 1907, he developed his prodigious strength by playing sports and performing various forms of farm labor. The results were nearly incredible. By age 16, he had the body of a cartoon superhero. In his prime, Foxx would stand 6 feet tall and weigh 200 pounds.

As a mere youth in 1922 and 1923, Jimmie played pitcher and third base in the Caroline County League. His reputation for speed and power reached the ears of the legendary Frank "Home Run" Baker, who was then managing the Easton team in the Eastern Shore League. Foxx joined Baker in 1924, and switched to catcher at his skipper's request. Playing 76 games, he batted .296 and slugged 10 homers. Baker was so impressed that he contacted the Yankees and Athletics to advise them of Jimmie's unlimited potential. Connie Mack of the A's acted first and signed Foxx to a $2,000 contract on July 30, 1924. The lad was instructed to finish the year with Easton, which he did in almost mythic style.

In a September playoff game against Martinsburg (champs of the Blue Ridge League), Jimmie whacked two tremendous homers, including one to the center field flagpole for the longest drive ever hit in that park. He then clinched the final playoff victory with a 9th inning single, thereby inducing Mack to summon him to the A's. On September 12, 1924, at Erie, Pennsylvania, Connie inserted Foxx into the starting lineup in an exhibition game against the Cincinnati Reds. He tripled, and played the entire game at catcher in an Athletics win. Before returning home to attend high school, Jimmie played a final exhibition game on September 28. Again, he caught the entire contest, and, this time, added a long left field double. Through all this, Jimmie Foxx was a 16-year-old kid! This is not romanticized fiction. All these events have been confirmed by primary sources. The

Jimmie Foxx

greatest prodigies (teenage boys with nearly superhuman power) in baseball history have been Mickey Mantle, Jimmie Foxx, and Babe Ruth. In this chronicle of the longest hitters in the annals of the game, they hold the top three spots. Obviously, prodigious strength at a young age is the first step to historic power performance.

Jimmie's high school class graduated without him in June 1925, because he had already rejoined the Philadelphia Athletics. After receiving a rousing farewell party from his entire hometown, Jimmie went to Fort Myers, Florida, to participate in spring training. By February 28, he was captaining one of two A's teams competing in an intra-squad game. The other team was led by 22-year-old catcher Mickey Cochrane from Boston University. Foxx had no chance to beat out the more mature Cochrane, which turned Jimmie into a position gypsy. In truth, that role followed him for the rest of his career. But, regardless of his defensive future, even then, Foxx was the strongest hitter on the club. On March 4, in another squad game, he belted a home run so far to left center field that it was hailed as the A's longest spring training drive.

Of course, Connie Mack never intended to regularly use the 17-year-old Foxx that year. He pinch hit nine times, and spent the months of July and August gaining experience with Providence in the International League. So it went through 1927. Jimmie would play a little here and there, mostly in pinch-hitting roles or in exhibition games, but he didn't return to the minor leagues. Foxx usually sat beside Connie Mack in the dugout, and learned his craft from the old master. Jimmie did manage to record his first big-league home run on May 31, 1927, by smacking the ball over Babe Ruth's head and into the left field upper deck at Philadelphia's Shibe Park.

Then came the transition year of 1928. It was the height of the great Yankee dynasty, but the Athletics were pretty good themselves. In fact, they almost beat the Yanks that year, and then whipped them the next three seasons. Their roster featured future Hall of Famers Foxx, Cochrane, Lefty Grove, Al Simmons, Ty Cobb, and Tris Speaker. Jimmie Foxx also had a breakout season in 1928. After experimenting at first base in '27, "Double X" played more at third base in '28, but, most importantly, he just played more. Along the way, he belted 13 home runs, including his first-ever tape measure drives in official Major League games. On June 25, 1928, at Griffith Stadium in Washington, D.C., Foxx bombed one nearly halfway up the center field bleachers above the 441 foot sign. Then, on July 25 at Shibe Park, Jimmie ripped the ball completely over the left field grandstand. Those drives respectively sailed about 480 feet and 470 feet. Jimmie Foxx had not yet turned 21 years old, but both he and his team had arrived at the doorstep of greatness.

Over the next three years, Jimmie averaged 33 homers a season. It was the start of an historic 12-year streak when he would slug 30 or more home runs each season. In 1929,

Foxx moved back to first base, and, despite sometimes filling in at third, it became his primary position for the remainder of his career. It was also the year that Jimmie blasted three balls over Shibe Park's left field roof; plus he added one off the center field fence and one over it. Here is where some clarification is necessary. It has been suggested by some historians that Foxx's accomplishments are somewhat tainted because of his "home and away splits." They refer to the fact that Jimmie performed significantly better during home games than away games, thereby inferring that he might not have been as good as his total numbers suggest. This fiction should be put to rest.

It's true that Jimmie Foxx recorded 56 percent of his career four-baggers in home games. From 1927 through 1935, with Shibe Park as his home turf, Jimmie hit 169 homers in Philly and only 133 on the road. But this criticism is valid only if the home park is easier than the historical norm. That isn't the case here. At Shibe Park, it was 334 feet to the left field foul pole, 372 feet to the left center field power alley, and 468 feet to the corner in dead center. The fence along that entire distance was 12 feet high, and the right field area was of comparable difficulty. For anybody who knows baseball, those dimensions are demonstrably more difficult than the average ballpark of today. The reason that Foxx hit more homers at Shibe is simple. During his career, it was more difficult for a right-handed power hitter in the

American League ballparks than for sluggers at any other time.

Left field in Yankee Stadium was a notorious graveyard. While a mere 301 feet along the foul line, the fence quickly arched to 400 feet in straight left field and 470 feet to the power alley. Of course, it was 490 feet to dead center. In Washington and Cleveland, it was 400 feet and 375 feet respectively to the left field bleachers along the lines with proportional distances to left center and center. At St. Louis, the bleachers were 351 feet distant from home plate, and Comiskey Park in Chicago was an absolute nightmare for all hitters. Those foul lines were 365 feet in both directions, with center field at 455 feet. The only place in the American League (except for a while in Detroit) where it was beneficial batting right-handed was Fenway Park in Boston. Jimmie eventually played there from 1936 through early 1942.

The left field wall at Fenway, now referred to as the "Green Monster," was just 309 feet away, rising 37 feet above the playing field. However, Foxx's time in Boston never offset the total degree of difficulty that he experienced during his entire career. It should also be recalled that the bullpens in right and right center field were not installed until 1940. Ted Williams had arrived the preceding season, and the Red Sox wanted to make it easier for him to hit homers in his home park. In later years, during his Hall of Fame career, Jim Rice blasted over 20 of his career home runs into those bullpens. During his first four years as a Red Sock (1936–1939), Foxx hit none, because opposite field homers had to fly all the way into the distant bleachers. Some other American League dimensions also changed during Jimmie's career, but slugging right-handed in the American League remained prohibitively difficult for as long as he played. Let's be completely clear on this topic: Jimmie Foxx did not have it easy hitting home runs in his time as a big leaguer.

Returning to 1929 and those three balls that Jimmie knocked over the left field roof at Shibe Park, a few more numbers are relevant. It was 378 feet to the back of the roof at its closest position and 65 feet above the street. Since Foxx rarely cleared that structure near the foul line, almost every roof-topper flew well over 450 feet. Jimmie ultimately blasted 24 homers over that roof with many leaving the field in deep left center field. Several topped that grandstand by as much as 40 feet and landed at various points north of the stadium. It should be added that Foxx smacked another 29 homers onto the top of the grandstand. So, in '29, when Jimmie started hitting tape measure shots regularly, it was a revelation. Up to that time, only Babe Ruth had done this, and most observers felt that he was a one-time phenomenon. With Jimmie Foxx now approaching the Babe's accomplishments, baseball would never be the same.

The Philadelphia Athletics won the World Series in both 1929 and 1930, and just missed in 1931. But Connie Mack was not a wealthy man, and began selling off his roster. The team would never return to glory, but Jimmie Foxx was still emerging. In '32, Jimmie smashed 58 home runs, nearly breaking Ruth's record of 60. Some even thought that he was clubbing them as far as the mighty Bambino. Prior to the Foxx onslaught, that would have been heresy. It all started on opening day on April 12 at Shibe Park versus the Yankees. The Babe hit a pair of gigantic homers of about 480 feet, but they were not the longest of the game. In the 7th inning, Jimmie pounded Lefty Gomez for an amazing drive over the center field wall beside the flagpole. It was the first time in baseball history that anyone, other than Ruth, hit a 500-foot center field home run. Then, at Yankee Stadium on June 25, Foxx lined a ball deep into the towering left field upper deck. This was also hit off Gomez, who was so incredulous that after the game he walked to the landing spot. He claimed that the ball broke the seat that interrupted its flight. This may be an overstatement, but contemporary accounts confirm that this drive was struck on a line drive trajectory. It certainly would have flown over 500 feet.

Jimmie was tremendous in 1932, but, as often happens with great performances, there has been some hyperbole. A screen had been placed atop the right field fence in St. Louis after Babe Ruth set the record in 1927. It has been said that Foxx batted seven balls off that barrier in '32, along with other drives in Cleveland and elsewhere that would have been homers in '27. That is not true. By studying game accounts for the entire season, it is apparent that Jimmie lost only one homer to the new screens. Foxx doesn't need any embellishment. What he did in 1932 stands on its own merits. As discussed, the configuration of American League ballparks was such that it was significantly harder to hit 58 homers right-handed than 60 homers left-handed. Ruth had other issues to deal with, but the stadium factor weighed against Jimmie. Regardless of the false data, Foxx made his mark in St. Louis by launching a 500-footer over the left center field bleachers on June 19. And contemplate this: Among Foxx's homers in that single year, 24 of them traveled 450 feet or farther. It was a season for the ages!

"The Beast" kept blasting. From 1933 through 1935, he averaged 42 homers a year, and many were leviathans. On May 18, 1934, in Chicago's Comiskey Park, Foxx rocketed a ball to the seventh row in the center field bleachers. Home plate had been moved forward 14 feet that year, but the 15-foot wall was still 440 feet away. Jimmie's shot was estimated at 475 feet, but everybody agreed that it was not his longest in the Windy City . . . not nearly. Until 1934, a ball had to travel 375 linear feet to reach the nearest edge of the *75-foot-high* grandstand roof. So, Comiskey offered an ideal 450-foot minimum-distance plateau for any ball that reached that point. Also remember that the roof was 52 feet wide. On July 18, 1930, August 31, 1931, and June 20, 1932, Jimmie thundered similar blows to the back of the Comiskey Park roof in left center. Each of them then bounced over the top and out

of sight. After home plate was repositioned, it was still over 360 feet to the closest corner, and Foxx still reached it on June 16, 1936, July 18, 1937, and July 28, 1938. The one in 1936 actually cleared the entire roof in left field on the fly. In later years (1983), home plate was moved out again, whereby the roof became much more accessible. But, when it was at its most distant (1927–1933), nobody mastered it as did Jimmie Foxx. His home runs there in 1930, 1931, 1932, and 1936 can each be realistically estimated at over 500 feet. That is distance-hitting on a scale that defies explanation.

Jimmie was traded to Boston in 1936, and spent the rest of his peak years with the Red Sox. He did fine in his first two years, bashing 41 and 36 home runs. Foxx was still rightfully regarded as the game's mightiest slugger. However, on a return trip to Shibe Park on September 19, 1936, an event took place that demonstrated Jimmie's exceptional speed. Wally Moses was a second-year outfielder with the reputation as the fastest runner in the American League. In fact, he would steal 56 bases during the 1943 season. Foxx was matched against him and others in a pregame 75-yard sprint. There was an apparent dead heat at the finish line, but Moses was proclaimed the victor. Jimmie, affable as always, didn't complain, but the *Boston Herald* declared that Foxx had won. No matter, the point was made; Jimmie Foxx could flat-out fly.

However, amidst all the glory, something else was going on that nobody seemed to notice. Foxx had been violently struck in

---

JIMMIE FOXX'S 10 LONGEST HOME RUNS

- June 16, 1936—Chicago off Cain—Over roof in left center to court across street—530 ft.
- May 14, 1932—Philadelphia off St. Louis's Hadley—Far over roof in left center onto house—525 ft.
- July 18, 1930—Chicago off Braxton—To back of grandstand roof in left center—520 ft.
- September 10, 1929—Philadelphia off Cleveland's Ferrell—High over roof in left center—515 ft.
- June 20, 1932—Chicago off Caraway—To back of grandstand roof in left center—515 ft.
- June 25, 1932—New York off Gomez—High into left field upper deck at far end—515 ft.
- August 22, 1931—Chicago off Caraway—To back of grandstand roof in left center—510 ft.
- August 16, 1940—Boston off Washington's Monteagudo—Over wall in left to back of parking lot—510 ft.
- April 12, 1932—Philadelphia off New York's Gomez—Far over wall in dead center field—505 ft.
- August 2, 1940—Detroit off Newsom—To top of second deck just left of center—505 ft.

---

the head with a pitched ball in Winnipeg, Canada, at the outset of a 1934 postseason world tour. X-rays were negative, but they showed an old skull fracture that Jimmie said dated back to 1928. Either way, the '34 incident caused a very serious injury, involving a severe concussion, and Foxx should have refrained from vigorous activity for at least a month. But, within a week, he was playing ball and boarding a ship for the Orient. The bottom line is that Jimmie Foxx, just shy of his 27th birthday, suffered a debilitating injury from which he never completely recovered. He would enjoy many more successful seasons, but always complained of "sinus troubles." With the benefit of 21st-century medical hindsight, we can surmise that it all

originated as early as 1928 and culminated in 1934 with his beaning in Canada.

In 1938, Jimmie Foxx hammered 50 home runs. One of the most interesting collided with the back wall atop the left center field bleachers at Cleveland's League Park on September 17. That was the closest that anyone ever came to clearing that structure in a game, although Jimmie had done it in BP on June 25, 1936. There are legends that he also landed a few of his Fenway homers on the old B & O railroad tracks in left field. Since those rails were positioned at a minimum distance of 505 feet along the left field line (and angled out sharply), those may have been "fish stories." He did come close on August 16, 1940, reaching the back of a parking lot for a 510-foot shot. We also know that Jimmie launched many balls to the rear of the garage roof in deep left and left center. There are eyewitness drawings for some of those blows, and the buildings and ballpark are still in place for precise analysis. It can be proven that Foxx launched dozens of baseballs in the 450 to 500-foot range at Fenway Park. An ideal example occurred on August 12, 1937, when Double X reached the roof just left of center field.

In 1939, when Ted Williams became Foxx's teammate, Jimmie clobbered 35 homers despite ending his season on September 9 with an appendectomy. Then in 1940, while catching 42 games due to team need, he added 36 circuits. Imagine a modern superstar volunteering to catch after years away from that grueling position. In fact, Foxx took over the catching duties while recovering from a severely wrenched knee! After just a few days of action, future Hall of Fame player-manager Joe Cronin rated Jimmie as the best receiver in the Junior Circuit. Although seldom recognized for his defensive prowess, Jimmie Foxx was an extraordinary athlete. Cronin further described Foxx as being as good an all-around player as anyone in the game's history.

His longest hit on the road that year was likely the one he walloped almost over the center field upper deck at Tiger Stadium on August 2. That season also featured Career Homer Number 500. Until 2007, when Alex Rodriguez set the new standard, Foxx was the youngest player ever to reach that mark. Jimmie was not yet 33 years old, and every-body assumed that he had at least another 200 left in him. In a 1986 interview, Ted Williams described why it didn't happen. He theorized that Jimmie's affection for Babe Ruth may have inadvertently led to his premature decline. According to Ted, Foxx felt that he had to emulate the Babe in every way. That included drinking and partying, which was not a good way to prolong anybody's career. Everyone knows that Ruth did party, but historians agree that he was never an alcoholic. Furthermore, Babe quieted down after he met his second wife. Besides, Ruth could somehow handle it. Apparently, Jimmie couldn't.

Combined with the serious head injury (already described), Foxx's poor habits led to a rapid downward spiral after the 1940 season. He was actually out of big-league baseball in 1943, but returned in '44 and '45 when World War II depleted the talent pool. He recorded his final two homers (533 and 534) at Forbes Field in Pittsburgh on September 9, 1945, and they were worthy of the man who hit them. Both were bombed over the distant left field wall and flew well over 400 feet. It's true that Jimmie had trouble adjusting to life after the fame and fortune of his playing days. But, in the same interview with Ted Williams in '86, the Splinter referred to his old buddy as "a real peach of a guy." He also stated, "You just can't imagine how far he could hit a baseball." Let's follow Ted's lead, and remember Jimmie Foxx as that smiling youth with the bulging biceps, who blasted baseballs to the realm of our imagination.

NUMBER 1: BABE RUTH—714 HOME RUNS—1915 TO 1935

There is no rational explanation for Babe Ruth. He was probably placed on earth in a time capsule dated 1895 by the same extra-terrestrials who built the pyramids 4,000 years earlier. Since he shouldn't have been able to do the things that he did on the ball field, that explanation is as good as any. The Babe really was larger than life. Of course, that is an overused cliché, but, in this case, it is appropriate. Ruth was the best player, best showman, best ambassador, and the mightiest batsman that baseball has ever known . . . or likely ever will know!

George Ruth was born in Baltimore, Maryland, in 1895, and sent to a local reform school at age seven. Fortunately, St. Mary's had a baseball team, where Ruth played pitcher and catcher until leaving just after his 19th birthday in February 1914. As he walked out the door, George stood 6'2" and weighed a lean 185 pounds. Playing for the International League Baltimore Orioles, George was an immediate sensation. In his first competition against professional ballplayers, during an intra-squad game in Fayetteville, Ruth blasted a 435-foot home run into a corn field. It broke the city's distance record established by legendary Olympian Jim Thorpe and left everyone numb with amazement. That was a stupefying distance for a 19-year-old kid in the dead ball era.

But sports fans around the country soon got accustomed to Babe Ruth doing seemingly impossible deeds. Working as a left-handed pitcher that first year, Ruth won a total of 31 games, including minor league contests, exhibition appearances, and Major League games. Along the way, also batting from the left side, he set distance records in at least three other cities. Then, in 1915, as a full-time rookie pitcher with the Boston Red Sox, Babe hit the first confirmed tape measure home run in Major League history. Some performance standards must be assigned to the concept of "tape measure," and, if a 450-foot minimum is appropriate, then Babe Ruth recorded the first one. It occurred on July 21, 1915, and roared over the right field pavilion at Sportsman's Park in St. Louis. The ball landed on the far side of Grand Avenue for a flight distance of 475 feet. In that instant, the sport of baseball was changed forever.

From 1915 through 1917, Ruth averaged 21 wins a year along with a minuscule ERA. He was regarded as the best left-hander in baseball, and his Red Sox were just as successful, winning the World Series in 1915 and 1916. But, in 1918, World War I caused a diminution in the big-league talent level, motivating Babe's manager to risk using him in the field when he wasn't pitching. It was a landmark decision. Ruth belted an AL lead-tying total of 11 home runs. Oddly, his longest blow of the year was not a home run. On July 8, 1918, at Boston's Fenway Park, Babe batted in the bottom of the 10th inning in a 0–0 tie. He savagely lined a ball deep into the right field bleachers for what would be a walk-off homer today. But, according to the rules of the time, when the runner on first base scored, the game ended, limiting Ruth to a triple. However, the distance wasn't compromised; it flew a whopping 490 feet. A pattern was emerging as Babe Ruth kept slamming them farther with each passing season.

In 1919, Babe just wanted to hit, but skipper Ed Barrow wasn't convinced. So, Ruth did everything humanly possible to make his move to the outfield permanent. On April 4 at Boston's spring training site at Plant Field in Tampa, Babe played left field against the New York Giants. In the 2nd inning, he teed off to right center field with all his vast power. The ball sailed on and on, finally landing at the far side of a racetrack in which the ball field was situated. The spot was marked, and the flight distance was measured the next day. Some disagreement over the exact number still exists, but the likely figure was 552 feet. Such a drive would have been inconceivable before the arrival of Babe Ruth. Then, two weeks later during a two-day exhibition appearance back in Baltimore, Ruth did the unthinkable again. He blasted home runs in six consecutive at-bats versus his old team, the Orioles. Two of those homers flew over 500 feet. Babe went on to shatter the Major League record by smashing 29 home runs that year, and rendered the sporting world incredulous.

Babe's escalating salary demands led to his off-season sale to the New York Yankees, where the world discovered that they hadn't

Babe Ruth

Courtesy of Linda Ruth Tosetti

seen anything yet. It is hard for fans in the 21st century to comprehend what it meant in 1920 when Babe Ruth almost doubled his nearly unbelievable home run record from the preceding year. Babe's 54 homers would be the equivalent of about 130 today. Folks thought they were dreaming. But he hit them, and oh how far he hit them! After bashing a few monster shots during spring training, Ruth took his time before logging his first official homer as a New Yorker. The Yankees shared the Polo Grounds with the Giants in those days, and it was ridiculously close down the right field line at 257 feet. However, the grandstand moved out at an angle that paralleled a line drawn between home plate and dead center field. So, when Babe crushed one far over the fourth flagpole from the foul line atop the right field roof, the ball had already flown 400 feet. This May 1, 1920 drive traveled about 505 feet. Before the season ended, Ruth miraculously added five more 500-footers, including blows in Boston, St. Louis, and Detroit.

The English language needs a new vocabulary to adequately describe what Babe Ruth did in 1921. Fighting a weight problem for the first time, the Bambino played at about 225 pounds. The strength inside that torso is virtually impossible to quantify. Ruth's first virtuoso blast was launched over the right center field scoreboard at Griffith Stadium in Washington, D.C., on May 6. That 490-footer was acclaimed as the town's longest-ever, but that distinction endured exactly one day. Turning around a Walter Johnson fastball on May 7, Babe thumped the ball far over the high wall in the deepest center field corner. Even Ruth was pleased with this drive of 520 feet. He acknowledged after the game that he had made perfect contact, and was benefited by the transferred energy of the Big Train's 100-mph heater. Later that month, Babe hit one even a little farther into the center field bleachers in St. Louis. Then, on June 13th and 14th, Ruth smacked almost matching shots into the center field seats at the Polo Grounds.

Playing at Navin Field, against nemesis Ty Cobb on July 18, it didn't seem possible that Babe could hit a baseball any harder than he already had. Wrong assumption. This was Babe Ruth, and the seemingly impossible was now commonplace. After walking four straight times, which surely raised Ruth's adrenaline level, the Babe tore into a Bert Cole offering in the 8th inning. The ball soared toward the corner of Cherry Street and Trumbull Avenue in dead center, and landed in the middle of the intersection. The groundskeeper immediately produced stadium blueprints proving that the ball had left the premises 560 feet from home plate. More will be said about this event in the final chapter. So it went for the entire schedule. Babe astonished Chicagoans at Comiskey Park on August 17 with his awesome poke high over the top of the right center field bleachers. When he pounded a 510-foot missile to deepest left center at Shibe Park in Philadelphia, Ruth had completed his tape measure sweep of every American League city. He finished with 59 home runs for another record. Babe also established a power performance standard that has never been approached by any other player.

Babe Ruth demonstrated his mortality both on and off the field in 1922. He dropped to "just" 35 homers, and received some appropriate criticism for not living up to his role as America's preeminent athlete. Happily, he took it to heart, and spent the winter at his farm chopping wood and embracing a spartan lifestyle. For the flamboyant Ruth, it could not have been easy. However, the results were spectacular. When Babe reported for the inaugural of Yankee Stadium on opening day 1923, he took the field at a svelte 201 pounds. He lined the first-ever home run in "The House That Ruth Built" into the right field bleachers, thereby initiating his best all-around season. The Babe has traditionally been feted for both his slugging and his pitching, but rarely for his fielding. In truth, when Ruth aged into his late thirties, he didn't deserve much defensive recognition. But, in 1923, those days were a long way off, and the Bambino was sensational as an outfielder. Game accounts are replete with glowing descriptions of Ruth ranging everywhere to make great catch after great catch. Although playing corner outfield, he still finished third in outfield putouts (378) in the American League. Babe also amassed career highs in outfield assists (20), stolen bases (17), and batting average (.393).

Of course, Ruth was still the longest hitter in baseball, despite slimming down and focusing on other aspects of his game. He proved that at Yankee Stadium on April 24 and June 12, when he lined balls respectively to the 55th row in the right field bleachers and the 35th row in right center. Those were drives of 480 and 495 feet. Babe hit one almost as far as he led the Yanks to their first World Series victory in October. Ruth added 46 homers in 1924 (five more than 1923) and won his only batting championship at .378. Along the way, he pummeled a 525-foot blast deep into the bleachers just right of center field. Nobody ever reached the scoreboard atop those seats at Yankee Stadium, but this Ruthian drive on May 31, 1924 came closest. Babe struck a ball 505 feet that cleared Comiskey Park's right center field bleachers on July 28, and rounded out the year by clubbing a pair of 500-footers at Fenway Park on September 8 and 11. Sadly, however, he lost control of his weight over the winter and reported out of shape for spring training in St. Petersburg. Somehow, he still performed superbly until collapsing at the Asheville, North Carolina, train station on April 7. He was diagnosed with a stomach abscess, which required major surgery. Despite returning to the lineup on June 1, it was a lost year for Ruth and the Yankees. Babe hit only 25 homers, and the team finished in seventh place. The good news was that Ruth amended his ways permanently, and played in 1926 with a sense of purpose that never left him.

After working out all winter with former boxer Artie McGovern, Babe arrived at spring training in excellent condition in 1926. He regained his stature as the game's top slugger by bashing 47 home runs and leading the Yanks back to the World Series. It didn't take long to show that his Herculean power was still intact. At Yankee Stadium on April 24, Ruth nearly cleared the bleachers in right center field, and, on May 19, he lined one to the 64th row in right field. They were blows of 510 and 515 feet. On the road, Babe was even mightier. He hit his longest-ever at Fenway Park on May 25 by launching the ball to the 44th row in the distant right field seats. If allowed to return to field level, that drive would have flown 540 feet. In Detroit on June 8, Ruth uncorked an amazing blast of 520 feet that carried over Trumbull Avenue in right field, landing on a taxi in Plum Street. It was all wonderful stuff, but may not have measured up to what the Babe did in his postseason barnstorming tour.

Those games were always ripe for exceptional displays of power because Ruth swung with all his might. Why not? The outcomes of the contests were relatively unimportant; the fans essentially came to see a Ruthian homer. On October 12, 1926, at Artillery Field in Wilkes-Barre, Pennsylvania, Babe Ruth hit what may have been the longest drive of his career. Putting on a batting exhibition after the actual game, Ruth pounded the ball toward right center with ungodly force. Knowing that

he had made perfect contact with his most powerful swing, Babe immediately dropped the bat and walked off the field. Afterwards, he readily stated that he couldn't hit a ball farther. When asked to compare the distance to his recent confirmed 530-footer during the World Series in St. Louis, Ruth said, "I believe the ball I hit here this afternoon went a lot farther." The exact distance is still being debated, but it was no fluke. Two days later in Scranton and 11 days later in South Bend, Babe Ruth smashed home runs well over 500 feet.

What else can be said about The Sultan of Swat and the New York Yankees in 1927? How about this: Among Ruth's record 60 home runs, there were 28 that were hit from 400 to 450 feet, another 17 that flew from 450 to

BABE RUTH'S 10 LONGEST HOME RUNS

- July 18, 1921—Detroit off Cole—Out of stadium in dead center field into street—575 ft.
- May 22, 1930—Philadelphia off Ehmke—Over two rows of houses in right field—550 ft.
- August 17, 1921—Chicago off Wieneke—High over bleachers in deep right center—545 ft.
- May 25, 1926—Boston off Zahniser—Line drive to 44th row in right field bleachers—540 ft.
- May 25, 1935—Pittsburgh off Bush—Over right field roof onto house across street—540 ft.
- May 25, 1921—St. Louis off Shocker—Deep into distant bleachers in dead center—535 ft.
- July 31, 1921—New York off Cleveland's Caldwell—Line drive far over right field roof—530 ft.
- October 6, 1926—St. Louis off Bell—Line drive halfway up bleachers in dead center—530 ft.
- May 27, 1920—Boston off Harper—To 40th row in right center field bleachers—525 ft.
- May 31, 1924—New York off Philadelphia's Gray—High into bleachers right of center—525 ft.

500 feet, as well as three more that traveled over 500 feet. Upon sweeping the World Series in four games, Babe Ruth was at the height of his legendary popularity. He and Lou Gehrig next embarked on a cross-country barnstorming tour, where Ruth bludgeoned another 19 massive four-baggers. Counting all games in 1927, official and unofficial, Babe smacked 90 homers that year. He seemed fictional, and no one thought that those events could ever be repeated. Yet in 1928, Ruth hammered 54 homers with the distances essentially equaling those of the year before. The Yankees again swept through the World Series in four games, after which, Babe and Lou toured the country once more in grand style. This time around, Ruth amassed 84 home runs, and perhaps, one of these should be singled out. On May 10, 1928, at Yankee Stadium, Babe whacked a ball to left field that came down at the base of the mezzanine. It was a drive of 465 feet that was aimed in the opposite direction of Ruth's optimum power.

In 1929 Ruth had a tough year. His first wife died in January, he missed three weeks with a nervous breakdown in mid-season, manager Miller Huggins passed away in September, and the Philadelphia Athletics defeated the Yankees for the pennant. But this was the post-1925 Bambino, and he could handle anything. Despite the extreme adversity, Ruth was personally magnificent, bashing 46 home runs and adding to his unique legacy. Actually, Babe's baseball life from 1929 through 1931 was remarkably consistent. He averaged 47 homers, slugged over .700, and batted close to .360 while the Yankees finished just behind the A's each year. Although not at his peak, Ruth was still a great player. And, of course, he could hit the ball farther than anyone on the planet. During that time, Babe delivered many long-distance drives, but his work at Shibe Park in 1930 best exemplifies his capability. In the first game of a doubleheader on May 21, Ruth drilled three home runs, with number two flying over a house across the street in right field. The next day, folks were still buzzing over that 505-footer, and wondering if it had been Babe's longest in Philadelphia. Those conversations ended in the 3rd inning of the first game of yet another twin-bill. Ruth again pounded the ball to right field, but, this time, the ball kept going past where the previous day's shot had landed. It ultimately cleared two rows of houses along with the yards and alleyway between and struck a window on the east side of Opal Street. That 550-foot thunderbolt was the exclamation point to six home runs hit in the space of 28 hours.

In 1932, Babe Ruth finally slowed down. Forbidden by the Yankees to play golf during the season, Ruth lost some valuable leg strength. He was replaced by Jimmie Foxx as baseball's longest hitter, but there was no shame in that. He still smacked 41 regular season homers with the most famous one he ever hit coming in the postseason. Almost everyone has heard of Babe's "called shot" in the '32 World Series, but few realize how far it went. Openly defying the Chicago Cubs and their hostile fans in Game Three at Wrigley Field, Ruth gestured that he was about to punish them. He did. We will never know exactly what Ruth expressed at that moment, but the defiance and intent were unmistakable. He then launched a 490-foot bomb to the flagpole beyond the center field fence. It was pure Ruthian magic. During 1933 and 1934, Babe slipped back a little further, but he could still pound them. He reached the 25th row of the center field bleachers at Fenway Park on September 23, 1933 (510 feet). Then, Ruth recorded his 700th career homer in Detroit on July 13, 1934, by driving a breathtaking 505-footer past Trumbull Avenue.

Babe's brief tenure with the Boston Braves in 1935 was a disappointment. He retired from the team and his sport on June 1 after hitting only six home runs. But the last three, struck on May 25 at Forbes Field in Pittsburgh, were a fitting climax to the greatest slugging career of all time. The first one went 385 feet and landed in the right field lower deck. Number two was a 500-foot line drive masterpiece, landing in the upper deck in deep right center. That would have been more than enough for anyone except Babe Ruth. Summoning all his still-formidable strength, the Bambino launched his third homer over the right field roof onto a house across the street. That building was later measured at 529 feet from home plate, meaning that Ruth's final big-league home run (714) flew approximately 540 feet. It's doubtful that anyone was surprised. The man's physical supremacy had been proven repeatedly over 22 years of incomparable performance. What else can be said about this guy? You could just shrug your shoulders and say nothing. Or you could attempt to quantify the man by talking continuously for the rest of your days. Why not settle for this: After the comparisons with all other players are complete, he stands alone. He was one of a kind, and there will never be another.

Eight

The Best of the Best

The careers of baseball's longest hitters have now been reviewed, and yet there are some lingering issues. The rankings were difficult to make. The incremental difference from one ranking to the next is usually very slight. In fact, most of the players fall into clusters, where their positions could reasonably be interchanged.

Also, there has been little focus on the great unofficial home runs. That includes spring training drives, exhibition clouts and, from the old days, homers struck during barnstorming games. They may not be as important as official homers, but they still have relevance, especially in this particular context. In unofficial appearances, most sluggers tend to swing a little harder, knowing that they don't have to attain maximum efficiency. As a result, they are more likely to blast the extra-long drives that fit into the telling of this particular story.

Finally, serious baseball fans probably want to learn more about the specifics of those rare blows that vie for the distinction as the single longest home run in Major League history. This text will conclude with a detailed discussion about the merits of each of the longest home runs in official Major League history.

DISCUSSION OF RANKINGS

Starting from the top, ranking Babe Ruth as the number one long-distance hitter in baseball history is relatively simple. Admittedly, acquiring all the data was not an easy task. However, once it was obtained, the process of selecting Ruth as the ultimate King of the Tape Measure was not a problem. His supremacy, although somewhat counterintuitive, is absolute. I don't know how or why it happened that way, but the Babe clearly hit the ball farther than anyone else.

Choosing between Jimmie Foxx and Mickey Mantle as number two, however, was extremely difficult. There is only a hair's breadth of difference between their respective power levels. The common tie-breaker is of no use since Mickey (536) hit only two more career homers than Jimmie (534). Actually, Mantle may have an edge over Foxx in optimum distance—about 540 feet to 530 feet. However, the longest-rated homer for Mickey is the one that he lined off the Yankee Stadium roof façade in 1963, and we can't be certain exactly how far it would have flown. Plus, Jimmie has the advantage in the total number of tape measure drives. He appears to have belted more 450-footers and 500-footers than Mickey.

A good case study can be made within the setting of the original Comiskey Park in Chicago. Foxx swung only from the right side, whereas Mantle was a switch hitter. That's not a problem with the Comiskey comparison, since it was symmetrical in design. In his career, Mickey reached the grandstand roof one time. That was in 1955, when he landed a ball atop the left field stands batting right-handed against Billy Pierce. However, Jimmie reached it six times, and cleared it completely on at least one occasion. In addition, the grandstands were situated approximately 351 feet away along the foul lines for the entirety of Mantle's career. On the occasion of Foxx's first three roof-toppers in 1930, 1931, and 1932, those foul line distances were 365 feet. Jimmie reached the center field bleachers once (1934), while Mickey never did it. Also, Foxx sent three balls to the opposite field upper deck (façade or seats), and Mantle didn't do it at all. In fairness to Mickey, he hit several balls that would have reached either the roof or center field bleachers if aimed in just a slightly different direction. But so did Jimmie.

Of course, it must also be pointed out that Mantle cleared the left field bleachers at Griffith Stadium in Washington, D.C., while Foxx never did it despite logging many more right-handed at-bats. Yet, we can't put too much emphasis on only one batted ball. Using models with a larger data pool seems to make more sense, and Comiskey Park is the best that we have. Both players batted roughly an equal number of times in that ballpark, where the measurements to the distance plateaus were exactly the same in both directions. The Foxx/Mantle distance debate could go on forever with both sides making valid points. I have given my admittedly ambiguous opinion, and I will let others continue the discussion.

The Foxx/Mantle distance debate could go on forever.

Frank Howard and Dick Allen are well positioned at rankings four and five. They actually rival Foxx and Mantle for optimum distance. However, neither Frank (382) nor Dick (351) recorded as many homers as the fellows ranked just ahead of them, and that gives Jimmie and Mickey the advantage. Howard and Allen are just about as close in overall power as Foxx and Mantle, and placing one man ahead is almost as hard. Even though Dick had better opposite field power than Frank, "Hondo" appears to have a slight overall advantage over "Crash."

At the number six ranking, we come to the bewildering figure of Mark McGwire. During his prime season in 1998, he may have surpassed the four men positioned directly ahead of him for peak performance. But there is a problem: McGwire was not always a true tape measure artist. In the first half of his career, Mark was not one of the longest hitters in the game. When healthy, he always hit lots of home runs, but he did not hit them unusually far. That didn't happen until 1995 at age 31. From then on, culminating in '98 and continuing to his retirement, McGwire was a distance freak. However, the guys ranked in front of him blasted balls for prodigious distances from day one in their big-league careers. For that reason, they deserve to stay ahead of Mark.

Willie Stargell seems to fit nicely at number seven, but the next few sluggers are tightly bunched. That includes Willie McCovey (#8), Harmon Killebrew (#9), and Reggie Jackson (#10). All three of those great batsmen hit well over 500 home runs, and each of them had comparable tape measure resumes. So, here is a familiar dynamic. As happens often throughout the ranking process, a small group of players fall into a tight cluster, making it difficult to quantify one over another. But, in order to move forward, best judgment has been summoned, and Willie, Harmon, and Reggie have been assigned their respective rankings. It is recognized, however, that their places, relative to each other, could be debated.

The great Josh Gibson has been installed at number 11. His ranking is also problematic. Josh, of course, played in the Negro Leagues before his premature death in 1947. As any baseball historian will tell you, it is significantly harder to research and evaluate Negro Leaguers than Major Leaguers. The documentation relating to their on-field play is much less inclusive. Primarily, that relates to newspaper coverage, which constitutes the bulk of contemporaneous description for any past player. In those days, the so-called black newspapers only published on a weekly basis, whereas there were multiple daily papers in every Major League city. Most of those publications provided little or no coverage for the Negro League teams. As a result, there just isn't the wealth of information relating to the old black players as there is for the old white players.

That was not Josh Gibson's fault, and he certainly shouldn't be further penalized for the social climate into which he was born. But, if we want to be fair to everybody, we can't just leapfrog Gibson over another player with better documented credentials. There is also a counterpoint, however. Despite the limited coverage for Josh and his teams, there is still sufficient confirmed data to place Gibson in the top 15. Plus, if you consider the following extrapolation, there is also some interesting anecdotal support for Josh. We know that black ballplayers have competed in Major League baseball for only about half its history. Despite that handicap, in the historical home run list, men of color rank first, second, fourth, fifth, sixth, and seventh. In this narrative, black men hold four of the top ten distance rankings. When you then consider that Josh Gibson enjoys the consensus position as the greatest power hitter in Negro League history, it seems logical that he deserves to be in the tape measure top 10. Hopefully, the case on behalf of Josh Gibson has been properly framed, and readers can make their own judgments.

Greg Luzinski holds down the number 12 spot, but hit the ball with about the same power as the guys ranked eight through ten. Since his career total of 307 homers is less than theirs, he has been assigned the lower bracket. The "Bull" was extremely strong, and, considering the millions of men who have aspired to play professional baseball, finishing 12th still places him in rarified air. Moving down the list (Williams #13, Kingman #14, Kiner #15, and Sosa #16) until number 17, everyone seems to be right where they belong. Then we encounter the next fellow from the old Negro Leagues, this time in the person of George "Mule" Suttles. Essentially, we can say most of the same things about Mule that we said about Josh. He may deserve to rank higher, but we just don't have enough data to place him above the better documented players.

In fact, all six ranked Negro League players fall into this category. That includes Norman "Turkey" Stearnes (#52), John Beckwith (#69), Louis Santop (#86), and Oscar Charleston (#92). We should also mention such "crossover" batsmen as Luke Easter (#31) and Larry Doby (#41). They both played in the big leagues, but arrived late due to pre-1947 segregation. Each man would probably have placed higher if given the chance to perform longer in the Major Leagues. However, we can

still honor them by simply telling their stories to the best of our knowledge.

The rankings then proceed smoothly until we come to Dan Brouthers at number 23. Here we encounter a similar caveat to the Negro Leaguers. Brouthers played in the 19th century, when the ball was significantly less resilient than it is now. In Chapter One, I estimated that balls of that era flew about 20 percent shorter than balls of today. The truth is that neither I nor anyone else knows the exact differential. We are sure that Major League balls have improved over time for flight performance, but we have no precise data to tell us the specific improvement. So, for Big Dan Brouthers and his contemporaries, we are guessing how they compare to the men who played after 1919. That is the final year of the so-called dead ball era. However, it is important to recall that it wasn't the most important year in the evolution to the "lively ball." That was 1911, when the manufacturers placed a cork center in official Major League baseballs.

Predictably, all offensive production soared in '11, but historians have designated 1920 as the first year of the lively ball era. It is believed that the ball was wound tighter that season due to the availability of higher quality yarn at the conclusion of World War I. Of course, that raises the question about the material being used before the Great War. Apparently, the ball could always have been wound tighter if officials wanted it that way, but they didn't have the inclination until

Babe Ruth started filling stadiums. When Babe smashed a then record 29 homers in 1919, owners took notice. As top quality Australian wool reached our shores for use in 1920, the manufacturers were instructed to put it to good purpose. At least, that's the way the story is usually told. There are many reputable historians who disagree. In fact, since there are very few official records relating to the history of Major League baseball, it is virtually impossible to know exactly when it improved, why it improved, or how much it improved.

However, one thing is certain: The balls that Dan Brouthers whacked in the late 1800s were a comparative lump of clay to the balls in use today. Accordingly, we must give both the 19th-century and dead ball era (1901–1919) sluggers the same consideration as the Negro League stars. We can rank them for power, but, while doing so, we must acknowledge that we don't know exactly how to compare them to the modern guys. Along with Brouthers, that list includes Roger Connor (#34), Buck Freeman (#39), Sam Thomson (#49), Ed Delahanty (#75), Buck Ewing (#87), Harry Stovey (#94), Honus Wagner (#97), and Sam Crawford (#100). In this class, Rogers Hornsby (#51) serves as the man crossing over the timeline, since he logged many at-bats (1916–1919) with the old ball. Each of these mighty athletes is ranked, but they may have finished higher if not for the coincidence of birth.

Proceeding down the list, each player has his own chronicle with self-evident stature until we come to ranking number 47. There, we encounter the prominent persona of Bo Jackson. His very first Major League home run went farther than anyone else's inaugural blast, and it appeared briefly that he might rank near the top of the historical power rankings. But, as almost everyone knows, Bo was a two-sport professional athlete who also starred as a National Football League running back. Within a few years, a degenerative hip injury (probably originating from his gridiron activity) forced him to retire from both sports. Before leaving, he amassed a highly impressive dossier of long-distance clouts. Other than his durability, he seemed to have only one serious limitation. Jackson used a so-called inside-out swing that directed most of his best shots to the opposite field. When Bo "turned" on a pitch, and pulled it to left or left center field, he generated more bat speed, thereby driving the ball for optimum distance. Bo Jackson possessed the power to rank significantly higher, but other factors held him back.

Scanning down the rankings, all seems reasonably self-evident until we reach number 53 with Rocky Colavito. He was a great

> **The balls that Dan Brouthers whacked in the late 1800s were a comparative lump of clay to the balls in use today.**

power hitter who recorded 374 big-league homers along with many tape measure shots. He launched about a dozen balls into the left field upper deck at Municipal Stadium in Cleveland while reaching almost all the other distance plateaus in the American League. However, hitting a baseball was not Rocky's primary claim to fame; he was better known for throwing them. This may be a treatise about long-distance hitting, but anyone reading these pages probably likes athletic power in all its forms. When it comes to throwing power for a position player, Rocky Colavito ranks at the top. In fact, Rocky was so dominant as a distance thrower, he was sometimes asked to display his prowess in unofficial exhibitions. As a minor leaguer on July 1, 1956, in San Diego, Colavito hurled a baseball the astounding distance of 435 feet, 10.5 inches. More will be added to this topic at the end of the book, where throwing power will be briefly chronicled.

Talking about Colavito establishes a natural segue to the great Roberto Clemente. He is ranked number 89 as a distance hitter, but was also known more as a power thrower. Along with Rocky, Roberto certainly belongs in the all-time top five for power throwing. His uncanny strength in heaving a baseball is legendary. Yet, hardly anybody recalls how far Clemente could hit a baseball. That is almost certainly due to his relatively modest career home run total as well as his prevailing image as a wondrously versatile athletic artist. Roberto belted 240 homers in 9,454

big-league at-bats, but was never regarded as a slugger. Consider, however, that Roberto cleared the distant center field wall at Pittsburgh's Forbes Field twice in the unlikely span of four days.

Clemente blasted matching 475-footers on June 5 and June 9, 1966 that soared over the 457 foot mark near the Barney Dreyfuss memorial. That display wasn't a short-term aberration. Much earlier in his career, on May 17, 1959, in Chicago's Wrigley Field, Roberto slugged a ball so far over the left center field bleachers that most observers estimated it at 500 feet. Near the end of his fabled playing days, at Veterans Stadium in Philadelphia on June 27, 1971, Clemente smashed a 470-foot thunderbolt. That drive was lined over the fence in dead center field and almost reached the upper deck. It's true that Roberto was a great right fielder with an amazing throwing arm. He was also a remarkable baserunner. Always recognized as a high average hitter who could be counted on in the clutch, Roberto Clemente should also be remembered as one of baseball's mightiest batsmen.

Every man in the top 100 deserves his own chapter. Each has a compelling story to tell about the awesome power in his bat. Plus, there are dozens more who didn't make the list, who also made a significant mark in the history of tape measure home runs. There just isn't sufficient space within the covers of a single book to talk about everybody. That would require a voluminous encyclopedia. Here, we have tried to chronicle the absolute best. At the same time, let's tip our hats to every player who has recorded a long-distance home run against a big-league pitcher. They have accomplished something that the rest of us can only fantasize about.

UNOFFICIAL LONG-DISTANCE DRIVES

Many of baseball's longest home runs were not hit in official games. Every Major League team annually plays many spring training contests. Occasionally, they play in-season exhibition games that are not part of their official schedules. In the old days, these exhibitions were commonplace. Big-league clubs routinely planned appearances on so-called off days against minor league squads, college nines, or anyone else who could provide reasonable competition. In addition, Major Leaguers, especially the guys with the marquee names, often "barnstormed" after the regular season. It seems out of sync today, but barnstorming was popular in the pre-television era when revenues were significantly lower. Plus, Major League baseball was played only east of the Mississippi River until 1958, and those October ball games were the only way that many fans could actually see their heroes. Unofficial ball games have been an important ingredient in our national pastime. Accordingly, we should discuss some of the greatest long-distance clouts that occurred in those circumstances.

As might be expected, the men already acknowledged are the same players who recorded the longest drives in unofficial games. In fact, they generally hit them even a little farther in the nonleague contests. There are two reasons for that. First, they probably swung harder when the outcome of the games didn't mean as much. This was especially true in the old barnstorming format. Nobody wanted to see Babe Ruth move runners into scoring position. The fans were there to see him knock the ball out of sight and he knew it. As a result, he disdained walks, and swung from his heels. The Babe wasn't any different in this regard than any other slugger. Mickey Mantle was well aware of his reputation as the longest hitter of his era, and spoke openly about the need to live up to it, especially in informal situations.

Second, exhibition games are often played in circumstances that are ripe for distance hitting. Spring games in Florida often feature strong breezes. Sometimes they blow in an adverse direction that limits distance. Just as often, the wind is behind the hitter, and carries the ball farther, occasionally much farther, than under calm conditions. Of course, spring games have also been played in Arizona for decades now, where higher altitudes enhance flight performance. The wind tends to whip at high speed in the desert as well.

Starting all the way back in the 19th century, the greatest sluggers hit the longest drives. Getting an early start for the 1890 season, the Philadelphia Phillies played Cap Anson's Chicago Colts on February 20 in Jacksonville. As was often the case back then, there were no outfield fences surrounding the field. Remember this was before the automobile, and many fans arrived by horse and carriage. On this occasion, they formed a ring around the outfield where they assumed that no one could hit a baseball. But, in the 3rd inning, Big Sam Thompson blasted one to right center field that flew over the parked carriages for a majestic triple. We don't know how far this drive traveled through the air, but 440 feet is a realistic estimate. Considering that baseballs didn't fly nearly as far in those days, this was a tremendous poke. Five years later, Dan Brouthers was working his way north with the Baltimore Orioles during spring training when they stopped in Raleigh, North Carolina, to play the Wake Forest College team. It was April 3, 1895, and Dan hit one so far to right field that it landed in an adjoining cemetery. After Brouthers retired, he cited this drive as one of the few longest of his distinguished career. It was probably a shot in the 450-foot range, which translates to well over 500 feet with the balls used after 1919. There were many other great unofficial distance drives in those early years, but these two may have been the mightiest.

In 1919 Babe Ruth shattered the then-existing season home run record. However, before opening day, he had already pounded several drives with astonishing force. The Babe Ruth mini-chapter included discussion about what happened on April 4 at Plant Field in Tampa. Babe's historic blow still resonates there today. A marker has been erected adjacent to the University of Tampa's administration building recording the distance at 587 feet. At the time of the original event, that building was the world-famous Tampa Bay Hotel, where Teddy Roosevelt stayed prior to embarking for fame and glory in Cuba during the Spanish-American War of 1898. Years later, both Ruth's Boston Red Sox and John McGraw's New York Giants were guests in that hotel at the time of Babe's epic homer. The distance of that drive was estimated at 552 feet earlier in this book, but there is a context.

The precise distance was reportedly measured the day after the event, but, for unknown reasons, there have been conflicting accounts about the results. Fortunately, there was extensive press coverage, and many eyewitness descriptions ran in newspapers from New York, Boston, Tampa, and St. Petersburg. Those stories are still available on microfilm records. In 2009, Lawrence "Tim" Reid and Bruce Orser compiled all the data and performed extensive research on the exact length. According to Tim and Bruce, the ball likely flew 552 feet, although

> **Before opening day, [Ruth] had already pounded several drives with astonishing force.**

estimates up to 570 feet are plausible. Their efforts were quite sophisticated in detail and methodology, using contemporary aerial photos along with modern survey technology. Accordingly, their findings are the most trustworthy to date. Ruth also added a pair of 500-footers during exhibition games in Baltimore later that same month. However, since all conversations about long-distance hitting begin and end with the Bambino, we will skip over his further exploits until the end of this section.

It should be acknowledged that there have been several reported unofficial home runs in the 600-foot category. However, with the possible exception of Babe Ruth, all such claims have been discredited. Even with Ruth, there is no concrete evidence that he ever reached that romanticized plateau. Each such legend will be discussed. The first home run traditionally reputed to have exceeded 600 feet was a minor league drive by Roy "Dizzy" Carlyle on July 4, 1929, in Emeryville, California. There are proponents of this event who ardently claim that Carlyle struck a baseball 618 feet on the fly. Their conviction is based upon a single eyewitness account from an unidentified teammate situated inside the park. He allegedly asserted that the ball landed in a rain gutter on the third house beyond the fence in center field. That building was measured at over 600 feet from home plate. I do not doubt the measurement, but I have strong reservations about the original confirmation of the landing point. The

scene has been carefully researched, and it was impossible for anyone to see the ball land from the playing field.

Additionally, I believe that it is essential to study the career "power performance curve" of any man who allegedly struck an historically long drive. In the case of Roy Carlyle, I don't have a problem with the fact that he hit only nine Major League home runs. I recognize that the longest hitter in baseball history could be an individual who never even made it to the big leagues. There may have been some freakishly strong specimen, who lacked diversified skills, but was capable of launching baseballs even farther than Babe Ruth. This mythic brute may have blasted 600-footers in some remote setting, where his deeds went unrecorded. Lacking the overall talent to make a living playing baseball, he could have retired into the forests to chop down trees for the rest of his days. Admittedly, that might have happened, although I doubt it. More importantly, this was not the case with old Dizzy Carlyle.

The fact is that we have a clear idea about his physical capabilities. In truth, he was a very strong man. He just wasn't strong enough to strike a baseball anywhere close to 600 feet. We know that Roy smacked a few balls in the 450-foot range, since he spent time on three different Major League rosters. I have personally studied accounts of his performances during spring training where his capabilities were specifically analyzed. There is a demonstrable deficit between the power alleged from the single 1929 event and the actual power level established from the thousands of swing variables throughout the totality of his baseball life. Let's put it this way: If a player is capable of hitting a ball over 600 feet, isn't it certain that he would have struck a few 500-footers?

Of course, that extrapolation is based on the assumption that the subject played a lot of baseball. Roy Carlyle may have played in only 174 official big-league contests, but he spent virtually his entire early adult life playing baseball. That includes college ball at Oglethorpe University as well as sojourns in both the Southern League and Pacific Coast League. Diz spent spring training with the 1927 New York Yankees, where, at age 26, he was in his physical prime. Despite reviewing six different detailed accounts of Carlyle during the spring of '27, there were no reports of any drives (including batting practice) flying over 450 feet. Roy continued to play minor league ball through 1934, but there were never any other examples of unusually long home runs. I'm sorry, but I cannot see any credence to the legend of Roy Carlyle's 600-foot home run. He was a great batsman, compiling a lifetime minor league batting average of .349, but proof of historic batting strength cannot be found.

Lou Gehrig supposedly launched a 600-footer later in the same year as the Carlyle episode. Lou was barnstorming with buddy Babe Ruth on October 27, 1929, when they stopped at Cameron Field in South Orange, New Jersey, to play a team from New Brunswick. Gehrig smacked a prodigious shot over the center field fence that was initially reported to have flown 600 feet, landing beyond the railroad tracks outside the park. Subsequent research rather easily debunks the original estimate. This was one of dozens of long homers over the years that had its flight distance confused with its total distance including the roll. Lou probably blasted his shot close to 500 feet in the air, but, when it passed the tracks, it was near the end of a series of bounces.

That brings us to the often-rumored Josh Gibson homer that allegedly flew out of Yankee Stadium. Such a drive, directed to left or center field, would have needed to fly well over 600 feet. As discussed in the Gibson section, that event simply never happened. Every legitimate baseball scholar who has looked into this myth, including Josh's biographer, knows that this story is apocryphal. It has been theorized that the legend started during a 1930s Negro League four-team doubleheader at Yankee Stadium. Some of the participants from game one were standing in the aisles behind home plate during the second contest. That is when Josh supposedly launched a magnificent drive over the protruding corner of the left field upper deck beyond the old bullpen. When the ball passed from view, some of the men, who were in the process of leaving the premises, incorrectly assumed that the ball had flown out of the giant enclosure.

Regardless of the origin of the myth, Josh Gibson's visits to Yankee Stadium were too well chronicled for any such event to have occurred without verifiable documentation. Anyone who has researched Josh (or any other Negro Leaguer) understands that some events are extremely difficult or even impossible to trace. That is especially true for games played in small towns. For example, Gibson's legendary blast in Monessen, Pennsylvania, required a quarter century of inquiry for confirmation of the exact date. However, there is simply no corollary between ball games at Tin Plate Field and Yankee Stadium. Ever since Josh first played there in the fall of 1930, when he blasted his historic 460-footer to left field, he was regarded as a celebrity by New York's African-American community. The black press attended all those games for the *Amsterdam News* (and other papers), and dutifully reported Gibson's home runs. Those stories are still available on microfilm, and each of them has been reviewed. The accounts from the *Pittsburgh Courier* (Josh's hometown paper) have similarly been studied, and there are no eyewitness accounts of any historic home runs at Yankee Stadium. For the record, Gibson walloped a few impressive shots at the great Bronx ballpark, even reaching the distant left center field bleachers on two occa-

sions. However, he never struck a baseball within 100 feet of flying out of The House That Ruth Built.

The discussion now brings us back to the extraordinary personage of Mickey Mantle. This guy was truly amazing. But, like all the other great sluggers, he has become a centerpiece for distortion and exaggeration. Mickey needs none of that nonsense. As a 19-year-old rookie with the Yankees, he came to Bovard Field in Los Angeles on March 26, 1951 to play an exhibition game against the University of Southern California. Some folks believe to this day that Mantle struck a 600-foot home run to right center during that contest. Essentially, they base their convictions on the recollections of Southern Cal's center fielder Tom Riach, who was interviewed many years later. It is alleged that Riach grabbed the top of the right center field fence after the ball had flown over his head. He did this to pull himself into position to witness the ball landing on the far side of an adjoining football field.

Assuming that Mr. Riach made such assertions, we are then left with the manageable task of simply measuring the distance. The figure does not exceed 600 feet. There are aerial photographs of Bovard Field that can be analyzed by any qualified person; the actual distance is about 550 feet. Earlier in

> **Gibson ... never struck a baseball within 100 feet of flying out of The House That Ruth Built.**

that same game, the switch-hitting Mickey allegedly blasted a monstrous homer far over the left field fence. That imposing drive has similarly been revered for its exceptional length. But that right-handed blow has less authentication than the subsequent left-handed shot, and may not have happened. However, a competent and reliable historian named Bruce Orser has tediously studied these events, and, in my judgment, has rendered the best evaluations to date.

I have known Bruce Orser for many years and find his work to be highly dependable. He has shared his findings with me, and I accept the results. If he is right, Mickey Mantle fell well short of hitting a 600-foot home run on that occasion. Still, anyone caring about the history of tape measure home runs can surely see the importance of Mickey's accomplishments. Mantle was just a teenager, and launched one of the longest drives in baseball history! By any standard, that demonstration of physical prowess is among the most remarkable in the annals of sports. For the record, I have personally investigated these events, and was able to interview renowned Southern Cal coach Ron Dedeaux. He was there that day, and saw Mickey's mighty wallop. Although greatly impressed with the young slugger's prodigious power, Dedeaux dismissed any notions of 600-foot flight distances as "ridiculous."

There are no contemporaneous newspaper accounts that provide any helpful information. All the Los Angeles and New York papers have been reviewed, as has the campus newspaper, but none contain any descriptions of either Mantle four-bagger. Several other members of the Southern Cal squad have been interviewed on this matter. They were all amazed by the magnitude of the right center field shot, but, as far as I know, only Riach claimed to have seen the landing point. I believe that Mr. Orser has taken the matter as far as it can go, and quantified the results as accurately as anyone can. It should also be noted that Bruce believes that Mantle's left field homer also occurred, and similarly flew close to 550 feet. Although I reject the more enhanced 600-foot version of events, I am in genuine awe of what teenage Mickey Mantle did on that March afternoon in 1951.

Not surprisingly, there are about as many legends of 600-foot homers centered on Babe Ruth as everyone else combined. There are three reasons for the myths. First, Babe Ruth hit the ball farther than any other player. Second, he probably played in more unofficial games than anyone else. And, third, his legend is so vast that it was inevitable that some of his deeds would be artificially enhanced. Accordingly, it's time to return the conversation to the Bambino and his montage of mythological events. They include, but are not limited to nine different incidents. Beginning on September 21, 1919, at Muzzy Field in Bristol, Connecticut, Ruth slammed a procession of mighty drives in various settings that have been reported to have flown 600 feet. However, there is no hard evidence to support that first alleged 600-footer in the Nutmeg State.

Next, playing an exhibition game against the Brooklyn Dodgers on April 8, 1920, in Winston-Salem, Babe actually bashed three titanic shots to right and right center field. These events occurred inside another oval half-mile track, which was surrounded by low fences. As a result, their actual flight distances were easy to observe. Several newspapers insisted that the longest of the three had flown farther than the more famous Tampa shot from the preceding spring. In fact, three of those papers asserted that the ball exceeded the Tampa blast by about 100 feet or more! Subsequent reviews of aerial photographs indicate that the actual distance was closer to 550 feet than 600 feet. Accordingly, I am not inclined to believe the more grandiose references.

We then come to the interesting oral history relating to an alleged 600-footer struck by Ruth in an undated San Francisco barnstorming appearance. This one is pretty juicy. We know that the Babe struck seven extracurricular homers in the City by the Bay, including two in 1919, three in 1924, and two in 1927. Yet, there is no exact date, or even a specific year, attached to the verbal accounts handed down through the generations. But five of those seven dingers can be eliminated because contemporary newspaper stories establish the lack of requisite length. That leaves us with two others, including Ruth's enormous shot to right field at Recreation Park on October 8, 1919.

One paper claimed that it flew 200 feet past the right field fence. That still doesn't add up to 600 feet. What about Babe's shot on a return visit to the same field on October 25, 1924? It cleared the clubhouse in right center field, but there just isn't enough detail in the available descriptions to accept a 600-foot designation. However, there are compelling accounts of batting practice feats that may have muddied the waters. During my long tenure of researching tape measure home runs, it has become clear that, in subsequent years, BP drives are often intermingled with competitive homers in the memory of those retelling the story. It is possible, therefore, that the lingering oral history of Babe Ruth's 600-foot Bay Area home run is based on a batting practice function. Over 100 such pregame blows have been identified in the nine times that the Bambino played in San Francisco. Ruth certainly smashed several balls well over 500 feet while visiting town, but there is no conclusive proof that any of them flew 600 feet.

Proceeding chronologically, Babe Ruth allegedly blasted 600-footers in Grand Rapids, Michigan, on July 20, 1923, and in Dunsmuir, California, on October 22, 1924. He must have been particularly potent during his barnstorming trip after the 1926 World Series, because there are legends of three different 600-foot blasts during the span of only 11 days! They began on October 12, 1926, in Wilkes-Barre, Pennsylvania, continued during a visit to Montreal, Canada, on October

17, and concluded with a stop in South Bend, Indiana, on October 23. The last of the nine primary examples of Ruthian 600-foot exhibition homers relates to Babe's tremendous poke over the outer wall at Sing Sing prison in Ossining, New York, on September 5, 1929. All of these drives have been carefully researched, and each was genuinely stupendous, flying well over 500 feet. However, only two seem to have plausible credentials for possibly landing 600 feet from where they started.

Those exceptions are Ruth's home run at Dunsmuir in 1924 and his demonstration drive at Wilkes-Barre in 1926. The first blow occurred as Babe was traveling from Portland to San Francisco during his 1924 barnstorming tour. Playing against a team of local Siskiyou County stars, Ruth slammed two homers, one of them flying to the top of an old fir tree in distant center field. Two months later, after returning to New York, Christy Walsh (Babe's business manager) summarized the fall tour in the December 12, 1924, edition of the *New York Telegram and Evening Mail*. Referring to the epic Dunsmuir blast, Walsh wrote, "He drove a ball to the top of a fir tree at Dunsmuir, a distance of 604 feet and five inches (measured by surveyor)." The local newspapers covering the event do not provide confirmation of that distance, but Walsh's remarks are

> **Those were intensely emotional days for the Sultan of Swat.**

compelling in their specificity. It's true that Christy was a promoter (with a little P. T. Barnum in him), but he was not a frivolous man. He was not known for exaggeration or fabrication, so his statement should not be ignored. On the other hand, since there is no corroboration to his assertion of a measured 604-footer, it is difficult to accept such an unlikely scenario.

Finally, we have Babe Ruth's demonstration homer at Artillery Field in Wilkes-Barre, Pennsylvania, on October 12, 1926. That one warrants a detailed analysis. I refer to this drive as a "demonstration homer" because Ruth was not actually involved in a competitive game when he hit it. Just two days earlier in New York, Babe had made the final out in the World Series by unsuccessfully attempting to steal second base during Game Seven with two outs in the 9th inning. Although most baseball experts of the time praised Ruth for having the courage to risk making the right play, he may have been even more anxious than usual to prove himself. Those were intensely emotional days for the Sultan of Swat. He had suffered through his worst year in 1925 and had vowed to make amends. During the off-season, Babe had worked out intensely with a hard-nosed trainer, reporting for spring training in the best condition of his professional life. Ruth enjoyed a great season, which featured his longest hitting since 1921.

In the World Series, Babe belted a record four home runs, but had seen few pitches in the strike zone. The Cardinals were managed by National League batting legend Rogers Hornsby, who had directed his staff not to throw the ball over the plate. As a result, Ruth walked 11 times, and usually swung at bad pitches even when he wasn't passed. During the seventh game, Babe had smacked a 3rd inning homer, but walked on his four other plate appearances. By his own admission, he had been extremely frustrated. Three of Ruth's home runs had been launched in one memorable performance in St. Louis on October 6. Word had reached Babe that his deeds had so inspired a sick child that the little fellow had rallied from the brink of death. Accordingly, Ruth went to see Johnny Sylvestri in Essex Falls, New Jersey, on his way to his first barnstorming appearance the day after the Series concluded. It was the next day, October 12, 1926, that Babe Ruth struck what might be the longest batted ball in baseball history.

I first became aware of the potentially unique nature of the event in the 1990s when researching the aftermath of Ruth's failed baserunning gambit from two days earlier. I was reading the accounts of various baseball insiders who generally exonerated the Babe for getting thrown out trying to steal second base. However, amidst the lingering World Series coverage was a small wire service article in the *Philadelphia Inquirer* trumpeting a 650-foot home run by Ruth during a barnstorming game in upstate Pennsylvania. At that time, I was convinced that no human being (absent hurricane force winds) could hit a baseball 600 feet. As a result, I felt no urgency in tracking down the specifics. I had already spent years in futile efforts to confirm a 600-footer by anyone, and didn't see much point in investing additional resources. Yet, I realized that it was something that I eventually had to do, and finally scheduled an appointment at the Luzerne County Historical Society in early February 2002. That's when things became interesting.

After six innings of the scheduled exhibition game that day, Babe Ruth had gone 0 for 2. Everyone in attendance was clamoring for Ruth to bat again, but the proceedings were running behind schedule due to the usual stoppages for autograph signings. Fortunately, Babe, the consummate showman, had an idea. He challenged the local pitchers to a duel, thereby signaling the end of the actual game. The accounts from the area newspapers were quite specific in describing what transpired. This was no batting practice scenario where the hurlers fed Ruth a series of easy fastballs down the middle of the plate. They gave it everything they had, including their best breaking balls. When Ernie Corchran of nearby Pittston took the mound, Ruth invited him to throw his best fastball. Corchran was no fool, and tried a few curveballs first. But Babe was no dummy either, and knew that a fastball would soon come his way. When it did, Ruth was waiting.

In an instant, the ball ascended high over the fence in deep right center field about 400 feet from home plate. According to witnesses, it was still rising as it left the park, and sped on and on until it sailed completely over a quarter-mile running track. The ball then collided with a fence on the far side of that track in front of a row of trees. How far did it fly? Even now, we can't be sure. The *Wilkes-Barre Record* said that it flew 200 feet past the fence, which was proven to stand more than 400 feet away. The Associated Press estimated 650 feet, while the *Scranton Republican* reported 700 feet. This we know for sure: As soon as Ruth made contact, he dropped the bat and walked off the field. Moments later in the clubhouse, he acknowledged that it was the longest drive that he had ever struck. When asked to compare it to his recent confirmed 530-footer in St. Louis, Babe responded that this one "traveled a lot farther." He asked to have the exact flight distance measured, but, although local officials agreed, the results were never publicized.

After exhausting all the old game accounts, I kept digging. I was both pleased and surprised to learn that the field still exists. It is now owned and maintained by Wilkes University, and still used for baseball. Upon contacting the staff at Wilkes for permission to inspect the field, they were most cooperative. The local media got involved and attended the inspection. As a result, when their stories appeared, I learned about a man who had seen everything happen those many years ago. His name was Joseph Gibbons, and he was born in Wilkes-Barre in 1916. He had attended the game as a 10-year-old boy with his father and uncle, and watched from his seat in the old grandstand near first base. Gibbons had been so amazed by the sight of Ruth's Herculean drive that he had talked about it for the rest of his life. He was kind enough to return to the field in October 2003 to assist in the evaluation process.

Upon arriving, Mr. Gibbons showed me exactly where he had been seated 77 years earlier, and it was easy to see that he had benefited from an unobstructed view of the entire flight of the ball. He then demonstrated the clarity of his memory by providing details of ballpark history that I had already confirmed from formal records. He pointed in the direction that the ball traveled, but admitted that he could no longer see far enough to visualize the landing point. Since there was a fence between us and that spot, we drove briefly to a parking lot adjacent to the field. Gibbons then exited the car, and walked directly to where he saw the ball land. He pointed to the place in a grassy area, and confidently proclaimed that this was where the ball landed. I reminded him that at least two other eyewitnesses had claimed that the ball had collided with a fence on the far side of a running track. He said that he knew that, and correctly reminded me that the original track had been relocated after being washed away by a flood from the nearby Susquehanna River. He couldn't personally confirm that the ball had hit the old fence on the fly, but was adamant that it had landed "within a few feet" from where he was standing. I had already confirmed the exact 1926 position of home plate, and then measured the distance to Mr. Gibbons's marker. It came out to 650 feet.

How reliable was Joseph Gibbons? I had the pleasure of meeting his children and grandchildren, and they assured me that his memory was in excellent condition at the time of our meeting. His account of what happened on October 12, 1926 had never varied. Gibbons served honorably in World War II and spent time in a German prison camp. Returning home, he continued his employment with Uncle Sam as a postal worker while raising a family and participating in amateur sports. After retirement, he golfed almost every day well into his eighties. Sadly, he passed away in January 2008, but not before playing his final role in this Ruthian drama. In June 2007, he returned for the last time to Artillery Field and was introduced to Linda Ruth Tosetti, the Babe's granddaughter. Looking into Linda's face, which bears a striking resemblance to that of her famous grand sire, Gibbons began to weep. He told Tosetti, "Your grandfather was the greatest guy in the world!" He couldn't

> **Drugash spoke in wonderment about [Ruth's homer] until the day he died.**

continue, and was unable to speak about the great blow in 1926. But that was okay; he had already gone on record about what he had seen.

So, what does it all mean? I have spent my entire adult life working with witnesses, and regard Joseph Gibbons as one of the most reliable. But he was a human being, capable of making mistakes, especially after 77 years. However, he was not alone. When discussing my then-recent findings at the Babe Ruth Museum on February 6, 2002, a man named Dan Corkran stepped forward. He had been a good friend of Joe Drugash, who had similarly been born in Wilkes-Barre at around the same time as Joe Gibbons. Drugash had also attended the 1926 game, and had told Corkran much the same thing that Gibbons told me. Drugash recalled that the ball had struck the fence on the far side of the running track, and spoke in wonderment about the event until the day he died. According to Corkran, it was a source of comfort for Drugash to reminisce about that specific recollection during his final days.

What else can be added? The official weather records for that day were taken in Scranton about 10 miles away. They show a 5-mph wind blowing in the same general direction as the Ruthian blast, but there could have been higher gusts in Wilkes-Barre. If the wind aided Ruth significantly, it would add credibility to the prospects of a 600-foot shot. What about the ball? Is it possible that the organizers used some kind of "rabbit ball" just for this occasion, one that would fly farther than an official Major League ball? That is extremely unlikely. First, we have no confirmation that such equipment even existed back then. Second, Babe Ruth was meticulous about the balls used in his barnstorming appearances. Games were arranged with the understanding that only official Major League balls were to be put in play. Eleven days later in South Bend, Ruth mildly rebuked local organizers for using unofficial balls. A second game was scheduled the next day, and Babe was quite insistent about using Major League baseballs.

Where does that leave us? How far did Babe Ruth actually hit that demonstration home run on October 12, 1926? I don't know for sure, and, after investigating the matter so rigorously, I wouldn't respect anyone who said that they did. But, there are few loose ends to this story. In fact, the biggest caveat is the basic question as to whether any mortal can hit a baseball 600 feet. Until researching this drive, I always insisted that the answer was "no." Now, I'm not sure of anything. When asked, I say that my best estimate is 605 feet. If it were anyone other than Babe Ruth, I would say "no way." But Ruth is the one man who established a power performance curve that often approached the

600-foot plateau. If anyone could do it, it was the Bambino.

LONGEST OFFICIAL HOME RUNS

Let's move on to the most compelling question of all. What is the longest home run in the history of official Major League Baseball? Although no one can answer that question with absolute certainty, there is one homer that clearly has the best credentials. In this category, we have reasonably definitive information about all the realistic contenders, and one stands apart. Again, all the usual suspects take center stage.

First, we must decide how best to tell the tale. Let's do all the debunking of historically exaggerated homers before talking about the drives that stand the test of close scrutiny. Second, we need to establish a standard for the list of absolute longest drives. Accordingly, we will talk about each home run that has been reported to have flown 540 feet or more. There haven't been many. As might be expected, by the time we eliminate the pretenders, the list will be extremely exclusive.

As always, Babe Ruth leads the way in both real and imaginary long-distance clouting. In their edition on May 26, 1921, the *New York Times* reported that Ruth's homer in St. Louis the day before had been a "200 yard drive into the center field bleachers." They based that estimate on the belief that those bleachers were then situated 550 feet from home plate. That assumption was wrong.

Although home plate was positioned farther from the center field boundary in Ruth's day than in later years, it was never 550 feet distant. This was a truly great poke, but 600 feet was absurd. In the matter of traditionally overstated homers, there is one other on Ruth's resume that needs to be identified. It occurred on June 8, 1926, at Detroit's Navin Field.

The story began with a massive shot far over the fence in right center field. This was long before the ballpark (later known as Tiger Stadium) was enclosed by towering grandstands, and occupants of the press box had a clear view of where the ball landed. It flew beyond Trumbull Avenue, which paralleled the right field wall, and crashed into an automobile on Cherry Street. The ball then bounced several times while a group of children went in pursuit. Sportswriter Ford Frick, who later became baseball's commissioner, was working the game, and observed everything. At the time, none of the New York or Detroit newspapers reported that the ball had flown 600 feet. That was because it hadn't. However, in his autobiography, Frick wrote passionately about this drive, and regarded it as the longest of Babe's career.

I don't know exactly what happened, but I believe that, over time, Frick and others confused this 1926 drive with another by the Babe in the same stadium in 1921. That is a rather common phenomenon in tape measure history. Oftentimes, witnesses either see or hear about two (or more) dif-ferent events, and inadvertently blend all the characteristics into one fictional occurrence. Naturally, the longer that time elapses, the more the corresponding confusion increases. I believe that is what has happened with this Ruthian home run. It has been reported as a 600-footer for many years, but it didn't travel nearly that far. It was a whopper, but 520 feet is closer to reality.

Despite being one of the longest hitters ever, Jimmie Foxx has not been the source of much distance hyperbole, probably because his entire career has been largely forgotten by baseball fans. It's truly a shame since this man was one of the most gifted athletes in our nation's history. The next slugger to be victimized by unwanted exaggeration is home run machine Ralph Kiner. "The Alhambra Kid" was a bona fide distance artist, but the 560-foot length traditionally attributed to his April 22, 1950 drive in Pittsburgh has been overrated.

Ralph struck the drive on his home turf at Forbes Field, lining the ball high over the left field wall. All the local press reports described an impressive blow of about 500 feet that traveled deep into adjoining Schenley Park. However, radio announcer Joe Tucker was late arriving at the ballpark, and saw the ball land near the "Pipes of Pan" statue situated 560 feet from home plate. Or did he? In 1987, Tucker's son Bob was kind enough to talk to me about his father's role in this event, and he remembered how excited his dad was that night after the game. I then asked Bob Tucker if his father ever specifically stated that he watched the entire flight of the ball from the point where it cleared the left field wall to where he thought it landed near the statue. He said "no." Clearly, Joe Tucker surmised that the ball had landed there on the fly, and he was rightfully energized by the experience. Since this home run is remarkably similar to another one that occurred a decade later, the two should be analyzed together.

On the night of May 25, 1960, Frank Howard tore into a pitch while playing for the Dodgers at Forbes Field. The ball soared high over the left field wall, and landed far out in Schenley Park. A late arriving radio man saw the ball land, and paced off the distance back to where it had cleared the wall. He took 54 steps to the 400 foot mark, and then assigned three feet for each step. It came out to 562 feet. That was within two feet of the Kiner blast that had landed in close proximity to the Howard shot. And guess who the radio personality was this second time around? None other than Mr. Joe Tucker!

A review of the initial newspaper accounts indicates a consensus opinion that the Howard ball had flown about 550 feet, which is reasonably close to Tucker's assertion of 562 feet. However, the June 15, 1960 edition of the *Sporting News* explained that Tucker had relied on another unidentified person to actually pinpoint the exact landing spot. He had just parked his car and was exiting the vehicle when the ball shot past him. By all accounts, Joe Tucker was a serious observer of baseball as well as an intelligent and honor-able man. He probably believed that both the Kiner and Howard homers flew about 560 feet. I have repeatedly encountered honest, well-intentioned individuals who have unwittingly provided false testimony about the length of great home runs. They see a ball strike ground level at a particular place, and, reacting to the inevitable excitement of the moment, assume that the ball had flown there.

When I interviewed Frank Howard about this matter years later, I specifically asked him to comment on the reputed 560-foot distance. In response, he stated simply, "That's ridiculous." Big Frank is genuinely proud of his accomplishments, but doesn't want credit for something that he didn't do. He believes that the distances attributed to most of the famous long-distance drives in baseball annals have been highly exaggerated. To illustrate his point, he talked about the time that he was offered a large sum of money (possibly $5,000) if he could reach the center field bleachers at Cleveland's Municipal Stadium. Constructed in 1932 at a distance of 470 feet from home plate, no ball was ever known to have landed there on the fly. It would have required a drive of about 485 feet, but, trying as hard he could, Howard was unable to do it. That does not mean that Frank could never have reached those distant seats, but it does mean that it would have taken one of his best shots. Frank Howard's story is a sobering reminder of how hard it is for anyone, including the strongest batsmen, to launch a ball 500 feet.

Obviously, Howard was capable of producing 500-footers, since he recorded a measured 506-foot shot in Anaheim in 1971. I have personally estimated his 1960 Forbes Field blast at 520 feet, and rate the 1950 Kiner shot at the same length. They were both awesome blows by two of the mightiest sluggers that the game has known. Yet, it is extremely unlikely that either home run flew close to 560 feet. In both cases, that reported distance was the result of a common and understandable perceptual error.

Now, it's time to return to Mickey Mantle. Like Babe Ruth, he was nearly superhuman in his abilities, and, like the Bambino, he played in the media capital of the known universe. Inevitably, he and Ruth have been magnetically drawn to the center of legend, myth, and outright exaggeration. Neither man courted credit for fictional deeds, but they had no control over the behavior of overly ardent admirers. As a result, they jointly lead the baseball world in both genuine and overstated long-distance homers. For Mickey, it starts with his legendary 565-foot blast over the left center field bleachers at Washington's Griffith Stadium on April 17, 1953. Mickey personally told me that he didn't think that the ball flew that far, and everyone who has seriously studied the event agrees with him. Nevertheless, this drive still exists in the minds of most old-time fans as a true 565-footer and the granddaddy of all tape measure home runs.

However, the facts say otherwise. Mickey belted a high, towering drive toward the bleachers in left center. With the help of a powerful tailwind, the ball carried completely over the 32 rows of seats and caromed off the right side of an old football scoreboard that was then serving as an ad sign. At that moment, the ball had flown 462 linear feet, and ricocheted out of sight at a height of 55 feet. Since those stands had not been cleared in their prior 28-year existence, this homer was instantly recognized as a genuinely historic blow. Yankee publicist Red Patterson saw his duty, and immediately went in search of the details.

Outside the ballpark, he found a neighborhood boy, whom he identified as 10-year-old Donald Dunaway. The child was holding the ball that he had recovered at 434 Oakdale Street, prompting Red to pace off the distance from that house back to the outer wall of the stadium where the ball had left the premises. Returning to the press box, Patterson reviewed the stadium dimensions, and initially estimated the flight distance at 563 feet. Then, two additional feet were soon added for the thickness of the outer wall, whereupon the final distance was computed at 565 feet. The news flashed around the country despite the fact that the actual event had been grossly misrepresented. The whole process was based upon the specious assumption that young Donald had found the ball where it had landed. But that is not what happened.

Many years later, in 1983, I tracked down Patterson when he was working for the

California Angels. I asked him directly if he had ever questioned Donald Dunaway about actually seeing the ball land on the fly. He acknowledged that he had not. Red then went on to say that he still thought that the ball had flown 565 feet. Not wanting to embarrass the man, I left it at that. So, how far did the ball actually fly? I can't say for sure, but several physicists with whom I have consulted agree that it could not have been more than 510 feet. That's very long indeed, but far from 565 feet.

As odd as that episode might be, it still doesn't compare to the folly of another misrepresented Mickey Mantle home run. While playing at Detroit's Tiger Stadium on September 10, 1960, Mickey launched one of his better shots over the right center field grandstand roof. Note the operative word is "better" as opposed to "best." The ball passed through a lattice framework of metal beams that supported a light tower and sailed out of sight 370 feet away and 95 feet above field level. At the time, it was regarded as another impressive Mantle "500-footer" but nothing of historic significance. However, some 20 years later, a group of researchers announced that the ball had flown 643 feet, and were campaigning to label this homer as the longest in baseball history. That is when I got involved.

A group of researchers announced that the ball had flown 643 feet . . . the longest ball in history. That is when I got involved.

I knew about this home run, since I had compiled a career home run log for Mickey. According to my research, it seemed more like a 490-foot blow. But since I took the history of tape measure home runs seriously, I felt compelled to evaluate their findings. Essentially, they were basing their conclusions on the testimony of a secondhand witness by the name of Sam Cameron. When the event actually occurred, Cameron was making a truck delivery in his capacity as an employee of the Brooks Lumber Company, which was located across Trumbull Avenue from the ballpark. In his absence, co-worker Paul Borders was working in the open lot behind the building, when he witnessed the Mantle blast land a few feet away. Borders was so impressed that he told Cameron about it, when Sam returned from his truck-driving duties.

By the 1980s, Borders had passed away, but Cameron was still working for the same employer. That is where he was tracked down by the zealous researchers. They interviewed Sam, who reportedly identified the landing place of the epic 1960 moon shot. The distance from home plate was then calculated at the astounding distance of 643 feet. All the while, I was having trouble reconciling that distance with the laws of physics. I reviewed every firsthand source that I could find, and, although all the contemporary witnesses were impressed, they consistently placed limitations on how far the ball could have flown. None of the newspaper accounts described the homer as a line drive. They all agreed where the ball went, and, in a highly unusual scenario, the *Detroit Free Press* even published a photograph showing the ball passing through the light tower.

What added to the irony was the fact that Reggie Jackson's legendary 1971 All-Star homer tracked along almost the exact same flight path. But, where Reggie's was knocked down by the tower, Mickey's sailed just a few feet away and escaped the confines of the stadium. The biggest difference was that everyone in attendance in 1971 hailed Jackson's shot as a vicious line drive that was still rising when it collided with the light standard. None of the contemporaneous accounts of the 1960 drive mentioned anything about a line drive trajectory. The more that I studied the matter, the more confused I became. After all, there was the matter of Sam Cameron and Paul Borders to consider, and their testimony could not be overlooked.

In August 1985, I had traveled from Philadelphia to Niagara Falls for a family vacation. We were having a good time, so there wasn't much enthusiasm when I suggested a side trip to Detroit. That little sojourn included my wife and four children, but only my 14-year-old son had any real interest. I had contacted the Brooks Lumber Company and made an appointment to interview Mr.

Cameron. I had also bribed young Bill into some small measure of support by arranging with the Detroit Tigers to inspect Tiger Stadium at the conclusion of the Cameron meeting. So, after my wife and other children took off in the family car to explore the Motor City, Bill (with glove and ball in hand) and I met Sam Cameron.

The interview quickly demonstrated to my son that adults can be as unreliable as children. After exchanging some brief social chit-chat, we focused on our business. Mr. Cameron took me to the exact spot where Borders had seen the ball land 25 years earlier. I then asked the single most important question that any serious historian must ask in such an inquiry: "Did Mr. Borders ever tell you that he saw the ball land here in uninterrupted flight?" Cameron thought for a few seconds and said, "No." I then queried, "Can you recall exactly what he said?" Again Cameron reflected before responding. "Yes. He said that he was standing here doing some work when, all of a sudden, the ball hit right at his feet and then rolled over to the corner of the garage over there." The spot in question was paved in asphalt, whereupon I followed with, "Are you sure that he used the word 'rolled'?" Sam said, "Yes." I then pointed to the corner of the garage about 40 feet away that Cameron had referenced and asked, "Was this area the same then as it is now? I mean that it's now paved with asphalt and that garage isn't very far away." Once more, Cameron searched his memory and responded,

"Except for a missing shed (which was not involved), everything is the same now as it was back then."

At that moment, I heard my 14-year-old son groan and say, "Come on Dad; let's get out of here. Let's go see Tiger Stadium." Even a 14-year-old kid needed only about one minute of discussion to see through the absurdity of the 643-foot assertion. Of course, his instincts were right. Subsequent tests confirmed that any ball flying 600 feet and landing on hard asphalt would generate a first bounce of more than 75 feet. Keep in mind, however, that none of this was Sam Cameron's responsibility. He seemed like an honorable and intelligent individual, and I certainly did not want to offend him. Accordingly, we stayed a while longer as I asked a series of other pertinent questions. They all led to the same inescapable conclusions: There was no confirmation of the Mantle home run landing anywhere near where Paul Borders had been standing. I never met Mr. Borders, and I don't feel that he fabricated his story. I believe that he really did see the ball "hit" at his feet. The ball almost certainly landed on Trumbull Avenue, where three different newspapers said that it did, and bounced onto the low roof of the lumber company. It then bounded across the roof to where it toppled off, and then "rolled" past Borders. I estimate that this magnificent home run by the wondrous Mickey Mantle traveled 500 feet in the air.

There have been many other overhyped homers by other sluggers, but there is only one more that merits inclusion in the debate about baseball's longest home runs. It was the famous Dave Kingman Wrigley Field blast on April 14, 1976. This blow seems ideally suited for discussion here, since it serves as a perfect transition from exaggeration to confirmation. To be more specific, Kingman's shot was grievously overestimated at the time, but still holds up as one of the longest four-baggers ever struck. Dave was playing for the Mets at the time and was facing the Cubs' John Dettore in the 6th inning. Kingman took one of his famous violent, uppercut swings, and made perfect contact. Kong sent the ball on a towering parabola toward left field, which happened to be the direction in which a 16-mph wind was blowing.

The drive carried high over the left field wall and easily cleared Waveland Avenue with a host of young men in pursuit. As always, there was a group of guys waiting outside the ballpark to chase down any homers leaving the stadium. However, this shot was going to require a lot more legwork than they were accustomed to giving. The ball eventually collided with the porch on the third house past Waveland on Kenmore Street. By a coincidence, occupant Naomi Martinez was watching the game on television, and was tracking the ball in flight toward her home when she heard the loud thump. It then caromed back toward Wrigley Field where it was retrieved by 25-year-old Richard Kieber. He was one of the fellows waiting on Waveland Avenue for just such an event and instantly hailed the Kingman blast as the longest that he had ever witnessed.

In their next-day editions, the *New York Times* estimated the drive at 630 feet, and the *Chicago Tribune* calculated the blow at 600 feet. It certainly was a monstrous homer, but there was just one problem with those estimates. They were wrong. Dave Kingman eventually played for the Chicago Cubs from 1978 through 1980 and hit many more tremendous shots past Waveland Avenue while competing at Wrigley Field. So, in the mid '80s, the Cubs' management was receptive to my suggestion that they measure the distance to the house where the legendary home run had actually landed. It turned out to be just over 530 feet, which places this remarkable wallop in the 540-foot category. What do we make of this episode? This is one of those rare events that has been grossly misrepresented, but still retains legitimate historical significance. Obviously, the original reports of a 600-foot flight distance are way out of line. Yet, a proven home run of 540 feet is rare enough to place it in the top 10 longest home runs in Major League history. Its dual nature of fiction and fact also helps to pivot the focus from counterfeit drives to the bona fide mega-shots.

Proceeding in reverse chronological order, the next of the 540-footers for dis-

> **Reggie Jackson had an established power curve that peaked at over 500 feet in those early days of his career.**

cussion is Reggie Jackson's All-Star blast at Tiger Stadium in Detroit. While pinch-hitting in the 3rd inning on July 13, 1971, Reggie pulverized a Dock Ellis fastball and sent it screaming toward the grandstand roof in right center field. Like most of baseball's longest homers, Jackson's shot was aided by a powerful tailwind. The ball was headed high over the roof when it collided with a transformer on a light tower atop the roof. It was only a brief moment before the entire sequence was over. Reggie trotted around the bases, while baseball's mightiest hitters blinked in disbelief. For example, Frank Howard, one of the sport's strongest-ever sluggers, declared Reggie's blow as the longest and hardest that he had ever witnessed.

What more do we know about it? It ricocheted off the transformer at a linear distance of 370 feet at a height of 95 feet above the playing field. Every firsthand observer (and there were many) swore that the ball was struck on a savage line drive trajectory. It is impossible to know exactly how far the ball would have flown if unimpeded, but I have estimated 540 feet. I acknowledge that I could be wrong, but that is my best guess. We know that Reggie Jackson had an established power curve that peaked at over 500 feet in those early days of his career. Plus, we know that he made optimum contact under optimum conditions. Due to the wind, the ball was really flying toward right center all evening. In fact, Johnny Bench, a right-handed hitter, has been quoted as describing his 2nd inning rocket off Vida Blue as the longest of his own exceptional career. Why is that relevant? It matters because Johnny's shot landed high in the right center field upper deck in close proximity to where Jackson's missile was knocked down. As a matter of fact, two other batters from the right side (Henry Aaron and Roberto Clemente) also landed homers in the right center field upper deck. Clearly, the conditions were ripe for an epic distance shot.

I am admittedly uncomfortable judging the Jackson homer at the same length as the Kingman homer, since Dave's has a confirmed linear distance that exceeded Reggie's by about 160 feet. However, this will be a recurring theme that should be addressed right now. Since thousands of Major League games have been played inside enclosed stadiums, it was inevitable that a significant number of the longest drives would be struck inside them. We can't discount them just because they were knocked down in mid-flight and are harder to judge than balls that leave the confines of different style stadiums. It is fair to remind ourselves that we have traditionally overestimated the distance of the "impeded" drives, but that should not induce us to simply dismiss them. Accordingly, I am sticking to my estimate of 540 feet for Reggie Jackson's 1971 All-Star homer.

We now move on to Dick Allen's epic blast at Philadelphia's Connie Mack Stadium on June 6, 1967. This is another of the four home runs that I have estimated at 540 feet in total flight distance. It was hit in the 5th inning of the second game of a so-called twi-night doubleheader against Joe Niekro of the Chicago Cubs. Allen was in one of his defiant moods that evening, since the Phillies had earlier traded his friend Bob Uecker. There was a double-decked left field grandstand that stood 65 feet high that was topped by three 10-foot billboards. The sign closest to the left field line displayed a Cadillac advertisement, whereas the board in left center advertised Coca-Cola. Moving toward center field, the last billboard exhibited a Philco promotion, and was situated just left of dead center at a linear distance of 420 feet from home plate.

When Dick unloaded his monstrous blow high over the "P" on that distant target, he ignited a firestorm of reaction. Every player offering an opinion about the ball's comparative value hailed it as the longest drive that they had ever seen. Each of the Philadelphia and Chicago newspapers the next day described it as a line drive. The *Philadelphia Daily News*, *Philadelphia Inquirer,* and the *Philadelphia Bulletin* estimated the shot at 550 feet. Larry Shenk was then a young publicist with the Phillies and had enjoyed considerable success in locating witnesses to prior Allen moon shots. In fact, he had reliably established Dick's May 29, 1965 roof-topper at the distance of 529 feet. That had also been recorded against the Chicago Cubs, and many of the same people who had witnessed the '65 blow were there for the '67 reprise. Everyone agreed that the latter version went farther.

Sadly, Shenk was unsuccessful in his quest that night, and we must use other criteria to form a final assessment. Since we know that Dick Allen could strike a baseball 529 feet, it is not a major stretch of his proven power curve to estimate another one at 540 feet. Additionally, physics tells us that a line drive disappearing from view 420 feet away and about 85 feet high could reasonably be expected to fly somewhere in the 540-foot range. It seems right to mention that Dick Allen was a personal favorite of mine, and I was listening to the radio broadcast of this home run. It was an experience that left a lasting impression on me, and it is difficult to remain objective about this particular event. I have given the basic facts, and will again let the readers decide what to believe.

It's now time to return to the familiar figure of Babe Ruth. Like most other long-distance hitters, the Bambino reached the apex of his power in his mid-twenties. We will soon review some of his exploits during the 1921 season when he was 26 years of age. However, even at age 40, during his final abbreviated season in 1935, Babe Ruth was still the Sultan of Swat. Despite his dwindling skills and prolonged slump during spring training, he still managed to thump a pair

of 500-footers on his way north. So it was on May 25, 1935, at Forbes Field in Pittsburgh, when Ruth belted the final three home runs of his fabled career. Number one was an impressive 380-foot shot into the lower deck of the right field grandstand. Number two was a grandiose smash deep into the upper deck in right center. That 500-foot bomb was instantly labeled the longest-ever in the Steel City, but nobody could foresee what would happen four innings later.

Ruth had already victimized Guy Bush for his epic second homer, and the veteran hurler was still on the mound in the 7th inning. Upon throwing a slow curve to Ruth, he turned to watch the ball soar majestically over the 86-foot-high right field grandstand roof. Babe then pigeon-toed his way around the bases for the 714th and last time. Everyone instantly started guessing where the ball had landed. In response, Pirate head usher Gus Miller soon left the ballpark to investigate. According to the *Pittsburgh Post-Gazette*, Miller "went to considerable pains in an effort to solve the riddle." They reported that the ball had descended onto the house-top at 318 Boquet Street, and then bounced onto the roof of yet another nearby home. Fifty years later, I asked the Engineering Department at the University of Pittsburgh to measure the distance from where home plate had been located in 1935 to the house at 318 Boquet Street. They graciously agreed to do so and computed the distance at 529 feet and 6.14 inches.

Unfortunately, there is a problem. It was also determined that the Boquet Street address was situated slightly into foul territory. If Babe's drive passed just inside the foul pole, it could possibly have hooked foul after leaving the ballpark. But that probably was not the case. Even more convincing than the *Post-Gazette's* initial reference to 318 Boquet Street are the multiple subsequent attributions to a different address. That would be 334 Joncaire Street. That house lies on a direct line from the place on the roof where the consensus of the news accounts tracked Ruth's drive. There is a considerable amount of neighborhood oral history that specifically pinpoints the Joncaire Street address as ground zero. A guy named Henry "Wiggy" DeOrio is even identified as the fellow who retrieved the ball and later donated it to the Hall of Fame. Accordingly, the distance was then computed from home plate to that house, and it came out to 527 feet. Therefore, from a distance perspective, either house functions pretty much the same.

But, could Babe's homer have realistically reached either home on the fly? All the Pittsburgh and Boston newspapers thought so. They agreed that Babe's clout passed high over the roof (the *Boston Globe* said by "50 feet") at a point close to the right field foul pole. We are then left with the usual question

about whether the ball might have landed on the street and bounced onto the house roof. In this case, that scenario is extremely unlikely. There were multiple reports about the ball bounding from the first roof to the next housetop, which would be a virtual impossibility on a second bounce. Then, there are the reactions of the eyewitnesses.

Honus Wagner said that it was the longest drive that he had ever seen. Paul Waner stated the blow flew "close to 600 feet if I'm not mistaken." The consensus opinion from the various papers declared that the ball was still rising as it passed out of sight, and the distance estimates ranged from 550 to 600 feet. Decades later, pitcher Guy Bush admitted that he couldn't recall the first homer that Ruth had belted off him even though it had been a leviathan drive in its own right. However, he could never forget the second blast. Bush acknowledged that, until it happened, he would have sworn that no human being could hit a baseball so far.

Finally, as Babe Ruth entered the Braves clubhouse prior to the game, he was handed a letter from a worried mother from McKeesport. Her son was seriously ill, and she was imploring Ruth to send him an autographed baseball. The Babe immediately complied as he had similarly done on other occasions. Considering his well-recognized love of

> **Until it happened, [pitcher Guy Bush] would have sworn that no human being could hit a baseball so far.**

children, especially those in need, it seems possible that Babe Ruth was particularly inspired when he took the field on May 25, 1935. It is a fact that Ruth launched three prodigious home runs in a 1926 World Series game after learning about the illness of young Johnny Sylvester of Essex Falls, New Jersey. Each blow got progressively longer, culminating in the final drive of 530 feet. The similarity to the 1935 episode is too dramatic to simply discard as mere coincidence. It may sound like movie fiction, but Babe Ruth established a documented record of elevating his game whenever performing with troubled children on his mind. For this and other reasons, I believe that the Babe was unusually energized when he walloped that final home run. All in all, 540 feet seems realistic.

Nine years earlier to the day, Babe Ruth had struck another prodigious drive that I have also estimated at 540 feet. Playing for the Yankees at Fenway Park in Boston, Babe connected off Tony Zahniser in the 7th inning of the first game of a twin-bill. Ruth directed his shot toward the open bleachers in deep right field, which were then situated over 400 feet from home plate. The ball roared onward and upward as though shot from a cannon and gained extra momentum due to a strong outgoing breeze. Ultimately, it crashed into either the 44th or 45th row of the towering 50-row stand of bleachers.

The Fenway bleachers on May 25, 1926, were not the same as those that exist today. The modern bleachers were constructed after the 1933 season as a result of a fire that had destroyed the Ruthian era seats. Both were comprised of 50 rows of benches, but the latter rows were built at a width of 30 inches with 6-inch risers. Although the exact specifications of the older bleachers are unknown, it is believed that they were about 24 inches wide. They were located in a similar configuration, but the original structure was a little more distant from home plate. Accordingly, comparisons between balls landing in the same row of both bleachers (old and new) appear to be legitimate.

How far did this one fly? As always, exactitude is difficult, but we have enough hard data to compute this one pretty closely. We know within one row exactly where this amazing drive landed, since all the contemporary newspaper accounts agreed. Both the *Boston Post* and the *Boston Globe* included sketches in their coverage. There was also solid evidence that the ball was struck on a line drive trajectory. The *New York Herald-Tribune* described the drive as a "screamer," and the *Boston Post* referred to it as a "bullet." Regarding the relative scope of this blast, the *New York Times* and the *Boston Herald* concluded that, if struck at Yankee Stadium, the ball would have flown completely over the right field bleachers. The only unknown variable is the exact distance to the front of the bleachers at the point where the ball entered. The best estimate is 410 feet. Next, there was an approximately 4-foot-wide walkway between the bleacher wall and the first row.

Allowing 2 feet for the width of each subsequent row and multiplying by 43, we arrive at 500 linear feet. That front bleacher wall was 10 feet high, and, assigning 6-inch risers for each of the 44 rows that the ball ascended, we reach a vertical distance of 32 feet. By factoring in the unusually rapid line drive trajectory, the final estimate is 540 feet. If that assessment is wrong, it could only be off by a few feet.

Mickey Mantle's turn is next in this discussion, featuring his historic "façade shot" at Yankee Stadium on May 22, 1963. Along with Mickey's 1953 Griffith Stadium blast over the left field bleachers, this may be the most heralded tape measure drive in baseball history. Just like Babe Ruth at Pittsburgh in 1935, everyone thought that Mantle had left his best distance days in the rear view mirror. But they were wrong. Facing Kansas City's Bill Fischer in a tie game in the 11th inning, Mickey smashed the longest home run of his Major League career. He was in his 32nd year at the time and had enjoyed his best tape measure season seven years earlier in 1956. It didn't matter.

Mantle blasted a line drive to deep right field that initially appeared destined to reach the towering grandstand roof. Nobody had ever done that since construction in 1938. Ultimately, the ball collided violently with the ornate roof façade 370 feet away and 110 feet high. It then ricocheted back toward the second baseman as Mickey circled the bases with a "walk-off" home run. The estimates

for an unimpeded flight began swirling right away, and they haven't stopped yet. Over the years, there have been appraisals ranging from 500 feet all the way to 640 feet. Those longer estimates are based on the assumption that the ball was still rising when it crashed into the façade, but that conjecture has essentially been discredited. So, how far would it have flown? I wish that I knew.

As discussed, drives knocked down near the apex of their flight are the most difficult to assess. This one is no exception. Mickey told me as well as dozens of other interviewers that he regarded this shot as the longest he ever hit. Considering the man's track record of impeccable honesty in such matters, we must take his testimony seriously. He acknowledged that he swung as hard as he could, and made optimum contact. When we also review Mantle's established power performance curve, we can point to many confirmed drives of well over 500 feet. My best estimate for this blow is 540 feet. In this range, we can revert back to March 1951 at Bovard Field in Los Angeles. If 19-year-old Mickey Mantle could launch a baseball 550 feet, why couldn't he hit a comparable shot at age 31?

Returning to our old friend Babe Ruth, we now visit Chicago's Comiskey Park on August 17, 1921. Babe was in town for the start of a three-game series with the White Sox when he faced Sox left-hander Jack Wieneke in the 6th inning. As things turned out, young Jack pitched only 25 innings that season, after which he never returned to the Major Leagues. It's natural to wonder if what happened on this occasion had some damaging effect. His fastball was sent flying toward the distant bleachers just right of center field, where home runs were hard to come by. In those days, the foul lines at symmetrical Comiskey Park were 365 feet long, and it was 455 feet to both corners of the center field fence. The open bleachers extended about 50 feet in depth (the grandstand was not completed until 1927) and rose to a height of about 30 to 35 feet above the field. They were a long way from home plate.

Nonetheless, Ruth's prolific drive soared high over those bleachers before descending onto a soccer field outside the park. On the matter of total distance, there was a wire service report stating that the ball had flown 675 feet. Of course, that figure was farcical. Although the New York papers heaped lavish praise on this shot, none of them ventured a guess about the flight distance. However, it is interesting that both the *Chicago Daily Tribune* and the *Chicago Herald & Examiner* cited 475 feet. It is interesting because subsequent analysis indicates that 475 feet coincides with the distance to the outer wall of the bleachers where the ball left the stadium. It seems probable, therefore, that the two Chicago writers met with club officials while

> **Ruth's prolific drive soared high over those bleachers before descending onto a soccer field outside the park.**

studying a stadium blueprint. When it was determined that this homer escaped Comiskey Park at the linear distance of 475 feet, they probably confused that figure with the actual total distance. Since the *Herald & Examiner* also published a photograph showing the ball's flight path, it is apparent that this drive could not possibly have flown only 475 feet.

The *New York World* asserted that the ball passed over the bleachers at the same height as the large, nearby scoreboard (60 feet) in dead center field. The *New York Times* stated that the ball cleared the seats by 10 feet, and that same *Chicago Daily Tribune* referred to a 15 to 20 foot clearance. At least three of the papers described the trajectory as a line smash. It should also be noted that there were some random references in other papers in the following weeks about Ruth's recent 610-foot home run in Chicago. As usual, we will never know the exact distance, but my best guess is 545 feet. I know that 475 feet is way too short and that 610 feet is way too long. According to my understanding of the laws of physics, a hard line drive traveling at 60 feet in height at a linear distance of 475 feet would likely fly about 545 feet.

The next home run on the list is, admittedly, a personal favorite. I can't avoid a natural emotional attachment, since my then-14-year-old father witnessed the event, telling me about it many years later. It occurred on May 22, 1930, at Shibe Park (aka Connie Mack Stadium) against Dad's beloved Philadelphia Athletics. He went to see the A's and Yanks play their second doubleheader in two days, but his uncle opted for the cheaper seats atop private houses across 20th Street in right field. My father didn't think much of that arrangement until the Bambino came to bat for the second time in the first game. It was the 3rd inning, and Babe was facing veteran Howard Ehmke. Dad's first impression of what he was witnessing was actually the explosive sound of Ruth's bat. Just a moment later, the ball came speeding toward him, but, to his astonishment, it kept flying until it passed swiftly over his head. Until that instant, young Bill Jenkinson assumed that his position atop that two-story house, about 440 feet away and 30 feet high, was too far removed from the action to ever be a part of it. The power of Babe Ruth's bat dramatically reversed that assumption.

As the ball passed directly over his head, my dad rolled his head backward, and followed it until it passed over both rows of houses and the intervening backyards and descended into Opal Street. The fact that this ball actually landed on Opal Street has been confirmed by the *Philadelphia Record*, the *New York World,* and the *Philadelphia Inquirer*. I have personally interviewed several other Philadelphians who similarly claimed to have witnessed the Opal Street landing, and that included award-winning *Inquirer* sportswriter Allen Lewis. As a boy, he was seated in the right field upper deck that day, and had a perfect view of the entire route that the ball traveled.

In later years, the Babe himself would invariably make reference to the event whenever he returned to Shibe Park. Walking onto the field to take batting practice, Ruth would gesture east over the right field fence, and say, "That's where I dropped the big one!" As late as 1949, there was a detailed article in the *Philadelphia Evening Bulletin* that discussed Ruth's pride in reaching Opal Street. As a result of all this cumulative data, there is really no doubt about the Opal Street destination. However, until just recently, there had been some lingering question about the precise direction in which the ball traveled. If the ball landed in the street close to the right field foul line, it would have flown as little as 505 feet. If it tracked further toward center field, and landed nearer to the northern end of the block, it could have flown close to 600 feet. Happily, in 2007, an unexpected gift arrived by way of some new information.

That was when I learned about Professor John J. Rooney of LaSalle University in Philadelphia. Dr. Rooney was born on March 19, 1923 and grew up across the street from Shibe Park. He is still going strong, and, as of this writing in 2009, continues to serve as director of LaSalle's master's program in psychology. On May 22, 1930, seven-year-old Jack Rooney was playing near home, and recalls the buzz that radiated around the neighborhood after the Ruthian bomb-shell. It was quickly reported that the ball had smashed into the second-story window of Russel Frain's house at #2735 on the east side of Opal Street. I talked to Dr. Rooney on multiple occasions, and he even identi-fied a boyhood friend, David Wasson, as an actual eyewitness. I subsequently visited the Philadelphia Public Library and reviewed all the names that he identified throughout his accounts in the Philadelphia Directories for the early 1930s. They were all listed right where Dr. Rooney said they would be, includ-ing the family of Herbert and Marie Frain at 2735 North Opal Street.

For the record, Ruth enjoyed the benefits of a 15 to 20-mph wind that was blowing from the WSW. When you consider that Babe directed his shot ENE, it is apparent that he got a big boost from the elements. Those houses are still there and have not changed. Accordingly, it has been relatively easy to study aerial photographs and determine the linear distance from home plate to the Frain residence. It is exactly 540 feet. Since the ball struck the window 15 feet above street level, I have added another 10 feet to the total flight estimate. I rate this one at 550 feet, which ranks it as the second longest drive in official Major League history.

For anyone who read my 2007 book about Babe Ruth, they may have noticed my refer-ence to the Bambino's imposing home run at the Polo Grounds on July 31, 1921. In that work, I estimated the blow at 560 feet, which

would have placed it in second place on the all-time list. However, after further consid-eration, I have lowered my original assess-ment to 530 feet. Essentially, I now feel that I placed too much reliance on a single source. All the papers that covered the game agreed that the ball was blasted far over the right field grandstand roof near its farthest point from home plate. But only the *New York Times* gave specific details about where it landed. The *Times* claimed that this massive drive grounded in the mud in adjoining Manhattan Field near the east curb line of 8th Avenue. That may be true, and, if so, the ball prob-ably did fly around 560 feet. However, with-out a second confirmation, I am unwilling to embrace that distance as reliable.

Now, finally, after multitudinous pages of preliminaries, we arrive at the ultimate moment. We are ready to discuss the single longest batted ball ever struck in a big-league ball game. Of course, anyone paying atten-tion has already figured out that we are talking about Babe Ruth's monstrous center field blast at Detroit's Navin Field (aka Tiger Stadium) on July 18, 1921. It has already been discussed in the Ruth mini-chapter, but there is still plenty more to talk about. First, it should be understood that the conditions were virtually perfect for Ruth. He was in the middle of the season when he was at the absolute peak of his physical abilities. Next, Babe was performing at Navin Field, which we now know to have been the best-ever stadium for launching historic long-range home runs.

Then, even by Navin Field standards, the weather was especially conducive to distance hitting with the wind blowing straight out from home plate to center field at 21 miles per hour. And last, Babe Ruth was playing against antagonist Ty Cobb, and that factor should not be underrated.

Eventually, during the 1924 World Series, these two athletic legends reconciled the worst of their differences, and got along reasonably well. However, in 1921, they were bitter enemies, and had spent the season insulting each other in a vicious feud. Ruth, of course, was not vicious by nature, but had a tough side when he needed it. When Cobb made it clear that he resented Ruth for supplanting him as the game's preeminent player, the Babe accepted his ground rules. They competed passionately for years, but never as ferociously as in 1921. During a June series at the Polo Grounds between the Tigers and Yankees, Ruth and Cobb nearly came to blows on several occasions. On this subsequent July meeting in Detroit, Ruth was ready for anything. He had been enjoying a good road trip, having performed well in both Chicago and St. Louis. However, when he arrived in the Motor City on July 16, his fortunes slipped downhill. In that first of the four-game set, Babe went 0 for 5, including two long drives that were caught in deep center field by Cobb. In game two, the next day, Ruth went 0 for 3, while also collecting two bases-on-balls. One of his outs that afternoon was yet another towering fly out to distant center field.

So, when Babe Ruth arrived at Navin Field on July 18, 1921, he was not a happy fellow. Cobb was the player/manager back then, and he decided to sit out game three. However, his presence was still a factor, since he had a standing rule not to give Ruth any good pitches to hit. In fact, Babe walked the first four times that he batted that day against Howard Ehmke, and appeared again in the 8th inning without having taken a single swing. For a guy with the impatient and spontaneous temperament that personified Babe Ruth, it was a difficult situation. He was clearly frustrated. But the Yankees were leading 8–1 at that point, and either Cobb relented or reliever Bert Cole simply made a mistake. With a one and one count, Babe saw one that he liked from the young left-hander, and swung with all his pent-up energy. He connected perfectly, dropping his massive bat to watch his handiwork as he jogged toward first base.

> **The horsehide sphere absorbed that frightful force, which launched it into a rising parabola toward dead center field.**

The horsehide sphere absorbed that frightful force, which launched it into a rising parabola toward dead center field. The ball climbed higher and higher, leaving center fielder Chick Shorten looking hopelessly upward. He quickly recognized that there was zero chance of getting anywhere near the eventual landing place. Navin Field had not been significantly renovated since its original construction in 1913. Accordingly, there had been no effort to build a center field fence that would establish a realistic home run barrier. Instead, both the left and right field fences extended on straight lines from their respective foul poles along courses that paralleled the adjoining streets. As a result, the farthest center field corner, where the fences met, stood a ridiculous 560 feet from home plate. It was so far away that the spot was simply regarded as out of play.

By a coincidence, Tigers' slugger Harry Heilmann had come closest to that remote angle with a batted ball just 10 days earlier. However, the right-handed Heilmann had smashed his historic drive four panels to the left of the extreme corner in straightaway center. It had been measured at 512 feet, and was regarded by many as the longest drive in baseball history. Certainly those who had witnessed it felt certain that they would never see its equal. But they forgot that Babe Ruth was scheduled to soon arrive at that same venue. The Bambino routinely did things that had previously been perceived as undoable. That became evident as his towering drive rode the wind, climbing higher and higher, while flying on and on. Within moments, the seemingly impossible happened, and the ball easily cleared the high concrete walls at the

intersection of Cherry Street and Trumbull Avenue. The reaction of the 9,000 fans in attendance was predictable.

According to the *New York Herald* "the fans gasped" at the sight of the ball, and the *Detroit Free Press* stated that they were "almost struck dumb." So, how far did it go? Immediately afterward, the Detroit Tiger management produced stadium blueprints that showed the distance to the center field corner as 560 feet. A total of 18 newspapers that covered the event unanimously agreed that Ruth's drive exited the ballpark at that precise location. There is no doubt on that point. The next logical question is: How far beyond that corner did the ball land? Sadly, on this issue, we can't be certain. We know that the concrete wall, which the Babe's homer cleared, was 15 feet in height.

On the matter of clearance, the newspapers registered some slight disagreement. The estimates ranged from 5 feet over the wall (*New York World*) to 10 feet (*New York Sun*). On the matter of the exact landing point, the *Detroit News* suggested that the ball probably landed "on the car tracks," which passed through the middle of the intersection. The *New York Evening Journal* said the "ball not only cleared the wall but the street beyond," and the *New York American* reported that the drive "cleared the street and probably traveled 600 feet." The *New York Daily News* admitted "where it struck beyond the park is unknown."

What does it all mean? We still don't know for sure. One important fact is certain;

there are no home runs in Major League history that have a confirmed linear distance that is nearly so long. Even if the original blueprints were wrong, this drive traveled at least 560 feet. How do we know? We know because we have aerial photographs from above the stadium, and they have been carefully studied by qualified experts. In truth, there has been some slight disagreement about that original 560-foot assertion, but the distance to the center field corner has never been calculated at less than 540 feet. Adding to the puzzle are some rather mysterious newspaper references later that same season. On August 23, 1921, the *Cleveland Plain Dealer* reported that this Ruthian rocket had flown 610 feet. Then, on September 10, 1921, the *Philadelphia Inquirer* claimed a 601-foot flight distance. Why they would have said 601 feet instead of rounding it off to an even 600 feet is interesting. It infers an exact measurement, but they offered no discussion of their methodology. The *Sporting News* published on September 15, 1921 called the homer a "585 foot shot."

What do I think? My best estimate is 575 feet. The laws of physics almost certainly would not have permitted this drive to reach the far side of the intersection. Such a blast would indeed have flown over 600 feet. However, even though two papers reported that the ball had flown completely across the corner of Cherry and Trumbull, they did not specifically state that they had actually observed the ball land. I interpret that to mean that they were guessing. The consensus opinion was that this drive passed out of sight at a height of 20 to 25 feet and a linear distance of between 550 and 560 feet. When you consider Babe Ruth's established power performance curve for that season, when he had hit other homers almost as far, 575 feet is not a reach. Factoring in the 21-mph wind blowing out to center field helps to establish the plausibility of an historic distance shot.

My only reservation is the 25-foot differential between this Ruthian drive ranked number one and his 1930 Philadelphia shot ranked number two at 550 feet. I do not profess to be an expert in assessing probability. But my limited understanding of that factor tells me that the incremental difference between Ruth's two longest homers should be less than 25 feet. He accrued so many performance variables during his career that I expected numbers one and two to be bunched closer together. But the data says otherwise. Plus, other top sluggers also had significant gaps between their first and second longest career home runs.

Of course, the most important trait of Babe's Detroit blockbuster is its confirmed linear distance. No other drive in the annals of the game is known to have traveled so far on the fly. In fact, other than Ruthian home runs, the shot with the next longest confirmed linear distance is Dave Kingman's 1976 Wrigley Field blast at 530 feet. The other candidates for longest-ever recognition are drives either knocked down in mid-flight or lost from view near their apex. That doesn't eliminate them from consideration, but it certainly compromises their stature. We know that we have traditionally overestimated the flight of balls knocked down in mid-flight. Most of the alleged longest home runs over the course of baseball history have shared that common characteristic. All those eye-popping upper-deckers by Frank Howard at RFK Stadium in Washington and by Mark McGwire at Busch Stadium in St. Louis certainly come to mind. When you carefully study the confirmed distances of Hondo and Big Mac's best shots in non-enclosed stadiums, you realize that 500 feet is extremely difficult to attain . . . even for them.

> **We tend to add too much distance to balls, especially line drives, that collide with ballpark super-structures.**

Remember Mark blasting away at the All-Star home run derby at Fenway Park in 1998. That was the peak year for McGwire's distance capability, but his best shots were falling short of 500 feet. They were not receiving extra credit by colliding with high altitude stadium structures, but were landing on a garage roof that was only about 20 feet above field level. At home in St. Louis, his upper deck drives were consistently being estimated at well over 500 feet. I am not implying that the Cardinal staff was deliberately overstating McGwire's accomplishments. In fact, I know that they were not. I talked to them on a regular basis back then, and we discussed their methods.

They were simply making the same mistake that we have all consistently made over time. We tend to add too much distance to balls, especially line drives, that collide with ballpark super-structures. That includes me.

Consider Dick Allen's monstrous blast off the Tiger Stadium roof façade on July 6, 1974. It crashed into that impediment in left center field at a height of 90 feet and at a linear distance of 420 feet. Allen's manager was the highly respected Chuck Tanner, and he stated vehemently that the ball was still rising at that moment. The *Chicago Tribune* concurred as did pitcher Dave Lemanczyk (along with many others). Such a drive would have required enough force to have flown over 700 feet if lofted at a slightly higher angle. So, were all these seemingly honest men lying? Of course not. They were simply overreacting to an astonishing display of power, which has been the case almost every time that such an event has occurred.

We will never know for sure which is the longest drive in Major League history. However, considering all factors, Babe Ruth's Detroit home run on July 18, 1921 certainly has the best qualifications. It definitely has the longest confirmed linear distance. It was authored by the man who clearly established the best power performance curve in the annals of the game. It was struck at a time of particular emotional intensity for the man who hit it. Ruth himself acknowledged that he had swung as hard as he could, and that he had made perfect contact. The ball was launched in the best stadium for optimum distance, and the atmospheric conditions were particularly favorable. It adds up to a pretty convincing package. I estimate 575 feet, but, with a guy like the Babe, almost anything was possible.

That's the story of the tape measure home run. I regret that not every great slugger could be properly recognized and that, since not every home run has been documented for posterity, there may be a few that have not been mentioned. Yet, we can be reasonably confident that all the truly historic drives have been discussed. It is unlikely that any 500-foot big-league home runs have not been identified. For the guys who hit them, I wish to say thank you. They have given us some of the best entertainment that the sports world has ever created. Their skill, dedication, and power—mostly their power—have provided America (and beyond) with decades of unforgettable experiences. We are naturally drawn to power, and they have displayed that quality in one of its most pleasing manifestations. So, thank you King Kong and Teddy Ballgame. We tip our hats to you, Bull and Josh. We will never forget you Mr. October. Wish you were still banging them Killer, Stretch, and Pops. You were amazing Big Mac. How do we repay you Crash and Hondo? Nobody can ever take your places Double X and Mighty Mick. And, hey there Sultan of Swat, how are things on planet Krypton? Wherever you guys are and whatever you're doing, you were the best. Thanks for the memories!

EPILOGUE

*U*pon flying into Tampa International Airport on Monday afternoon, March 10, 2008, I was met at the arrival gate by Tim Reid. After stopping briefly to pick up my auto rental, I followed Tim into downtown Tampa to visit a place that I had wanted to see for many years. Reid, along with cousin Bob Ward, is the co-chair of the Committee To Commemorate Babe Ruth, and he had organized a series of events that had induced me to make the trip south from Philadelphia.

What was the destination of this pilgrimage that I wanted to make before checking into my hotel? It was the campus of the University of Tampa where their athletic field occupies the same space as the original Plant Field. That was where Babe Ruth launched his historic 552-foot home run on April 4, 1919, while playing against the New York Giants for the Boston Red Sox. The university now uses the former world-renowned Tampa Bay Hotel as its administration building. Nearby, they also maintain a plaque to memorialize Babe's big blast.

Upon arriving at the field, Tim pointed out the 1919 location of home plate, and then led me on a not-so-short walk to a place outside the premises. Pursuant to Reid's

and baseball historian Bruce Orser's careful research, we were then standing on the spot where Ruth's epic shot had landed. For a baseball historian, it was a riveting moment. By applying a little imagination, I could visualize The Bambino jogging around the bases. The only dynamic that blurred the image was the shocking distance from where I stood transfixed to where the infield had been situated. It came readily to my mind that 552 feet was farther than any human being should be able to hit a baseball.

On Tuesday, March 11, I stayed in Tampa, and spent a few hours at the library researching Ruth and others who had made their mark on the local sports culture. Despite reading about such powerful performers as Jimmie Foxx, Mickey Mantle, and Dick Allen, it was Babe Ruth who generated the most dramatic descriptive prose. It was yet another reminder in a 30-year process that this unlikely figure somehow bashed baseballs harder and farther than anyone else.

Then on Wednesday, I drove over the I-275 causeway into St. Petersburg where I rejoined Tim along with Linda Ruth Tosetti (Babe's granddaughter) and her husband Andy. The Tampa Bay Rays had arranged for

Linda to throw out the first pitch before their exhibition game with the New York Yankees, and had been kind enough to invite all of us to come along. For the record, it was the last game that the Yanks would ever play in the modern incarnation of Waterfront Park known as Al Lang Field. Rays' senior advisor and broadcast legend Dick Crippen met us at the ticket window outside the stadium and was leading us inside when an elderly ticket-taker discovered Linda's identity. That recognition triggered a spontaneous reaction inside the gentleman's memory. He called out to Linda, "I saw your grandfather play a game in Albany back in the '30s, and he hit a home run over the right field fence that landed on a roller coaster."

Of course, I couldn't resist. I turned around, and asked the man for more details about the event. He remembered that everyone in his group had stood at their seats for about 10 minutes staring and pointing in disbelief at the implausible place where the Ruthian rocket had landed. I subsequently checked my records, and confirmed that Babe hit three homers in Albany in that time period (two on April 23, 1934 and one on July 26, 1938, while coaching for the Brooklyn Dodgers), but I was unable to obtain specifics about the landing places. But that was okay. Over the years, I had learned that it was impossible to confirm every legend involving Babe Ruth. Later that night, it occurred to me that I had been in the Tampa Bay area for three days, and, on each of those days, I

had some type of experience relating to Babe Ruth's extraordinary power. That seemed remarkable to me, but the trip still had one day to go.

On Thursday morning, March 13, 2008, I met Tim Reid, Bob Ward, and a group of other folks in a parking lot adjacent to First Street where the old Waterfront Park had been located. As stated, it was later renamed Al Lang Field, and eventually relocated slightly to the south of its original position. Babe Ruth played many exhibition games there during the 11 years that he had trained in St. Pete. We were all there to meet Mr. Mike Mastry, who, at age 92, still recalled the day that he had seen Ruth pound a batting practice shot off the West Coast Inn. That hotel was situated across First Street beyond the distant outfield wall in deepest right center field. It was an intriguing recollection since Mastry started chasing Babe's BP drives as early as 1930. In fact, young Mike had gotten to know Ruth very well due to Babe's willingness to autograph packages of baseballs each spring during the Great Depression. Following Ruth's advice, Mastry would purchase the cheapest balls, selling at 25 cents apiece in boxes of 12. After Babe affixed his signature to them, the industrious teenager would then sell the balls for up to $5 each, thereby helping to feed his family during those tough times.

I knew about the Mastry meeting in advance and had scrupulously researched the matter. I discovered that many newspapers had reported unusually long batting practice drives by Babe Ruth over the years that the Bambino had competed at Waterfront Park. There were particularly dramatic accounts of a blow off Ben Cantwell on March 5, 1935. However, none of them mentioned the West Coast Inn. There were occasional references to "hotels," but no specific identification of that one particular building. Of further interest, Tim had identified a passage in Red Smith's 1973 book titled *Red Smith on Baseball,* where Ruth had personally confirmed the incident. In the spring of 1948, during Ruth's final visit to his beloved St. Petersburg, he had been interviewed by Francis Stann of the *Washington Star*. When asked what he remembered best about his days at Waterfront Park, Babe reportedly pointed to the West Coast Inn, and said, "The day I hit the f.... ball against that hotel."

Think about that. Of all the amazing things that Babe Ruth had accomplished in that historic ballpark, he named a batting practice shot as the deed that he recalled with the most passion. It must have been a whopper! And that was why we were all there that day. Tim had engaged the services of George F. Young Surveyors, who had performed the original surveys for both the West Coast Inn and Waterfront Park early in the 19th century. They proceeded to locate both the original position of home plate as well as the closest corner of the hotel. They then calculated the distance between the two fixed points at the astounding distance of 624

feet. We weren't quite sure what to make of it, since it seemed unlikely that even Babe Ruth could hit a baseball that far on the fly. Perhaps Mr. Mastry had seen the ball strike against the hotel, as did The Babe himself, without realizing that it had first bounced on the street. Even then, the ball would have flown over 550 feet in the air. Again, I was living a surreal Babe Ruth moment.

Just for fun, we next drove across town to Huggins-Stengel Field, which was originally called Crescent Lake Ballpark. It had been built in 1925 to serve as a practice field for the New York Yankees when they first came to St. Pete for spring training. Basically, Babe and the Yanks played exhibition games at Waterfront Park, but they practiced and played inter-squad games at Crescent Lake Park. As of 2008, the right field fence was marked at 430 feet, and I paced off another 140 feet to the nearest edge of the lake itself. I had read numerous accounts of Ruth slamming balls into that lake, but I knew that the swampy corners had not been filled in until 1928. In other words, Crescent Lake wasn't 570 feet from home plate during the first three years of Babe Ruth's visits. Plus, most of those newspaper accounts spoke only in general terms about Ruth "knocking the ball into the lake." It seemed likely that they meant that those balls bounced into the water.

It is also true, however, that author Kevin McCarthy wrote in his book titled *Babe Ruth in Florida* that The Babe had landed six drives in Crescent Lake during batting practice on

March 7, 1928. It is widely recognized that no other player ever reached the water on the fly although Mickey Mantle and Darryl Strawberry came close. So what is the truth? Did Babe Ruth ever really bash a baseball 570 feet through the air into Crescent Lake?

I had separated from the group and was contemplating these cosmic issues on the bank of the lake when one of my friends called to me. I rejoined our party of explorers, which had gathered near a paved walkway about halfway between the outfield fence and the lake. They were talking to an elderly gentleman, a complete stranger, who had been walking his dog. He was asked to repeat his question from a moment earlier. Just then, Tim Reid also rejoined the group as the man queried, "Would you like me to show you where Babe Ruth hit the longest ball in baseball history?" Of course, we had just come from the formal survey at old Waterfront Park where Tim had invested a lot of time and resources. He just smiled and blinked, stating rather numbly, "I thought we just came from there." In truth, we were all a little numb.

The man went on to explain that he was a member of the "Kids and Cubs" baseball league, which does not allow participation until age 75. Some years earlier, he had a teammate who had played in the Philadelphia Athletics farm system back in the 1930s. When the Yankees were a little short-handed one time, Connie Mack had loaned him to the Yanks to help them play a full inter-squad game. He was playing first base when Babe Ruth came to bat, and watched in disbelief as the Bambino knocked one into the lake . . . on the fly! The wooden fence wasn't around in those days, and he claimed that he had a clear view of the ball splashing into the water. He turned around just in time to see Ruth rounding first base and smiling at him. Babe winked at him and asked, "How'd you like that kid?"

By that time, I had been researching Ruth for almost three decades, and thought that I had heard everything. But this was too much. Fortunately, everybody felt the same way, and all we could do was laugh. The well-intentioned gentleman insisted that his story was genuine, and we assured him that we believed him. We offered a brief explanation about the origin of our group, whereupon he smiled politely and continued walking his dog. If anyone else had been credited with a 570-foot home run into a lake, I wouldn't have believed it for a second. But this was Babe Ruth, and I have learned not to put limits on his capabilities.

Will we ever see his like again? When I concluded the Babe Ruth chapter, I said no. Yet, I must, at least, acknowledge the possibility of a successor. Since 2006, an enterprising fellow named Brian Domenico has used his considerable abilities to organize an annual event known as the "Power Showcase." Like many of us, Brian loves the long ball, but has been disillusioned by the apparent inclusion of steroids in the picture. Unlike most of us, Brian is doing something about it. Every winter, he invites all the best high school sluggers from around the baseball world to a home run hitting contest staged inside Tropicana Field in St. Pete. However, there is one stipulation. In order to participate, each young man must agree to be tested for performance-enhancing drugs if he finishes at the top. In January 2009, the single longest drive during the Power Showcase was computed at 502 feet. Admittedly, those young studs use aluminum bats, which propel the ball farther than the wooden clubs used in professional ball. But 502 feet is still quite a wallop. And here's the kicker; that award-winning shot was authored by a 16-year-old kid from Las Vegas by the name of Bryce Harper.

Apparently, Bryce has been leaving witnesses gasping over the length of his drives for a few years now. He stands 6'3" and weighs 205 pounds. By all accounts, he possesses a great attitude, high intelligence, and a disciplined work ethic. He has loving parents and seems headed in the right direction. Could he finally be the one to rival Babe Ruth as the mightiest hitter that baseball has ever produced? That seems unlikely to me, but check back in 10 years. If Bryce is the real heir to the Sultan of Swat, it will be time to write the next edition of *Baseball's Ultimate Power*.

APPENDIXES

Appendix A

Top 100 Tape Measure Sluggers

In order to achieve the best historical overview of how all the great power hitters compare to each other, all players (except those still active) are included in this list. It combines Major League players (including the 19th-century sluggers) with Negro League players.

1.	Babe Ruth	23.	Dan Brouthers	45.	Jim Rice
2.	Jimmie Foxx	24.	Ron Kittle	46.	Boog Powell
3.	Mickey Mantle	25.	Lou Gehrig	47.	Bo Jackson
4.	Frank Howard	26.	Mike Piazza	48.	Fred McGriff
5.	Dick Allen	27.	Wally Berger	49.	Sam Thompson
6.	Mark McGwire	28.	Norm Cash	50.	Gus Zernial
7.	Willie Stargell	29.	Frank Robinson	51.	Rogers Hornsby
8.	Willie McCovey	30.	George Foster	52.	Turkey Stearnes
9.	Harmon Killebrew	31.	Luke Easter	53.	Rocky Colavito
10.	Reggie Jackson	32.	Willie Mays	54.	Rob Deer
11.	Josh Gibson	33.	Wally Post	55.	Jay Buhner
12.	Greg Luzinski	34.	Roger Connor	56.	Dave Winfield
13.	Ted Williams	35.	Eddie Mathews	57.	Stan Lopata
14.	Dave Kingman	36.	Darryl Strawberry	58.	Greg Vaughn
15.	Ralph Kiner	37.	Andres Galarraga	59.	Tony Perez
16.	Sammy Sosa	38.	Henry Aaron	60.	Kevin Mitchell
17.	Mule Suttles	39.	Buck Freeman	61.	Carl Yastrzemski
18.	Joe Adcock	40.	Kirk Gibson	62.	Al Simmons
19.	Barry Bonds	41.	Larry Doby	63.	Eddie Murray
20.	Cecil Fielder	42.	Mike Schmidt	64.	Dave Nicholson
21.	Jose Canseco	43.	Hank Greenberg	65.	Jim Gentile
22.	Dick Stuart	44.	Jimmy Wynn	66.	Willie Horton

67. Bob Cerv	84. Johnny Mize	**HONORABLE MENTIONS**
68. Bill Nicholson	85. Hack Wilson	Bob Bailey
69. John Beckwith	86. Louis Santop	Harold Baines
70. Duke Snider	87. Buck Ewing	Steve Balboni
71. Jeff Bagwell	88. Stan Musial	Ernie Banks
72. Albert Belle	89. Roberto Clemente	Ellis Burks
73. Pete Incaviglia	90. Johnny Bench	Wes Covington
74. Orlando Cepeda	91. Joe Carter	Mike Epstein
75. Ed Delahanty	92. Oscar Charleston	Harry Heilmann
76. Roger Maris	93. Joe DiMaggio	Glenallen Hill
77. Rudy York	94. Harry Stovey	Kent Hrbek
78. Dave Parker	95. Todd Hundley	Ryan Klesko
79. Juan Gonzalez	96. Eric Davis	Ted Kluszewski
80. Jack Clark	97. Honus Wagner	Jim Lemon
81. George Bell	98. Mickey Tettleton	Mel Ott
82. Steve Bilko	99. Andre Dawson	Rafael Palmeiro
83. Nate Colbert	100. Sam Crawford	Larry Parrish
		George Scott
		Mo Vaughn
		Leon Wagner
		Earl Williams

Appendix B

Top 100 Longest Drives in Major League Games

1. Babe Ruth—July 18, 1921—Detroit—575 ft.
2. Babe Ruth—May 22, 1930—Philadelphia—550 ft.
3. Babe Ruth—August 17, 1921—Chicago—545 ft.
4. Babe Ruth—May 25, 1926—Boston—540 ft.
4. Babe Ruth—May 25, 1935—Pittsburgh—540 ft.
4. Mickey Mantle—May 22, 1963—New York—540 ft.
4. Dick Allen—June 6, 1967—Philadelphia—540 ft.
4. Reggie Jackson—July 13, 1971—Detroit—540 ft.
4. Dave Kingman—April 14, 1976—Chicago—540 ft.
10. Babe Ruth—May 25, 1921—St. Louis—535 ft.
10. Frank Howard—September 24, 1967—Washington—535 ft.
10. Dick Allen—July 6, 1974—Detroit—535 ft.
10. Mark McGwire—May 12, 1998—St. Louis—535 ft.
10. Mark McGwire—May 16, 1998—St. Louis—535 ft.
15. Babe Ruth—July 31, 1921—New York—530 ft.
15. Babe Ruth—October 6, 1926—St. Louis—530 ft.
15. Jimmie Foxx—June 16, 1936—Chicago—530 ft.
15. Mickey Mantle—April 17, 1956—Washington—530 ft.
15. Frank Howard—July 7, 1969—Washington—530 ft.
15. Adam Dunn—August 10, 2004—Cincinnati—530 ft.
21. Dick Allen—May 29, 1965—Philadelphia—529 ft.
22. Bob Cerv—May 16, 1958—Kansas City—528 ft.
23. Babe Ruth—May 27, 1920—Boston—525 ft.
23. Babe Ruth—May 31, 1924—New York—525 ft.
23. Babe Ruth—May 24, 1930—New York—525 ft.
23. Jimmie Foxx—May 14, 1932—Philadelphia—525 ft.
23. Mickey Mantle—July 6, 1953—Philadelphia—525 ft.
23. Frank Howard—April 24, 1970—Washington—525 ft.

239

29. Ted Williams—June 9, 1946—Boston—522 ft.

29. Frank Howard—April 25, 1966—Washington—522 ft.

29. Harmon Killebrew—June 3, 1967—Minnesota—522 ft.

32. Babe Ruth—May 23, 1920—New York—520 ft.

32. Babe Ruth—May 7, 1921—Washington—520 ft.

32. Babe Ruth—September 2, 1921—New York—520 ft.

32. Babe Ruth—June 8, 1926—Detroit—520 ft.

32. Babe Ruth—August 16, 1927—Chicago—520 ft.

32. Jimmie Foxx—July 18, 1930—Chicago—520 ft.

32. Ralph Kiner—April 22, 1950—Pittsburgh—520 ft.

32. Dick Stuart—May 1, 1959—Pittsburgh—520 ft.

32. Frank Howard—May 25, 1960—Pittsburgh—520 ft.

32. Wally Post—April 14, 1961—St. Louis—520 ft.

32. Willie Stargell—July 3, 1967—Pittsburgh—520 ft.

32. Reggie Jackson—July 5, 1969—Minnesota—520 ft.

32. Sammy Sosa—June 24, 2003—Chicago—520 ft.

45. Carl Yastrzemski—May 9, 1969—California—518 ft.

46. Mark McGwire—September 16, 1997—St. Louis—517 ft.

47. Frank Howard—July 30, 1965—Kansas City—516 ft.

48. Babe Ruth—May 13, 1924—New York—515 ft.

48. Babe Ruth—May 19, 1926—New York—515 ft.

48. Babe Ruth—October 6, 1926—St. Louis—515 ft.

48. Babe Ruth—June 22, 1927—Boston—515 ft.

48. Babe Ruth—May 25, 1928—Philadelphia—515 ft.

48. Babe Ruth—July 23, 1928—Boston—515 ft.

48. Jimmie Foxx—September 10, 1929—Philadelphia—515 ft.

48. Jimmie Foxx—June 20, 1932—Chicago—515 ft.

48. Jimmie Foxx—June 25, 1932—New York—515 ft.

48. Mickey Mantle—September 12, 1953—New York—515 ft.

48. Mickey Mantle—August 23, 1956—New York—515 ft.

48. Dick Stuart—June 5, 1959—Pittsburgh—515 ft.

48. Norm Cash—July 29, 1962—Detroit—515 ft.

48. Frank Howard—July 18, 1965—New York—515 ft.

48. Dick Allen—August 19, 1966—Philadelphia—515 ft.

48. Willie McCovey—September 4, 1966—St. Louis—515 ft.

48. Greg Luzinski—May 21, 1977—Houston—515 ft.

48. Willie Stargell—May 20, 1978—Montreal—515 ft.

48. Dave Kingman—August 14, 1981—New York—515 ft.

48. Kirk Gibson—June 14, 1983—Detroit—515 ft.

48. Bo Jackson—September 14, 1986—Kansas City—515 ft.

69. Harry Heilmann—July 8, 1921—Detroit—512 ft.

69. Mickey Mantle—August 12, 1964—New York—512 ft.

71. Mark McGwire—July 17, 1998—St. Louis—511 ft.

71. Jim Thome—July 3, 1999—Cleveland—511 ft.

73. Babe Ruth—August 23, 1919—Detroit—510 ft.

73. Babe Ruth—September 9, 1921—Philadelphia—510 ft.

73. Babe Ruth—September 11, 1924—Boston—510 ft.

73. Babe Ruth—September 8, 1925—Boston—510 ft.

73. Babe Ruth—April 24, 1926—New York—510 ft.

73. Babe Ruth—August 6, 1926—Cleveland—510 ft.

73. Lou Gehrig—May 4, 1929—Chicago—510 ft.

73. Jimmie Foxx—August 22, 1931—Chicago—510 ft.

73. Babe Ruth—September 23, 1933—Boston—510 ft.

73. Jimmie Foxx—August 16, 1940—Boston—510 ft.

73. Ralph Kiner—May 8, 1949—Boston—510 ft.

73. Larry Doby—May 24, 1951—Washington—510 ft.

73. Mickey Mantle—April 17, 1953—Washington—510 ft.

73. Joe Adcock—June 17, 1956—Brooklyn—510 ft.

73. Mickey Mantle—September 12, 1956—Boston—510 ft.

73. Roberto Clemente—May 17, 1959—Chicago—510 ft.

73. Dick Allen—June 15, 1966—Cincinnati—510 ft.

73. Willie McCovey—May 22, 1967—Philadelphia—510 ft.

73. Harmon Killebrew—June 4, 1967—Minnesota—510 ft.

73. Frank Howard—May 18, 1968—Detroit—510 ft.

73. Reggie Jackson—April 20, 1969—Kansas City—510 ft.

73. Dick Allen—June 21, 1969—Philadelphia—510 ft.

73. Willie Stargell—August 19, 1969—Pittsburgh—510 ft.

73. Willie Stargell—August 9, 1970—Pittsburgh—510 ft.

73.	Willie Stargell—July 4, 1979—St. Louis—510 ft.	100.	Andres Galarraga—May 31, 1997—Florida—509 ft.
73.	Kirk Gibson—May 10, 1985—Chicago—510 ft.	100.	George Foster—July 29, 1978—Cincinnati—509 ft.
73.	Cecil Fielder—August 25, 1990—Detroit—510 ft.	100.	Mark McGwire—August 26, 1998—St. Louis—509 ft.

Knowledgeable readers will recognize that there are few homers on this list that were hit by contemporary players. There are three reasons for this scenario. First, the older ballparks were prone to higher wind factors, thereby creating more opportunities for historically long drives. Second, it is possible that, in the past, a higher percentage of America's exceptionally strong men played baseball instead of other sports. Third, although this book has downsized most of the estimates for baseball's historic home runs, it is impossible to judge many of them reliably. There is virtually no film library to use in conjunction with modern scientific analysis for estimating drives recorded prior to the advent of current communications technology.

Stadium Photographs

This section includes photographs of forty prominent Major League stadiums. Each photo includes three markers (Shea Stadium is the lone exception with four) showing the longest known home runs recorded to each sector of the field: left field, center field and right field. ⊙ are placed wherever the photo shows the exact landing point. It is important to understand that the photographs reflect the stadium configuration only at the moment in which they were taken. In almost every case, the stadiums changed significantly over the years. The arrows show approximately where the home runs would have landed if hit at the time that the stadium is pictured. In some cases, the arrows also indicate the flight path of the ball when the photo does not include a view of the landing place. Beneath each photo are captions identifying the homers.

ANAHEIM

Courtesy of the National Baseball Hall of Fame and Museum

Angels Stadium   1966 to present
Left Center Field—Joe Adcock—September 2, 1966—495 ft.
Center Field—Frank Howard—August 25, 1971—506 ft.
Right Center Field—Carl Yastrzemski—May 9, 1969—518 ft.

ATLANTA

Atlanta-Fulton County Stadium   1966 to 1996
Left Field—Jeff Burroughs—April 17, 1974—495 ft.
Center Field—Steve Balboni—September 1, 1985—485 ft.
Right Field—Eddie Murray—August 20, 1982—475 ft.

ARLINGTON

Arlington Stadium   1972 to 1993
Left Center Field—Greg Luzinski—September 3, 1972—500 ft.
Center Field—Willie Stargell—July 15, 1979—455 ft.
Right Field—Willie McCovey—June 22, 1969—500 ft.

BALTIMORE

Courtesy of the Philadelphia Athletics Historical Society

Memorial Stadium   1954 to 1991
Left Center Field—Harmon Killebrew—May 24, 1964—471 ft.
Center Field—Boog Powell—June 22, 1962—469 ft.
Right Center Field—Jim Gentile—May 26, 1965—470 ft.

BOSTON

Courtesy of the Philadelphia Athletics Historical Society

Fenway Park   1912 to present
Left Field—Jimmie Foxx—August 16, 1940—510 ft.
Center Field—Babe Ruth—June 22, 1927—515 ft.
Right Field—Babe Ruth—May 25, 1926—540 ft.

BOSTON

Courtesy of the Atlanta Braves

Braves Field 1915 to 1952
Left Field—Ralph Kiner—May 8, 1949—510 ft.
Center Field—Rogers Hornsby—June 4, 1928—478 ft.
Right Field—Babe Ruth—May 18, 1930—490 ft.

CHICAGO

Courtesy of the Philadelphia Athletics Historical Society

Comiskey Park 1910 to 1990
Left Field—Jimmie Foxx—June 16, 1936—530 ft.
Left Center Field—Jimmie Foxx—July 18, 1930—520 ft.
Right Center Field—Babe Ruth—August 17, 1921—545 ft.

CHICAGO

Courtesy of the National Baseball Hall of Fame and Museum

U.S. Cellular Field   1991 to present
Left Field—Frank Thomas—July 23, 2002—495 ft.
Center Field—Jim Thome—June 4, 2008—464 ft.
Right Field—Joe Borchard—August 30, 2004—504 ft.

CHICAGO

Courtesy of the Philadelphia Athletics Historical Society

Wrigley Field   1916 to present
Left Field—Dave Kingman—April 14, 1976—540 ft.
Left Center Field—Roberto Clemente—May 17, 1959—510 ft.
Right Center Field—Eddie Mathews—April 22, 1953—500 ft.

CINCINNATI

Crosley Field   1912 to 1970
Left Center Field—Dick Allen—June 15, 1966—510 ft.
Center Field—Frank Robinson—June 22, 1965—503 ft.
Right Field—Willie McCovey—September 9, 1960—480 ft.

CINCINNATI

Riverfront Stadium   1970 to 2002
Left Field—George Foster—July 29, 1978—509 ft.
Center Field—George Foster—June 2, 1979—473 ft.
Right Field—Dave Parker—August 5, 1977—482 ft.

CLEVELAND

Courtesy of the Philadelphia Athletics Historical Society

League Park   1910 to 1946
Left Field—Jimmie Foxx—September 17, 1938—495 ft.
Center Field—Lou Gehrig—May 19, 1927—470 ft.
Right Center Field—Babe Ruth—August 6, 1926—510 ft.

CLEVELAND

Courtesy of the Philadelphia Athletics Historical Society

Municipal Stadium   1932 to 1993
Left Center Field—Jose Canseco—June 28, 1987—490 ft.
Center Field—Joe DiMaggio—August 6, 1938 (triple)—465 ft.
Right Center Field—Luke Easter—June 23, 1950—505 ft.

DETROIT

Courtesy of the Philadelphia Athletics Historical Society

Tiger Stadium 1913 to 1999
Left Center Field—Dick Allen—July 6, 1974—535 ft.
Center Field—Babe Ruth—July 18, 1921—575 ft.
Right Center Field—Reggie Jackson—July 13, 1971—540 ft.

HOUSTON

Courtesy of the National Baseball Hall of Fame and Museum

Astrodome 1965 to 1999
Left Field—Greg Luzinski—May 21, 1977—515 ft.
Center Field—Mike Schmidt—June 10, 1974 (single)—500 ft.
Right Center Field—Willie Stargell—May 28, 1966—490 ft.

KANSAS CITY

Municipal Stadium   1955 to 1967, 1969 to 1972
Left Field—Bob Cerv—May 16, 1958—528 ft.
Center Field—Frank Howard—July 30, 1965—516 ft.
Right Field—Harry Simpson—June 24, 1956—512 ft.

KANSAS CITY

Kauffman Stadium   1973 to present
Left Center Field—Bo Jackson—September 14, 1986—515 ft.
Center Field—Jermaine Dye—August 2, 2006—455 ft.
Right Field—Reggie Jackson—July 20, 1976—500 ft.

LOS ANGELES

Courtesy of the Philadelphia Athletics Historical Society

Dodger Stadium 1962 to present
Left Center Field—Mark McGwire—May 22, 1999—484 ft.
Center Field—Dick Allen—June 7, 1976—475 ft.
Right Field—Willie Stargell—August 5, 1969—506 ft.

MILWAUKEE

Courtesy of the Atlanta Braves

County Stadium 1953 to 1965, 1970 to 2000
Left Field—Cecil Fielder—September 14, 1991—502 ft.
Center Field—Joe Adcock—August 3, 1958—470 ft.
Right Field—Eddie Mathews—April 30, 1965—485 ft.

MINNEAPOLIS/BLOOMINGTON

Courtesy of the Philadelphia Athletics Historical Society

Metropolitan Stadium   1961 to 1981
Left Field—Harmon Killebrew—June 3, 1967—522 ft.
Center Field—Harmon Killebrew—April 30, 1961—475 ft.
Right Center Field—Reggie Jackson—July 5, 1969—520 ft.

MINNEAPOLIS

Courtesy of the National Baseball Hall of Fame and Museum

Metrodome   1982 to present
Left Field—Mark McGwire—June 9, 1996—475 ft.
Center Field—Pedro Munoz—April 6, 1994—473 ft.
Right Field—Ben Ogilvie—July 27, 1983—481 ft.

MONTREAL

Olympic Stadium   1977 to 2004
Left Field—Vladimir Guerrero—July 28, 2003—502 ft.
Center Field—Andre Dawson—April 26, 1987—460 ft.
Right Field—Willie Stargell—May 20, 1978—515 ft.

NEW YORK (BROOKLYN)

Ebbets Field   1913 to 1957
Left Field—Joe Adcock—June 17, 1956—510 ft.
Center Field—Duke Snider—April 18, 1955—470 ft.
Right Field—Duke Snider—July 17, 1955—470 ft.

NEW YORK (QUEENS)

Shea Stadium   1964 to 2008
Special Mention—Left Field—Tom Agee—April 10, 1969—490 ft.
Left Center Field—Dave Kingman—August 14, 1981—515 ft.
Center Field—Dick Allen—May 30, 1966—493 ft.
Deep Right Center Field—Mark McGwire—August 22, 1999—495 ft.

NEW YORK

Polo Grounds   1911 to 1957, 1962 to 1963
Left Center Field—Willie Mays—July 7, 1955—480 ft.
Center Field—Babe Ruth—June 14, 1921—490 ft.
Right Center Field—Babe Ruth—July 31, 1921—530 ft.

NEW YORK

Courtesy of the Philadelphia Athletics Historical Society

Yankee Stadium   1923 to 2008
Left Field—Tie—Jimmie Foxx—June 25, 1932, Mickey Mantle—
September 12, 1953, and Frank Howard—July 18, 1965—515 ft.
Right Center Field—Babe Ruth—May 31, 1924—525 ft.
Right Field—Mickey Mantle—May 22, 1963—540 ft.

OAKLAND

Courtesy of the National Baseball Hall of Fame and Museum

Oakland-Alameda County Coliseum   1968 to present
Left Center Field—Jose Canseco—September 26, 1985—495 ft.
Center Field—Reggie Jackson—June 23, 1972—475 ft.
Right Field—Reggie Jackson—July 20, 1973—480 ft.

PHILADELPHIA

Courtesy of the Philadelphia Athletics Historical Society

Baker Bowl   1887 to 1938
Left Field—Joe Medwick—May 12, 1937—480 ft.
Center Field—Cliff Lee—April 14, 1922—460 ft.
Right Center Field—Fred Luderus—July 22, 1913—455 ft.

PHILADELPHIA

Courtesy of the Philadelphia Athletics Historical Society

Connie Mack Stadium   1909 to 1970
Left Center Field—Dick Allen—June 6, 1967—540 ft.
Center Field—Babe Ruth—May 25, 1928—515 ft.
Right Center Field—Babe Ruth—May 22, 1930—550 ft.

PHILADELPHIA

Courtesy of the Philadelphia Phillies

Veterans Stadium   1971 to 2003
Left Center Field—Andruw Jones—June 21, 1997—508 ft.
Center Field—Greg Luzinski—May 16, 1972—505 ft.
Right Field—Willie Stargell—June 25, 1971—505 ft.

PITTSBURGH

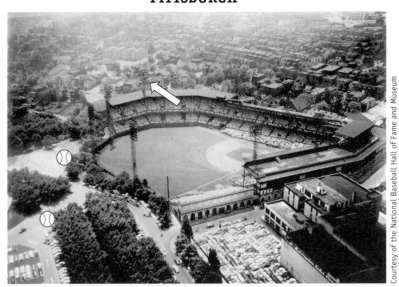

Courtesy of the National Baseball Hall of Fame and Museum

Forbes Field   1909 to 1970
Left Field—Tie—Ralph Kiner—April 22, 1950, Dick Stuart—May 1, 1959, and Frank Howard—May 25, 1960—520 ft.
Center Field—Willie Stargell—July 3, 1967—520 ft.
Right Field—Babe Ruth—May 25, 1935—540 ft.

PITTSBURGH

Courtesy of the National Baseball Hall of Fame and Museum

Three Rivers Stadium   1970 to 2000
Left Field—Greg Luzinski—April 18, 1979—480 ft.
Center Field—Greg Luzinski—August 5, 1979—490 ft.
Right Field—Willie Stargell—August 9, 1970—510 ft.

ST. LOUIS

Courtesy of the Philadelphia Athletics Historical Society

Sportsman's Park   1909 to 1966
Left Field—Wally Post—April 14, 1961—520 ft.
Center Field—Babe Ruth—May 25, 1921—535 ft.
Right Center Field—Babe Ruth—October 6, 1926—515 ft.

ST. LOUIS

Courtesy of the National Baseball Hall of Fame and Museum

Busch Memorial Stadium   1966 to 2005
Left Center Field—Mark McGwire—May 12, 1998—535 ft.
Center Field—Mark McGwire—May 16, 1998—535 ft.
Right Center Field—Willie McCovey—September 4, 1966—515 ft.

SAN DIEGO

Courtesy of the National Baseball Hall of Fame and Museum

Jack Murphy Stadium   1969 to 2003
Left Center Field—Nate Colbert—May 31, 1973—502 ft.
Center Field—Dick Allen—June 14, 1969—466 ft.
Right Field—Barry Bonds—June 5, 2002—482 ft.

SAN FRANCISCO

Courtesy of the National Baseball Hall of Fame and Museum

Candlestick Park   1960 to 1999
Left Center Field—Sammy Sosa—August 10, 1998—480 ft.
Center Field—Orlando Cepeda—August 28, 1963—458 ft.
Right Center Field—Willie McCovey—September 16, 1966—505 ft.

SEATTLE

Courtesy of the National Baseball Hall of Fame and Museum

Kingdome   1977 to 1999
Left Field—Mark McGwire—June 24, 1997—505 ft.
Center Field—Bo Jackson—July 31, 1993—472 ft.
Right Center Field—Roy Howell—June 10, 1977—480 ft.

TORONTO

Rogers Centre   1989 to present
Left Field—Manny Ramirez—June 3, 2001—491 ft.
Center Field—Jose Canseco—May 22, 1990—480 ft.
Right Center Field—Jim Thome—May 31, 1998—483 ft.

WASHINGTON, D.C.

Griffith Stadium   1911 to 1961
Left Center Field—Mickey Mantle—April 17, 1953—510 ft.
Center Field—Mickey Mantle—April 17, 1956—530 ft.
Right Center Field—Babe Ruth—May 7, 1921—520 ft.

WASHINGTON, D.C.

Courtesy of the National Baseball Hall of Fame and Museum

RFK Stadium   1962 to 1971, and 2005 to 2007
Left Center Field—Frank Howard—September 24, 1967—535 ft.
Center Field—Frank Howard—July 7, 1969—530 ft.
Right Field—Mike Epstein—June 29, 1969—490 ft.

LONGEST HOME RUNS FOR NON-PICTURED STADIUMS

Arlington, Ameriquest Field, 1994 to present
- Paul Sorrento on May 19, 1999—To top of grass embankment in center field—491 ft.

Atlanta, Turner Field, 1997 to present
- Mark Teixeira on September 21, 2007—To top of bleachers in deep right center field—477 ft.

Baltimore, Oriole Park at Camden Yards, 1992 to present
- Darryl Strawberry on June 17, 1998—Halfway up Jumbotron scoreboard just right of center field—485 ft.

Cincinnati, Great American Ballpark, 2003 to present
- Adam Dunn on August 10, 2004—Far over fence and out of stadium just right of center—530 ft.

Cleveland, Jacobs Field, 1994 to present
- Jim Thome on July 3, 1999—Over center field fence and hit pillar in Heritage Park—511 ft.

Denver, Mile High Stadium, 1993 to 1994
- Andres Galarraga on April 27, 1993—Far over fence in deep right center field—464 ft.

Denver, Coors Field, 1995 to present
- Andres Galarraga on August 28, 1997—To concourse atop bleachers in deep left center field—506 ft.

Detroit, Comerica Park, 2000 to present
- Magglio Ordonez on September 25, 2007—To second tier in deep left center field—462 ft.

Houston, Colt Stadium, 1962 to 1964
- Willie Mays on July 23, 1962—To top of left field bleachers—452 ft.

Houston, Minute Maid Park, 2000 to present
- Lance Berkman on July 26, 2006—To top of lower deck in deep right center field—465 ft.

Los Angeles, Los Angeles Coliseum, 1958 to 1961
- Frank Howard on July 9, 1960—To 37th row of bleachers in deep left center field—485 ft.

Miami, Dolphins Stadium, 1993 to present
- Andres Galarraga on May 31, 1997—Over exit in left field upper deck—509 ft.

Milwaukee, Miller Park, 2001 to present
- Russell Branyon on July 27, 2004—Over bleachers to concourse in right center field—480 ft.

Montreal, Jarry Park, 1969 to 1976
- Dick Allen on July 3, 1970—Halfway up center field backdrop—485 ft.

New York (Queens), Citi Field, 2009 to present
- Mark Reynolds on August 1, 2009—High into second deck in deep left center field—462 ft.

New York, Yankee Stadium II, 2009 to present
- Raul Ibanez on May 22, 2009—To top of right center field bleachers—477 ft.

Philadelphia, Citizens Bank Park, 2004 to present
- Ryan Howard on April 23, 2006—Over brick backdrop in center field—486 ft.

Phoenix, Chase Field, 1998 to present
- Adam Dunn on September 27, 2008—Line drive off scoreboard in center—504 ft.

Pittsburgh, PNC Park, 2001 to present
- Sammy Sosa on April 12, 2002—Far over fence in left center field to flagpole—484 ft.

St. Louis, Busch Stadium, 2006 to present
- Albert Pujols on June 30, 2009—Into left field upper deck—465 ft.

St. Petersburg, Tropicana Field, 1998 to present
- Darryl Strawberry on October 1, 1999—Off pipe hanging from roof in right field—490 ft.

San Diego, Petco Park, 2004 to present
- Adrian Gonzalez on April 26, 2009—High onto bleachers in deep right center field—470 ft.

San Francisco, Seals Stadium, 1958 to 1959
- Ernie Banks on August 17, 1958—Far over left center field wall into parking lot—470 ft.

San Francisco, AT&T Park, 2000 to present
- Barry Bonds on September 9, 2002—To base of backdrop in center field—491 ft.

Seattle, Safeco Field, 1999 to present
- Raul Ibanez on June 20, 2007—Into cafe in right field second deck—462 ft.

Toronto, Exhibition Stadium, 1977 to present
- Fred McGriff on September 2, 1988—Far over right field fence onto football field—473 ft.

Washington, D.C., Nationals Park, 2008 to present
- Adam Dunn on July 4, 2009—To top of right field second deck—458 ft.

Tape Measure Calendar

Each year, professional baseball is commonly played from early March to about the end of October. That time frame encompasses spring training contests, regular season games, and postseason competition, including the World Series and even "barnstorming" games from baseball's early days. To further enjoy the history of long-distance hitting, the following calendar has been assembled to identify the longest known drive from each date in baseball annals. As long as the pitcher was trying his best to retire the batter in a competitive situation, the at-bat qualifies for inclusion in this list. Batting practice, for example, is not included. After each date, there is the name of a great slugger who has hit the mightiest tape measure drive on that date. Also listed are the place, brief description, and approximate flight distance for each of those drives. In some cases, the long balls have actually been measured for exact distance. Unless otherwise noted, the designated drives resulted in home runs. However, occasionally, some of the following blows wound up as triples, doubles, or even fly outs.

For some dates, more than one home run has been listed. For example, there are two homers noted for April 13. The longest-ever home run on that date was struck by the mighty Jimmie Foxx in 1937. But, the wondrous Henry Aaron recorded his longest career four-bagger on that same date in 1970. That event should not be ignored. So, in order to make this document as informative as possible, both of the aforementioned blows are assigned to the date of April 13. When other dates have two or more highly significant home runs recorded, they are similarly represented. Occasionally, two different drives are judged to have flown the exact same distance. In such infrequent cases, both blasts are included.

Another example is the date of May 22. Babe Ruth smashed a tremendous drive to the second street east of Shibe Park on that date, and it appears to be the longest ball ever struck on May 22. However, on that same day in 1963, Mickey Mantle blasted what was probably the longest homer of his remarkable career. Again, this is a case where the reader needs to know about both drives. Therefore, they are both listed on the calendar. On the subject of Ruth and Mantle, it should be understood that they could easily dominate this chronicle. Along with Jimmie Foxx, they are the strongest batsmen ever, and their deeds alone could occupy almost every single date from March through October. Since diversity is a primary objective, whenever two balls are relatively close in flight distance, the benefit of doubt goes to the other player. Even though Foxx, Mantle, and Ruth show up more frequently than any other sluggers, they would be even more prominent if not for the deliberate effort to limit their domination.

One final point about the calendar should be addressed. Although all the official home runs for every great slugger have been studied, the same attention has not been given to the unofficial careers of other players. Specifically, due to their apparent superiority, the exhibition games of Ruth, Foxx, and Mantle have been scrutinized more than those of the other power hitters. Accordingly, their names appear more often in March and October than even their transcendent skills would suggest.

- March 3: Dick Allen (fly out)—1968—Clearwater—Flied out to deep center field—425 ft.

- March 4: Jimmie Foxx—1925—Fort Myers—Far over left center field fence—460 ft.

- March 5: Bo Jackson—1989—Haines City—Over scoreboard in left center—515 ft.

- March 6: Babe Ruth (triple)—1930—St. Petersburg—Over center fielder's head—450 ft.

- March 7: Jimmie Foxx—1928—Fort Myers—To a palm tree in deep left field—465 ft.

- March 8: Babe Ruth—1921—Shreveport—Far over center field fence at flagpole—495 ft.

- March 8: Dan Pasqua—1987—Miami—Over right field fence and landed across street—471 ft.

- March 9: Jimmie Foxx—1933—Fort Myers—Far over distant center field fence—515 ft.

- March 10: Joe DiMaggio—1946—St. Petersburg—To distant center field—455 ft.

- March 11: Mickey Mantle—1956—St. Petersburg—Bounced into bay in left field (LH)—465 ft.

- March 12: Dave Kingman—1975—Fort Lauderdale—Over both fences in left center field—490 ft.

- March 13: Jimmie Foxx—1940—Winter Haven—Over left field bleachers and hedge—465 ft.

- March 14: Frank Howard—1961—Fort Myers—Into horse corral past center field—475 ft.

- March 15: Jimmie Foxx—1936—Tampa—Over fence and trees in left center—480 ft.

- March 16: Babe Ruth (double)—1931—St. Petersburg—To palm trees in right center—485 ft.

- March 17: Hank Greenberg (double)—1935—Tampa—Between palm trees in center—480 ft.

- March 17: Earl Williams—1972—West Palm Beach—Far over left center field fence—475 ft.

- March 18: Jimmie Foxx (triple)—1939—Sarasota—To deep left center field—450 ft.

- March 19: Babe Ruth (ground rule double)—1926—St. Petersburg—To right field—495 ft.

- March 20: Mickey Mantle—1956—St. Petersburg—Far over center field wall—480 ft.

- March 20: Ted Williams—1940—St. Petersburg—Onto softball field in deep right field—460 ft.

- March 21: Mickey Mantle—1956—St. Petersburg—Into yard across street in right field—475 ft.

- March 21: Bobby Bonds—1971—Phoenix—Over high scoreboard in deep right center—470 ft.

- March 21: Dave Kingman—1975—Vero Beach—Over left field embankment and trees—465 ft.

- March 22: Jimmie Foxx—1934—Lakeland—Far over left field wall into trees—460 ft.

- March 22: Dave Kingman—1981—Fort Lauderdale—Over left field fence to 2nd field—480 ft.

- March 22: Dave Kingman—1983—St. Petersburg—To Bayfront Center past left field—517 ft.

- March 23: Frank Howard—1966—Pompano Beach—Into parking lot in left field—508 ft.

- March 24: Babe Ruth—1918—Hot Springs—Over fence, street, and pond in right—505 ft.

- March 24: Bob Cerv—1952—Bradenton—Far over left field scoreboard—470 ft.

- March 24: Orlando Cepeda—1966—Mesa—To distant center field—500 ft.

- March 25: Babe Ruth—1934—St. Petersburg—High drive over fence in right center—500 ft.

- March 26: Mickey Mantle—1951—Los Angeles (Bovard Field)—To left and right: 520 ft. and 550 ft.

- March 27: Babe Ruth (fly out)—1928—St. Petersburg—Flied out to fence in center—460 ft.

- March 28: Willie McCovey—1977—Tempe—Halfway up center field scoreboard—455 ft.

- March 29: Babe Ruth (double)—1925—Montgomery—Onto track in right center—497 ft.

- March 30: Dick Allen—1969—St. Petersburg—Over fence and trees in center field—505 ft.

- March 31: Babe Ruth—1924—Mobile—Far over fence in dead center field—510 ft.

- April 1: Stan Lopata—1956—Clearwater—Line drive far over high center field wall—500 ft.

- April 1: Nate Colbert—1970—Mesa—To building far beyond fence in left center—495 ft.

- April 2: Adam Dunn—2007—Cincinnati—To top of seats just right of centerfield—455 ft.

- April 3: Jimmie Foxx—1934—Jacksonville—Lined far over left field fence—505 ft.

- April 4: Babe Ruth—1919—Tampa—Onto race track in deep right center—552 ft.

- April 4: Darryl Strawberry—1988—Montreal—Off rim of roof above right field—505 ft.

- April 5: Jimmie Foxx—1929—Richmond—Over left center field fence into river—490 ft.

- April 6: Dick Allen—1965—Clearwater—Line drive far over wall in center—510 ft.

- April 6: Pedro Munoz—1994—Minnesota—Into seats past fence in dead center field—473 ft.

- April 7: Jimmie Foxx—1937—Sebring—Very far over left fielder's head—530 ft.

- April 7: Jeff Burroughs—1974—Texas—Almost to top of left field bleachers—495 ft.

- April 8: Babe Ruth (ground rule double)—1920—Winston: Salem—To right field—550 ft.

- April 9: Mickey Mantle—1953—Pittsburgh—Over right field grandstand roof—510 ft.

- April 10: Tommy Agee—1969—New York—To fifth level in left field grandstand—490 ft.

- April 11: Shawn Green—2006—Arizona—High into seats in right center—474 ft.

- April 12: Jimmie Foxx—1932—Philadelphia—Far over fence in dead center field—505 ft.

- April 13: Jimmie Foxx—1937—Durham—Over fence and onto hill in center field—510 ft.

- April 13: Hank Aaron—1970—Atlanta—Into left field upper deck—470 ft.

- April 14: Dave Kingman—1976—Chicago—To third house beyond street in left field—540 ft.

- April 14: Wally Post—1961—St. Louis—Hit "Eagle" atop scoreboard in left field—520 ft.

- April 15: Reggie Jackson—1983—Minnesota—Far over center field fence—472 ft.

- April 15: Orlando Cepeda—1959—San Francisco—Off light tower in deep left center—470 ft.

- April 16: Ted Williams—1946—Washington—To 10th row in center field bleachers—470 ft.

- April 17: Mickey Mantle—1956—Washington—Over center field wall onto house—530 ft.

- April 17: Mickey Mantle—1953—Washington—Over left center field bleachers—510 ft.

- April 17: Wily Mo Pena—2005—Cincinnati—High into second deck in deep left center—502 ft.

- April 18: Babe Ruth—1919—Baltimore—Far over right center field fence into trees—500 ft.

- April 18: Derrek Lee—2005—Cincinnati—To top of backdrop in dead center field—482 ft.

- April 18: Duke Snider—1955—Brooklyn—To railing at back of upper deck in center—470 ft.

- April 19: Jim Gentile—1965—Kansas City—Almost over scoreboard in right center—505 ft.

- April 19: Reggie Abercrombie—2006—Cincinnati—Above exit in left field upper deck—493 ft.

- April 20: Reggie Jackson—1969—Kansas City—To top of scoreboard in right center—510 ft.

- April 20: Babe Ruth—1931—New York—To top of right field bleachers—505 ft.

- April 21: Hank Greenberg—1938—Chicago—Onto left field grandstand roof—480 ft.

- April 21: Troy Glaus—2000—St. Petersburg—Into left field upper deck—470 ft.

- April 22: Ralph Kiner—1950—Pittsburgh—Over left field scoreboard into park—520 ft.

- April 23: Ryan Howard—2006—Philadelphia—Over backdrop in dead center field—486 ft.

- April 24: Frank Howard—1970—Washington—To exit in left center field upper deck—525 ft.

- April 25: Frank Howard—1966—Washington—To second row in center field upper deck—522 ft.

- April 26: Richie Sexson—2004—Arizona—Off Jumbotron scoreboard in center field—495 ft.

- April 26: Eric Chavez—2001—Chicago—Over right field bleachers—490 ft.

- April 27: Dan Pasqua—1991—Chicago—To top of right field bleachers—470 ft.

- April 28: Mickey Mantle—1953—St. Louis—Over left field bleachers—500 ft.

- April 28: Mark McGwire—1996—Detroit—Onto left field grandstand roof—462 ft.

- April 29: Joe Adcock—1953—New York—To 10th row in center field bleachers—476 ft.

- April 30: Eddie Mathews—1965—Milwaukee—To screen atop bleachers in deep right—485 ft.

- April 30: Willie Mays—1961—Milwaukee—To top of left field bleachers—460 ft.

- May 1: Dick Stuart—1959—Pittsburgh—Far over left field wall and landed in park—520 ft.

- May 2: Willie Stargell—1977—Atlanta—Off façade of right field upper deck—465 ft.

- May 3: Ruben Rivera—1999—Philadelphia—Into 600 level in left field—465 ft.

- May 4: Lou Gehrig—1929—Chicago—Over right field grandstand roof—510 ft.

- May 5: Jim Rice—1977—Boston—Over wall in left center; hit building across street—495 ft.

- May 6: Dave Nicholson—1964—Chicago—Onto grandstand roof in left center—490 ft.

- May 7: Babe Ruth—1921—Washington—Far over high wall in deep right center—520 ft.

- May 8: Ralph Kiner—1949—Boston—Over left field scoreboard and RR tracks—510 ft.

- May 9: Carl Yastrzemski—1969—California—To base of light tower in right center—518 ft.

- May 9: Alfonso Soriano—2006—Cincinnati—Far over center field fence—491 ft.

- May 10: Kirk Gibson—1985—Chicago—Over right field grandstand roof—510 ft.

- May 11: Willie Stargell—1964—Pittsburgh—Lined off girder near right field roof—505 ft.

- May 11: Glenallen Hill—2000—Chicago—Onto roof across street in left field—500 ft.

- May 12: Mark McGwire—1998—St. Louis—Into left center field upper deck—535 ft.

- May 13: Babe Ruth—1924—New York—To 40th bleacher row in right center—515 ft.

- May 14: Jimmie Foxx—1932—Philadelphia—Far over roof in left center—525 ft.

- May 15: George Brett—1982—Kansas City—Almost to top of right field bleachers—458 ft.

- May 16: Mark McGwire—1998—St. Louis—Off press level façade in center—535 ft.

- May 16: Bob Cerv—1958—Kansas City—Far into parking lot beyond left field fence—528 ft.

- May 16: J. D. Drew—2003—St. Louis—Off "Diamond Vision" in right center top deck—507 ft.

- May 17: Roberto Clemente—1959—Chicago—Far over bleachers in left center—510 ft.

- May 18: Frank Howard—1968—Detroit—Onto 94: foot: high left field roof—510 ft.

- May 19: Ray Lankford—1996—Colorado—High into right field third deck—483 ft.

- May 19: Paul Sorrento—1999—Texas—Deep into right field upper deck—491 ft.

- May 20: Willie Stargell—1978—Montreal—Into right field upper deck—515 ft.

- May 21: Greg Luzinski—1977—Houston—Lined to fifth row in left field upper deck—515 ft.

- May 22: Babe Ruth—1930—Philadelphia—Far over right field fence to Opal St.—550 ft.

- May 22: Mickey Mantle—1963—New York—Lined off right field roof façade—540 ft.

- May 23: Babe Ruth—1920—New York—Far over roof in deep right field—520 ft.

- May 24: Babe Ruth—1930—New York—To top of bleachers in right center—525 ft.

- May 24: Larry Doby—1951—Washington—Over scoreboard in right center and onto roof—510 ft.

- May 25: Babe Ruth—1926—Boston—To 45th row in right field bleachers—540 ft.

- May 25: Babe Ruth—1935—Pittsburgh—Far over right field grandstand roof—540 ft.

- May 25: Frank Howard—1960—Pittsburgh—Far over wall in left center—520 ft.

- May 25: Larry Doby—1949—Washington—Far over scoreboard in right center—500 ft.

- May 26: Bobby Darwin—1974—Minnesota—Into left field upper deck—490 ft.

- May 27: Babe Ruth—1920—Boston—To 40th row in bleachers in right center—525 ft.

- May 28: Luke Easter—1958—Buffalo—Over scoreboard in right center onto porch—520 ft.

- May 29: Dick Allen—1965—Philadelphia—Far over roof in left center—529 ft.

- May 30: Mickey Mantle—1956—New York—Off right field roof façade—495 ft.

- May 31: Babe Ruth—1924—New York—Into bleachers just right of center—525 ft.

- May 31: Andres Galarraga—1997—Florida—High into left field upper deck—509 ft.

- June 1: Babe Ruth—1929—New York—To 25th bleacher row in right center—505 ft.

- June 1: Jason Giambi—2002—New York—High into right field upper deck—480 ft.

- June 2: Willie Mays—1962—New York—Lined off light tower atop left field roof—470 ft.

- June 3: Harmon Killebrew—1967—Minnesota—To second row in left field upper deck—522 ft.

- June 3: Manny Ramirez—2001—Toronto—Into fifth left field deck right of exit—491 ft.

- June 4: Harmon Killebrew—1967—Minnesota—Off left field upper deck façade—510 ft.

- June 5: Dick Stuart—1959—Pittsburgh—Far over 457 ft. sign in deep left center—515 ft.

- June 6: Dick Allen—1967—Philadelphia—Over roof in deep left center—540 ft.

- June 7: Wally Berger—1930—Boston—Far over left field bleachers onto RR tracks—475 ft.

- June 8: Babe Ruth—1926—Detroit—Onto taxi in Trumbull Ave. beyond right field—520 ft.

- June 8: Fred McGriff—1987—New York—To 16th row in right field upper deck—490 ft.

- June 9: Ted Williams—1946—Boston—To 33rd row of bleachers in deep right field—522 ft.

- June 10: Dick Allen—1965—Philadelphia—Far over left field grandstand roof—504 ft.

- June 10: Jimmy Wynn—1967—Cincinnati—Over scoreboard in left center; hit factory—507 ft.

- June 10: Mike Schmidt (single)—1974—Houston—Off loudspeaker on roof in center—500 ft.

- June 11: Babe Ruth (double)—1934—West Point—To tennis court in right center—535 ft.

- June 12: Rogers Hornsby—1922—Philadelphia—Into clubhouse window in center—460 ft.

- June 13: Jose Canseco—1994—Cleveland—To back bullpen wall in left center—488 ft.

- June 14: Kirk Gibson—1983—Detroit—Over right field roof and landed across street—515 ft.

- June 14: Cecil Fielder—1993—Detroit—Onto back of left field grandstand roof—495 ft.

- June 15: Dick Allen—1966—Cincinnati—Lined over scoreboard in left center—510 ft.

- June 16: Jimmie Foxx—1936—Chicago—Over left center field grandstand roof—530 ft.

- June 16: Dan Brouthers—1894—Baltimore—Far over fence in right center—440 ft. (dead ball)

- June 17: Joe Adcock—1956—Brooklyn—Over left field grandstand roof—510 ft.

- June 18: Hank Aaron—New York—1962—Into distant center field bleachers—460 ft.

- June 19: Harmon Killebrew—1959—Washington—To 28th row in left field bleachers—490 ft.

- June 19: Jim Rice—1977—Boston—Far over Green Monster in deep left center—470 ft.

- June 20: Jimmie Foxx—1932—Chicago—Onto back of roof in left center—515 ft.

- June 21: Dick Allen—1969—Philadelphia—Far over left center field roof—510 ft.

- June 21: Andruw Jones—1997—Philadelphia—Into upper deck in deep left center—508 ft.

- June 22: Babe Ruth—1927—Boston—Into alley between bleachers in right center—515 ft.

- June 22: Frank Robinson—1965—Cincinnati—Far over center field wall into street—503 ft.

- June 22: Buck Ewing—1889—Cleveland—Past distant left field fence—440 ft. (dead ball)

- June 23: Babe Ruth—1921—Boston—To 35th bleacher row in right field—510 ft.

- June 23: Luke Easter—1950—Cleveland—Into upper deck in deep right center—505 ft.

- June 23: Manny Ramirez—2001—Boston—High off left field light tower—501 ft.

- June 24: Sammy Sosa—2003—Chicago—Far over left center field bleachers—520 ft.

- June 24: Harry Simpson—1956—Kansas City—To far side of Brooklyn Ave. in right—505 ft.

- June 25: Jimmie Foxx—1932—New York—Deep into upper deck near left center—515 ft.

- June 25: Willie Stargell—1971—Philadelphia—To exit in right field 600 level—505 ft.

- June 26: Dick Stuart—1959—Los Angeles—Halfway up seats in left center—495 ft.

- June 26: Mo Vaughn—2002—New York—High off scoreboard in right center—484 ft.

- June 27: Tony Perez—1965—Milwaukee—Over modern (1960) left field bleachers—492 ft.

- June 28: Jose Canseco—1987—Cleveland—Lined off second deck façade in deep left—490 ft.

- June 29: Wily Mo Pena—2005—St. Louis—High off backdrop in dead center field—492 ft.

- June 30: Lou Gehrig—1931—Detroit—Onto building across street in right field—500 ft.

- July 1: Harmon Killebrew—1972—Chicago—Onto left field grandstand roof—470 ft.

- July 2: Cecil Fielder—1993—Detroit—Onto grandstand roof in deep left field—485 ft.

- July 3: Willie Stargell—1967—Pittsburgh—Far over wall in center field—520 ft.

- July 3: Jim Thome—1999—Cleveland—Far over center field fence: through a gate—511 ft.

- July 4: Willie Stargell—1979—St. Louis—Into upper deck in right center—510 ft.

- July 4: Joe Adcock—1966—Detroit—Lined under left field grandstand roof—505 ft.

- July 5: Reggie Jackson—1969—Minnesota—Off top of scoreboard in right center—520 ft.

- July 6: Dick Allen—1974—Detroit—Lined off roof façade in deep left center—535 ft.

- July 6: Mickey Mantle—1953—Philadelphia—Far over grandstand roof in left center—525 ft.

- July 7: Frank Howard—1969—Washington—To fourth row in center field upper deck—530 ft.

- July 8: Harry Heilmann—1921—Detroit—Far over fence in deep left center—512 ft.

- July 8: Babe Ruth (triple)—1918—Boston—Walk: off drive into right field bleachers—490 ft.

- July 9: Willie Horton—1965—Kansas City—Over light tower in left center field—475 ft.

- July 9: Dick Allen—1967—Philadelphia—Over high wall just right of center field—475 ft.

- July 10: Mike Piazza—1999—New York—Over left field bullpen and landed on tent—482 ft.

- July 11: Greg Luzinski—1973—Philadelphia—To fifth row in left field upper deck—495 ft.

- July 12: Willie Mays—1956—St. Louis—Off light tower atop left field scoreboard—475 ft.

- July 13: Reggie Jackson—1971—Detroit—Lined off light tower on roof in right center—540 ft.

- July 13: Leon Durham—1980—New York—Hit car in players' lot in right field—474 ft.

- July 14: Ralph Kiner—1950—Pittsburgh—Over wall in deep left center—470 ft.

- July 15: Rudy York—1940—Philadelphia—Over left field grandstand roof—470 ft.

- July 16: Bob Robertson—1971—Pittsburgh—Into left field upper deck—468 ft.

- July 17: Mark McGwire—1998—St. Louis—Into exit in left field upper deck—511 ft.

- July 18: Babe Ruth—1921—Detroit—Out of stadium in dead center field—575 ft.

- July 18: Jimmie Foxx—1930—Chicago—Onto grandstand roof in left center field—520 ft.

- July 19: Carlos Delgado—1998—Toronto—Into right field fifth deck—467 ft.

- July 20: Reggie Jackson—1976—Kansas City—To back wall in right field bullpen—500 ft.

- July 21: Joe Adcock—1962—Philadelphia—Over left center field grandstand roof—490 ft.

- July 21: Boog Powell—1972—Kansas City—Far over right field fence to light tower—460 ft.

- July 22: Nate Colbert—1970—San Diego—To third row in upper deck in deep left field—502 ft.

- July 23: Babe Ruth—1928—Boston—Onto garage in deep left center—515 ft.

- July 23: Frank Thomas—2002—Chicago—To top of left field bleachers—495 ft.

- July 24: Josh Gibson—Monessen, PA—1938—Far over center field fence and garage—536 ft.

- July 24: Hank Greenberg—1938—Philadelphia—Over left field grandstand roof—495 ft.

- July 25: Frank Howard—1970—Anaheim—Far over left center field fence—495 ft.

- July 25: Jay Buhner—1991—New York—To driveway past left field bullpen—492 ft.

- July 25: Luke Easter—1950—Cleveland—High into right field upper deck—480 ft.

- July 26: Boog Powell—1970—Minnesota—Off scoreboard in deep right center—470 ft.

- July 26: Manny Ramirez—2007—Cleveland—Far over center field fence—481 ft.

- July 27: Joe Carter—1996—Toronto—To second row in left field fifth deck—483 ft.

- July 27: Ben Ogilvie—1983—Minnesota—High into right field upper deck—480 ft.

- July 27: Russell Branyan—2004—Milwaukee—Far over fence in deep right center—480 ft.

- July 28: Babe Ruth—1924—Chicago—Over bleachers in deep right center—505 ft.

- July 28: Vladimir Guerrero—2003—To base of middle deck in left field—502 ft.

- July 29: Norm Cash—1962—Detroit—Over right center field roof; landed across street—515 ft.

- July 29: George Foster—1978—Cincinnati—High into left field upper deck—509 ft.

- July 30: Frank Howard—1965—Kansas City—Far over center field fence—516 ft.

- July 31: Babe Ruth—1921—New York—Far over roof near right center field—530 ft.

- August 1: Greg Luzinski—1976—New York—Over left field bullpen and hit bus—485 ft.

- August 1: Carlos Delgado—2001—Toronto—To restaurant above center field fence—478 ft.

- August 2: Jimmie Foxx—1940—Detroit—To top of upper deck in deep left center—505 ft.

- August 3: Harmon Killebrew—1962—Detroit—Onto left field grandstand roof—505 ft.

- August 3: Rocky Colavito—1959—Los Angeles—To 33rd row in left field bleachers—460 ft.

- August 4: Todd Hundley—1996—New York—Far over right field bullpen—480 ft.

- August 5: Willie Stargell—1969—Los Angeles—Over right field pavilion—506 ft.

- August 6: Babe Ruth—1926—Cleveland—Across street in deep right center field—510 ft.

- August 7: Ted Williams—1958—Boston—To 25th row in right field bleachers—495 ft.

- August 7: Josh Gibson—1945—Philadelphia—Over left field grandstand roof—480 ft.

- August 8: Barry Bonds—2003—San Francisco—Over right field arcade into cove—475 ft.

- August 9: Willie Stargell—1970—Pittsburgh—Lined off upper deck façade in right—510 ft.

- August 10: Adam Dunn—2004—Cincinnati—Out of stadium in dead center field—530 ft.

- August 11: Luke Easter—1954—Hollywood, CA—Far over center field fence—500 ft.

- August 11: Frank Robinson—1962—Cincinnati—Over scoreboard in left center—490 ft.

- August 12: Mickey Mantle—1964—New York—To 12th row in center field bleachers—512 ft.

- August 13: Alex Rodriguez—2005—New York—Over back wall of old left field bullpen—487 ft.

- August 14: Dave Kingman—1981—New York—Over fence in left center to outer wall—515 ft.

- August 15: Babe Ruth—1928—New York—Almost to top of right field bleachers—505 ft.

- August 16: Babe Ruth—1927—Chicago—Over right field grandstand roof—520 ft.

- August 16: Jimmie Foxx—1940—Boston—Over left field wall to back of parking lot—510 ft.

- August 17: Babe Ruth—1921—Chicago—High over bleachers in deep right center—545 ft.

- August 18: Dave Winfield—1988—New York—Over monuments in left center—478 ft.

- August 19: Dick Allen—1966—Philadelphia—Lined over left field grandstand roof—515 ft.

- August 19: Willie Stargell—1969—Pittsburgh—Over right field grandstand roof—510 ft.

- August 20: Sammy Sosa—1999—Chicago—Far over left center field bleachers—501 ft.

- August 21: Mike Schmidt—1974—Cincinnati—Lined into yellow seats in left field—470 ft.

- August 22: Jimmie Foxx—1931—Chicago—Onto grandstand roof in left center field—510 ft.

- August 23: Mickey Mantle—1956—New York—To 20th row in left field upper deck—515 ft.

- August 24: Ralph Kiner—1949—Boston—Lined over left field scoreboard—475 ft.

- August 25: Cecil Fielder—1990—Detroit—Onto left field roof right of light tower—510 ft.

- August 25: Frank Howard—1971—California—Far over center field fence—506 ft.

- August 26: Mark McGwire—1998—St. Louis—To top of center field backdrop—509 ft.

- August 27: Barry Bonds—2002—Colorado—Over center field fence and trees—492 ft.

- August 28: Andres Galarraga—1997—Colorado—Over bleachers in deep left center—506 ft.

- August 28: Greg Luzinski—1983—Chicago—Onto back of left field grandstand roof—500 ft.

- August 29: Barry Bonds—2004—Atlanta—To top of lower deck in right center—467 ft.

- August 30: Joe Borchard—2004—Chicago—Over right field bleachers onto walkway—504 ft.

- August 31: Larry Walker—1997—Colorado—To fifth row in right field third deck—493 ft.

- August 31: Albert Pujols—2003—Cincinnati—To top of batter's eye in dead center—477 ft.

- August 31: Ralph Kiner—1949—New York—Into second deck in deep left center field—475 ft.

- September 1: Reggie Jackson—1968—Anaheim—High into right center field bleachers—489 ft.

- September 1: Steve Balboni—1985—Arlington—Into upper seats of bleachers in center—485 ft.

- September 2: Babe Ruth—1921—New York—Far over right field grandstand roof—520 ft.

- September 2: Fred McGriff—1988—Toronto—Far over right field fence into field—473 ft.

- September 3: Joe Adcock—1961—Chicago—Far over bleachers in left center—500 ft.

- September 3: Greg Luzinski—1972—To club level in left center—500 ft.

- September 4: Willie McCovey—1966—St. Louis—Into right center field upper deck—515 ft.

- September 5: Jonny Gomes—2007—Tampa Bay—High over center field fence—460 ft.

- September 6: Babe Ruth—1927—Boston—Over wall near flagpole in center field—505 ft.

- September 7: Carlos Delgado—2008—New York—Over corner of right field third deck—460 ft.

- September 8: Babe Ruth—1925—Boston—To 35th row in right field bleachers—510 ft.

- September 9: Babe Ruth—1921—Philadelphia—Into tree just left of center field—510 ft.

- September 9: Barry Bonds—2002—San Francisco—To backdrop past fence in center—491 ft.

- September 10: Jimmie Foxx—1929—Philadelphia—Over roof in left center—515 ft.

- September 11: Babe Ruth—1924—Boston—Lined halfway into bleachers in center—510 ft.

- September 12: Mickey Mantle—1953—New York—Lined into upper deck near left center—515 ft.

- September 13: Jim Rice—1988—Boston—High off light tower in deep left center—485 ft.

- September 13: Ron Kittle—1985—Seattle—To third row in left field upper deck—483 ft.

- September 14: Bo Jackson—1986—Kansas City—To top of embankment in left center—515 ft.

- September 14: Cecil Fielder—1991—Milwaukee—Over bleachers in left to concourse—502 ft.

- September 15: Frank Robinson—1957—Cincinnati—Hit building beyond left center—485 ft.

- September 16: Mark McGwire—1997—St. Louis—To top of scoreboard in left center—517 ft.

- September 17: Jimmie Foxx—1938—Cleveland—To back fence atop left field seats—485 ft.

- September 18: Andres Galarraga—2001—San Francisco—To top of seats in left center—480 ft.

- September 19: Ron Kittle—1983—Chicago—Onto left field grandstand roof—485 ft.

- September 20: Mark McGwire—1995—Oakland—To aisle atop left field bleachers—467 ft.

- September 20: Danny Tartabull—1992—Kansas City—To bullpen wall in left field—465 ft.

- September 21: Mike Piazza—1997—Los Angeles—Onto pavilion roof in left center—478 ft.

- September 22: Jose Canseco—1985—Chicago—To light tower on left field roof—480 ft.

- September 23: Babe Ruth—1933—Boston—To 25th row in center field bleachers—510 ft.

- September 24: Frank Howard—1967—Washington—Far into left center upper deck—535 ft.

- September 25: Mike Schmidt—1981—Chicago—Into upper bleachers in center field—480 ft.

- September 26: Mike Piazza—1997—Colorado—Over bleachers in deep left center—504 ft.

- September 26: Jose Canseco—1985—Oakland—To 34th bleacher row in left center—495 ft.

- September 27: Adam Dunn—2008—Arizona—Line drive off scoreboard in center—504 ft.

- September 27: Hank Greenberg—1938—Detroit—Into upper deck in deep left center—460 ft.

- September 27: Josh Gibson—1930—New York—Lined into back of left field bullpen—460 ft.

- September 28: Babe Ruth—1928—Detroit—Far over bleachers in right center field—505 ft.

- September 29: Mike Piazza—2005—New York—Over left center field bleachers—450 ft.

- September 30: Juan Gonzalez—1992—Oakland—Into exit in left field second deck—460 ft.

- October 1: Babe Ruth—1932—Chicago—Over center field fence ("called shot")—490 ft.

- October 1: Darryl Strawberry—1999—Tampa Bay—Off pipe on right field roof—490 ft.

- October 2: Adam Dunn—2001—Chicago—Far over bleachers in right center—490 ft.

- October 2: Willie McCovey—1966—Pittsburgh—Lined over gate in right center field—465 ft.

- October 3: Bob Robertson—1971—San Francisco—Into distant bleachers in left center—465 ft.

- October 4: Greg Luzinski—1977—Los Angeles—Far over center field fence—455 ft.

- October 5: Prince Fielder—2008—Milwakee—Onto concourse in deep right center—462 ft.

- October 5: Lou Gehrig—1928—New York—Into bleachers in deep right center—465 ft.

- October 6: Babe Ruth—1926—St. Louis—High into center field bleachers—530 ft.

- October 7: Mike Shannon—1964—St. Louis—Off scoreboard atop left field bleachers—490 ft.

- October 7: Jose Canseco—1989—Toronto—To fifth row in left field fifth deck—484 ft.

- October 8: Reggie Jackson—1981—Milwaukee—Near top of right field bleachers—445 ft.

- October 9: Babe Ruth—1921—New York—Over far corner of right field roof—475 ft.

- October 10: Mickey Mantle—1958—Philadelphia (Home Run Contest)—Over roof near center—530 ft.

- October 10: Joe DiMaggio—1937—New York—Lined off pole atop left field roof—455 ft.

- October 11: Babe Ruth—1923—New York—Far over right field grandstand roof—465 ft.

- October 12: Babe Ruth—1926—Wilkes: Barre—Demonstration drive to right center—605 ft.

- October 13: Lou Gehrig—1929—New York—Over right field bleachers—450 ft.

- October 14: Babe Ruth—1926—Scranton—Over farthest corner on center field fence—520 ft.

- October 15: Babe Ruth—1927—Kansas City—Over distant and high right field wall—480 ft.

- October 16: Reggie Jackson—1977—Los Angeles—High off right field foul pole—430 ft.

- October 16: Babe Ruth—1922—Sleepy Eye, MN—Far over center field fence (twice)—520 ft.

- October 17: Babe Ruth—1928—Elmira—Far over right field fence against wind—500 ft.

- October 18: Reggie Jackson—1977—New York—Over center field fence to backdrop—465 ft.

- October 19: Babe Ruth—1924—Seattle—Over right field fence and gas station—540 ft.

- October 20: Barry Bonds—2002—Anaheim—Into exit in right center field bleachers—485 ft.

- October 21: Babe Ruth—1924—Portland—Over right field fence and foundry—515 ft.

- October 22: Barry Bonds—2002—San Francisco—Over center field fence to backdrop—437 ft.

- October 22: Babe Ruth—1924—Dunsmuir, CA—Over fence and trees in center field—580 ft.

- October 23: Babe Ruth—1926—South Bend—Almost to racetrack in right center—550 ft.

- October 24: Babe Ruth—1927—Stockton—Over right field scoreboard into trees—490 ft.

- October 25: Babe Ruth—1924—San Francisco—Over clubhouse in right center—495 ft.

- October 26: Barry Bonds—2002—Anaheim—High into right field bleachers—440 ft.

- October 26: Babe Ruth—1927—San Jose—Over center field fence by great distance—530 ft.

- October 27: Lou Gehrig—1929—South Orange, NJ—Over RR tracks in center field—500 ft.

- October 28: Babe Ruth—1924—Santa Barbara—To trees past right center field fence—505 ft.

- October 29: Babe Ruth—1922—Denver—Over center field fence near scoreboard—500 ft.

- October 30: Babe Ruth—1928—Sioux City—High into left field bleachers—400 ft.

- October 31: Babe Ruth—1924—Anaheim—To distant right center field—535 ft.

Power Rankings by Position

FIRST BASE

1. Jimmie Foxx
2. Dick Allen
3. Mark McGwire
4. Willie McCovey
5. Harmon Killebrew

SECOND BASE

1. Rogers Hornsby
2. Alfonso Soriano
3. Jeff Kent
4. Tony Lazzeri
5. Dan Uggla (tie)
5. Bobby Grich (tie)

THIRD BASE

1. Eddie Mathews
2. Mike Schmidt
3. Al Rosen
4. Ron Santo
5. Matt Williams

SHORTSTOP

1. Alex Rodriguez
2. Honus Wagner

3. Ernie Banks
4. Cal Ripken
5. Miguel Tejada (tie)
5. Hanley Ramirez (tie)

CATCHER

1. Mike Piazza
2. Stan Lopata
3. Johnny Bench
4. Todd Hundley
5. Mickey Tettleton (tie)
5. Dave Duncan (tie)

PITCHER

1. Earl Wilson
2. Don Drysdale
3. Red Ruffing
4. Wes Ferrell
5. Bob Lemon (tie)
5. Schoolboy Rowe (tie)
5. Walter Johnson (tie)

LEFT FIELD

1. Frank Howard
2. Willie Stargell

3. Greg Luzinski
4. Ted Williams
5. Ralph Kiner

CENTER FIELD

1. Mickey Mantle
2. Larry Doby
3. Willie Mays
4. Jimmy Wynn
5. Duke Snider

RIGHT FIELD

1. Babe Ruth
2. Reggie Jackson
3. Sammy Sosa
4. Jose Canseco
5. Frank Robinson

DESIGNATED HITTER

1. Ron Kittle
2. Frank Thomas
3. David Ortiz
4. Travis Hafner
5. Richie Sexson

The Longest of This and the Longest of That

The following lists identify the 10 longest known drives in various categories. It is impossible to know the exact length of every batted ball in Major League history, but I've tried to be as inclusive as possible.

It will be noted that Babe Ruth's name dominates these lists. Why? First and most importantly, he hit the ball harder than any other player in the annals of his sport. Second, as it relates to these lists (especially the first few), he benefited from the era in which he played. Although Ruth lost many career homers due to the distant center field boundaries of his times, it did allow him to appear more often on lists for non-homers. Mickey Mantle also appears often for the same reasons. He was historically powerful, and his home field for his entire career was Yankee Stadium.

When Mickey played, the great Bronx ball yard maintained a 466-foot distance to the farthest point in center field. In Babe's day, it was 490 feet. Modern players don't have to deal with such prohibitive dimensions, but, as a result, they can't hit extra-long balls that remain in play. As a general rule, therefore, many of these lists focus on the older players.

TEN LONGEST SINGLES

1. Mike Schmidt—June 10, 1974—Houston—Off speaker on center field roof—500 ft.
2. Mickey Mantle—August 10, 1956—New York—Bounced into seats in center—450 ft.
3. Babe Ruth—October 7, 1928—St. Louis—To center field fence on one bounce—440 ft.
4. Whitey Lockman—July 3, 1951—New York—To center field wall on one bounce—435 ft.
5. Jimmie Foxx—August 8, 1936—Washington—To flagpole in center field—425 ft.
6. Barry Bonds—June 14, 2006—Arizona—Almost over high center field wall—422 ft.
7. Bibb Falk—June 8, 1923—New York—To track in left center—420 ft.
8. Willie Horton—June 5, 1979—Seattle—Off speaker on left field roof—415 ft.
9. Paul O'Neill—September 2, 1995—New York—Off 408 foot sign in center field—413 ft.
10. Vladimir Guerrero—May 24, 1998—Montreal—Off top of center field fence—412 ft.

TEN LONGEST DOUBLES

1. Babe Ruth—August 5, 1927—New York—To center field fence on one bounce—475 ft.
2. Frank Howard—October 2, 1963—New York—To bleacher screen in deepest left center—470 ft.
3. Bob Cerv—July 2, 1961—New York—To screen atop 457 foot sign in deep left center—467 ft.
4. Mickey Mantle—August 16, 1959—New York—Off bleacher wall in center field—465 ft.
5. Wally Post—May 17, 1957—Cincinnati—Into opening atop scoreboard in left center—460 ft. (tie)
5. Mickey Mantle—June 14, 1964—New York—To bleacher wall in deep left center field—460 ft. (tie)
7. Hack Miller—June 9, 1922—New York—To Grant Memorial in deep center field—458 ft.
8. Red Ruffing—July 12, 1938—New York—To flagpole in deepest center field—456 ft.
9. Willie McCovey—July 29, 1964—Philadelphia—To 447 foot sign in center field—455 ft.
10. Ted Kluszewski—May 1, 1951—Pittsburgh—To top of wall in right center—453 ft.

TEN LONGEST TRIPLES

1. Babe Ruth—July 8, 1918—Boston—Walk-off triple to top of right field bleachers—490 ft.
2. Lou Gehrig—June 7, 1929—New York—To screen in dead center—485 ft.
3. Babe Ruth—April 19, 1923—New York—One bounce to wall in deepest left center—475 ft.
4. Mickey Mantle—April 18, 1954—New York—To wall in dead center field—470 ft.
5. Babe Ruth—April 20, 1923—New York—Over track in deep left center—468 ft.
6. Jimmie Foxx—May 13, 1929—Detroit—To top of gate in center field—465 ft. (tie)
6. Joe DiMaggio—August 6, 1938—Cleveland—To base of bleacher wall in center field—465 ft. (tie)
7. Bob Johnson—June 10, 1934—New York—Bounced to 490 foot sign in center field—462 ft.
8. Lou Gehrig—July 16, 1929—Detroit—High off flagpole in center field—460 ft. (tie)
8. Ralph Kiner—May 21, 1950—New York—Over track in Grant Memorial in center field—460 ft. (tie)
8. Stan Lopata—May 30, 1955—New York—Over track to Grant Memorial in center field—460 ft. (tie)
8. Bill Skowron—May 24, 1961—New York—Off 457 foot sign in deep left center field—460 ft. (tie)

TEN LONGEST INSIDE-THE-PARK HOME RUNS

1   Lou Gehrig—May 19, 1927—Cleveland—Lined off center field scoreboard—478 ft.

2   Babe Ruth—July 20, 1924—New York—Lined past flagpole in center field—475 ft.

3   Dusty Cooke—June 25, 1930—New York—Over track in dead center field—470 ft.

4. Dee Fondy—June 7, 1953—New York—To path in front of clubhouse in center—465 ft. (tie)

4. Mickey Mantle—June 30, 1961—New York—Off center field wall near 461 foot sign—465 ft. (tie)

6. Al Simmons—April 19, 1930—Philadelphia—Off top of center field fence—462 ft.

7. Ben Paschal—September 22, 1925—New York—One bounce to bleacher wall in left center—460 ft. (tie)

7. Lou Gehrig—July 22, 1926—New York—To flagpole in center field—460 ft. (tie)

7. Bill Skowron—April 10, 1962—New York—Off center field wall near 461 foot sign—460 ft. (tie)

10. Bill Terry—September 20, 1932—New York—Almost to Grant Memorial in dead center—455 ft. (tie)

10. Gil Hodges—May 16, 1962—New York—Off wall beyond bullpen in deep left center—455 ft. (tie)

TEN LONGEST FLY OUTS

1. Babe Ruth—July 8, 1931—New York—Two steps from farthest center field corner—480 ft.

2. Mickey Mantle—July 9, 1958—New York—To center field wall at 461 foot sign—465 ft.

3. Babe Ruth—May 25, 1921—St. Louis—To center field bleacher wall—463 ft.

4. Hank Greenberg—August 2, 1939—To DiMaggio past center field flagpole—460 ft. (tie)

4. Mickey Mantle—May 10, 1958—New York—To center field wall near 461 foot sign—460 ft. (tie)

4. Jim Lemon—May 11, 1958—New York—To Mantle near 461 foot sign in center field—460 ft. (tie)

7. Lou Gehrig—June 3, 1932—Philadelphia—To Simmons beside center field flagpole—458 ft.

8. Ralph Kiner—June 2, 1951—New York—To Mays at bleacher wall in deep left center—455 ft. (tie)

8. Joe Adcock—July 17, 1955—New York—To Mays at bleacher wall in deep left center—455 ft. (tie)

8. Wally Post—July 31, 1956—New York—To Mays at bleacher wall in deep left center—455 ft. (tie)

Note: On August 9, 1956, at the Polo Grounds in New York, the Philadelphia Phillies hit 1,300 feet of fly outs in the 6th inning off pitcher Joe Margoneri. Catcher Stan Lopata flied out to Dusty Rhodes in left center field about 450 feet from home plate. Shortstop Granny Hamner hit a 430-footer to Willie Mays in center, and left fielder Del Ennis also flied to Mays at a distance of about 420 feet.

TEN LONGEST OPPOSITE FIELD HOME RUNS

1. Babe Ruth—September 9, 1921—Philadelphia—To tree across street in deep left center—510 ft.
2. Mark McGwire—August 22, 1999—New York—Near top of scoreboard in right center—485 ft.
3. Dick Allen—May 8, 1969—Philadelphia—Onto roof across street in right center—470 ft.
4. Babe Ruth—May 10, 1928—New York—Under mezzanine in deep left field—465 ft. (tie)
4. Mark McGwire—August 22, 1998—Pittsburgh—To top of lower seats in right center—465 ft. (tie)
4. Johnny Bench—July 13, 1971—Detroit—High into right center field upper deck—465 ft. (tie)
7. Bo Jackson—July 17, 1990—New York—Near top of right center field bleachers—464 ft.
8. Mickey Mantle—September 17, 1952—Detroit—Off press level in right center—460 ft. (tie)
8. Willie Stargell—July 8, 1966—Pittsburgh—Over wall in deep left center field—460 ft. (tie)

10. Joe Adcock—April 14, 1960—Philadelphia—Over scoreboard in right center—455 ft.

TEN LONGEST SPRING TRAINING HOME RUNS

1. Babe Ruth—April 4, 1919—Tampa—Over racetrack in right center—552 ft.
2. Mickey Mantle—March 26, 1951—Los Angeles—Far beyond fence in right center—550 ft.
3. Jimmie Foxx—April 7, 1937—Sebring—Very far over left fielder's head—530 ft.
4. Dave Kingman—March 22, 1983—St. Petersburg—To Bayfront Center past left field fence—517 ft.
5. Jimmie Foxx—March 9, 1933—Fort Myers—Far over distant center field fence—515 ft.
6. Bo Jackson—March 5, 1989—Haines City—Over left center field scoreboard—515 ft.
7. Babe Ruth—March 31, 1924—Mobile—Far over fence in dead center field—510 ft. (tie)
7. Mickey Mantle—April 9, 1953—Pittsburgh—Over right field grandstand roof—510 ft. (tie)
7. Dick Allen—April 6, 1965—Clearwater—Far over high center field wall—510 ft. (tie)
10. Frank Howard—March 23, 1966—Pompano Beach—To parking lot in left field—508 ft.

Note: On April 8, 1920, in Winston-Salem, Babe Ruth smashed three tremendous drives to right field. Two were designated ground rule doubles, and one was incorrectly ruled foul. After the game against the Brooklyn Dodgers, officials investigated the landing points. It was determined that all three were fair balls and flew a total distance of about 1,600 feet.

TEN LONGEST POSTSEASON HOME RUNS

1. Babe Ruth—October 6, 1926—St. Louis—Line drive halfway up bleachers in dead center—530 ft.
2. Babe Ruth—October 6, 1926—St. Louis—Broke window across street in right center—515 ft.
3. Mickey Mantle—October 6, 1960—Pittsburgh—Over brick wall in deep right center—495 ft. (tie)
3. Sammy Sosa—October 8, 2003—Chicago—To TV platform atop center field bleachers—495 ft. (tie)
5. Babe Ruth—October 1, 1932—Chicago—"Called Shot" to flagpole in center field—490 ft. (tie)
5. Mike Shannon—October 7, 1964—St. Louis—High off scoreboard atop left field bleachers—490 ft (tie)
7. Barry Bonds—October 20, 2002—Anaheim—Into tunnel in right center field bleachers—485 ft.
8. Jose Canseco—October 7, 1989—Toronto—To fifth row in left field fifth deck—484 ft.
9. Frank Howard—October 6, 1963—Los Angeles—To eighth row in left field loge level—480 ft.
10. Babe Ruth—October 9, 1921—New York—Between grandstand and roof in right center—475 ft.

TEN LONGEST ALL-STAR HOME RUNS

1. Reggie Jackson—July 13, 1971—Detroit—Line drive off tower on roof in right center—540 ft.
2. Ted Williams—July 8, 1941—Detroit—Line drive off right field roof façade—475 ft.
3. Hank Sauer—July 8, 1952—Philadelphia—Over left field grandstand roof—465 ft. (tie)
3. Johnny Bench—July 13, 1971—Detroit—High into right center field upper deck—465 ft. (tie)
5. Bo Jackson—July 11, 1989—California—Onto black backdrop in center field—462 ft.
6. Willie Mays—July 10, 1956—Washington—Halfway up left field bleachers—460 ft. (tie)
6. Rocky Colavito—August 3, 1959—Los Angeles—To 33rd row in left field bleachers—460 ft. (tie)
6. Stan Musial—July 13, 1948—St. Louis—Onto pavilion roof in deep right center field—455 ft. (tie)
6. Frank Howard—July 23, 1969—Washington—Into center field mezzanine—455 ft. (tie)

10. Al Rosen—July 13, 1954—Cleveland—
    Far over left center field fence—450 ft.

TEN LONGEST FIRST CAREER HOME RUNS

1. Bo Jackson—September 14, 1986—
   Kansas City—To top of embankment in
   deep left center—515 ft.
2. Reggie Abercrombie—April 19, 2006—
   Cincinnati—High into left field upper
   deck—493 ft.
3. Harmon Killebrew—June 24, 1955—
   Washington—To 24th row in left field
   bleachers—470 ft. (tie)
3. Ron Swoboda—April 14, 1965—New
   York—Far over left field bullpen—470
   ft. (tie)
5. Willie Horton—September 14, 1963—
   Detroit—High into upper deck in deep
   left center field—462 ft.
6. Bill Dietrich—May 12, 1934—Philadelphia—Over left field grandstand roof—
   460 ft.
7. Greg Luzinski—September 7, 1971—
   Philadelphia—To fourth row in left field
   upper deck—457 ft.
8. Tony Eusebio—April 13, 1994—
   Florida—Over 434 foot sign in center
   field—453 ft.
9. Mickey Mantle—May 1, 1951—Chicago—Into lower deck just right of center field—452 ft.
10. Jose Canseco—September 9, 1985—
    Oakland—Deep into center field bleach-
    ers—450 ft.

TEN LONGEST FINAL CAREER HOME RUNS

1. Babe Ruth—May 25, 1935 (#3)—Pittsburgh—Over right field grandstand
   roof—540 ft.
2. Darryl Strawberry—October 1, 1999—
   Tampa Bay—Off pipe on roof in right
   field—490 ft.
3. Mo Vaughn—April 30, 2003—St. Louis—
   Into right field upper deck—460 ft.
4. Bo Jackson—August 9, 1994—California—Over fence in center to concrete
   wall—450 ft.
5. Rogers Hornsby—April 21, 1937—St.
   Louis—Lined into center field bleachers—445 ft.
6. Ted Williams—September 28, 1960—
   Boston—Over bullpen in deep right
   center field—430 ft. (tie)
6. Jimmy Wynn—April 7, 1977—New
   York—Far over center field fence—430
   ft. (tie)
8. Joe Adcock—September 7, 1966—Kansas City—Over high wall in deep left
   center field—427 ft.
9. Rocky Colavito—September 24, 1968—
   New York—Into left field bullpen—
   422 ft.
10. Jimmie Foxx—September 9, 1945—
    Pittsburgh—Over left field score-
    board—420 ft.

Note: In Philadelphia on August 18, 1890, Dave Orr hit a ball far over the left field fence, a distance of approximately 400 feet. This was a significant clout in the dead ball era.

TEN LONGEST HOME RUNS BY A TEENAGER

1. Mickey Mantle—May 4, 1951—St. Louis—Over pavilion in right and across street—475 ft.
2. Harmon Killebrew—June 24, 1955—Washington—To 24th row in left field bleachers—470 ft.
3. Mickey Mantle—September 8, 1951—New York—To top of right field bleachers—462 ft.
4. Mickey Mantle—May 1, 1951—Chicago—Into lower deck just right of center field—452 ft.
5. Jimmie Foxx—June 8, 1927—Philadelphia—Line drive high into left field upper deck—447 ft.
6. Tony Conigliaro—June 6, 1964—Kansas City—Line drive over center field fence—443 ft.
7. Tony Conigliaro—July 5, 1964—Boston—High over left field wall and screen—428 ft.
8. Mel Ott—May 18, 1928—St. Louis—Over right field pavilion into street—425 ft.
9. Mickey Mantle—September 13, 1951—New York—Into right field upper deck—423 ft.
10. Mickey Mantle—July 7, 1951—Boston—Into right center field bleachers—420 ft.

Note: Only official home runs are included on this list. However, readers should be reminded of Mantle's extraordinary performance in Los Angeles on March 26, 1951. At age 19, Mickey blasted a 550-foot home run during an exhibition game.

TEN LONGEST HOME RUNS BY PLAYER OVER 40

1. Babe Ruth—May 25, 1935 (#3)—Pittsburgh—Over right field grandstand roof—540 ft.
2. Babe Ruth—May 25, 1935 (#2)—Pittsburgh—Lined into right center field upper deck—500 ft.
3. Andres Galarraga—September 18, 2001—San Francisco—To top of bleachers in left center—480 ft.
4. Barry Bonds—May 7, 2006—Philadelphia—To façade on third deck in right field—470 ft.
5. Barry Bonds—August 29, 2004 (#1)—Atlanta—To top of lower deck in right center—467 ft.
6. Barry Bonds—August 29, 2004 (#2)—Atlanta—Deep into right center field bullpen—462 ft.
7. Barry Bonds—September 12, 2004—Arizona—To base of center field scoreboard—460 ft. (tie)
7. Matt Stairs—October 13, 2008—Los Angeles—Near top of right field pavilion—460 ft. (tie)
9. Ted Williams—April 18, 1960—Washington—Over high center field wall—456 ft.

10. George Brett—August 19, 1993—Minnesota—Into right field top deck—454 ft. (tie)

10. Reggie Jackson—April 30, 1987—Oakland—To top of right field bleachers—454 ft. (tie)

Note: On August 20, 1915, Honus Wagner hit a ball to the top of the seats in center field in Philadelphia's Baker Bowl, a 430-foot dead ball era shot.

TEN LONGEST PINCH-HIT HOME RUNS

1. Mickey Mantle—July 6, 1953—Philadelphia—Far over grandstand roof in left center—525 ft.

2. Joe Adcock—September 2, 1966—Anaheim—Off light tower in deep left center field—495 ft.

3. Leon Wagner—April 30, 1961—Los Angeles—Far over right field wall—473 ft.

4. Ron Swoboda—April 14, 1965—New York—Far over left field bullpen—470 ft. (tie)

4. Reggie Jackson—June 10, 1983—California—Deep into right center field bleachers—470 ft. (tie)

6. Frank Howard—July 22, 1961—St. Louis—Lined off scoreboard atop bleachers in left—465 ft. (tie)

6. Willie McCovey—October 2, 1966—Pittsburgh—Line drive over gate in right center—465 ft. (tie)

7. Willie Smith—June 10, 1969—Atlanta—To fourth row in right field upper deck—464 ft.

8. Willie Horton—September 14, 1963—Detroit—High into upper deck in deep left center field—462 ft.

9. Matt Stairs—October 13, 2008—Los Angeles—Near top of right field pavilion—460 ft. (tie)

9. Tony Solaita—September 13, 1977—Texas—Far over center field fence—460 ft. (tie)

TEN LONGEST HOME RUNS BY A PITCHER

1. Babe Ruth—May 25, 1915—St. Louis—Over right field bleachers; landed across street—475 ft.

2. Babe Ruth—June 9, 1916—Detroit—Deep into bleachers just right of center field—465 ft. (tie)

2. Babe Ruth—August 10, 1917—Boston—To eighth row in center field bleachers—465 ft. (tie)

4. Wes Ferrell—July 31, 1935—Washington—Near top of left field bleachers—462 ft.

5. Bill Dietrich—May 12, 1934—Philadelphia—Over left field grandstand roof—460 ft. (tie)

5. Red Ruffing—June 17, 1936—Cleveland—Deep into left center field bleachers—460 ft. (tie)

5. Jerry Casale—April 15, 1959—Boston—Over wall in left center; landed on building—460 ft. (tie)

5. Earl Wilson—May 22, 1964—Boston—Over wall and screen in left center—460 ft. (tie)

5. Earl Wilson—August 26, 1965—New York—Into left field upper deck—460 ft. (tie)

10. Kip Wells—April 25, 2003—Pittsburgh—Off backdrop past center field fence—457 ft.

TEN LONGEST WALK-OFF HOME RUNS

1. Mickey Mantle—May 22, 1963—New York—Line drive off right field roof façade—540 ft.

2. Dick Allen—August 19, 1966—Philadelphia—Line drive over sign on left field roof—515 ft.

3. Babe Ruth—July 8, 1918—Boston (official triple)—Deep into right field bleachers—490 ft.

4. Mark McGwire—July 11, 1998—St. Louis—High into left field upper deck—485 ft.

5. Babe Ruth—September 22, 1927—New York—To 60th row in right field bleachers—480 ft.

6. Jimmie Foxx—August 23, 1938—Boston—Onto roof across street in left field—475 ft. (tie)

6. Willie Stargell—July 9, 1967—Pittsburgh—Onto right field grandstand roof—475 ft. (tie)

8. Sammy Sosa—May 5, 1996—Chicago—Broke window across street in left field—468 ft. (tie)

8. Adam Dunn—May 17, 2008—Cincinnati—To top row in right field bleachers—468 ft. (tie)

10. Eric Davis—August 2, 1987—Cincinnati—To façade on left field upper deck—466 ft.

Appendix G

Power Personified

The five lists included in this section are intended to create enjoyment and good-natured debate. With only one exception, which is explained, they include only players with Major League experience. The years of big-league participation are provided after each player's name. Unlike the main body of this book, the lists are not regarded as definitive. I have laboriously studied the topic of tape measure home runs for 30 years. Even though I acknowledge that no historian, myself included, can ever know everything about any topic, I like to think that this treatise is "definitive" on the matter of long-distance hitting. Along the way, I acquired information about related topics, but I do not consider myself an expert on any of them. Accordingly, this section is dedicated to having fun!

TEN GREATEST INDIVIDUAL COMBINATIONS OF BATTING, THROWING, AND RUNNING

Sitting at the top of the first list is a name that everyone will recognize. Frankly, Mickey Mantle came immediately into my mind the second that I first considered the question of baseball's greatest all-around power athlete. He is ranked third in batting power, first in running speed, and had a powerful throwing arm until he lost some zip due to a late-1950s shoulder injury. Who else could be number one?

It seemed just as obvious to insert Bo Jackson at number two. Whether blazing down the sidelines scoring touchdowns, launching mighty home runs, or throwing anything, Bo seemed omnipotent. The rest of the names speak for themselves. Don't be misled by Honus Wagner's 19th-century background. He was an absolute juggernaut in every form of athletic strength, and could excel in any era. How about Babe Ruth at number nine? Remember this: Besides being a legendary batsman and thrower, the Bambino could run well during the first two-thirds of his career. Check his defensive statistics if you have any doubts. And how could Jim Thorpe not be included? Although not successful as a Major League player, he still brought vast physical talent onto the field. His historic success as an Olympic decathlete proves that point. Enjoy the debate!!

1. Mickey Mantle—1951–1968
2. Bo Jackson—1986–1991 and 1993–1994
3. Willie Mays—1951–1952 and 1954–1973
4. Jimmie Foxx—1925–1942 and 1944–1945
5. Roberto Clemente—1955–1972
6. Jose Canseco—1985–2001
7. Darryl Strawberry—1983–1999
8. Honus Wagner—1897–1917
9. Babe Ruth—1914–1935
10. Jim Thorpe—1913–1917

HONORABLE MENTIONS

Harry Stovey—1880–1893
Ed Delahanty—1888–1903
Joe Jackson—1908–1920
Joe DiMaggio—1936–1942 and 1946–1951
Pete Reiser—1940–1942 and 1946–1952
Duke Snider—1947–1964
Henry Aaron—1954–1976
Frank Robinson—1956–1976
Bobby Bonds—1968–1981
Dave Winfield—1973–1995
Andre Dawson—1976–1996
Eric Davis—1984–2001
Ken Griffey Jr.—1989–2009

NEGRO LEAGUES

John Henry "Pop" Lloyd—1914–1932
Oscar Charleston—1915–1941
John Beckwith—1920–1935
Norman "Turkey" Stearnes—1923–1940

TEN MOST POWERFUL THROWING ARMS (POSITION PLAYERS)

This ranking was a little tougher. After researching the issue for a couple of months, Rocky Colavito seemed like the natural choice. However, there was a minor problem. Rocky is a personal favorite of mine, and I didn't want to appear biased. But, after interviewing other retired Major Leaguers and carefully examining what little hard information was available, Colavito emerged as a clear number one.

The only time that Rocky's throws were measured was on July 1, 1956, in San Diego. His longest of five tosses was 435 feet, 10.5 inches. The only two men known to better that are Glen Gorbous (Omaha: 445 feet, 10 inches in 1957) and Don Grate (Minneapolis: 445 feet, 1 inch in 1953). But consider that Colavito's first two throws didn't count. The first one sailed into an adverse wind (415 feet, 7 inches), prompting officials to move him into a neutral, crosswind position. He then hurled one from beside home plate over the 426 foot sign in center field that landed on top of the batting cage! If that toss had hit the ground and been measured, the consensus is that it would have topped Rocky's 435-footer by a considerable margin. Grate and Gorbous were magnificent, but it is believed that they both threw for distance on multiple occasions, thereby gaining an advantage in this function. Shortly after the San Diego exhibition, Colavito was summoned back to the Major Leagues, where he remained for the rest of his career. Big-league general managers didn't like risking the health of their players, and, by the 1950s, rarely allowed such demonstrations.

Additionally, Rocky Colavito is known to have accepted a challenge and flung a baseball over the high scoreboard in Indianapolis in either 1954 or 1955. He stood at home plate and cleared that 40-foot-high structure at the 385 foot marker in left center. In the June 13, 1956 edition of the *Sporting News*, there is an item telling of two other noteworthy events. First, Colavito once stood behind the third base line at Washington's Griffith Stadium and threw a ball over the beer sign atop the high right center field wall. On another occasion, Rocky positioned himself beside the Indian dugout in Cleveland and zoomed one completely over the immense right field grandstand roof. During an interview with well-known Detroit sportswriter Joe Falls back in the 1980s, Joe stated that the longest throw that he had ever witnessed was authored by Rocky Colavito. He recalled Rocky receiving a little razzing from the Tiger fans for a recent slump. When Colavito then caught a fly ball in medium left field, he vented his frustration by heaving the ball high over the towering right field roof. There are even more stories of great throws in actual game situations, but the point has been made. Rocky Colavito could really hum it.

It is not known if the great Roberto Clemente ever had any of his throws actually measured; I could find no record of such an event. However, there are many legends about the strength of his arm. When you look at the number of outfield assists that he accumulated during his career, it is obvious that he had a gun. In fact, there seems to be a consensus that Roberto had the most functional throwing arm for a position player in big-league history. That standing would include power, accuracy, and quickness of release. I had the privilege of seeing Clemente throw, and it was a sight that I will always treasure.

It was hard to get noticed when playing with Babe Ruth, but Bob Meusel was always able to do it. As most fans know, Ruth started as a pitcher, and then became an outfielder while earning a reputation as one of the best throwers of his era. But he could never throw like Bob Meusel. When the two men, who were good friends, barnstormed together, it was Babe's batting strength and Bob's rifle arm that were the primary attractions. In fact, arm strength must have run in the family, since brother Emil "Irish" Meusel reportedly possessed the best throwing arm in the National League.

I also saw Ellis Valentine, Jesse Barfield, and Shawon Dunston throw, and they all had cannons. In fact, I was there at Veterans Stadium in Philadelphia for the 1976 All-Star Game, where Valentine dueled with Dave Parker and others in a pregame throwing exhibition in right field. Of course, Honus Wagner and Sheldon LeJeune are from the distant past, but their reputations have endured over the intervening generations. LeJeune owned the long toss record for many years, having heaved the ball 426 feet, 9.5 inches in Cincinnati on October 9, 1910. Wagner was a monster in all aspects of physical function, and used to throw runners out while flinging handfuls of dirt that he inadvertently scooped up with the ball. There are dozens of other great throwers who could vie for inclusion in this list, and you are invited to name your own top ten.

1. Rocky Colavito—1955–1968—Outfielder
2. Roberto Clemente—1955–1972—Outfielder
3. Bob Meusel—1920–1930—Outfielder
4. Don Grate—Minor League Outfielder—Pitched in MLB briefly in 1945 and 1946
5. Glen Gorbous—1952 and 1956–1957—Outfielder
6. Ellis Valentine—1975–1985—Outfielder
7. Jesse Barfield—1981–1993—Outfielder
8. Sheldon "Larry" LeJeune—1911 and 1915—Outfielder
9. Shawon Dunston—1985–2002—Shortstop, but played some outfield late in his career.
10. Honus Wagner—1897–1917—Primarily a shortstop, but played other positions

HONORABLE MENTIONS
John Hatfield—1871–1876
Dave Parker—1973–1990
Vladimir Guerrero—1996–2009

NEGRO LEAGUES
Louis Santop—1916–1926
Martin Dihigo—1923–1945

STRONGEST ARMS BY POSITION
1B: George Kelly—1915–1917 and 1919–1930 and 1932
2B: Manny Trillo—1973–1989
3B: Ned Williamson—1878–1890 (also played shortstop)
SS: Honus Wagner—1897–1917 and Shawon Dunston—1985–2002 (tie)
OF: Rocky Colavito—1955–1968
OF: Roberto Clemente—1955–1972
OF: Bob Meusel—1920–1930
C: Johnny Bench—1967–1983

TEN FASTEST STARTING PITCHERS
Since none of the older pitchers were ever evaluated with radar guns, we have virtually no way of accurately comparing the modern guys with the old-timers. I have chosen Walter Johnson as the fastest ever due to anecdotal information, but there is a mountain of it. First, look at his astonishingly successful big-league record, and then consider that he was primarily a one-pitch pitcher. The "Big Train" could throw breaking pitches, but, by all accounts (including his own), rarely threw them because of the effectiveness of his blazing fastball. There are so many quotations about his "un-hittable" fastball that you eventually have to take them seriously.

Many of the men who faced Johnson stayed in the game for decades as coaches and managers. Every one of them who ventured an opinion on the subject unhesitatingly identified Walter Johnson as the fastest pitcher they ever saw. Don't buy into that nonsense that Johnson couldn't have been physically transcendent because of the era in which he pitched. Walter was a physiological marvel. He stood 6'3", and possessed a chiseled 220-pound physique. He also had the longest arms in baseball, which afforded him an immensely effective lever system.

Perhaps the most valuable pre–radar gun computation occurred at Griffith Stadium in Washington, D.C., on August 20, 1946. As previously arranged with the United States Army, Bob Feller threw three pitches into a specially designed chronograph as he completed his warm-up tosses prior to his start against the Senators. The device had been created to calculate the speed of bullets, and was accurate to 1/10,000th of a second. Feller was clocked at 98.6 miles per hour. That wasn't bad considering that Rapid Robert had started his Major League career in 1936, and had logged a lot of innings in between. Naturally, Senators' owner Clark Griffith, who witnessed Feller's efforts, offered his opinion on the matter of ultimate speed. Walter Johnson had played for him, and, according to Griffith, as great as Feller was, he could not hold a candle to the Big Train.

This section was intended to include only Major League ballplayers along with the top Negro Leaguers. However, no meaningful discussion of baseball's fastest pitchers can ignore the legendary figure of Steve Dalkowski. Born in Connecticut in 1939, this immensely talented left-hander never pitched an inning in an official big-league game. Dalkowski played in the minors from 1957 through 1965, and participated in many Baltimore Oriole spring training and exhibition games. Along the way, he left a legacy of overwhelming speed that seems more like fiction than reality. Yet, after doing the research, one thought keeps recurring: Steve Dalkowski may have thrown baseballs as hard as any other man!

Then, why didn't he make it to the majors? Sadly, Dalkowski was erratic with both his pitching control and his personal behavior. During his first professional season in 1957, pitching in the Class-D Appalachian League, Steve struck out 24 opposing hitters on August 21. Yet, he lost the game 8-4. Along with all those K's, Dalkowski walked 18 men, and flung six wild pitches. Unfortunately, that was typical of the man's career, which resulted in a 46–80 won-loss record and 5.59 ERA. On the positive side, there is a wealth of testimonials left by well-known Major League players and managers who confirmed his amazing velocity.

Cincinnati Reds manager Birdie Tebbetts referred to Dalkowski's fastball as his radio pitch, meaning "you can hear it, but you can't see it." Baltimore Orioles manager Paul Richards said, "I honestly think I have never seen anyone throw harder than

Steve Dalkowski." Veteran Eddie Robinson (1942 and 1946–1957) was quoted, "I've batted against the fastest from Feller on down. I believe this boy is faster." There are even stories that Ted Williams once faced Dalkowski in batting practice during spring training at Scottsdale, Arizona. According to myth, Williams watched one pitch speed past him, whereupon he walked away claiming that Dalkowski was the "fastest ever." In an interesting interview in the *Hartford Courant* on December 14, 1975, Dalkowski certainly remembered it that way. He stated, "He got scared. He couldn't believe it."

Remarkably, Steve Dalkowski stood 5'11", and weighed only 175 pounds in his prime. Considering that Steve's size is roughly equivalent to that of current San Francisco Giant speed-baller Tim Lincecum, it is apparent that you don't have to be physically large to hurl a baseball at high velocity. It's true that most of the pitchers on the following list tended to be big, powerful men, but, big or not, they all had an uncanny ability to whip their arms with extraordinary torque. Their common skill is one of the most romanticized in the world of sports, and the debate about their relative power will continue.

1. Walter Johnson—1907–1927
2. Nolan Ryan—1966–1993
3. Bob Feller—1936–1941 and 1945–1956
5. Lefty Grove—1925–1941
6. Randy Johnson—1988–2009
7. Sandy Koufax—1955–1966
8. J. R. Richard—1971–1980
9. Sam McDowell—1961–1975
10. Herb Score—1955–1962
11. Smoky Joe Wood—1908–1915 and 1917 and 1919–1920

HONORABLE MENTIONS

Amos Rusie—1889–1896 and 1897–1898 and 1901

Dazzy Vance—1915 and 1918 and 1922–1935

Jim Maloney—1960–1971

Vida Blue—1969–1986

Dwight "Doc" Gooden—1984–2000

Roger Clemens—1984–2007

Justin Verlander—2005–2009

NEGRO LEAGUES

Smokey Joe Williams—1918–1932

Bullet Joe Rogan—1920–1938

Cannonball Dick Redding—1916–1931

Satchel Paige—1927–1947 and 1950 (MLB: 1948–1949 and 1951–1953 and 1965)

Slim Jones—1933–1938

TEN FASTEST RUNNERS

In order to discuss the fastest runners in baseball, it is necessary to first establish the standard for "fastest" in this context. The single most important application of foot speed in baseball is running from home plate to first base after making contact with the ball. Usually, contact occurs while swinging, but, occasionally, it happens during bunting. There is an important distinction between the two functions. It is generally much harder to accelerate toward first base after swinging than after bunting. Some "slap hitters" are the exceptions. Certain left-handed batsmen, who focus on speed over power, develop a style where they are "falling" toward first as they swing. This approach tends to compromise batting power, but helps to catapult the runner down the first base line. Of course, it is significantly easier to reach first base when batting from the left side rather than from the right.

Running from home to first is primarily important because it is the function of foot speed that is used most often in baseball. Running out extra-base hits or advancing around the bases on a teammate's hit is also a valuable example of this skill. Watching a particularly speedy player record a triple or inside-the-park homer is one of baseball's most exhilarating visual experiences, and most of us wish that it happened more often. Depending on the position, speed can be critical in achieving defensive prowess as well. Running fast is helpful for any outfielder, but, in center field, it is essential.

Mickey Mantle was timed at 3.1 seconds from home to first after swinging the bat from the left side. That is particularly impressive when considering how hard Mantle swung. This phenomenon was not a one-time aberration. It was recorded by many different observers over a period of several years.

Let's be honest. We normally expect African-American athletes to dominate in the field of sprinting. They generally prevail in almost every test of foot speed, including my informal list. However, Mickey Mantle was one of those rare talents who superseded all the traditional athletic norms. Although we will never know the identity of baseball's fastest player with certainty, Mantle has the best resume to place him at the top.

Most readers will be surprised to see Joe Caffie's name in the number two position. I was not familiar with him either until I started making inquiries into this topic. He was first mentioned to me by Rocky Colavito when I was talking to Rocky about his great throwing arm. I asked for some nominees in the area of running speed, and Colavito instantly thought of Caffie. I then did the follow-up research, and, frankly, I was overwhelmed. Joe only played two big-league seasons, but he could fly. In the April 20, 1957 edition of the *Pittsburgh Courier*, Luke Easter was quoted, "We clocked him in three seconds flat from home plate to first base. I have seen a lot of fast ones, but this Caffie is the fastest."

Moving down the list, the most familiar name is probably Deion Sanders. Like Bo Jackson, Deion was best known for flying around the football field, but he also left his mark on the baseball diamond. Some of the older fellows may not be readily recognizable to modern fans, but they all possessed blazing speed. For example, George Washington Case won a match race against rookie speedster Gil Coan at

Griffith Stadium on August 21, 1946. Running in baseball cleats across the grass outfield in his uniform, Case was timed at 10 seconds flat for 100 yards. Folks from the track world were skeptical of that time, so Bill Veeck (Case's Cleveland Indians owner) put up $1,000 for Jesse Owens to challenge his fleet outfielder.

The showdown was arranged for September 8, 1946 at Cleveland's Municipal Stadium. At the time, Owens was 32 years old, but reported himself in "top condition" as a result of several other exhibition races that summer. Jesse won the contest, but it was highly competitive. Owens was clocked at 9.9 seconds, while the 31-year-old Case duplicated his earlier time of 10-flat. The existing world record (then still co-held by Jesse) was 9.4 seconds, but remember that those record-making sprints were performed on tracks with shorts and track shoes. A time of 10-flat under the subject conditions indicates that Case was really hauling!

Also consider Pedro Ramos who, despite being a pitcher, had quite a motor. He challenged Phillies' speed king Richie Ashburn to a duel during spring training in 1959. Although denied permission by his manager, Ashburn agreed to an 80-yard runoff in Orlando on March 30. After losing by 5 yards, Richie wished that he hadn't bothered. Ramos then threw down the gauntlet to Mickey Mantle, whereupon the Mighty Mick picked it up. Unfortunately, Yankee skipper Casey Stengel forbade Mantle's participation. Too bad. That would have been like Secretar-iat going head to head with Man O' War. All of the fellows listed below could run like the wind, and there are many others who could also be included.

1. Mickey Mantle—1951–1968
2. Joe Caffie—1956–1957
3. Willie Davis—1960–1979
4. Sam Jethroe—1950–1952 and 1954
5. Vada Pinson—1958–1975
6. Deion Sanders—1989–2001
7. George Case—1937–1947
8. Willie Wilson—1976–1994
9. Pedro Ramos—1955–1967 and 1969–1970
10. Ichiro Suzuki—2001–2009 and Carlos Gomez—2007–2009 (tie)

HONORABLE MENTIONS

"Sliding" Billy Hamilton—1888–1901
Evar Swanson—1929–1930 and 1932–1934
Richie Ashburn—1948–1962
Miguel Dilone—1974-1985
Rickey Henderson—1979–2003
Vince Coleman—1985–1997
Bo Jackson—1986–1991 and 1993–1994
Kenny Lofton—1991–2007
Carl Crawford—2002–2009
Jacoby Ellsbury—2007–2009

NEGRO LEAGUES

James "Cool Papa" Bell—1922–1946
Bernardo Baro—1917–1929

FASTEST RUNNERS BY POSITION

1B: Jimmie Foxx—1925–1942 and 1944–1945

2B: Jackie Robinson—1947–1956

3B: Chone Figgins—2002–2009

SS: Jose Reyes—2003–2009

OF: Mickey Mantle—1951–1968

OF: Joe Caffie—1956–1957

OF: Willie Davis—1960–1979

C: Jason Kendall—1996–2009

P: Pedro Ramos—1955–1967 and 1969–1970

TEN LONGEST HITTERS POUND FOR POUND

This is a topic that we rarely consider, but perhaps we should pay more attention. In boxing and wrestling, we arrange for competition according to equivalent body mass. Of course, we can't do that in Major League Baseball, but we can, at least, recognize those men who generated the most power for their size. Some of the weights attributed to the men on the following list may not reflect their maximum career bulk. Those numbers, however, show the weight at which they competed for the longest time.

Jimmy Wynn seems like the logical number one in this category. His weight of 168 pounds has been confirmed for his entire big-league career, yet his legacy of long drives is remarkable. Remember that his 507-foot blast in Cincinnati on June 10, 1967 has been confirmed. The exact landing place has been recorded on film, and the flight distance has been actually measured. Right behind the

"Toy Cannon" is 19th-century legend Lip Pike. By all accounts, he weighed only about 160 pounds, but he propelled balls for prodigious distances. It is a shame that we do not have exact data for the comparative flight capabilities of baseballs used in the 1800s and subsequent eras. If we did, the ranking process would be more reliable. Suffice to say that all the listed individuals could really pack a punch.

Jimmy Wynn—168 pounds—1963–1977

Lipman Pike—160 pounds—1871–1878 and 1881 and 1887

Buck Freeman—175 pounds—1891 and 1898–1907

Hank Thompson—172 pounds—1947 and 1949–1956

Ernie Banks—175 pounds—1953–1971

Willie Mays—176 pounds—1951–1952 and 1954–1973

Eric Davis—178 pounds—1984–2001

Harry Stovey—180 pounds—1880–1893

Chet Laabs—175 pounds—1937–1947

Mel Ott—178 pounds—1926–1947

NEGRO LEAGUES

Charles "Chino" Smith—168 pounds—1925–1930

Norman "Turkey" Stearnes—170 pounds—1923–1940

SOURCES

This section is intended primarily for the more dedicated baseball enthusiasts. They may wish to confirm my estimates of baseball's longest drives, which constitutes the foundation of this book. Accordingly, we will include a discussion of the sources themselves along with a list of those sources for the ten longest drives of each subject player. We will also discuss ballpark configurations as well as the technical or scientific components of the estimation process.

Almost all the sources for the home runs of the older players are eyewitness accounts printed in the thousands of newspapers published in North America. In the case of Babe Ruth's, during his years (1920–1934) as a New York Yankee, there were about 15 daily newspapers printed in the Big Apple. Since that era slightly overlapped the onset of radio coverage and completely predated television, those newspaper accounts tended to be highly descriptive. On average, there were about five daily papers in the other Major League towns as well. All those old newspaper editions are still available either on microfilm in libraries or, more and more, on the Internet. Accordingly, if anyone takes the time to look them up, it is a relatively

straightforward task to determine where all 714 Ruthian homers landed. With the advent of TV and, ultimately, with the proliferation of computer technology, the importance of newspaper research has declined. It still plays a key role in developing information about the older players, but you don't need papers to follow the modern guys. Just turn on your television or computer, and you are all set.

For all home runs, whether I have seen them personally or not, I have implemented the standard of supplying the reader with two primary sources (mostly newspaper accounts) for confirmation. If the subject event is truly historic in nature, in my research I strived for as many sources as possible. For example, since I maintain that Babe Ruth's center field blast in Detroit on July 18, 1921 is baseball's longest-ever home run, I have tracked down as many eyewitness accounts as I could. There are 18 of them. That event, however, is unique, and another example might be more revealing. How about Jimmie Foxx's tremendous shot over Comiskey Park's left center field rooftop on June 16, 1936? For that event, which is historically significant but not one of a kind, I have accrued seven accounts.

Let's say that I'm researching Henry Aaron's home run off Sandy Koufax at Milwaukee's County Stadium on June 27, 1958. By referencing the *Los Angeles Times*, which is available in many libraries around the country, I found an account saying that the ball flew into the left center field bleachers for a ride of 395 feet. A good shot for sure, but nothing exceptional. Considering the usual degree of reliability for that publication along with the specificity of the description, I saw no need to research that one further. And so it went for 30 years. Using a sliding scale of historical relevance, I have obtained anywhere from one to 18 accounts of all or most of the home runs of every great slugger. Whenever the first source asserted a drive of 450 feet or more, I always strived to obtain at least one additional source.

An example is Willie Stargell's rocket over the right field grandstand roof at Pittsburgh's Forbes Field on August 19, 1969. Working at Pennsylvania's State Library in Harrisburg, I obtained my initial description from the *Pittsburgh Press*. That paper provided some convincing data that Willie's blow completely cleared the 86-foot-high structure. Such a drive would be genuinely historic, and almost certainly would have flown over 450 feet. As a result, I went directly back to the service desk, and requested the microfilm reel for the *Pittsburgh Post-Gazette* for the same date. Sure enough, the *Post-Gazette* confirmed the depiction from the *Press*, which pretty much sealed the deal in my mind.

That brings us to another important source, which is the player himself. Staying with the Willie Stargell model, I met "Pops" at the Hilton Hotel in downtown Pittsburgh in 1983. This was not a typical interview, mostly for two reasons. Willie was retired at that point, and he was an unusually personable fellow. We had lunch inside the Hilton, which contrasts to the usual five-minute pregame locker room chat one typically gets with active players. Stargell seemed genuinely interested in my research, and conversed at length about himself and the other great distance hitters that he had seen. Afterward, he even took the time to drive me across the Allegheny River to Three Rivers Stadium. Willie and I climbed to the right field upper deck to where many of his longest homers had traveled. It was an enjoyable and informative experience.

Yet, as an historian, I couldn't simply accept Willie's account of his deeds. So, after returning home, I checked my notes against Stargell's career home run log, and identified those shots that he had described. During lunch, Willie had cited his 1967 center field bomb off Don Drysdale at Forbes Field as his personal longest. While exploring Three Rivers, where he played during the second half of his career, he had singled out his upper-deckers off Ron Taylor and Gary Gentry as his mightiest at that site. It was a relatively simple matter to determine that he was referring to his homers of July 3, 1967, August 9, 1970, and May 31, 1973. Then, a follow-up trip to the library along with more sessions with the *Pittsburgh*

Press and *Pittsburgh Post-Gazette* provided the formal historical confirmation.

With television, we have an immensely important tool in assessing the topic of tape measure home runs. Who wouldn't want to see the event themselves? As a child growing up in the 1950s, I got to see some of the four-baggers recorded by such legends as Willie Mays and Frank Robinson. But, back then, the benefit was marginal. There were single black-and-white camera angles and no instant replays. More to the point, there was virtually no out of town coverage. Little by little, TV technology has steadily improved to where we are today. Starting with the founding of ESPN in 1979, interested fans were able to see more of the most important plays from every game. That was a major breakthrough. You might have needed to stay up late to see Reggie Jackson smacking one for the California Angels, but it was doable.

Naturally, if a guy played in your home television market, you had it much easier. Living near Philadelphia, I didn't miss many of Mike Schmidt or Greg Luzinski's four-baggers. As of this writing in 2009, Ryan Howard plays for my hometown Phillies. Between the national cable networks and local coverage, it is unlikely that I will ever need to look up any of Ryan's long clouts at the library. I've had little trouble seeing every one to date, usually with multiple views.

Finally, we address the latest and, possibly, most effective source ever devised for evaluating long-distance home runs. Clearly, that is the Internet. There are actually sites where a baseball fan can view any contemporary home run in any park anytime he or she chooses to do so. In my opinion, the best is Greg Rybarczyk's Hit Tracker. Greg is a talented guy whose reliable system has made my research much simpler and more productive. Wow! When I think of all those three-hour drives from Philly to Washington, D.C., along with those ten-hour days at the Library of Congress, I have to laugh. Chronicling the current group of sluggers will never require such relatively primitive methodology. If you're sincere about understanding the history of Major League Baseball, it is all good.

Before moving to the topic of ballparks, we should at least mention one other source. Most of us don't see many of any player's career home runs, while actually present at the stadium. But, "being there" is the most enjoyable way of recording the image of any sporting event. Plus, it's usually highly effective in establishing reliable factual context. I recall Dick Allen's walk-off homer at Philadelphia's Connie Mack Stadium on August 19, 1966. Sitting in the lower seats just past first base, my cousin Tom Stock and I had an ideal view of the ball soaring high over the billboard atop the left field roof. If I hadn't been there, I would not have clearly heard the gunshot-like sound, and I would not have fully comprehended the seemingly bullet-like speed with which the ball left the premises. Exiting the ballpark immediately after the game, we could hear everybody expressing their disbelief that any human being could hit a baseball with such unnatural force. I understood their perspective. I had just experienced the same sensual overload.

Regarding Major League ballparks, it is essential that anyone researching long-distance hitting familiarize themselves with this topic. Admittedly, it is a tough job. Over the life of any stadium, there are changes and alterations. Many good books are available on the subject, but my personal favorite is Phil Lowry's *Green Cathedrals* (Walker & Company, 2006). It contains descriptions, dimensions, histories of alterations, and photographs of every big-league stadium from the 19th century onward. Predictably, there are also different Web sites that provide similar information. Regardless how it is done, a student of tape measure home runs must be familiar with the landing areas of those homers. Some ballparks, especially in the old days, were constructed on a smaller scale, whereby many four-baggers landed outside the confines of the stadium. In those cases, it is necessary to learn about the streets and buildings in the neighborhoods beyond the outfield fences. In this regard, I have a secret weapon.

Bruce Orser is a first-class baseball historian, who is also a wizard at using the Internet to locate aerial photographs of all the ballparks as well as their adjoining neighborhoods. If I can establish an accurate description of where a ball lands outside the stadium, Bruce can reliably determine (within about

10 feet) how far it flew. A good example is Larry Doby's classic smash over the right center field wall at Washington's Griffith Stadium on May 24, 1951. Larry told me that the ball landed on the roof of a house during a 1985 interview at RFK Stadium in D.C. Since I was already in town, I first confirmed the landing point from the *Washington Post*. Next, I ventured to the stadium site, where the ballpark was long gone, but the houses were still intact. Some routine investigation brought me into contact with an elderly gentleman who had lived in the neighborhood since Doby had been coming to town. He remembered that at least one of Larry's epic blasts had landed on a particular house, and he showed me where it was. However, since Griffith Stadium had been turned into a parking lot, I had to wait for Bruce Orser's computer magic to figure out the actual flight distance.

This methodology is particularly effective for evaluating balls landing outside the confines of the stadiums. It is much less useful, however, for balls that are interrupted in mid-flight by the typical modern, enclosed ballparks. In order to compute the total flight distance of such drives (if left unimpeded), a researcher must rely on stadium knowledge along with a rudimentary understanding of the laws of physics. Once a ball has reached its apex (highest point) and is descending back to field level, it travels in a rapidly declining trajectory. In other words, it doesn't fly nearly as far as we normally think. For the record, virtually every ball that has ever collided with a stadium structure after it passed over an outfield fence has been on a downward path. The only viable exception is the old Polo Grounds, where the grandstand roof façades were unusually close to home plate along the foul lines.

So, how do we figure out how far such drives would have flown? First, we establish where the ball collided with the stadium by using our sources. Second, we implement our stadium knowledge, and determine two measurements: the linear distance from home plate and the height above the playing field where the ball was interrupted. Returning to our sources, we must also determine the approximate trajectory of the ball. Was it a high fly, average drive, or a line drive? This is very important. Finally, we resort to that dreaded science of physics to finish the process.

You start with the linear distance and then add a factor of the vertical distance above field level. This is where the physics enters the picture. If the ball is a high fly, you multiply the vertical distance by a factor of .5 (one-half), and add it to the linear distance to compute how far the ball would have flown. For example, if you know that Albert Pujols hit a high fly homer that collided with an upper deck façade 400 feet away at a height of 50 feet, you can estimate that it would have flown 425 feet. Start with the 400 feet and then multiply 50 feet by one-half before adding them together.

In the case of average trajectory, the multiplier is .7 (seven-tenths), and, with line

drives, the factor is 1.1 (one and one-tenth). By way of example, if that same Pujols shot had been a line drive instead of a high fly ball, we would multiply the height of 50 feet by one and one-tenth. By adding the result of 55 feet to 400 feet, we would estimate the total flight distance at 455 feet. If you think that these types of home runs are the hardest to judge, you get high marks. They are. First, it is often difficult to agree on the trajectory of a batted ball. Different witnesses will sometimes disagree on this issue. Additionally, there is not uniform agreement among physicists on the exact multipliers that should be used. I have consulted with several, and have basically provided their consensus figures. Again, an example seems appropriate.

In this case, why not use one of the most famous home runs in baseball history? It also happens to be arguably the most difficult ever to estimate. Specifically, let's talk about Mickey Mantle's legendary roof façade shot at Yankee Stadium on May 22, 1963. That ball was clearly on a line drive trajectory when it smashed into the ornate right field roof façade 370 linear feet away at a height of 110 feet above field level. If you apply the standard formula, you arrive at 491 feet. But, we know that this particular drive did not fit into a neat little box. Mickey emphatically categorized it as the hardest ball he ever hit, and all eyewitnesses confirm that it was struck on a vicious line trajectory. Accordingly, we should increase the standard line drive multiplier of 1.1. But, by how much?

We know that the ball nearly bounced back to the second baseman. This is a clear indicator that it was still flying at a high rate of speed at the moment of impact. Some highly qualified scientists have studied the existing film footage and attempted to calculate the elapsed time before the ball hit the façade. The problem is that the film is not definitive; it doesn't follow the entire flight path. As a result, different physicists have offered different estimates. They have ranged from 600 feet down to 500 feet. My personal estimate is 540 feet. Hopefully, this example demonstrates the degree of difficulty in estimating home runs knocked down in mid-flight.

That is the basic story of how I have estimated the home runs discussed in this book. I will now identify one or two of the sources for all of the 10 longest home runs attributed to each of the top sluggers. As the reader will note, there is generally only one source for most of the modern homers. This phenomenon has already been explained. With improving technology and communication, I have witnessed a higher percentage of home runs in recent years. In those instances, the source is simply identified "Author Eyewitness." Everyone is encouraged to make their own estimates. You might enjoy the process; obviously I did. Here are the sources in the order in which the players appeared in the book:

HANK AARON

April 13, 1970—Hank Aaron Interview, 1985 and *Sporting News*, May 9, 1970.

May 25, 1962—Hank Aaron Interview, 1985 and *Milwaukee Journal*, May 26, 1962.

June 18, 1962—Hank Aaron Interview, 1985 and *New York Times*, June 19, 1962.

April 20, 1966—*Philadelphia Bulletin* and *Philadelphia Inquirer*, April 21, 1966.

July 26, 1966—*Atlanta Constitution* and *St. Louis Post-Dispatch*, July 27, 1966.

July 13, 1963—*Milwaukee Journal* and Associated Press, July 14, 1963.

May 7, 1955—*Milwaukee Journal* and Associated Press, May 8, 1955.

July 20, 1960—*Milwaukee Journal* and *Washington Post*/AP, July 21, 1960.

September 10, 1963—*Milwaukee Journal* and *Cincinnati Enquirer*, September 11, 1963.

April 14, 1961—*Milwaukee Journal* and *Chicago Tribune*, April 15, 1961.

WILLIE MAYS

July 7, 1955—*New York Herald-Tribune* and *New York Times*, July 8, 1955.

June 14, 1957—*New York Herald-Tribune* and *New York Times*, June 15, 1957.

July 12, 1956—*New York Herald-Tribune* and *New York Times*, July 13, 1956.

June 2, 1962—*San Francisco Chronicle* and *New York Times*, June 3, 1962.

May 5, 1962—*San Francisco Chronicle* and *Oakland Tribune*, May 6, 1962.

June 27, 1957—*New York Herald-Tribune* and *New York Times*, June 28, 1957.

September 8, 1961—*San Francisco Chronicle* and *Oakland Tribune*, September 9, 1961.

July 27, 1954—*Sport Magazine*, June, 1961 and *New York Times*, July 28, 1954.

April 30, 1961—*San Francisco Chronicle* and *Milwaukee Journal*, May 1, 1961

April 14, 1965—*Philadelphia Bulletin* and *Philadelphia Inquirer*, April 15, 1965.

FRANK ROBINSON

June 22, 1965—Frank Robinson Interview, 1982 and *Sporting News*, July 10, 1965.

August 11, 1962—*Cincinnati Enquirer* and *New York Times*, August 12, 1962.

September 15, 1957—*New York Times* and *Chicago Daily Defender*, September 16, 1957.

May 11, 1965—*Philadelphia Bulletin* and *Philadelphia Inquirer*, May 12, 1965.

July 27, 1969—*Chicago Tribune* and *Baltimore Sun*, July 28, 1968.

June 26, 1970—*Washington Post* and *Baltimore Sun*, June 27, 1970.

May 6, 1965—*Los Angeles Times* and *Cincinnati Enquirer*, May 7, 1965.

May 27, 1959—*Philadelphia Bulletin* and *Philadelphia Inquirer*, May 28, 1959.

September 8, 1957—*Cincinnati Enquirer* and *Hartford Courant*/AP, September 9, 1957

July 15, 1971—*Los Angeles Herald-Examiner* and *Washington Post*, July 16, 1971.

FRED McGRIFF

June 8, 1987—Author Eyewitness and *New York Times*, June 9, 1987.

September 2, 1988—Fred McGriff Interview, 1995 and Author Eyewitness.

August 28, 1992—Author Eyewitness.

July 20, 1989—Author Eyewitness and *Toronto Globe and Mail*, July 22, 1989.

May 5, 1999 (#2)—Author Eyewitness.

July 17, 1990—Author Eyewitness.

May 6, 1994—Author Eyewitness and *Atlanta Journal*, May 7, 1994.

July 17, 1989—Author Eyewitness and *Toronto Globe and Mail*, July 18, 1989.

June 17, 1995—Author Eyewitness.

August 6, 1992—Author Eyewitness.

BO JACKSON

September 14, 1986—Bo Jackson Interview, 1993 and Author Eyewitness.

May 22, 1987—Author Eyewitness and Texas Rangers Media Relations.

July 31, 1993—Author Eyewitness and Seattle Mariners Media Relations.

June 10, 1987—Author Eyewitness and Minnesota Twins Media Relations.

July 17, 1990 (#2)—Author Eyewitness and *New York Times*, July 18, 1990.

May 23, 1989—Author Eyewitness and *Kansas City Times-Star*, May 24, 1989.

July 1, 1990—Author Eyewitness.

May 20, 1994—Author Eyewitness and *Los Angeles Times*, May 21, 1994.

September 21, 1991—Author Eyewitness.

June 28, 1987—Author Eyewitness and Associated Press, June 29, 1987.

JOHN "BOOG" POWELL

June 3, 1964—Boog Powell Interview, 1992 and *Baltimore Sun*, June 4, 1964.

July 18, 1966—*Chicago Tribune* and *Baltimore Sun*, July 19, 1966.

July 6, 1969—*Baltimore Sun* and *Detroit Free Press*, July 7, 1969.

June 15, 1967—*Baltimore Sun* and *Kansas City Star*, June 16, 1967.

July 26, 1970—*Baltimore Sun* and *Minneapolis Tribune*, July 27, 1970.

June 22, 1962—*Baltimore Sun* and *Boston Globe*, June 23, 1962.

May 14, 1963—*Baltimore Sun* and *Washington Evening Star*, May 15, 1963.

June 25, 1969—*Baltimore Sun* and *Washington Evening Star*, June 26, 1969.

July 21, 1972—*Baltimore Sun* and *Kansas City Star & Times*, July 22, 1972.

June 21, 1968—*Baltimore Sun* and *Los Angeles Times*, June 22, 1968.

JIM RICE

May 5, 1977—*Boston Globe* and *Boston Herald*, May 6, 1977.

September 13, 1988—Author Eyewitness and *Boston Globe*, September 14, 1988.

July 18, 1975—*Boston Globe* and *Boston Herald*, July 19, 1975.

July 13, 1977—*Boston Globe* and *Cleveland Plain Dealer*, July 14, 1977.

June 19, 1977—*Boston Globe* and *New York Times*, June 20, 1977.

July 2, 1983—*Boston Globe* and *New York Times*, July 3, 1983.

June 16, 1980—*Boston Globe* and *San Francisco Chronicle*, June 17, 1980.

May 4, 1977—*Boston Globe* and *Boston Herald*, May 5, 1977.

April 22, 1983—*Boston Globe* and *San Francisco Chronicle*, April 23, 1983.

August 19, 1985—Author Eyewitness and *Boston Globe*, August 20, 1985.

JIMMY WYNN

June 10, 1967—Jimmy Wynn Interview, 1991 and Author Eyewitness.

July 23, 1967—*Pittsburgh Press* and *Chicago Daily Defender*/UPI, July 24, 1967.

April 12, 1970—*Atlanta Constitution* and *Houston Post*, April 13, 1970.

June 6, 1965—Jimmy Wynn Interview, 1991 and *St. Louis Post-Dispatch*, June 7, 1965.

August 1, 1966—*Philadelphia Inquirer* and *Philadelphia Bulletin*, August 2, 1966.

June 6, 1967—*St. Louis Post-Dispatch* and *Hartford Courant*/AP, June 7, 1967.

September 9, 1967—*Los Angeles Times* and *Houston Post*, September 10, 1967.

September 7, 1968—*Washington Post*/AP and *Chicago Tribune*/UPI, September 8, 1968.

April 7, 1977—*New York Times* and *Milwaukee Journal*, April 8, 1977.

August 28, 1965—*Houston Post* and *Pittsburgh Press*, August 29, 1965.

HANK GREENBERG

May 22, 1937—*Detroit News* and *Boston Post*, May 23, 1937.

July 24, 1938—*Detroit Free Press* and *Philadelphia Inquirer*, July 25, 1938.

July 6, 1947—Hank Greenberg Interview, 1984 and *Pittsburgh Post-Gazette*, July 7, 1947.

April 21, 1938—*Detroit Free Press* and *Chicago Tribune*, April 22, 1938.

September 14, 1934—*Detroit News* and *Washington Post*, September 15, 1934.

August 23, 1938—*Detroit News* and *Philadelphia Inquirer*, August 24, 1938.

August 21, 1933—*Detroit Free Press* and *Philadelphia Inquirer*, August 22, 1933.

June 30, 1940—*Detroit Free Press* and *Detroit News*, July 1, 1940.

May 27, 1938—*Chicago Tribune* and *Detroit Free Press*, May 28, 1938.

September 27, 1938—*Detroit Free Press* and *Washington Post*, September 28, 1938.

MIKE SCHMIDT

June 10, 1974—Author Eyewitness and *Philadelphia Inquirer*, June 11, 1974.

September 25, 1981—*Philadelphia Inquirer* and *Philadelphia Daily News*, September 26, 1981.

April 17, 1975—*Philadelphia Daily News* and *Philadelphia Bulletin*, April 18, 1975.

April 17, 1976—*Philadelphia Inquirer* and *Philadelphia Bulletin*, April 18, 1976.

August 21, 1974—*Philadelphia Bulletin* and *Philadelphia Daily News*, August 22, 1974.

August 31, 1986—Author Eyewitness and *Philadelphia Inquirer*, September 1, 1986.

June 1, 1974—Author Eyewitness and *Philadelphia Bulletin*, June 2, 1974.

May 22, 1986—Author Eyewitness and *Philadelphia Daily News*, May 23, 1986.

June 14, 1977—*Philadelphia Inquirer* and *Philadelphia Bulletin*, June 15, 1977.

July 18, 1975—*Camden Courier-Post* and *Philadelphia Daily News*, July 19, 1975.

LARRY DOBY

May 24, 1951—Larry Doby Interview, 1985 and *Pittsburgh Courier*, June 2, 1951.

May 25, 1949—*Sporting News*, June 8, 1949 and *Washington Post*, May 26, 1949.

May 29, 1955—*Kansas City Star* and *Chicago Daily Tribune*/AP, May 30, 1955.

June 19, 1956—*Chicago Daily Tribune* and *Chicago Daily Defender*, June 20, 1956.

May 19, 1949—*New York Times* and *Cleveland Plain Dealer*, May 20, 1949.

July 1, 1956—*Chicago Daily Tribune* and *Cleveland Plain Dealer*, July 2, 1956.

June 10, 1954—*Washington Post* and *Cleveland Plain Dealer*, June 11, 1954.

June 4, 1952—*Cleveland Plain Dealer* and *Cleveland Press*, June 5, 1952.

August 2, 1950 (#3)—*Cleveland Plain Dealer* and *Washington Post*, August 3, 1950.

May 8, 1948—Larry Doby Interview, 1985 and *Cleveland Plain Dealer*, May 9, 1948.

KIRK GIBSON

June 14, 1983—Author Eyewitness and *Boston Globe*, June 15, 1983.

May 10, 1985—*Chicago Tribune* and *Chicago Sun-Times*, May 11, 1985.

June 16, 1985—*New York Times* and *Los Angeles Times*, June 17, 1985.

July 13, 1986—Author Eyewitness.

September 10, 1986—Author Eyewitness.

May 1, 1994—Author Eyewitness and *Chicago Tribune*, May 2, 1994.

September 6, 1986—Author Eyewitness and Oakland Athletics Media Relations.

April 22, 1984—Author Eyewitness and *Chicago Tribune*, April 23, 1984.

August 30, 1993—Author Eyewitness and Seattle Mariners Media Relations.

August 3, 1985—Author Eyewitness.

ANDRES GALARRAGA

May 31, 1997—Author Eyewitness and Florida Marlins Media Relations.

August 28, 1997—Author Eyewitness and *Sporting News*, September 8, 1997.

September 18, 2001—Author Eyewitness and *San Francisco Chronicle*, September 19, 2001.

April 19, 1998—Author Eyewitness.

September 1, 1990—Author Eyewitness and *Los Angeles Times*, September 2, 1990.

July 6, 1993—Author Eyewitness.

May 26, 1997—Author Eyewitness.

April 27, 1993—Author Eyewitness and *Chicago Tribune*, April 28, 1993.

September 4, 1993—Author Eyewitness.

June 25, 1995 (#3)—Author Eyewitness and San Diego Padres Media Relations.

DARRYL STRAWBERRY

April 4, 1988—Darryl Strawberry Interview, 1990 and *New York Times*, April 5 and 6, 1988.

October 1, 1999—Author Eyewitness and *New York Times*, October 2, 1999.

June 17, 1998—Author Eyewitness and *New York Times*, June 18, 1998.

May 22, 1987—Darryl Strawberry Interview, 1990 and Author Eyewitness.

October 1, 1985—*New York Times* and *New York Daily News*, October 2, 1985.

July 17, 1988—Author Eyewitness and *New York Times*, July 18, 1988.

May 1, 1988—Author Eyewitness and *New York Times*, May 2, 1988.

May 12, 1992—Author Eyewitness and *Los Angeles Times*, May 13, 1992.

July 25, 1990—Author Eyewitness and *New York Times*, July 26, 1990.

September 5, 1987—*New York Times* and *Los Angeles Times*, September 6, 1987.

EDDIE MATHEWS

April 22, 1953—Eddie Mathews Interview, 1995 and *Milwaukee Sentinel*, April 23, 1953.

June 24, 1955—*Milwaukee Journal* and *New York Times*, June 25, 1955.

April 30, 1965—*Milwaukee Sentinel* and *Philadelphia Inquirer*, May 1, 1965.

August 11, 1956—*Milwaukee Journal* and *Milwaukee Sentinel*, August 12, 1956.

July 14, 1960—*Pittsburgh Post-Gazette* and *New York Times*, July 15, 1960.

July 22, 1956—*Philadelphia Inquirer* and *Philadelphia Bulletin*, July 23, 1956.

September 21, 1959—*Pittsburgh Post-Gazette* and *New York Times*, September 22, 1959.

August 25, 1967—*Kansas City Star* and *Detroit News*, August 26, 1967.

August 15, 1966—*Houston Post* and *Atlanta Journal*, August 16, 1966.

April 17, 1960—*Philadelphia Inquirer* and *Philadelphia Bulletin*, April 18, 1960.

WALLY POST

April 14, 1961—Curt Simmons Interview, 1993 and *St. Louis Post-Dispatch*, April 15, 1961.

August 23, 1956—*Sporting News*, September 5, 1956 and *New York Times*, August 24, 1956.

August 19, 1955—*Cincinnati Enquirer* and *St. Louis Post-Dispatch*, August 20, 1955.

April 16, 1955—*Cincinnati Enquirer* and *Milwaukee Sentinel*, April 17, 1955.

April 29, 1956 (#3)—*Cincinnati Enquirer* and *Chicago Tribune*, April 30, 1956.

May 22, 1955—*Cincinnati Enquirer* and *St. Louis Post-Dispatch*, May 23, 1955.

April 29, 1956 (#2)—*Cincinnati Enquirer* and *Washington Post*/AP, April 30, 1956.

June 24, 1955—*Philadelphia Inquirer* and *Philadelphia Bulletin*, June 25, 1955.

August 29, 1955—*Philadelphia Inquirer* and *Philadelphia Bulletin*, August 30, 1955.

June 18, 1961—*Philadelphia Bulletin* and *Philadelphia Inquirer*, June 19, 1961.

LUKE EASTER

June 23, 1950 (#2)—*Washington Post*, June 24, 1950 and *Sporting News*, July 5, 1950.

July 25, 1950—*Cleveland Plain Dealer* and *Philadelphia Inquirer*, July 26, 1950.

August 19, 1950—*Chicago Tribune* and *Cleveland Plain Dealer*, August 20, 1950.

June 16, 1951—*Washington Post* and *Cleveland Plain Dealer*, June 17, 1951.

June 28, 1950—*St. Louis Post-Dispatch* and *Cleveland Plain Dealer*, June 29, 1950.

September 13, 1950—*Cleveland Press* and *Cleveland Plain Dealer*, September 14, 1950.

September 10, 1952—*Cleveland Press* and *Cleveland Plain Dealer*, September 11, 1952.

August 24, 1952—*Cleveland Plain Dealer* and *Washington Post*, August 25, 1952.

April 17, 1952—*Cleveland Plain Dealer* and *Chicago Tribune*, April 18, 1952.

June 7, 1952—*Philadelphia Bulletin* and *Philadelphia Inquirer*, June 8, 1952.

GEORGE FOSTER

July 29, 1978—George Foster Interview, 1986 and *Cincinnati Enquirer*, July 30, 1978.

August 3, 1977—*Chicago Tribune* and *Los Angeles Times*, August 4, 1977.

June 14, 1976—*Cincinnati Enquirer*, June 15, 1976 and Cincinnati Reds Media Relations.

June 27, 1985—Author Eyewitness and *New York Times*, June 28, 1985.

September 7, 1977—*Cincinnati Enquirer*, September 8, 1977 and *Sporting News*, September 24, 1977.

June 2, 1979—Author Eyewitness and *Philadelphia Inquirer*, June 3, 1979.

August 31, 1980—Author Eyewitness and *Cincinnati Enquirer*, September 1, 1980.

September 6, 1979—*Cincinnati Enquirer*, September 7, 1979 and Cincinnati Reds Media Relations.

August 14, 1981—*Cincinnati Enquirer*, August 15, 1981 and Cincinnati Reds Media Relations.

June 15, 1977—*Philadelphia Bulletin* and *Philadelphia Inquirer*, June 16, 1977.

NORM CASH

July 29, 1962—*Detroit Free Press*, July 30, 1962 and *Sporting News*, August 11, 1962.

June 11, 1961—*Detroit Free Press* and *Hartford Courant*/AP, June 12, 1961.

July 31, 1966—*Kansas City Star-Times* and *Detroit Free Press*, August 1, 1966.

August 26, 1967—*Kansas City Star* and *New York Times*/UPI, August 27, 1967.

July 20, 1962—*Kansas City Star-Times* and *Detroit Free Press*, July 21, 1962.

July 27, 1962—*Detroit Free Press* and *Los Angeles Times*, July 28, 1962.

August 15, 1966—*New York Times* and *Chicago Tribune*/UPI, August 16, 1966.

May 17, 1969—*Detroit Free Press* and *Detroit News*, May 20, 1969.

May 11, 1962—*Detroit Free Press*, May 12, 1962 and *Sporting News*, May 23, 1962.

May 18, 1963—*Detroit Free Press* and *Detroit News*, May 19, 1963.

WALLY BERGER

June 16, 1935—*Boston Globe* and *Cincinnati Enquirer*, June 17, 1935.

June 23, 1930—*Boston Globe*, June 24, 1930 and *St. Louis Post-Dispatch*, June 23, 1930.

August 10, 1932—*Pittsburgh Post-Gazette* and *Boston Herald*, August 11, 1932.

June 23, 1931—*Boston Globe* and *Cincinnati Enquirer*, June 24, 1931.

September 5, 1932—*Boston Globe* and *Brooklyn Daily Eagle*, September 6, 1932.

June 25, 1933—*Boston Globe* and *Chicago Tribune*, June 26, 1933.

June 7, 1930—Associated Press and *Pittsburgh Sun Telegraph*, June 8, 1930.

July 1, 1937—*New York Times* and *Philadelphia Inquirer*, July 2, 1937.

May 1, 1930 (#2)—*Pittsburgh Sun-Telegraph* and *Boston Globe*, May 2, 1930.

May 30, 1931—*Philadelphia Inquirer* and *Boston Herald*, May 31, 1931.

MIKE PIAZZA

September 26, 1997—Author Eyewitness and *Los Angeles Times*, September 27, 1997.

September 4, 1998—Author Eyewitness and *New York Times*, September 5, 1998.

July 10, 1999—Author Eyewitness and *New York Times*, July 11, 1999.

September 14, 1998—Author Eyewitness and *New York Times*, September 15, 1998.

September 21, 1997—Author Eyewitness and *Los Angeles Times*, September 22, 1997.

June 6, 1994—Author Eyewitness and *Los Angeles Times*, June 7, 1994.

August 16, 1999—Author Eyewitness and *New York Times*, August 17, 1999.

July 27, 2001—*Philadelphia Inquirer* and *New York Times*, July 28, 2001.

July 30, 1998—Author Eyewitness and *New York Times*, July 31, 1998.

July 30, 1999—Author Eyewitness and *Chicago Tribune*, July 31, 1999.

LOU GEHRIG

May 4, 1929—*New York World* and *New York Herald-Tribune*, May 5, 1929.

June 30, 1931—*New York Herald-Tribune* and *New York Times*, July 1, 1931.

August 28, 1935—*Chicago Tribune* and *New York Herald-Tribune*, August 29, 1935.

September 7, 1936—*New York Times* and *New York Evening Post*, September 8, 1936.

July 22, 1926—*New York World* and *New York Herald-Tribune*, July 23, 1926.

April 19, 1930—*New York Times* and *New York World*, April 20, 1930.

May 19, 1927—*New York Herald-Tribune* and *New York Times*, May 20, 1927.

September 10, 1925—*New York Herald-Tribune* and *New York Times*, September 11, 1925.

May 1, 1934—*New York Sun* and *New York Times*, May 2, 1934.

April 27, 1929—*Philadelphia Inquirer* and *New York Herald-Tribune*, April 28, 1929.

RON KITTLE

July 2, 1984—Ron Kittle Interview, 1990 and *Chicago Tribune*, July 3, 1984.

August 8, 1985—*Chicago Tribune* and *Chicago Sun-Times*, August 9, 1985.

September 6, 1983—*Chicago Tribune*, September 7, 1983 and Chicago White Sox Media Relations.

September 19, 1983—*Chicago Tribune*, September 20, 1983 and Chicago White Sox Media Relations.

September 13, 1985—Author Eyewitness and *Chicago Tribune*, September 14, 1985.

August 1, 1984—*Chicago Tribune*, August 2, 1984 and Chicago White Sox Media Relations.

April 18, 1990—Author Eyewitness and *Washington Post*, April 19, 1990.

April 29, 1984—*Chicago Tribune*, April 30, 1984 and Chicago White Sox Media Relations.

August 8, 1983—Ron Kittle Interview, 1990 and *Chicago Tribune*, August 9, 1983.

June 27, 1990 (#2)—Author Eyewitness.

DICK STUART

May 1, 1959—*Pittsburgh Press* and *Pittsburgh Post-Gazette*, May 2, 1959.

June 5, 1959—*Pittsburgh Press* and *Pittsburgh Post-Gazette*, June 6, 1959.

June 26, 1959—*Pittsburgh Press* and *Pittsburgh Post-Gazette*, June 27, 1959.

June 14, 1963—*Boston Globe* and UPI, June 15, 1963.

September 10, 1958—*Pittsburgh Post-Gazette* and *Los Angeles Times*/UPI, September 11, 1958.

July 3, 1961—*Cincinnati Enquirer* and *Pittsburgh Post-Gazette*, July 4, 1961.

June 7, 1962—*Pittsburgh Press* and *Los Angeles Times*, June 8, 1962.

April 13, 1963—*Washington Evening Star* and *Hartford Courant*/AP, April 14, 1963.

July 2, 1965—*Philadelphia Inquirer* and *Philadelphia Bulletin*, July 3, 1963.

June 12, 1960—*Pittsburgh Press* and *Pittsburgh Post-Gazette*, June 13, 1960.

JOSE CANSECO

September 26, 1985—*San Francisco Chronicle* and *Chicago Tribune*, September 27, 1985.

June 28, 1987—*San Francisco Chronicle* and *San Francisco Examiner*, June 29, 1985.

June 13, 1994—Author Eyewitness and *Seattle Times*, June 14, 1994.

October 7, 1989—Author Eyewitness and Associated Press, October 8, 1989.

September 22, 1985—*Chicago Tribune* and *Chicago Sun-Times*, September 23, 1985.

May 22, 1990—Author Eyewitness and *San Francisco Chronicle*, May 23, 1990.

September 15, 1992—Author Eyewitness.

April 22, 2000—Author Eyewitness and *Los Angeles Times*, April 23, 2000.

July 19, 1997—*San Francisco Chronicle* and *Minneapolis Star Tribune*, July 20, 1997.

April 12, 1999—Author Eyewitness.

CECIL FIELDER

August 25, 1990—Author Eyewitness and *Detroit News & Free Press*, August 26, 1990.

September 14, 1991—Author Eyewitness and *Detroit News*, September 15, 1991.

June 14, 1993—Author Eyewitness and *Detroit Free Press*, June 15, 1993.

July 2, 1993—Author Eyewitness.

May 16, 1993—Author Eyewitness.

May 4, 1994—Author Eyewitness and *Detroit Free Press*, May 5, 1994.

July 4, 1991—Author Eyewitness.

May 13, 1998—Author Eyewitness.

April 10, 1994—Author Eyewitness.

May 28, 1995—Author Eyewitness and *Detroit News*, May 29, 1995.

BARRY BONDS

August 27, 2002—Author Eyewitness.

September 9, 2002—Author Eyewitness and *Los Angeles Times*, September 10, 2002.

October 20, 2002—Author Eyewitness.

September 9, 2001—Author Eyewitness.

June 5, 2002—Author Eyewitness and San Diego Padres Media Relations.

June 8, 2002—Author Eyewitness.

June 6, 2000—*San Francisco Chronicle* and *Los Angeles Times*, June 7, 2000.

September 13, 2003—Author Eyewitness.

August 8, 2003—Author Eyewitness.

July 7, 2003—Author Eyewitness.

JOE ADCOCK

June 17, 1956—*Milwaukee Journal* and *New York Herald-Tribune*, June 18, 1956.

July 4, 1966—Joe Adcock Interview, 1984 and *Los Angeles Times*, July 6, 1966.

September 3, 1961—*Milwaukee Sentinel* and *Chicago Tribune*, September 4, 1961.

September 2, 1966—*Los Angeles Times* and *Washington Evening Star*, September 3, 1966.

July 21, 1962—*Philadelphia Inquirer* and *Milwaukee Journal*, July 22, 1962.

April 29, 1953—*New York Herald-Tribune* and *New York Times*, April 30, 1953.

July 3, 1959—*Pittsburgh Press*, July 5, 1959 and *Milwaukee Sentinel*, July 4, 1959.

August 3, 1958—*Milwaukee Sentinel* and *Milwaukee Journal*, August 4, 1958.

July 18, 1953—*Milwaukee Sentinel* and *Milwaukee Journal*, July 19, 1953.

September 10, 1961—*Milwaukee Sentinel* and *Pittsburgh Post-Gazette*, September 11, 1961.

SAMMY SOSA

June 24, 2003—Author Eyewitness and *Chicago Tribune*, June 25, 2003.

August 20, 1999 (#1)—Author Eyewitness.

October 8, 2003—Author Eyewitness.

August 10, 2002 (#1)—Author Eyewitness.

May 4, 1999—Author Eyewitness and *Chicago Tribune*, May 5, 1999.

April 12, 2002—Author Eyewitness and *Chicago Tribune*, April 13, 2002.

July 20, 2003—Author Eyewitness and *Chicago Tribune*, July 21, 2003.

August 30, 1998—Author Eyewitness.

August 10, 1998—Author Eyewitness and *New York Times*, August 11, 1998.

September 13, 1998—Author Eyewitness.

RALPH KINER

April 22, 1950—Ralph Kiner Interview, 1987 and *Pittsburgh Press*, April 23, 1950.

May 8, 1949—*Boston Globe* and *Pittsburgh Press*, May 9, 1949.

August 5, 1951 (#3)—*Philadelphia Bulletin* and *Pittsburgh Post-Gazette*, August 6, 1951.

September 3, 1949—*Pittsburgh Press* and *Chicago Tribune*, September 4, 1949.

August 15, 1950—*Pittsburgh Press* and *Pittsburgh Post-Gazette*, August 16, 1950.

August 24, 1949—*Boston Globe* and *Pittsburgh Press*, August 25, 1949.

August 31, 1949—*Pittsburgh Press* and *Pittsburgh Post-Gazette*, September 1, 1949.

July 14, 1950—*Pittsburgh Press* and *New York Daily Mirror*, July 15, 1950.

July 20, 1949 (#2)—*Pittsburgh Press* and *New York Times*, July 21, 1949.

June 11, 1950 (#2)—*Philadelphia Bulletin* and *Philadelphia Inquirer*, June 12, 1950.

DAVE KINGMAN

April 14, 1976—*New York Times* and *Chicago Tribune*, April 15, 1976.

August 14, 1981—*Philadelphia Daily News* and *Philadelphia Bulletin*, August 15, 1981.

August 15, 1978—*Atlanta Journal* and *Chicago Tribune*, August 16, 1978.

May 13, 1977—*Los Angeles Times* and *New York Times*, May 14, 1977.

June 1, 1977—Montreal Expos Media Relations and *New York Times*, June 2, 1977.

September 12, 1973—*San Francisco Chronicle* and *San Francisco Examiner*, September 13, 1973.

April 20, 1979—*Chicago Tribune* and *Montreal Gazette*, April 21, 1979.

April 27, 1976—*New York Daily News* and *New York Times*, April 28, 1976.

June 21, 1977—*San Diego Union* and *Pittsburgh Press*, June 22, 1977.

September 2, 1986—Author Eyewitness and *New York Times*, September 3, 1986.

TED WILLIAMS

June 9, 1946—Ted Williams Interview, 1986 and *Boston Globe*, June 10, 1946.

May 7, 1941 (#2)—*Boston Herald* and *Boston Post*, May 8, 1941.

May 18, 1946—*Boston Post* and *Boston Globe*, May 19, 1946.

August 7, 1958—*Boston Globe* and *Washington Post*, August 8, 1958.

May 4, 1939 (#2)—*Detroit News* and *Boston Globe*, May 5, 1939.

September 3, 1954—*Philadelphia Bulletin* and *Philadelphia Inquirer*, September 4, 1954.

May 29, 1954—*Boston Herald* and *New York Times*, May 30, 1954.

July 23, 1955—*Chicago Tribune* and *Boston Globe*, July 24, 1955.

July 2, 1958—*Boston Globe* and *Washington Post*, July 3, 1958.

April 16, 1946—Ted Williams Interview, 1986 and *Boston Globe*, April 17, 1946.

GREG LUZINSKI

May 21, 1977—*Philadelphia Bulletin* and *Philadelphia Inquirer*, May 22, 1977.

May 16, 1972—Author Eyewitness and *Philadelphia Bulletin*, May 17, 1972.

September 3, 1972—*Philadelphia Bulletin* and *Philadelphia Inquirer*, September 4, 1972.

August 28, 1983—*Chicago Tribune* and *Chicago Sun-Times*, August 29, 1983.

July 11, 1973—*Philadelphia Bulletin* and *Philadelphia Inquirer*, July 12, 1973.

August 5, 1979—Author Eyewitness and *Philadelphia Inquirer*, August 6, 1979.

May 8, 1976—*Los Angeles Times* and *Philadelphia Inquirer*, May 9, 1976.

August 1, 1976—*Philadelphia Bulletin*, August 2, 1976 and *Sporting News*, August 21, 1976.

April 18, 1979—*Philadelphia Daily News* and *Philadelphia Inquirer*, April 19, 1979.

June 26, 1983—*Chicago Tribune* and *Chicago Sun-Times*, June 27, 1983.

J. D. DREW

May 16, 2003—*St. Louis Post-Dispatch*, July 17, 2003 and St. Louis Cardinals Media Relations.

April 12, 2002—*St. Louis Post-Dispatch*, April 13, 2002 and St. Louis Cardinals Media Relations.

September 10, 2003—Author Eyewitness.

May 17, 2001—Author Eyewitness and *Tribune-Review* (Pittsburgh), May 18, 2001.

July 26, 2008—Author Eyewitness and Hit Tracker.

May 31, 2003—Author Eyewitness and *St. Louis Post-Dispatch*, June 1, 2003.

May 7, 2005—Author Eyewitness.

July 2, 2005—Author Eyewitness.

July 3, 2009—Author Eyewitness.

August 12, 2004—Author Eyewitness and *Atlanta Journal-Constitution*, August 13, 2004.

ALBERT PUJOLS

August 31, 2003—Author Eyewitness.

July 13, 2007—Author Eyewitness.

June 30, 2009—Author Eyewitness.

April 25, 2009—Author Eyewitness.

September 26, 2004—Author Eyewitness.

July 15, 2007—Author Eyewitness.

April 23, 2002—Author Eyewitness.

May 3, 2003—Author Eyewitness.

May 25, 2002—Author Eyewitness.

April 3, 2006—Author Eyewitness.

PRINCE FIELDER

May 12, 2006—Author Eyewitness.

September 24, 2007—Author Eyewitness.

May 29, 2006—Author Eyewitness.

June 30, 2009—Author Eyewitness

April 18, 2006—Author Eyewitness.

May 21, 2007—Author Eyewitness.

October 5, 2008—Author Eyewitness.

September 16, 2008—Author Eyewitness.

July 13, 2007—Author Eyewitness.

September 16, 2006—Author Eyewitness.

FRANK THOMAS

July 23, 2002—Author Eyewitness and *Chicago Tribune*, July 24, 2002.

April 4, 1998—Frank Thomas Interview, 2002 and Author Eyewitness.

May 16, 1992—Author Eyewitness.

July 5, 1994—Frank Thomas Interview, 2002 and Author Eyewitness.

May 20, 1995—Author Eyewitness.

July 3, 2005—Author Eyewitness and *Chicago Tribune*, July 4, 2005.

August 4, 2003—Author Eyewitness.

September 8, 1997 (#2)—Author Eyewitness.

April 7, 2007—Author Eyewitness.

July 23, 1993—Author Eyewitness and *Chicago Tribune*, July 24, 1993.

WILY MO PENA

April 17, 2005—Author Eyewitness and Cincinnati Reds Media Relations.

June 29, 2005—Author Eyewitness.

July 31, 2006—Author Eyewitness and *Boston Globe*, August 1, 2006.

August 14, 2004—Author Eyewitness and *Cincinnati Enquirer*, August 15, 2004.

April 17, 2007—Author Eyewitness and Hit Tracker.

August 8, 2006—Author Eyewitness.

August 12, 2006—Author Eyewitness.
September 18, 2004—Author Eyewitness.
August 10, 2006—Author Eyewitness.
July 2, 2005—Author Eyewitness.

ALEX RODRIGUEZ

August 13, 2005—Author Eyewitness and New York Yankees Media Relations.
June 15, 2006—Author Eyewitness and New York Yankees Media Relations.
August 9, 2008—Author Eyewitness.
June 30, 2008—Author Eyewitness.
April 6, 1998—Author Eyewitness.
June 17, 2007—Author Eyewitness and *New York Times*, June 18, 2007.
July 10, 2004—Author Eyewitness and *New York Times*, July 11, 2004.
July 17, 2005—Author Eyewitness.
April 16, 2008—Author Eyewitness.
August 15, 2005—Author Eyewitness and *New York Times*, August 16, 2005.

MANNY RAMIREZ

June 23, 2001—Author Eyewitness and Boston Red Sox Media Relations.
June 3, 2001—Author Eyewitness.
July 26, 2007—Author Eyewitness.
October 7, 2007—Author Eyewitness.
September 19, 1999—Author Eyewitness and *New York Times*, September 20, 1999.
July 1, 1997—Author Eyewitness.
April 19, 2005—Author Eyewitness.
October 1, 2005—Author Eyewitness and *Boston Globe*, October 2, 2005.

October 1, 2005—Author Eyewitness and *Boston Globe*, October 2, 2005.
May 4, 2004—Author Eyewitness and *Cleveland Plain Dealer*, May 5, 2004.

RYAN HOWARD

April 23, 2006—Author Eyewitness.
June 20, 2006—Author Eyewitness.
April 5, 2008—Author Eyewitness.
June 27, 2007—Author Eyewitness.
May 30, 2009—Author Eyewitness.
August 31, 2006—Author Eyewitness.
June 30, 2007—Author Eyewitness.
July 15, 2006—Author Eyewitness.
August 30, 2007—Author Eyewitness.
August 19, 2006—Author Eyewitness.

JIM THOME

July 3, 1999—*Cleveland Plain Dealer*, July 4, 1999 and Cleveland Indians Media Relations.
May 31, 1998—Author Eyewitness.
July 17, 2000—Author Eyewitness.
May 30, 2002—Author Eyewitness and *Cleveland Plain Dealer*, May 31, 2002.
May 8, 2001—Author Eyewitness.
July 6, 2001—Author Eyewitness and *Cleveland Plain Dealer*, July 7, 2001.
July 26, 2002—Author Eyewitness.
April 7, 2000—Author Eyewitness and *Cleveland Plain Dealer*, April 8, 2000.
June 4, 2008—Author Eyewitness.
July 7, 2001—Author Eyewitness.

ADAM DUNN

August 10, 2004—Adam Dunn Interview, 2005 and *Cincinnati Enquirer*, August 11, 2004.

September 27, 2008—Author Eyewitness and Hit Tracker.

October 2, 2001—Adam Dunn Interview, 2005 and *Chicago Tribune,* October 3, 2001.

April 6, 2006—Author Eyewitness.

September 20, 2001—Author Eyewitness.

July 28, 2009—Author Eyewitness.

September 11, 2007—Author Eyewitness.

May 4, 2005—Author Eyewitness and Cincinnati Reds Media Relations.

May 17, 2008—Author Eyewitness.

June 16, 2005—Author Eyewitness.

REGGIE JACKSON

July 13, 1971—Reggie Jackson Interview, 1986 and Author Eyewitness.

July 5, 1969—Reggie Jackson Interview, 1986 and *Oakland Tribune*, July 6, 1969.

April 20, 1969—Reggie Jackson Interview, 1986 and *Oakland Tribune*, April 21, 1969.

July 20, 1976—*Baltimore Sun* and *Washington Post*, July 21, 1976.

September 1, 1968—*San Francisco Examiner* and *Los Angeles Times*, September 2, 1968.

June 16, 1969—*Oakland Tribune* and *San Francisco Chronicle*, June 17, 1969.

July 20, 1973—*San Francisco Examiner* and *San Francisco Chronicle*, July 21, 1973.

July 6, 1971—*Chicago Tribune* and *Chicago Sun-Times*, July 7, 1971.

June 23, 1972—*Oakland Tribune* and *San Francisco Examiner*, June 24, 1972.

April 15, 1983—Author Eyewitness and *Los Angeles Times*, April 16, 1983.

HARMON KILLEBREW

June 3, 1967—Harmon Killebrew Interview, 1988 and *Sporting News*, June 17, 1967.

June 4, 1967—*Minneapolis Star*, June 5, 1967 and *Sporting News*, June 17, 1967.

August 3, 1962—Harmon Killebrew Interview and *Minneapolis Tribune*, August 14, 1962.

August 6, 1960—Harmon Killebrew Interview, 1988 and *Washington Star*, August 7, 1960.

June 19, 1959—*Washington Star* and *Washington Post*, June 20, 1959.

July 11, 1959—*Washington Post* and *New York Times*/UPI, July 12, 1959.

May 10, 1961—*Minneapolis Star* and *Minneapolis Tribune*, May 11, 1961.

June 18, 1963—*Chicago Tribune* and *Minneapolis Tribune*, June 19, 1963.

June 20, 1966—*Minneapolis Star* and *Minneapolis Tribune*, June 21, 1966.

April 30, 1961—*Minneapolis Star* and *Minneapolis Tribune*, May 1, 1961.

WILLIE McCOVEY

September 4, 1966—Bob Gibson Interview, 1987 and *St. Louis Post-Dispatch*, September 6, 1966.

May 22, 1967—*Philadelphia Bulletin* and *Oakland Tribune*, May 23, 1967.

September 16, 1966—*San Francisco Chronicle* and *New York Daily News*, September 17, 1966.

June 6, 1969—*Philadelphia Daily News* and *Philadelphia Bulletin*, June 7, 1969.

June 22, 1969—*Atlanta Constitution* and *San Francisco Examiner*, June 23, 1969.

September 8, 1965—*San Francisco Chronicle* and *Oakland Tribune*, September 9, 1965.

September 26, 1963—*Philadelphia Bulletin* and *San Francisco Chronicle*, September 27, 1963.

September 9, 1960—*San Francisco Chronicle* and *Cincinnati Enquirer*, September 10, 1960.

September 9, 1961—*Los Angeles Times* and *San Francisco Chronicle*, September 10, 1961.

May 10, 1962—*St. Louis Post-Dispatch* and *San Francisco Chronicle*, May 11, 1962.

WILLIE STARGELL

July 3, 1967—Willie Stargell Interview, 1983 and *Pittsburgh Post-Gazette*, July 4, 1967.

May 20, 1978—*Pittsburgh Press* and United Press International, May 21, 1978.

August 19, 1969—*Pittsburgh Press* and *Pittsburgh Post-Gazette*, August 20, 1969.

August 9, 1970—*Pittsburgh Press* and *Pittsburgh Post-Gazette*, August 10, 1970.

July 4, 1979—*Pittsburgh Press* and *St. Louis Post-Dispatch*, July 5, 1979.

August 5, 1969—*Pittsburgh Post-Gazette* and *Los Angeles Times*, August 6, 1969.

May 11, 1964—*Pittsburgh Press* and *Cincinnati Enquirer*, May 12, 1964.

April 20, 1970—*Houston Post* and *Pittsburgh Press*, April 21, 1970.

June 25, 1971—Willie Stargell Interview, 1983 and *Philadelphia Bulletin*, June 26, 1971.

May 31, 1973—*Atlanta Journal* and *Pittsburgh Press*, June 1, 1973.

MARK McGWIRE

May 12, 1998—Mark McGwire Interview, 1999 and Author Eyewitness.

May 16, 1998—Mark McGwire Interview, 1999 and Author Eyewitness.

September 16, 1997—Author Eyewitness and St. Louis Cardinals Media Relations.

July 17, 1998—Author Eyewitness and St. Louis Cardinals Media Relations.

August 26, 1998—Author Eyewitness and St. Louis Cardinals Media Relations.

June 24, 1997—Mark McGwire Interview, 1999 and Author Eyewitness.

September 2, 1997—Author Eyewitness and St. Louis Cardinals Media Relations.

April 23, 2000—Author Eyewitness and St. Louis Cardinals Media Relations.

August 30, 1998—Author Eyewitness and St. Louis Cardinals Media Relations.

August 22, 1997—Author Eyewitness and St. Louis Cardinals Media Relations.

DICK ALLEN

June 6, 1967—*Philadelphia Daily News* and *Philadelphia Inquirer*, June 7, 1967.

July 6, 1974—*Detroit Free Press* and *Chicago Tribune*, July 7, 1974.

May 29, 1965—*Philadelphia Bulletin* and *Philadelphia Inquirer*, May 30, 1965.

August 19, 1966—Author Eyewitness and *Philadelphia Inquirer*, August 20, 1966.

June 15, 1966—*Philadelphia Daily News* and *Philadelphia Inquirer*, June 16, 1966.

June 21, 1969—Willie Stargell Interview, 1983 and *Philadelphia Bulletin*, June 22, 1969.

August 22, 1964—*Philadelphia Inquirer* and *Philadelphia Bulletin*, August 23, 1964.

June 10, 1965—Bill Conlin Interview, 1995 and *Philadelphia Bulletin*, June 11, 1965.

June 16, 1967—Author Eyewitness and *Philadelphia Inquirer*, June 17, 1967.

May 1, 1973—Dick Allen Interview, 1986 and *Baltimore Sun*, May 2, 1973.

FRANK HOWARD

September 24, 1967—*Washington Post* and *Los Angeles Times*/UPI, September 25, 1967.

July 7, 1969—*Washington Post* and *Hartford Courant*/AP, July 8, 1969.

April 24, 1970—*Los Angeles Times* and *Washington Post*, April 25, 1970.

April 25, 1966—*Chicago Daily Tribune* and *Washington Post*, April 26, 1966.

May 25, 1960—*Los Angeles Times*, May 26, 1960 and *Sporting News*, June 15, 1960.

July 30, 1965—*Washington Post* and *Chicago Tribune*/AP, July 31, 1965.

July 18, 1965—*New York Herald-Tribune* and *Washington Post*, July 19, 1965.

May 18, 1968—*Washington Post* and United Press International, May 19, 1968.

August 25, 1971—*Los Angeles Times* and *Washington Post*, August 26, 1971.

August 16, 1963—*Los Angeles Herald-Examiner* and *Los Angeles Times*, August 17, 1963.

MICKEY MANTLE

May 22, 1963—Author Eyewitness and *New York Times*, May 23, 1963.

April 17, 1956 (#1)—*New York Herald-Tribune* and *New York Times*, April 18, 1956.

July 6, 1953—*Philadelphia Inquirer* and *Philadelphia Bulletin*, July 7, 1953.

September 12, 1953—*New York Times* and *Washington Post*/AP, September 13, 1953.

August 23, 1956—*New York Times* and *Chicago American* (second edition), August 24, 1956.

August 12, 1964—*New York Times* and *Chicago Daily Tribune* (sketch), August 13, 1964.

April 17, 1953—*Sporting News*, April 29, 1953 and *Washington Post*, April 18, 1953.

September 21, 1956—*Boston Herald* and *New York Herald-Tribune*, September 22, 1956.

June 21, 1955—*New York Times* and *Hartford Courant*/AP, June 22, 1955.

April 28, 1953—*St. Louis Post-Dispatch* and *New York Herald-Tribune*, April 29, 1953.

JIMMIE FOXX

June 16, 1936 (#1)—*Boston Globe* and *Chicago Tribune*, June 17, 1936.

May 14, 1932—*Philadelphia Record* and *Philadelphia Inquirer*, May 15, 1932.

July 18, 1930—*Philadelphia Public Ledger* and *Philadelphia Bulletin*, July 19, 1930.

September 10, 1929—*Philadelphia Record* and *Philadelphia Inquirer*, September 11, 1929.

June 20, 1932—*Philadelphia Bulletin* and *Chicago Herald & Examiner*, June 21, 1932.

June 25, 1932—*New York Herald-Tribune* and *Philadelphia Inquirer*, June 26, 1932.

August 22, 1931—*Chicago Daily News* and *Philadelphia Inquirer*, August 23, 1931.

August 16, 1940 (#1)—*Boston Post* and *Boston Herald*, August 17, 1940.

April 12, 1932—*Philadelphia Public Ledger* and *Philadelphia Record*, April 13, 1932.

August 2, 1940—*Boston Herald* and *Boston Globe*, August 3, 1940.

BABE RUTH

July 18, 1921—*Detroit Free Press* and *New York Sunday Herald*, July 19, 1921.

May 22, 1930—*Philadelphia Record* and *New York World*, May 23, 1930.

August 17, 1921—*New York World* and *Chicago Daily Tribune*, August 18, 1921.

May 25, 1926—*Boston Post* (sketch) and *Boston Herald*, May 26, 1926.

May 25, 1935—*Pittsburgh Post-Gazette*, May 27, 1935 and *Boston Globe*, May 26, 1935.

May 25, 1921—*St. Louis Globe-Democrat* and *New York Times*, May 26, 1921.

July 31, 1921—*New York Times* and *New York Tribune*, August 1, 1921.

October 6, 1926—*St. Louis Post-Democrat* and *New York Evening Journal*, October 7, 1926.

May 27, 1920—*Boston Post* (sketch) and *New York Herald*, May 28, 1920.

May 31, 1924—*Philadelphia Record* and *New York Herald-Tribune*, June 1, 1924.

SELECTED BIBLIOGRAPHY

Adair, Robert K. *The Physics of Baseball*. New York: Harper & Row Publishers, 1990.

Alexander, Charles. *John McGraw*. New York: Viking Penguin Inc., 1988.

Alexander, Charles. *Ty Cobb*. New York, Oxford: Oxford University Press, 1984.

Allen, Bob with Gilbert, Bill. *The 500 Home Run Club*. Champaign, IL: Sports Publishing Inc., 1999.

Bak, Richard. *Turkey Stearnes and the Detroit Stars: The Negro Leagues in Detroit, 1919–1933*. Detroit: Wayne State University Press, 1994.

Canseco, Jose. *Juiced: Wild Times, Rampant 'Roids, Smash Hits, and How Baseball Got Big*. New York: Regan Books, 2005.

Canter, Len. *Babe Ruth*. New York: Baronet Books, 1996.

Casway, Jerrold. *Ed Delahanty in the Golden Age of Baseball*. Notre Dame: University of Notre Dame Press, 2004.

Cobbledick, Gordon. *Don't Knock the Rock: The Rocky Colavito Story*. Cleveland and New York: The World Publishing Story, 1966.

Considine, Bob. *The Babe Ruth Story*. New York: E.P. Dutton and Co., Inc., 1948.

Cramer, Richard Ben. *Joe DiMaggio: The Hero's Life*. New York: Simon & Schuster, 2000.

Creamer, Robert W. *Babe: The Legend Comes to Life*. New York: Simon & Schuster, 1974.

Curran, William. *Big Sticks: The Phenomenal Decade of Ruth, Gehrig, Cobb and Hornsby*. New York: Harper Collins Publishers, 1990.

DeValeria, Dennis and DeValeria, Jeanne Burke. *Honus Wagner: A Biography*. Pittsburgh: University of Pittsburgh Press, 1998.

Eig, Jonathan. *Luckiest Man: The Life and Death of Lou Gehrig*. New York: Simon & Schuster, 2005.

Fleming, G.H. *Murderers' Row: The 1927 New York Yankees*. New York: William Morrow and Company, Inc., 1985.

Frommer, Harvey. *Shoeless Joe and Ragtime Baseball*. Dallas: Taylor Publishing Company, 1992.

Gallagher, Mark. *Explosion: Mickey Mantle's Legendary Home Runs*. New York: Arbor House, 1987.

Gilliam, Richard, ed. *Joltin' Joe DiMaggio*. New York: Carroll & Graf Publishers, 1999.

Hochman, Stan. *Mike Schmidt: Baseball's King of Swing*. New York: Random House, 1983.

Hogan, Lawrence D. *Shades of Glory*. Washington, D.C.: National Geographic, 2006.

Holway, John B. *Josh and Satch: The Life and Times of Josh Gibson and Satchel Paige*. New York: Carroll & Graf, 1991.

Holway, John B. *Black Diamonds: Life in the Negro Leagues from the Men Who Lived It*. New York: Stadium Books, 1991.

Holway, John B. *The Complete Book of Baseball's Negro League: The Other Half of Baseball History*. Fern Park, FL: 2001. Hastings House Publishers.

Honig, Donald. *Baseball When the Grass Was Real*. New York: Coward, McCann and Geoghegan, Inc., 1975.

Honig, Donald. *The New York Yankees: An Illustrated History*. New York: Crown Publishers, Inc., 1981.

Jackson, Reggie with Lupica, Mike. *Reggie: The Autobiography of Reggie Jackson*. New York: Villard Books, 1984.

Kashatus, William. *Connie Mack's '29 Triumph*. Jefferson, NC and London: MacFarland and Company, Inc., 1999.

Lally, Richard. *Bombers: An Oral History of the New York Yankees*. New York: Crown Publishers, 2002.

Linn, Ed. *Hitter: The Life and Turmoils of Ted Williams*. San Diego: Harcourt Brace & Company, 1993.

McConnell, Bob and Vincent, David, eds. *The Home Run Encyclopedia*. New York: Macmillan, 1996.

Meany, Tom. *Babe Ruth: The Big Moments of the Big Fellow*. New York: Grosset and Dunlap, 1947.

Miller, Ernestine. *The Babe Book: Baseball's Greatest Legend Remembered*. Kansas City: Andrews McMeel Publishing, 2000.

Montville, Leigh. *The Big Bam: The Life and Times of Babe Ruth*. New York: Doubleday, 2006.

Nelson, Don. *Baseball's Home Run Hitters: The Sultans of Swat*. New York: Leisure Press, 1984.

Neyer, Rob and Epstein, Eddie. *Baseball Dynasties: The Greatest Teams of All Times*. New York, London: W.W. Norton and Company, 2000.

Nicholson, Lois P. *Babe Ruth: Sultan of Swat*. Woodbury, CT: Goodwood Press, 1994.

Pearlman, Jeff. *Love Me, Hate Me: Barry Bonds and the Making of an Antihero*. New York: Harper Collins Publishers, 2006.

Peterson, Robert. *Only the Ball Was White: A History of Legendary Black Players and All-Black Professional Teams.* New York: Gramercy Books, 1970.

Pirrone, Dorothy Ruth. *My Dad, The Babe: Growing Up with an American Hero.* Boston: Quinlan Press, 1988.

Plimpton, George, ed. *Home Run.* San Diego and New York: Harcourt, Inc., 2001.

Ribowsky, Mark. *A Complete History of the Negro League, 1884–1955.* Secaucus, NJ: A Citadel Press Book, 1997.

Ribowsky, Mark. *The Complete History of the Home Run.* New York: Citadel Press, 2003.

Riley, James A. *The Negro Leagues.* Philadelphia: Chelsea House Publishers, 1997.

Ritter, Lawrence and Rucker, Mark. *The Babe: The Game that Ruth Built.* New York: Total Sports, 1997.

Robinson, Ray. *Iron Horse: Lou Gehrig in His Time.* New York, London: W.W. Norton and Company, 1990.

Rust, Art. *Get That Nigger Off the Field: An Informal History of the Black Man in Baseball.* New York: Delacorte Press, 1976.

Schmidt, Mike with Waggoner, Glen. *Clearing the Bases.* New York: Harper Collins Publishers, 2006.

Shaughnessy, Dan. *The Curse of the Bambino.* New York: Penguin Books, 1990.

Smelser, Marshall. *The Life That Ruth Built: A Biography.* Lincoln and London: University of Nebraska Press, 1975.

Smith, Curt. *Storied Stadiums: Baseball's History Through Its Ballparks.* New York: Carroll and Graf Publishers, 2001.

Snyder, Brad. *Beyond the Shadow of Senators*. Chicago, New York: Contemporary Books, 2003.

Sobol, Ken. *Babe Ruth and the American Dream*. New York: Ballantine Books, 1974.

Sowell, Mike. *The Pitch That Killed*. New York: Macmillan Publishing Co., 1989.

Stargell, Willie and Bird, Tom. *Willie Stargell: An Autobiography*. New York: Harper & Row Publishers, 1984.

Staten, Vince. *Ol' Diz: A Biography of Dizzy Dean*. New York: Harper Collins Publishers, 1992.

Vincent, David. *Home Run: The Definitive History of Baseball's Ultimate Weapon*. Washington, D.C.: Potomac Books, Inc., 2007.

Wagenheim, Kal. *Babe Ruth: His Life and Legend*. Chicago: Olmstead Press, 2001.

Wood, Allan. *Babe Ruth: And the 1918 Red Sox*. San Jose, New York, Lincoln, Shanghai: Writers Club Press, 2000.

Note: As discussed, the primary sources of information for this book are the thousands of newspaper articles published in the hundreds of different newspapers that have been reviewed.

INDEX

A

Aaron, Henry, 10, 13, 14, 16–19
  greatest batting/throwing/running and, 294–95
  mini-biography, 16–19
  tape measure calendar dates, 266, 269, 274
  ten longest home runs, 18
  top slugger ranking, 237
Abercrombie, Reggie, 270, 290
Adcock, Joe, 10, 92–95
  longest final career homer, 290
  longest fly out, 287
  longest homers by stadium, 243, 252, 254
  longest opposite field homer, 288
  longest pinch-hit homer, 292
  mini-biography, 92–95
  tape measure calendar dates, 271, 274, 275, 276, 279
  ten longest home runs, 95
  top 100 longest homer of, 241
  top slugger ranking, 237
Agee, Tommy, 255, 269
Allen, Dick (Richie), XIV, 10, 164–68
  longest home run, XV, 219–20
  longest homers by stadium, 248, 250, 252, 255, 257, 260, 264
  longest opposite field homer, 293
  longest spring training homer, 288
  mini-biography, 164–68
  monstrous blast in Detroit, 230
  power ranking by position, 283
  tape measure calendar dates, 267, 269, 272, 273, 274, 275, 278
  ten longest home runs, 168
  top 100 longest homers of, 239, 240, 241
  top slugger ranking, 195, 237
  writing of this book and, XV
All-Star homers, longest, 289–90
Ashburn, Richie, 133, 301

B

Bagwell, Jeff, 238
Bailey, Bob, 238
Baines, Harold, 238
Balboni, Steve, 238, 244, 279
ball, history of, 4–5
Banks, Ernie, 10, 238, 265, 283, 302
Barfield, Jesse, 296, 297
Barnes, Ross, 2, 3
Baro, Bernardo, 301
Beckwith, John, 67–70, 71, 197, 238, 295
Bell, Buddy, 89
Bell, George, 238
Bell, Gus, XIII, 89
Bell, James "Cool Papa," 71, 77, 301
Belle, Albert, 238
Bench, Johnny, 219, 238, 283, 288, 289, 297
Berger, Wally, 44–45, 237, 273
Berkman, Lance, 142, 264
Bilko, Steve, 238
Blue, Vida, 219, 299
Bonds, Barry, 12, 89–92, 133
  greatest batting/throwing/running and, 294–95
  longest homer by player over 40, 291
  longest homers by stadium, 260, 265
  longest postseason homer, 289
  longest single, 285
  mini-biography, 89–92
  tape measure calendar dates, 277, 278, 279, 282
  ten longest home runs, 91
  top slugger ranking, 237
Bonds, Bobby, 268
book overview, 13
Borchard, Joe, 247, 279
Branyan, Russell, 142, 265, 276
Brett, George, 271, 292
Brouthers, Dan, 3, 5, 54, 61–64, 197, 198, 201, 237, 274
Buhner, Jay, 237, 276
Burks, Ellis, 238
Burroughs, Jeff, 244, 269

C

Caffie, Joe, 300, 301, 302
calendar, longest homers by date, 266–82
Canseco, Jose, 12, 83–86
  greatest batting/throwing/running and, 294–95
  longest first career homer, 290
  longest homers by stadium, 249, 256, 262
  longest postseason homer, 289
  mini-biography, 83–86
  power ranking by position, 284
  tape measure calendar dates, 273, 275, 280, 281
  ten longest home runs, 85
  top slugger ranking, 237
Carlyle, Roy "Dizzy," 202–3
Carter, Joe, 238, 276
Casale, Jerry, 293
Case, George Washington, 301–2
Cash, Norm, 10, 43–44, 237, 240, 277
Cepeda, Orlando, 152, 238, 261, 268, 270
Cerv, Bob, 238, 239, 251, 268, 272, 286
Charleston, Oscar, 68, 77, 197, 295
Chavez, Eric, 270
Clark, Jack, 109, 238
Clemens, Roger, 95, 299
Clemente, Roberto, 157, 199, 238, 241, 247, 272, 295, 296, 297
Coan, Gil, 300–301
Cobb, Ty, 8, 55, 71, 181, 189, 227
Colavito, Rocky, XIV, 198–99, 237, 277, 290, 295–96, 297, 300
Colbert, Nate, 238, 260, 269, 276
Coleman, Vince, 301
Conigliaro, Tony, 291
Connor, Roger, 3, 4, 5, 54, 58–60, 198, 237
Cooke, Dusty, 287
Covington, Wes, 238
Crawford, Carl, 301
Crawford, Sam, 7, 55, 198, 238
criteria for rankings, 14–15
Cruz, Nelson, 142
current sluggers, 111–42
  Adam Dunn, 12, 138–41, 239, 264, 265, 269, 277, 280, 281, 293
  Albert Pujols, 12, 114–16, 265, 279

Alex Rodriguez, 12, 126–29, 186, 277, 283
Frank Thomas, 12, 120–23, 247, 276, 284
honorable mentions, 141–42
J. D. Drew, 111–13, 272
Manny Ramirez, 12, 129–32, 262, 273, 274, 276
Prince Fielder, 117–19
Ryan Howard, 12, 132–35, 138, 265, 270
Thome, Jim, 12, 123, 132, 133, 135–38, 241, 247, 262, 264, 275
Wily Mo Pena, 12, 123–26, 270, 275

D
Dalkowski, Steve, 298–99
date, longest homers by, 266–82
Davis, Eric, 238, 293
Davis, Willie, 301, 302
Dawson, Andre, 238, 254, 295
"Dead Ball Era," 4–5, 52, 56, 187, 197, 198, 290, 292
Deer, Rob, 237
Delahanty, Ed, 5, 50–52, 54, 198, 238, 295
Delgado, Carlos, 141, 142, 276, 277, 279
Dietrich, Bill, 290, 292
Dihigo, Martin, 74, 297
Dilone, Miguel, 301
DiMaggio, Joe, 115, 174, 238, 249, 267, 281, 286, 295
Doby, Larry, 10, 33–34, 197, 237, 241, 272, 284
doubles, longest, 286
Drew, J. D., 111–13, 272
Drysdale, Don, 23, 152, 156, 157, 283
Duncan, Dave, 283
Dunn, Adam, 12, 138–41, 239, 264, 265, 269, 277, 280, 281, 293
Dunston, Shawon, 296, 297
Durham, Leon, 275
Dye, Jermaine, 251

E
Easter, Luke, 10, 40–42, 197, 237, 249, 272, 274, 276, 277, 300
Ellsbury, Jacob, 301
Ennis, Del, XII, XIV, 288
Epstein, Mike, 238, 263

Eusebio, Tony, 290
Ewing, William "Buck," 6–7, 51, 75–76, 198, 238, 274

F
Falk, Bibb, 285
Falls, Joe, XV, XVI, 296
fastest runners, 299–302
fastest starting pitchers, 297–99
Feller, Bob, 298, 299
Ferrell, Wes, 283, 292
Fielder, Cecil, 12, 82–89, 237, 242, 252, 273, 275, 278, 280, 281
Fielder, Prince, 117–19
Figgins, Chone, 302
final career homers, longest, 290
first career homers, longest, 290
fly outs, longest, 287–88
Fondy, Dee, 287
Foster, George, 12, 42–43, 237, 242, 248, 277
Foxx, Jimmie, 180–86, 212
Babe Ruth and, XII, XV–XVI, 9, 183–84, 186
fastest runner by position, 302
greatest batting/throwing/running and, 294–95
longest final career homer, 290
longest homers by stadium, 245, 246, 249, 256
longest homers by teenagers, 291
longest single, 285
longest spring training homers, 288
longest triple, 286
longest walk-off homers, 293
Mickey Mantle and, 194–95
power ranking by position, 283
strength of, 9
tape measure calendar dates, 266, 267, 268, 269, 271, 274, 276, 277, 278, 279, 280
ten longest home runs, 185
top 100 longest homers of, 239, 240, 241
top slugger ranking, 237
Freeman, John "Buck," 7, 55–57, 198, 237, 302

G
Galarraga, Andre, 36–37, 237, 242, 264, 272, 278, 280, 291
Gehrig, Lou, 9, 47–48

Babe Ruth and, 192
exaggerated blast, 203
longest fly out, 287
longest triples, 286
mini-biography, 47–48
stadium photo of homer, 249
tape measure calendar dates, 271, 275, 281, 282
top 100 longest homers of, 241
top slugger ranking, 237
Gentile, Jim, 237, 245, 270
Giambi, Jason, 273
Gibson, Josh, 9–10, 71, 74, 75–79
legendary home runs, 203–4
mini-biography, 75–79
tape measure calendar dates, 276, 277, 280
top slugger ranking, 196–97, 237
Gibson, Kirk, 12, 34–35, 237, 241, 242, 271, 273
Glaus, Troy, 270
Gomes, Jonny, 279
Gonzalez, Adrian, 265
Gonzalez, Juan, 238, 281
Gooden, Dwight "Doc," 299
Gorbous, Glen, 295, 297
Grate, Don, 295, 297
greatest batting/throwing/running individuals, 294–95
Green, Shawn, 93, 269
Greenberg, Hank, 10, 31–32, 99, 237, 268, 270, 276, 280, 287
Grich, Bobby, 283
Griffey, Ken, Jr., 12, 89, 123, 142, 295
Griffey, Ken, Sr., 89
Grove, Lefty, 165, 181, 299
Guerrero, Vladimir, 142, 254, 277, 285, 297

H
Hafner, Travis, 142, 284
Hamilton, Billy, 7–8, 51, 301
Hamilton, Josh, 142
Harper, Bryce, 236
Hatfield, John, 297
Heilmann, Harry, 228, 238, 241, 275
Henderson, Rickey, 301
Hill, Glenallen, 238, 271
Hodges, Gil, XIV, 287
Hornsby, Rogers, 198, 208, 237, 246, 273, 283, 290
Horton, Willie, 237, 275, 285, 290, 292
Howard, Frank, XIV, 169–73, 230

exaggerated accounts of
homers, 213
500-foot blasts, 213–14
longest All-Star homer, 289
longest double, 286
longest homers by stadium, 243,
251, 256, 258, 263, 264
longest pinch-hit homer, 292
longest postseason homer, 289
longest spring training
homer, 288
mini-biography, 169–73
power ranking by position, 283
tape measure calendar dates,
267, 268, 270, 272, 275, 276,
277, 278, 280
ten longest home runs, 172
top 100 longest homers of, 239,
240, 241
top slugger ranking, 195, 237
Howard, Ryan, 12, 132–35, 138,
265, 270
Howell, Roy, 261
Hrbek, Kent, 238
Hundley, Todd, 238, 277, 283

I
Ibanez, Raul, 265
Incaviglia, Pete, 238
inside-the-park homers, longest, 287

J
Jackson, Bo, 12, 26–27, 198, 237,
288, 289, 290, 294, 295, 301
Jackson, Joe, 7, 295
Jackson, Reggie, 10, 143–47
legendary All-Star homer,
144–45, 216, 218–19
longest All-Star homer, 289
longest homer by player over
40, 292
longest homers by stadium, 250,
251, 253, 256, 261
longest pinch-hit homer, 292
mini-biography, 143–47
power ranking by position, 284
tape measure calendar dates,
267, 269, 270, 275, 276, 279,
280, 281, 282
ten longest home runs, 146
top 100 longest homers of, 239,
240, 241
top slugger ranking, 196, 237

Jethroe, Sam, 301
Johnson, Bob, 286
Johnson, Randy, 116, 162, 299
Johnson, Walter, 189, 283, 297–98, 299
Jones, Andruw, 258, 274
Jones, Charley, 2–3
Jones, Slim, 299

K
Kelly, George, 297
Kendall, Jason, 302
Kent, Jeff, 283
Killebrew, Harmon, XIV, 10, 147–51
longest first career homer, 290
longest homers by stadium,
245, 253
longest teenager homer, 291
mini-biography, 147–51
power ranking by position, 283
tape measure calendar dates,
273, 274, 275, 277
ten longest home runs, 150
top 100 longest homers of,
240, 241
top slugger ranking, 196, 237
Kiner, Ralph, 10, 98–101
legendary blast, 212–13, 214
longest fly out, 287
longest homers by stadium, 246,
258
longest triple, 286
mini-biography, 98–101
power ranking by position, 284
tape measure calendar dates,
270, 271, 276, 278, 279
ten longest home runs, 101
top 100 longest homers of,
240, 241
top slugger ranking, 237
Kingman, Dave, 12, 101–4
longest homers by stadium, 247,
255
longest spring training
homer, 288
mini-biography, 101–4
by others, 230
tape measure calendar dates,
267, 268, 269, 278
ten longest home runs, 104
top 100 longest homers of,
239, 241
top slugger ranking, 237
Wrigley Field blast, 217–18, 229

Kittle, Ron, 48–49, 237, 280, 284
Klesko, Ryan, 238
Kluszewski, Ted, XIII, 92, 238, 286
Koufax, Sandy, XIV, 166, 170, 299

L
Laabs, Chet, 302
Lajoie, Nap, 7, 52, 54
Lankford, Ray, 272
Lazzeri, Tony, 283
Lee, Cliff, 257
Lee, Derrek, 270
LeJeune, Sheldon "Larry," 296–97
Lemon, Bob, 283
Lemon, Jim, 238, 287
Lloyd, John Henry "Pop," 66, 69,
71, 295
Lockman, Whitey, 285
Lofton, Kenny, 301
longest home runs. See official home
runs, longest
longest rankings
All-Star homers, 289–90
doubles, 286
final career homers, 290
first career homers, 290
fly outs, 287–88
hitters pound for pound, 302
homers by pitchers, 292–93
homers by players over 40,
291–92
homers by stadium. See
stadiums, longest home runs
and photographs
inside-the-park homers, 287
official home runs. See official
home runs, longest
opposite field homers, 288
pinch-hit homers, 292
postseason homers, 289
singles, 285
spring training homers, 288–89
teenager homers, 291
top 100 longest drives, 239–42
triples, 286
walk-off homers, 293
Lopata, Stan, 237, 269, 283, 286,
287–88
Luderus, Fred, 257
Luzinski, Greg, XV, 12, 108–10
longest first career homer, 290
longest homers by stadium, 244,
250, 258, 259

mini-biography, 108–10
power ranking by position, 284
tape measure calendar dates,
    272, 275, 277, 278, 279, 281
ten longest home runs, 110
top 100 longest homer of, 241
top slugger ranking, 197, 237

M
Maloney, Jim, 299
Mantle, Mickey, XV, 173–79
    author recalling, XIV
    500-foot blasts, 204–5,
        214–17, 223
    "Golden Age" of tape measure
        homers and, 10
    greatest batting/throwing/run-
        ning and, 294–95
    Jimmie Foxx and, 181, 194–95
    John Beckwith and, 69
    living up to longest hitter repu-
        tation, 200
    longest doubles, 286
    longest first career homer, 290
    longest fly outs, 287
    longest homers by stadium,
        256, 262
    longest inside-the-park
        homers, 287
    longest opposite field homer, 288
    longest pinch-hit homer, 292
    longest preseason homer, 289
    longest single, 285
    longest spring training
        homers, 288
    longest teenager homers, 291
    longest triple, 286
    longest walk-off homers, 293
    mini-biography, 173–79
    power ranking by position, 284
    speed of, 300, 301, 302
    strength of, 9
    tape measure calendar dates,
        266–67, 268, 269, 270, 271,
        272, 275, 277, 278, 279, 281
    ten longest home runs, 179
    top 100 longest homers of, 239,
        240, 241
    top slugger ranking, 237
Maris, Roger, 144, 177, 238
Mastry, Mike, 233–34
Mathews, Eddie, 38–39, 237, 247, 252,
    271, 283

Mays, Willie, 10, 13, 19–21
    greatest batting/throwing/run-
        ning and, 294–95
    Joe Adcock and, 94
    longest All-Star homer, 289
    longest fly out, 287
    longest fly outs to, 287–88
    longest homers by stadium,
        255, 264
    longest pound-for-pound
        hitter, 302
    mini-biography, 19–21
    power ranking by position, 284
    Ralph Kiner and, 100
    tape measure calendar dates,
        271, 273, 275
    ten longest home runs, 21
    top slugger ranking, 237
McCovey, Willie, XIV, 10, 151–55
    longest double, 286
    longest homers by stadium, 244,
        248, 260, 261
    longest pinch-hit homer, 292
    mini-biography, 151–55
    power ranking by position, 283
    tape measure calendar dates,
        268, 279, 281
    ten longest home runs, 154
    top 100 longest homers of, 241
    top slugger ranking, 237
McDowell, Sam, 299
McGraw, John, 7–8, 57, 63
McGriff, Fred, 12, 25–26, 237, 265,
    273, 279
McGwire, Mark, 160–64, 230
    Andres Galarraga and, 37
    breaking single-season record,
        112
    longest homers by stadium, 252,
        253, 255, 260, 261
    longest opposite field homers, 288
    longest walk-off homer, 293
    power ranking by position, 283
    Sammy Sosa and, 2, 96, 163
    tape measure calendar dates,
        271, 276, 278, 280
    ten longest home runs, 162
    top 100 longest homers of, 239,
        240, 241, 242
    top slugger ranking, 195–96, 237
Medwick, Joe, 257
Meusel, Bob, 296, 297
Miller, Hack, 286

Mitchell, Kevin, 237
Mize, Johnny, 238
Munoz, Pedro, 253, 269
Murray, Eddie, 237, 244
Musial, Stan, 238, 289

N
Negro League, 13, 65–79
    fastest runners, 301
    fastest starting pitchers, 299
    George "Mule" Suttles, 71,
        72–75, 197, 237
    greatest batting/throwing/
        running individuals, 295
    John Beckwith, 67–70, 71, 197,
        238, 295
    longest hitters pound for
        pound, 302
    Louis Santop, 65–67, 197,
        238, 297
    most powerful throwing arms
        (position players), 297
    Norman "Turkey" Stearnes,
        70–72, 197, 237, 295, 302
    See also Gibson, Josh
Nicholson, Bill, 238
Nicholson, Dave, 237, 271

O
official home runs, longest, 211–31
    by Babe Ruth, 211–12, 220–29
    best qualified for longest drive
        in history, 230–31
    by Dave Kingman, 217–18, 229
    by Dick Allen, 219–20
    by Frank Howard, 213–14
    by Jimmie Foxx, 212
    by Mickey Mantle, 214–17, 223
    by Ralph Kiner, 212–13
    by Reggie Jackson, 216, 218–19
Ogilvie, Ben, 253, 276
O'Neill, Paul, 285
opposite field homers, longest, 288
Ordonez, Magglio, 264
Orr, Dave, 4, 290
Ortiz, David, 131, 141, 284
Ott, Mel, 238, 291, 302
Owens, Jesse, 301

P
Paige, Satchel, 71, 77, 299
Palmeiro, Rafael, 238
Parker, Dave, 238, 248, 296, 297

Parrish, Larry, 238
Paschal, Ben, 287
Pasqua, Dan, 267, 271
Pena, Wily Mo, 12, 123–26, 270, 275
Perez, Tony, 237, 274
Piazza, Mike, 12, 45–47, 237, 275, 280, 281, 283
Pike, Lipman, 2, 302
pinch-hit homers, longest, 292
Pinson, Vada, 301
pitchers
    fastest starting pitchers, 297–99
    longest homers by, 292–93
position power rankings, 283–84
Post, Wally, XIII, 39–40, 237, 240, 259, 269, 286, 287
postseason homers, longest, 289
pound for pound, longest hitters, 302
Powell, Boog, 10, 27–28, 237, 245, 276
power rankings by position, 283–84
Pujols, Albert, 12, 114–16, 265, 279

R
Ramirez, Hanley, 283
Ramirez, Manny, 12, 129–32, 262, 273, 274, 276
Ramos, Pedro, 176, 301, 302
rankings
    criteria for, 14–15
    discussion of, 194–200
    fastest runners, 299–302
    fastest starting pitchers, 297–99
    greatest batting/throwing/running individuals, 294–95
    most powerful throwing arms (position players), 295–97
    power rankings by position, 283–84
    tape measure calendar dates, 266–82
    top 100 tape measure sluggers, 237–38
    unofficial long-distance drives, 200–211
    See also longest rankings
Redding, Dick "Cannonball," 65, 299
Reid, Tim, 201–2, 232, 234, 235
Reiser, Pete, 295
Reyes, Jose, 302
Reynolds, Mark, 142, 264
Rice, Jim, 12, 28–29, 182, 237, 271, 274, 279
Richard, J. R., 299

Ripken, Cal, 283
Rivera, Ruben, 271
Robertson, Bob, 276, 281
Robinson, Frank, XIII, 10, 13, 22–24
    greatest batting/throwing/running and, 295
    mini-biography, 22–24
    power ranking by position, 284
    stadium photo of homer, 248
    tape measure calendar dates, 274, 277, 280
    ten longest home runs, 24
    top slugger ranking, 237
Robinson, Jackie, 33, 79, 302
Rodriguez, Alex, 12, 126–29, 186, 277, 283
Rogan, Bullet Joe, 299
Rosen, Al, 283, 290
Rowe, Schoolboy, 283
Ruffing, Red, 283, 286, 292
runners, fastest, 299–302
Rusie, Amos, 60, 299
Ruth, Babe, XII, 187–93
    by Babe Ruth, 230–31
    Bob Meusel and, 296
    changing baseball, 8–9
    dominating lists, 266–67, 285
    drive into Crescent Lake, 234–35
    final three home runs, 220–23
    greatest batting/throwing/running and, 294–95
    Jimmie Foxx and, XII, XV–XVI, 9, 183–84, 186
    legendary Tampa homer, 201–2, 232
    longest double, 286
    longest final career homer, 290
    longest fly outs, 287
    longest homers by pitchers, 292
    longest homers by player over 40, 291
    longest homers by stadium, 245, 246, 249, 250, 255, 256, 257, 258, 259, 262
    longest inside-the-park homer, 287
    longest opposite field homers, 288
    longest postseason homers, 289
    longest single, 285
    longest spring training homers, 288, 289
    longest triples, 286

longest walk-off homers, 293
    Louis Santop and, 66–67
    Mike Mastry and, 233–34
    mini-biography, 187–93
    mythical 600-foot homers, 205–7
    possible 600-foot homers, 207–11
    power ranking by position, 284
    prodigious home runs, 200–202, 205–12, 220–29, 230–31, 232, 233–35, 266
    tape measure calendar dates, 266–82
    Ted Williams and, 105
    ten longest home runs, 191
    top 100 longest homers of, 239, 240, 241
    top slugger ranking, 194, 237
    Ty Cobb and, 8
Ryan, Nolan, 145, 167, 299

S
Sanders, Deion, 300, 301
Santo, Ron, 283
Santop, Louis, 65–67, 197, 238, 297
Schmidt, Mike, XV, 12, 32–33, 237, 250, 273, 278, 280, 283, 285
Score, Herb, 148, 299
Scott, George, 238
Sexson, Richie, 141, 142, 270, 284
Shannon, Mike, 281, 289
Sheffield, Gary, 142
Simmons, Al, 237, 287
Simpson, Harry, 251, 274
singles, longest, 285
600-foot home runs
    Babe Ruth and, 205–11
    Roy Carlyle and, 202–3
Skowron, Bill, 286, 287
Smith, Charles "Chino," 302
Smith, Willie, 292
Snider, Duke, 238, 254, 270, 284, 295
Solaita, Tony, 292
Soriano, Alfonso, 127, 271, 283
Sorrento, Paul, 264, 272
Sosa, Sammy, 12, 95–98
    longest homers by stadium, 261, 265
    longest preseason homer, 289
    longest walk-off homer, 293
    Mark McGwire and, 2, 96, 163
    mini-biography, 95–98
    power of, 7

power ranking by position, 284
tape measure calendar dates, 274, 278
ten longest home runs, 98
top 100 longest homer of, 240
top slugger ranking, 237
spring training homers, longest, 288–89
stadiums, longest home runs and photographs, 243–63
   Anaheim, 243
   Arlington, 244, 264
   Atlanta, 244, 264
   Baltimore, 245, 264
   Boston, 245–46
   Chicago, 246–47
   Cincinnati, 248, 264
   Cleveland, 249, 264
   Denver, 264
   Detroit, 250, 264
   Houston, 250, 264
   Kansas City, 251
   Los Angeles, 252, 264
   Miami, 264
   Milwaukee, 252, 264
   Minneapolis (and Bloomington), 253
   Montreal, 254, 264
   New York, 254–56, 264–65
   Oakland, 256
   Philadelphia, 257–58, 265
   Phoenix, 265
   Pittsburgh, 258–59, 265
   San Diego, 260, 265
   San Francisco, 261, 265
   Seattle, 261, 265
   St. Louis, 259–60, 265
   St. Petersburg, 265
   Toronto, 262, 265
   Washington, D.C., 262–63, 265
Stairs, Matt, 291, 292
Stargell, Willie, 10, 155–60
   on Dick Allen homer, 167
   longest opposite field homer, 288
   longest walk-off homers, 293
   mini-biography, 155–60
   power ranking by position, 283
   stadium photos of homers, 244, 250, 252, 254, 258, 259
   tape measure calendar dates, 271, 272, 274, 275, 277, 278
   ten longest home runs, 159
   top 100 longest homers of, 240, 241, 242

top slugger ranking, 196, 237
Stearnes, Norman "Turkey," 70–72, 197, 237, 295, 302
Stovey, Harry, 5, 198, 238, 295, 302
Strawberry, Darryl, 12, 37–38, 237, 264, 265, 269, 281, 290, 295
strength and conditioning, 4, 5–7
Stuart, Dick, 10, 80–83, 237, 240, 258, 271, 273
Suttles, George "Mule," 71, 72–75, 197, 237
Suzuki, Ichiro, 301
Swanson, Evar, 301
Swoboda, Ron, 290, 292

T
tape measure calendar dates, 266–82
tape measure home runs, 1–15
   "Dead Ball Era" and, 4–5, 52, 56, 187, 197, 198, 290, 292
   fascination with, 1, 2, 4, 9, 12–13
   "Golden Age" of, 10–11
   history of ball, 4–5
   origin/evolution of baseball and, 1–13
   overview of author's odyssey with, XII–XVI
   physics of, 10–11
   rankings of. See longest rankings; official home runs, longest; rankings
   strength, conditioning and, 4, 5–7
Tartabull, Danny, 280
teenager homers, longest, 291
Teixeira, Mark, 264
Tejada, Miguel, 283
Terry, Bill, 287
Tettleton, Mickey, 238, 283
Thomas, Frank, 12, 120–23, 247, 276, 284
Thome, Jim, 12, 123, 132, 133, 135–38, 241, 247, 262, 264, 275
Thompson, Hank, 302
Thompson, Sam, 5, 51, 52–55, 62, 201, 237
throwing arms, most powerful, 295–97
top rankings. See longest rankings; official home runs, longest; rankings
Trillo, Manny, 297
triples, longest, 286
two Bucks, 7

U
Uggla, Dan, 283
unofficial long-distance drives, 200–211
Upton, Justin, 142

V
Valentine, Ellis, 296, 297
Vance, Dazzy, 299
Vaughn, Greg, 237
Vaughn, Mo, 238, 274, 290
Verlander, Justin, 299

W
Wagner, Honus, 7, 66, 198, 221, 238, 283, 292, 294, 295, 296–97
Wagner, Leon, 238, 292
Walker, Larry, 279
walk-off homers, longest, 293
Wells, Kip, 293
Williams, Earl, 238, 268
Williams, Matt, 283
Williams, Smokey Joe, 65, 299
Williams, Ted, 9, 105–8, 182
   author recalling, XII–XIII
   Jimmie Foxx and, 186
   longest All-Star homer, 289
   longest final career homer, 290
   longest homer by player over 40, 291
   mini-biography, 105–8
   power ranking by position, 284
   practice regimen, 9
   Steve Dalkowski and, 299
   tape measure calendar dates, 268, 270, 273, 277
   top 100 longest homer of, 240
   top slugger ranking, 197, 237
Williamson, Ned, 297
Wilson, Earl, 283, 293
Wilson, Hack, 9, 238
Wilson, Willie, 301
Winfield, Dave, 237, 278, 295
Wood, Smoky Joe, 299
Wynn, Jimmy, 10, 29–31, 237, 273, 284, 290, 302

Y
Yastrzemski, Carl, 237, 240, 243, 271
York, Rudy, 238, 276

Z
Zernial, Gus, XII, 237

ABOUT THE AUTHOR

Bill Jenkinson is one of the country's most respected and trusted baseball historians. He has served as either official or de facto consultant for the Major League Baseball Hall of Fame, Major League Baseball, Society for American Baseball Research, Babe Ruth Museum, and ESPN. Jenkinson has written articles for various Major League teams including the Baltimore Orioles, Boston Red Sox, Cincinnati Reds, and Philadelphia Phillies. He has written several pieces for the nationally distributed *Sports Weekly* and was asked to contribute a chapter about the history of long-distance home runs for SABR's *Home Run Encyclopedia*. He has given countless radio and television interviews on ESPN and other sports networks in the United States and abroad.

With the 2007 publication of his book *The Year Babe Ruth Hit 104 Home Runs,* Jenkinson has received a steady stream of inquiries about Babe Ruth from around the world.

Besides researching and writing baseball history, Jenkinson enjoys reading, the arts, travel, playing sports, and all other fields of history. Born in Philadelphia in 1947, he lives with his wife Marie in Willow Grove, Pennsylvania. They have four children and four grandchildren.